COLONIAL RACIAL CAPITALISM

Colonial Racial Capitalism

SUSAN KOSHY, LISA MARIE CACHO, JODI A. BYRD,
AND BRIAN JORDAN JEFFERSON, EDITORS

DUKE UNIVERSITY PRESS *Durham and London* 2022

Printed in the United States of America on acid-free paper ∞
Project editor: Lisa Lawley
Designed by Matthew Tauch
Typeset in Arno Pro and Alegreya Sans by
Westchester Publishing Services

Library of Congress Cataloging-in-Publication Data
Names: Koshy, Susan, editor. | Cacho, Lisa Marie, editor. | Byrd, Jodi A.,
editor. | Jefferson, Brian Jordan, [date] editor.
Title: Colonial racial capitalism / Susan Koshy, Lisa Marie Cacho,
Jodi A. Byrd, and Brian Jefferson, editors.
Description: Durham : Duke University Press, 2022. | Includes
bibliographical references and index.
Identifiers: LCCN 2022000016 (print)
LCCN 2022000017 (ebook)
ISBN 9781478016106 (hardcover)
ISBN 9781478018742 (paperback)
ISBN 9781478023371 (ebook)
Subjects: LCSH: Indians, Treatment of—North America—History. |
Settler colonialism—United States—History. | Indians of North
America—Economic conditions. | Indians of North America—
Colonization—History. | Imperialism—Social aspects—North
America—History. | Capitalism—North America—History. |
Racism—North America—History. | Racism Economic aspects—
North America. | North America—Race relations—History. |
BISAC: SOCIAL SCIENCE / Ethnic Studies / American / African
American & Black Studies | SOCIAL SCIENCE / Ethnic Studies /
American / Native American Studies
Classification: LCC E91 .C656 2022 (print) | LCC E91 (ebook) |
DDC 970.004/97—dc23/eng/20220518
LC record available at https://lccn.loc.gov/2022000016
LC ebook record available at https://lccn.loc.gov/2022000017

Support for this research was provided by the Unit for
Criticism and Interpretive Theory at the University of Illinois,
Urbana-Champaign.

CONTENTS

ACKNOWLEDGMENTS

This one is for Cedric Robinson. For everything he taught me about race, politics, institutions, fighting, and living. I feel blessed to have known Cedric as a friend and mentor for the nine years I was at UC–Santa Barbara. His expansive intellect, his transfigurative political commitments, his luminous integrity, and his mischievous humor were a gift, teaching lessons I continue to learn. I hope that the work in this volume as well as the work that it took to produce this volume will carry forward the spirit of his work and testify to its horizon-shifting powers.

Before this book took shape as a publication, it was an event. This project was first conceived as a conference on racial capitalism organized through the Unit for Criticism and Interpretive Theory at the University of Illinois, Urbana-Champaign, in March 2019. I would like to thank my co-organizers—Jodi Byrd, Lisa Marie Cacho, Brian Jordan Jefferson, and Jodi Melamed—for their creativity and dynamism in planning the conference. For their inspiring contributions to the conference as keynote speakers and for the example of their scholarship and activism, my deepest gratitude to Michael Dawson and Ruth Wilson Gilmore. To the contributors to this volume, many of whom took time away from other long-term projects to work on this collection, no thanks will suffice for your remarkable scholarship and collaborative spirit. I also want to thank the unit's graduate assistants, Alyssa Bralower, Sarah Richter, and Lettycia Terrones, who worked tirelessly to make the conference a success.

This edited volume grows out of the mind-stretching experience of writing and thinking about colonial racial capitalism with my co-editors, Lisa Marie Cacho, Jodi Byrd, and Brian Jordan Jefferson. I am grateful to Lisa for her keen insights, deft revisions, and writerly instincts. My thanks to Jodi, who maintained a consistent focus on the frames of Indigeneity and settler colonialism. I appreciate Brian's work in providing clarity, balance, and precision to our thinking at every stage. To Md. Alamgir Hossain, who worked over the summer editing the manuscript, special thanks for his dedicated work. Finally, for her care and thoughtfulness in preparing this manuscript for publication, thanks to the Unit for Criticism's supremely capable research assistant, Ashli Anda.

For the advice, encouragement, and life-giving conversations that carried me through this work, my thanks to my family—Vinod, Tanya, Sunjay, and Vinay.

SUSAN KOSHY

I feel like I will always be learning how to theorize, articulate, and write about colonial racial capitalism, and I'd like to acknowledge a few people for their brilliance and their patience in thinking through and talking about these concepts with me over the years. Lisa Lowe, Yen Espiritu, Denise Ferreira da Silva, and George Lipsitz are all exceptional mentors who taught challenging classes and provided generous feedback while I was a graduate student. I was also lucky to learn from the other graduate students at UCSD during that time, especially David Coyoca, Ruby Tapia, Rod Ferguson, Grace Hong, Tony Tiongson, Ofelia Cuevas, and the Marlborough House Marxists: Helen Jun, Albert Lowe, Barry Masuda, Boone Nguyen, and Randall Williams. I am very grateful to my fellow coeditors: Jodi Byrd, Brian Jordan Jefferson, and Susan Koshy. I'd like to give Susan a special thanks for taking charge, organizing all of us, doing a lot of the hard writing, and keeping us on track. I also want to acknowledge Jodi Byrd for all her patience and support in helping me to rethink racial capitalism in relation to settler colonial studies and Indigenous studies over the last several years. I'd like to acknowledge a few people for helping me think specifically about my coauthored chapter in this volume. I'd like to thank Ruth Nicole Brown for helping me to write about hard things, and I want to thank her for the work that she does because everything she does is the answer to that all-important question: "So what do we do now?" I want to thank Chandan Reddy for his own work, brilliance, and generosity in helping us to theorize administrative power. And last, I extend much appreciation to Jodi Melamed, my coauthor, longtime interlocutor, and much-loved friend. I am so grateful for Jodi's genius, clarity, big-picture theorizing, and real-world activism. I love the work we produce together, and I love the collaborative process we take to get our shared thoughts out into the world.

LISA MARIE CACHO

I want to thank all my coeditors, and Lisa especially, for the collaborative work on the introduction. I also want to thank Chandan Reddy, Jodi Melamed, Iyko Day, and Alyosha Goldstein, but everyone is already in the collection, so I'm just feeling lucky to have been able to think with everyone for this conversation.

JODI A. BYRD

I would like to thank all who helped organize and participated in the Racial Capitalism conference in Champaign-Urbana in 2019: Alyosha Goldstein, Cheryl Harris, Marisol LeBrón, Kimberly Kay Hoang, Iyko Day, Laura Pulido, Ruth Wilson Gilmore, Michael Dawson, Jodi Byrd, Jodi Melamed, Lisa Marie Cacho, Susan Koshy, Lee Gaines, Chandan Reddy, Alyssa Bralower, and Sarah Richter. I would also like to extend thanks to all the students, faculty, and members of the community who came and provided lively discussion. This volume would not have been possible without such robust and collective input.

BRIAN JORDAN JEFFERSON

We are deeply grateful to our production team at Duke for their meticulous attention to all aspects of this volume. Courtney Berger's unflagging support for this book and her deft guidance at every stage kept us on track, despite the many troubles of the pandemic. Many thanks also to Sandra Korn, Lisa Lawley, and Donald Pharr for seeing this book through production and into the world.

Susan Koshy, Lisa Marie Cacho,
Jodi A. Byrd, and Brian Jordan Jefferson

Introduction

As Robin Kelley points out in his introduction to the 2020 reissue of *Black Marxism*, Cedric Robinson did not coin the term *racial capitalism*, that it in fact "originated in South Africa around 1976"—an origin point within a settler colonial apartheid state that, importantly, signals the convergence of settler colonialism, imperialism, anti-Blackness, and capitalism the following essays address.[1] For many, however, the concept of racial capitalism has been most influentially formulated in Cedric Robinson's monumental study *Black Marxism* (1983). Robinson's paradigmatic challenge to Marx's progressive teleology was transformative, and it extended the critique of South African thinkers and activists, many in the Black Consciousness movement and the Pan Africanist Congress, who were concerned that "dismantling apartheid without overthrowing capitalism would leave in place structures that reproduce racial inequality and the exploitation of all workers."[2] The political and analytical interventions that the framework of racial capitalism made in the work of Neville Alexander, Barnard Magubane, James A. Turner, John S. Saul, Stephen Gelb, and others were specific to South Africa. Robinson's contribution was to generalize and theorize racial capitalism on a world scale. His thesis was that capitalism was racial capitalism everywhere.

Fundamentally, Robinson's reworking of Marxism asserts that racism is not extrinsic to capitalism; it does not merely exacerbate or justify class-based inequalities. Critiquing key assumptions of Marxism, Robinson explains that capitalism did not overthrow the fixed social hierarchies of feudalism but instead extended and incorporated these unequal social and/or colonial relations. Furthermore, he argues, these inequalities had always been decidedly "racial." According to Robinson, racism did not emerge at the moment that Europeans justified the enslavement and colonization of non-Europeans but functioned long before to naturalize economic, social, and political inequalities within Europe that became entrenched within capitalism. As he writes, "The tendency of European civilization through capitalism was thus not to homogenize but to differentiate—to exaggerate regional, subcultural, and dialectical differences into 'racial' ones."

In the conversation that concludes this book, Ruth Wilson Gilmore reminds us that Robinson did not see the "racial" as synonymous with skin color. According to Robinson, racial logics naturalize capitalist inequalities and the violence that maintains them by naming the differences that justify unequal social relations as innate—as "biological," "cultural," "environmental," and so forth. These differences refer to unequal social relations, which can—but do not always or necessarily—correspond to skin color. Hence, Gilmore challenges us to renew the analytic of racial capitalism by asking us to think, "What is the 'racial' in racial capitalism?" How do we combine the specificity of how difference functions within specific locations to naturalize capitalist inequalities and their attendant violences with the general trend of capitalism in the world today? As Gilmore urges, "If we seriously want to enliven, and make useful, and keep useful the concept of racial capitalism, we have to get over thinking that what it's about is white-people capitalism. There *is* white-people capitalism, but that's not all of capitalism."[3] For Gilmore, Robinson's work offers indispensable guidance in addressing this challenge in that he demonstrates that although capitalism has always been racial capitalism, *racial* does not necessarily mean Black or require white.

For instance, analyses of hierarchies of global space in postcolonial studies illuminate a key racial logic inherent to Marxist stagism. The division of the world into centers and peripheries, modern and backward regions, and civilized and uncivilized peoples rested on what Enrique Dussel terms "the fallacy of developmentalism," the idea that the European model of economic and political governance was a universal one that must be followed by all other cultures.[4] The "failure" of Third World countries to develop along the pathways set up and exemplified by Euro-American nations, especially after gaining political independence, was taken as proof of a natural incapacity to reach humanity's highest goals through the exercise of universal reason. This failure served as warrant for continued Western intervention in the markets and governments of "less-developed" countries. As Denise Ferreira da Silva explains, developmentalism served as an alibi for expropriating the productive capacity of lands and bodies outside Europe by condensing three racial truths: "(a) that the targets of the development project (illiteracy, poverty, famine) resulted from certain peoples' and places' *natural* incapacity to move forward on their own, (b) those who could: white/Europeans had the moral obligation to help those (Asians, Africans, Latin Americans, and Pacific Islanders) who could not develop, and (c) this natural incapacity preempts attributions of the failures of development to past and current operations of colonial mechanisms of expropriation."[5] In other words, the production of racially marked hierarchies of space allows accumulation through dispossession to be resignified as a problem of development. For this reason, Ferreira da Silva explains, colonial racial critique offers a crucial corrective to Marxist theory: "Racial critique yields an anticolonial analysis of global capitalism without historical materialism's 'original' Eurocentrism."[6]

The racial grammar that shaped developmentalism in the twentieth century is being reconfigured in the twenty-first century in ways that highlight the urgency of connecting the critique of colonial and racial capitalism. Several epochal shifts have undermined Euro-American hegemony and the authority of linear models of development: the rapid economic rise of East and Southeast Asian countries; the relocation of industry to former colonies or semi-colonies; the counterweight of new Chinese development projects reshaping investment and infrastructure in Asia, Africa, Europe, and Latin America (e.g., the massive Belt and Road Initiative launched in 2013); the heightened global consciousness of the links between Western-style development and planetary environmental catastrophes; the transcontinental effects of the 2008 financial crisis; and most recently the cascading crises of the coronavirus pandemic alongside the resurgence of Indigenous and Black-allied activism and leadership against militarized police and the extractive industries that continue to expropriate resources and lives. The reorientation of the global extractive economy away from Euro-America and toward China, the paradoxical conditions of increasing Western and Asian foreign investments in emerging economies and the hyper-exploitation of racialized populations within them, the creation of permanent surplus populations mostly in the South but also in the North, and the hyper-exploitation of migrant labor within postcolonial states, between them, and in the North point to the emergence of new racializing regimes of accumulation and shifting geographical contours and formations of race. These changes bring to the fore the geographical fluidity of accumulation and racialized difference as the circuits linking North-South, South-South, South-East, and North-East proliferate and diversify at dizzying velocity.

Further complicating emerging global racial formations is the ambivalent role of postcolonial elites in the aftermath of decolonization. As Heidi Nast notes, "Since independence, for instance, postcolonial elites have, for economic reasons, worked to identify tacitly and racially with global hegemons. Yet, to stabilize and enhance their own local, national or regional political positions, they have spoken *in racialized opposition* to these same global hegemons, drawing on racialized commonalities with their own 'people.' The ambivalence and contradictions of such positioning has permitted a kind of racialized relay system in which political risk is dispersed across global and local racial formations, allowing capital to accumulate in ever more centripetal ways."[7] The strategic positioning of postcolonial states and elites, sometimes glossed as "neoliberalism with Southern characteristics" and sometimes seen as simply too heterogeneous and divergent to be captured by this label, raises crucial questions about racial capitalism now.[8]

In addition to rethinking primitive accumulation as endemic to capitalist development, we need to rethink the analytic of "dispossession" so that we can reframe and recenter land within analyses of colonial racial capitalism. One of the interventions that North American Indigenous studies has made to conversations about capitalism and racialization is to highlight how the dispossessive regimes of accumulation through differentiation, elimination, expropriation, enslavement, and incarceration have themselves always been settler colonialist. What is more, these regimes have always been an attack on collective life and its emphasis on relationality, kinship, and responsibility that shapes so many Indigenous philosophies. As mentioned above, Marx's so-called primitive accumulation carries with it a temporal and spatial teleology that assumes successive transformations of the means of production and political economies as necessary conditions of possibility. And even those necessary conditions of possibility rely on taken-for-granted assumptions about land and property as givens.

In linking capitalism to settler colonialism, scholars in Indigenous and settler colonial studies center land alongside labor within the horizons of expropriation. But as Chickasaw scholar Jodi Byrd cautions, although settler colonial studies and critiques of racial capitalism often understand land as necessary for life, Indigenous studies understands that *land is life*.[9] Accordingly, Yellowknives Dene scholar Glen Coulthard argues for a shift from understanding capitalism as a social relation to understanding capitalism as a colonial relation, an analytic reframing that he suggests might help us "occupy a better angle from which to both anticipate and inter-rogate practices of settler-state dispossession justified under otherwise egalitarian principles and espoused with so-called 'progressive' political agendas in mind."[10] From this better angle, we can push Robinson's ana-lytic of racial capitalism back to the significance of the term's South African settler colonialist origins to examine how Indigenous dispossession is not the precondition for racial capitalism to emerge but always has been part of its very structure. To understand racial capitalism as additionally a colonial relation, as Coulthard encourages us, is to understand that racial capital-ism exploits and expropriates not only labor but also land. For Coulthard, Marx's theory of primitive accumulation "thoroughly links the totalizing power of *capital* with that of *colonialism*."[11] Hence, primitive accumula-tion redirects attention to "the history and experience of *dispossession*, not proletarianization."[12]

In attempting to apprehend the difference that Indigenous disposses-sion makes to Marxist understandings of land, labor, accumulation, and property, Rob Nichols addresses what appears to be a contradiction out-side of Indigenous studies: If the Earth cannot be owned, how can land be stolen from its rightful owners? He argues that, first, dispossession "trans-forms nonproprietary relations into proprietary ones" and that, second, the dispossessed "are figured as 'original owners' but only *retroactively*, that is, refracted backward through the process itself." As he elaborates, "It is thus not (only) about the *transfer of* property but the *transformation into* prop-erty." Naming this process "recursive dispossession," Nichols pinpoints why Indigenous lands, stolen into property and possession, are so difficult to apprehend outside the systems of property and possession. As he ex-plains, recursive dispossession works through "transformation," "transfer-ence," and "retroactive attribution." Indigenous peoples' relations to land are transformed (from a relation of responsibility to a relation of rights) only so that land-as-a-property relation can be transferred or sold to settlers. The act of selling belatedly names Indigenous peoples as "original owners." Dispossession, Nichols demonstrates in *Theft Is Property!*, "produces what it presupposes."[13]

This shift is important for rethinking how primitive accumulation was not a stage of capitalist development but is, in fact, ongoing and necessary for settler-state capital accumulation through its colonial relation.[14] The shift is also important for theorizing and learning from Indigenous resis-tance: "The theory and practice of Indigenous anticolonialism, including Indigenous anticapitalism, is best understood as a struggle primarily inspired by and oriented around *the question of land*—a struggle not only *for* land in the material sense, but also deeply *informed* by what the land *as system of reciprocal relations and obligations* can teach us about living our lives in relation to one another and the natural world in nondominating and nonexploitative terms—and less around our emergent status as 'right-less proletarians.'"[15] As Coulthard explains, to see capitalism as a colonial relation is not just to see capital accumulation through the lens of ongoing dispossession but also to see anticapitalist activism in unceded and occupied Indigenous lands beyond workers' struggles—in other words, to see "indigenous land-based direct action" as fundamentally revolutionary and anticapitalist.[16]

For us, staging our analytic as colonial racial capitalism allows a centering of relations of racism, settler and franchise colonialisms, and capitalism across a variety of historical and geographical contexts and engages their relation to the persistence of violence, precarity, and inequality in capitalist modernity. Our analytic of colonial racial capitalism brings together genealogies of decolonial, Indigenous, and Black radical critique to explore how colonization and imperialism partitioned the globe into racially differentiated lands and peoples, naturalizing and justifying the expropriation of some bodies and lands for the benefit of others. As Chandan Reddy notes, "For the last three hundred years, Westernization and capitalism have refined and continuously expanded 'society' for the human community while abandoning for death any life whose first and primary crime has been its mere existence—that is, whose crime is that it exists without value or meaning for westernized-man."[17]

The essays in this volume move across a range of contexts, from the strategies of Indigenous dispossession encoded in legal definitions of the corporation and the tribe, to the historical erasure of the colonial violence of the Mexican-American War in public memorials, to the cognitive mapping of nuclear wastelands of colonial modernity located on Indigenous lands and in the global South, to mechanisms of debt and development as race-neutral means of asset-stripping Black communities, to the colonial legacies shaping the Vietnamese state's protection of natural resources in the mining sector against Western and Chinese investors. The analyses link the logics and violences of domination and dispossession to interconnections among colonialism, racial capitalism, and formations of social difference. As they construct new links across fields, extend the analytic to unforeseen situations, and direct it toward new materialities, these essays open up possibilities for solidarity, action, and reflection that work against the processes of violent partition and repartition through which colonial racial capitalism is reproduced.

Colonial Racial Capitalism

Racial capitalism *is* colonial capitalism, especially where settler and imperial thefts of land, the production of hierarchies of global space, and the expropriation of labor occur by means of recursive processes that require possession and rights in order to produce dispossession and rightlessness. As Jodi Melamed observes, "Capital can only be capital when it is accumulating, and it can only accumulate by producing and moving through relations of severe inequality among human groups—capitalists with the means of production/workers without the means of subsistence, creditors/debtors, conquerors of land made property/the dispossessed and removed."[18] Thus, although liberal multiculturalism premised on anti-Black settler colonial expropriation now promises inclusion and equality through rights-based forms of administrative rule, colonial racial capitalism depends upon a simultaneous violent disenfranchisement, dispossession, and removal of certain bodies, subjectivities, and possible collectivities to secure and maintain speculative financialization. In the context of US and Canadian settler colonial societies, the ever-expanding logic of accumulation through dispossession depends upon colonial relations with Indigenous peoples as its condition of possibility, and as Joanne Barker observes, "In a state whose capitalism is *always already* reaching out globally, of course Indigenous peoples cannot have equal or commensurate claims to any lands and resources that might compete with corporate-as-the-government's interests to expand, extract, and profit some more. Of course."[19]

This analytic of colonial racial capitalism therefore intervenes in and refracts a broader re-theorization of the relationship between capitalism and violence in Marxist theory that has been under way since the beginning of the twenty-first century.[20] The new work on capitalist violence issues from a convergence of multiple efforts to grapple with the devastating inequalities and cascading crises unleashed by global financialization: growing income inequality and precarity; the gutting of the welfare state in the global North and the social provisioning capacities of developing states in the global South; the debt crises of the 1980s in Latin America and Africa and the Asian financial crisis in 1997; the subprime mortgage crisis and the global financial meltdown in 2008; the expulsion of surplus populations into survival economies, prisons, slums, and migrant circuits; mass incarceration and the militarization of policing and border control; the digitization of social control, logistical operations, financial markets, property valuation, and urban development; the reproduction of racial and colonial wastelands; and "landgrabs" by old and new imperial powers in the South. The scope and scale of these brute inequalities have focused unprecedented attention on two cornerstones of Marxist theory: primitive accumulation and the relation between expropriation and exploitation.

The reappraisals of so-called primitive accumulation highlight the limitations of classical Marxist readings that treat it as a historically prior stage in the development of capitalism (land enclosures, slavery, Indigenous genocide and removal, colonial conquest and plunder) in which the use of extra-economic force to separate people from the means of production and subsistence is superseded in "mature" capitalism by the "the silent compulsion of economic relations [that] sets the seal on the domination of the capitalist over the worker."[21] Working largely from Marx's changing accounts of originary accumulation or Rosa Luxemburg's study of force as a permanent and intrinsic feature of capitalism that is repeatedly activated as accumulation is extended to the entire world, these accounts reframe primitive accumulation as an "inherent-continuous" element of capitalist processes.[22] These reformulations bring the work into closer alignment with scholarship on slavery and colonialism in Black, Indigenous, and postcolonial studies, which have long identified the enduring salience of extra-economic coercion in historical and contemporary capitalism.[23] As Samir Amin notes, "Whenever the capitalist mode of production enters into relations with pre-capitalist modes of production, and subjects these to itself, transfers of value take place from the pre-capitalist to the capitalist formations, as a result of the mechanisms of *primitive accumulation*. . . . It is these forms of primitive accumulation, modified but persistent, to the advantage of the centre, that form the domain of the theory of accumulation on a world scale."[24] Crucially, recent reassessments in Marxism, like Robinson's prior work, have hinged on a move away from Eurocentric models of capitalist development and toward "the colonial relation of dispossession as a co-foundational feature of our understanding of and critical engagement with capitalism."[25]

Among the most comprehensive efforts to rethink the relationship between capitalism and violence is Onur Ulas Ince's study of "capital-positing violence" and "capital-preserving violence." As a preliminary step,

Ince insists that understanding primitive accumulation requires that "the analytic aperture is widened to capture global networks of production and exchange as the historical condition of capitalism, which in turn entails abandoning the nation-state for the 'colonial empire' as the politico-legal unit of analysis." This scalar shift brings into view the otherwise obscured interdependence between slave and free labor that underwrote industrial capitalism as well as the racialized and gendered divisions between waged, disposable, unpaid, and unfree labor structuring the current international division of labor. Ince defines *capital-positing violence* as the brutal force used to separate people from their means of production and to dispossess them. This wholesale expropriation and expulsion of communities occurs when capitalism forcibly incorporates noncapitalist social forms to its logic of accumulation. By contrast, capital-preserving violence is less overt and hides beneath the silent compulsion of economic relations. Exercised primarily in quotidian forms through the law of the market, "capital-preserving violence, as the institutionalization of coercion *within* capitalism, thus encompasses not only the domain of law but a whole panoply of infra-legal administrative techniques of micro-coercion, both public and private, necessary for the reconstitution of 'capital-positing labor' from one day to the next."[26] Nevertheless, despite their outward difference, Ince insists that the two modalities of violence are interlinked and aimed at creating and maintaining the institutional and normative conditions for accumulation.

Black scholars, Indigenous scholars, feminist scholars, and scholars of color have vitally reframed current debates by underscoring the centrality and notable neglect of social reproduction and ecology in Marxist reconsiderations of expropriation. These sites of expropriation are not generally perceived as such because they are associated with the unpaid reproductive and social labor of women and natives and the extraction and commodification of natural resources and capacities in racial and gendered spaces marked as underdeveloped or unproductive. Nevertheless, along with expropriated labor, they form the disavowed foundation of processes of capitalism.

More to the point, the discounted value of racialized and gendered bodies, capacities, resources, and geographies is not accidental but is actively produced both economically and epistemologically. As Jennifer Morgan, Alys Weinbaum, Carole Boyce Davies, Sarah Haley, Erik McDuffie, and Marisa Fuentes argue in their respective scholarship, the development of racial capitalism has depended not only on Black women's labor and Black women's activism but also on the archival erasure of Black women's physical, intellectual, and resistance work.[27] The erasure of those who labor in the service of social reproduction is crucial to the workings of colonial racial capitalism.[28] Archival erasure naturalizes the devaluation of marginalized populations, the work they do, and the places they live, which not only keeps wages low and unlivable but also keeps resource-rich land exploitable and unprotected. Concurrently, this disavowal is also reinscribed in false dichotomies and hierarchies within analyses of political-economic processes that focus on paid, "productive" work at the expense of those whose work is arbitrarily considered "reproductive." Such archival erasures and theoretical elisions obfuscate the racialized and gendered nature of contemporary forms of unfree labor. As Ellie Gore and Genevieve LaBaron remind us, "Understanding women's unfree labour requires a broad understanding of social reproduction as embodied and enacted at individual and household levels, and the ways in which these are tied to processes of value production. . . . Understanding how and why women become vulnerable to unfree labor in global supply chains requires us to centralise dynamics of social oppression and social reproduction—not simply labour exploitation in economistic terms."[29] What links the distinct sites of expropriated labor in the peripheries and the core, of the unpaid and underpaid labor of social reproduction, and of low-cost food, energy, and raw materials is that they serve as sites where "capital, science, and empire . . . succeed in releasing new sources of free or low-cost human and extra-human natures for capital." These sites, vital to the incessant capitalist quest for and production of "cheap natures," sustain accumulation by driving down costs and providing fixes for periodic crises.[30] They are key sites of expropriation because they are thinly protected by contractual obligations; differentially devalued by racial and colonial legacies of conquest, plunder, dispossession, and genocide; and disadvantaged through their low position on a Eurocentric animacy hierarchy.

For Macarena Gómez-Barris, these key sites of expropriation exist in what she refers to as the "extractive zone." This is where colonial racial capitalists actively and violently exploit and destroy social and ecological life as well as the Indigenous, queer, and feminist epistemologies that value relationality, land, plants, animals, and humans. As she writes, "The 'extractive zone' names the violence that capitalism does to reduce, constrain, and convert life into commodities, as well as the epistemological violence of training our academic vision to reduce life to systems." In addition to "mega-extractive projects, such as large dams and mines," extractive capitalism, according to

Gómez-Barris, is expanded through "prisons and security regimes."[31] Prisons, according to Gilmore, are extractive because "prisons enable money to move because of the enforced *inactivity* of people locked in them. It means people extracted from communities, and people returned to communities but not entitled to be of them, enable the circulation of money on rapid cycles. What's extracted from the extracted is *the* resource of life—time."[32] The racial and colonial logics, mechanisms, and procedures of the carceral state not only create "surplus" populations but also confine and criminalize the histories, relationships, and knowledges that challenge the common sense of exploitability and disposability. As Melamed points out, "We need a more apposite language and a better way to think about capital as a system of expropriating violence on collective life itself."[33] Incarceration extracts time, the resource of life, and it extracts and criminalizes knowledge, the resource of communities with long histories of struggle and resistance. For this reason, it is important to work against the devaluation and erasure of Indigenous, Black radical, and subaltern epistemologies because the destruction of these worldviews is vital to the reproduction of colonial racial capitalism precisely because they offer alternatives that have always existed. Indigenous, decolonial, and Black radical critiques consider colonization, racialization, and capitalism as coevolving and co-constitutive; as Minneapolis-based poet Douglas Kearney observed in the days following George Floyd's murder by police, class is critical to analyses of power and access within systems of privilege, but it is "more fluid than perceived race. Police don't check your credit rating before they shoot, club, rough-ride, or strangle your life away because, you see, they already know what they think you're worth."[34]

It is no accident that the extractive violences of colonial racial capitalism target those people and *places* that are most vulnerable to devaluation and criminalization. As Gómez-Barris writes, "It is often in the heart of resource-rich territories that Indigenous peoples exist in complex tension with extractive capitalism and land defense. In these geographies, Indigenous peoples often multiply rather than reduce life possibilities, protecting land and each other at often extremely high personal and communal cost."[35] Hence, examining how racialized and gendered people whose labor is considered unfree, reproductive, unproductive, or nonproductive are devalued, exploited, disavowed, contained, criminalized, incarcerated, and dispossessed requires examining how land itself is reduced to only a property relation. To counter this academic tendency, it is necessary to attend to land as the site of expropriation, dispossession, and extraction as well as to apprehend land as the often unnamed but vital actor that is always exceeding and resisting the violence of colonial racial capitalism.

The framework of colonial racial capitalism centers land not only as the site of expropriation and the place that social relations are enacted but also as the unnamed actor that sometimes ostensibly but often invisibly facilitates, mediates, and influences our social relations to state agents, one another, the places we live, and the nonhuman lives and entities all around us. It matters whether land is perceived as life, as private property, as terra nullius, or as waste because such perceptions determine whether the land—as well as its life, all the lives it sustains, and all the worldviews that value it—is worthy of protection or vulnerable to extraction, expropriation, violence, and dispossession. At the same time, we want to emphasize that we need to see land beyond a property formation because if land is seen only as owned or as not yet owned rather than as a relation, an actor, or kin, then land, as well as all those the land sustains, will always be misunderstood as valuable only in economic terms—as something to be extracted from, possessed, exploited, damaged, owned, used, and abused. We consider land relationally and, in so doing, assert as a grounding assumption that land has its own capacities for agency, vitality, care, and consent that should be respected and protected. Therefore, we need to examine our relationships and responsibilities to land beyond its potential to be parceled, enclosed, dispossessed, owned, and circulated as property.

Racism and colonialism naturalize not just brutal economic inequalities but also the legal and extralegal violences and killings that come from making dehumanization and devaluation seem endemic to impoverished places and/or a product of people's choices rather than as central to regimes of accumulation. Thus, the framework of colonial racial capitalism is well suited to grappling with the centrality of dispossession to the reproduction of capitalist relations when it focuses on those peoples and places that are recurring targets of capital-positing violence or where the boundary between capital-positing and capital-preserving violence is weak and permeable. This raises a number of crucial questions that lie at the heart of the chapters in this collection. When do resistances to capital's endless drive for accumulation pose such a substantial threat as to unleash the direct force held in check "in the ordinary run of things"?[36] More importantly, which sites and populations bear the brunt of capital-positing violence at specific historical moments? How does this violence operate, and how can it be resisted?

To address these questions through the framework of colonial racial capitalism requires thinking about how the racial and colonial are enmeshed.

This approach also entails disregarding the structural separation of economy from the ostensibly noneconomic realm of social reproduction/kinship and ecology to examine their deep interconnections. Finally, colonial racial capitalism as a framework recenters Indigenous and settler colonial critique within what is often taken for granted within Marxist analyses: who labors and is made to labor (and who is presumed not to) in the presence and function of land in all its settler dispropriative and counter-resistance registers as relation, as kin, as prior possession, as property, and as the constitutive and literal theft of ground upon which colonial and racial relations are enacted, policed, surveilled, speculated, and monetized. The presumptions about land and labor bifurcated between Indigeneity and Blackness, we argue, also compel the driving common sense and taken-for-grantedness of racial capitalist critiques.

The framework of colonial racial capitalism counters the separation of exchange, exploitation, and expropriation in dominant social theory. It not only thematizes the structural interdependence of these three arenas; it also offers a systemic analysis of the excesses of capitalist violence that have and continue to target marginalized racial groups and peripheral spaces and populations. In doing so, it offers a more expansive and complex understanding of capitalist violence encompassing spectacular forms of violence such as genocide, occupation, and removal, and the slower violence of the destruction of collective knowledges, resources, languages, relationships, and capacities. The chapters in this volume analyze the interconnections among colonialism, racism, and capitalism from the conquest period of "war capitalism" in the Americas, through industrial capitalism, to contemporary financial capitalism.[37] The various chapters cover both settler colonialism in North America (Barker, Goldstein, Harris, Day, Cacho and Melamed, Pulido) and franchise colonialism in Africa, Asia, and Puerto Rico (Hoang, LeBrón, Jefferson, Day), exploring the logics, mechanisms, and structures of Indigenous dispossession, conquest, and slavery in the New World and the repressive and extractive modes of occupation, resource control, and underdevelopment of colonial territories.

Importantly, the chapters do not solely offer a negative critique, taking seriously Ruth Wilson Gilmore's guidance to go beyond reciting the horrors of capitalism to improvising resistance and rehearsing freedom for the future. To become "good readers" requires divining possibilities for different futures in the call of political movements and the expressive forms of art (Barker, LeBrón, Cacho and Melamed, Harris, Day, Pulido) and then putting this knowledge into action. Many of the essays channel dynamically substantive traditions of radical thought in Black, Latinx, Indigenous, Asian American, and decolonial studies toward addressing the challenges of the present. They resurrect and redescribe Indigenous and racial histories, epistemologies, and struggles that have been systematically occluded, erased, or distorted in dominant accounts. They recover and reveal refugia of resistance, delineating the values, practices, and ontologies through which Indigenous, enslaved, and colonized peoples define relationships to one another, to purposeful activity, to sustenance, and to the Earth.

Structure of the Book

We have organized the volume into four sections: "Accumulation," "Administration," "Aesthetics," and "Rehearsing for the Future." These sections are not conceived as autonomous and separate but as intertwined. Notably, many of the chapters could easily fit within two or even three sections because capital accumulation often relies on administrative procedures to abstract and obscure violence, and certain forms of art making are explicitly imagined and designed to counter the violences of capitalist exploitation and expropriation, as well as the legal and extralegal coercion that upholds extractive capitalisms. In other words, the chapters chosen to represent each section best highlight the specific organizing concepts, but they also work cross-sectionally to illuminate the interaction among capitalist accumulation, its law- and rule-making processes, and artistic acts of contestation and rememory.

The first section, "Accumulation," documents the persistence of so-called primitive accumulation in Indigenous histories of land theft, removal, and allotment (Barker); in the interconnected histories of Indigenous dispossession through adoption, foster care, and inheritance laws and Black subordination through heirs' property laws after Reconstruction (Goldstein); and in Black dispossession through debt and forced labor after slavery, which was modeled on earlier systems of Indian debt peonage (Harris). Working through Indigenous and Black history from the eighteenth century to the present, these chapters show how colonial relations of dispossession and servitude are inextricably linked to the processes and institutions of capital accumulation. They also reveal how Indigenous and Black dispossession beyond the land/labor divide was enabled and justified by a liberal legal system that covers over the violent illiberal origins of colonial racial capitalism.

The second section looks at administration as a dominant form of colonial racial capitalist power in the neoliberal present, clarifying a shift from lawmaking power to "the rule-making and rule-enforcing mode of governance" as state bureaucracies become more complex.[38] These chapters home in on the infra-legal mechanisms of rules, rights, and procedures used by states and institutions in the North and the South to manage racial difference and colonial legacies of uneven development in a time of neoliberal globalization. The chapters uncover telling differences in the use of administrative power, from the opacity of rules strategically used by Vietnamese state officials to parlay with Western and Chinese investors to the abstraction and purported objectivity of smart governance algorithms used for property valuation and waste management to the "transparent" police procedures employed by the US administrative state to justify the killing and criminalization of Black, Indigenous, gender-nonconforming, and other marginalized communities (Hoang, Cacho, Melamed, Lebrón, and Jefferson).

The third section, "Aesthetics," contrasts the archival erasure of racial and colonial dispossessive violence in official commemorations and its recollection in counter-hegemonic visual art. In focusing on how visual culture represents the nexus of military, technological, and economic violence in contexts of conquest and occupation, this section examines how the aesthetic can be marshaled by states to inculcate "colonial unknowing" and also be mobilized in decolonial visions to "reverse, displace, and seize the apparatus of value-coding."[39] This section centers artistic visions of land and ecology in memorial sites, murals, sculptures, dioramas, and photographs showing how, on the one hand, settler colonial and imperial commemorations project landscapes improved by development and technological modernization and, on the other hand, how oppositional art represents the making of wastelands and the extirpation of Indigenous and Native peoples as its necessary and brutal condition (Day, Pulido).

The concluding section, "Rehearsing for the Future," takes the form of a conversation between Michael Dawson and Ruth Wilson Gilmore in which they reflect on their trajectories as scholars and activists and discuss strategies for challenging racial capitalism now.

The first section considers the persistence of history in the present as the chapters pull back from contemporary flash points—the Occupy Wall Street (OWS) movement, the court challenges to the Indian Child Welfare Act (ICWA), the Flint water crisis, and the subprime loan crisis—to locate events in the long duration of settler colonial capitalist expansion. All three chapters in the opening section, Joanne Barker's "The Corporation and the Tribe," Alyosha Goldstein's "'In the Constant Flux of Its Incessant Renewal': The Social Reproduction of Racial Capitalism and Settler Colonial Entitlement," and Cheryl I. Harris's "The Racial Alchemy of Debt: Dispossession and Accumulation in Afterlives of Slavery," analyze foundational legal rulings and policies through which the US government expropriated and manipulated the land, labor, and kinship ties of Indigenous and Black communities to support capitalist development and white settlement. Barker's chapter powerfully illustrates this dynamic, tracing the concurrent evolution of the legal definitions of the "corporation" and the "tribe" between 1790 and 1887 to reveal how the courts stripped away Indian trade rights and sovereignty over land, resources, and capacities in service of white settlement and corporate interests. The steady expansion of corporate status and rights at the same time that Indian sovereignty was being systematically undermined worked "to establish and protect imperialist social relations and conditions . . . between powerful financial interests, both government and corporate, and Indigenous peoples." Barker documents the massive loss of land, life, and lifeways that followed, revealing dispossession as a world-historical reorientation to the nomos of capital. This legal history, distinct from but connected to the struggles of other oppressed racial groups, holds lessons for later generations struggling against capitalism. Specifically, Barker notes that movements like ows, which bracket the centrality of Indigenous territorial-based claims to sovereignty in their pursuit of economic justice, can offer only partial remedies rather than radical transformation.

Alyosha Goldstein's chapter picks up where Barker's legal history ends, with the 1887 General Allotment Act, but he shifts the focus of analysis to social reproduction. His chapter shows how policies of adoption, foster care, and inheritance served as instruments of ongoing Native dispossession. Specifically, he explores how the notion of filius nullius ("nobody's child"), enacted in a range of child-removal policies, works in tandem with terra nullius, implemented through federal policies for Indian removal, allotment, termination, and relocation in the nineteenth and twentieth centuries. The dynamic and shifting policies encouraged the adoption of Native children by non-Native parents and thereby "insinuate[d] settler futurity over and against Indigenous life and relations." Adoption policies worked in concert with laws of inheritance to dispossess Native people and Blacks through the fractionation of Native landed property in the post-Allotment period (1887–1934) and through the partition of heirs' property that disproportionately affected Blacks after Reconstruction. Both mechanisms "simultaneously advance a particular normative relation to ownership while holding the possibility of possession itself in abeyance and presuming the inevitability of loss as part of their instantiation." The violence that the chapter traces reaches through time, enacting its dispossessive force across generations as it shifts shape from a strategy of war to a civilizing strategy of uplift. Crucially, social reproduction and ecology, both often analytically sequestered from the economic because of their presumptively "natural" functions, capacities, and resources, are revealed in this chapter as paradigmatic sites of what Rob Nixon calls "slow violence" (see also Day).[40] The slow violence of laws restructuring kinship relations and inheritance dispossess marginalized groups of the resources and relationships on which their future depends while making their continued impoverishment appear to be endemic to the communities themselves rather than to external forces.

Cheryl I. Harris's "The Racial Alchemy of Debt: Dispossession and Accumulation in Afterlives of Slavery" traces how racial dispossession by debt has structured social relations and political economy in the afterlives of slavery. Whereas debt is formally race-neutral, Harris argues, it operates as a form of "racial alchemy" that obscures racially differentiated processes and burdens and abstracts systemic racial violence. Furthermore, both historically and contemporaneously, debt has turned racial subordination into a commodity that can be bought, sold, and speculated on. She analyzes this recurring pattern of dispossession through debt in its early form as Indigenous debt peonage and later in coerced labor systems such as convict leasing and chain gangs, tracing the changing forms of this extractive infrastructure across different carceral regimes up to the recent subprime mortgage and the Flint water crisis. Indian debt peonage, she argues, was intimately related to systems of coerced labor applied to Blacks. The settler colonial project of Indigenous land dispossession prepared the way for the cash-crop economies worked by enslaved and coerced Black labor. Debt peonage circumvented the formal abolition of Indian slavery and vagrancy laws aimed at disciplining Indian labor and created a template for the laws and work contracts imposed on Blacks after slavery. Abolition ended the value of Black people as chattel, but the imposition of Black Codes across the South and the system of convict leasing and the later chain gangs "transformed freed people into assets yet again, 'propertizing' and assigning value to Black bodies by virtue of their indebtedness." These systems were "implemented through formally color-blind laws and a ruthlessly targeted system of racialized administration." She concludes by examining how the Flint water crisis illustrates how neoliberalism not only dispossesses racial collectivities but can recycle what is devalued as throwaway or waste land by monetizing it. Harris's discussion of the centrality of the carceral state to racial capitalist and colonial extraction is taken up in the next section by Cacho and Melamed and by LeBrón, and the analysis of the accumulative strategies of wastelanding is further explored in the chapters by Jefferson and Day.

The chapters in the second section—Kimberly Kay Hoang's "In Search of the Next El Dorado: Mining for Capital in a Frontier Market with Colonial Legacies," Lisa Marie Cacho and Jodi Melamed's "'Don't Arrest Me, Arrest the Police': Policing as the Street Administration of Colonial Racial Capitalist Orders," Marisol LeBrón's "Policing Solidarity: Race, Violence, and the University of Puerto Rico," and Brian Jordan Jefferson's "Programming Colonial Racial Capitalism: Encoding Human Value in Smart Cities"—all focus on administration as a dominant vector of capital-preserving violence today. The chapters in the first section focus on lawmaking as a key mechanism of primitive accumulation or capital-positing violence, while the chapters that examine contemporary neoliberal capitalism broaden the frame to encompass the law and a whole array of administrative techniques.

In their recent work, Jodi Melamed and Chandan Reddy identify the importance of administrative power in contemporary capitalism, noting that it is the means through which racial violence becomes an "open secret" as violence takes the guise of routine calculations and everyday procedures that appear transparent and race-neutral. They specify three mechanisms through which administered racial violence and colonial power operate: (1) police procedures, (2) a liberal rights regime centered on accumulation rather than freedom, and (3) geo-economic strategies of command and control materialized in logistical operations.

The first chapter in this section illuminates administrative power within the context of the regional asymmetries of global financialization by looking at foreign direct investment flows into Vietnam, an emerging market economy in socialist transition, imagined by Western investors through a colonial prism as the "next El Dorado." The chapter provides us a detailed example of what Gómez-Barris has identified as a "mega-extractive project"; such projects, she explains, are "one of today's central modes of perpetuating racial capitalism in the Global South."[41] Using an extended case method, Hoang examines the face-off between the Vietnamese government and Western foreign investors over control of Vietranium (pseudonym) mining, a highly protected nationalistic sector of the economy. Woven into both parties' conflicting accounts of a failed $150 million investment venture is the gap between the white fantasy of a "lucrative new frontier" for investment and the political reality of Vietnam's paradoxically weak yet opaque legal and administrative regime that lures foreign investors in for quick profits but thwarts their efforts to obtain them. The chapter maps the complicated and unstable trialectics of Vietnamese negotiations with Western and Chinese capital, each marked by distinct histories of colonial domination. Hoang offers us a detailed account of how transnational capitalists move money across national borders and how a postcolonial, socialist nation-state both encourages and resists foreign investors' efforts to extract the nation's natural resources. She argues that the defeat of Western foreign investors by a country with a weak legal system and limited technological expertise appears counterintuitive but on closer scrutiny exposes the inadequacies of colonizer/colonized and center/periphery binaries prevalent in postcolonial studies. With the rise of East and Southeast Asian economies and the regional dominance of inter-Asian capital flows (in the wake of US President Donald Trump's withdrawal from the Trans-Pacific Partnership), Hoang suggests that new paradigms are needed to grapple with the reconfiguration of postcoloniality, sovereignty, and nationalism in countries like Vietnam. In the "Vietranium" project, the government allowed Western investors to assume risk in raising capital and testing for the profitability of mining operations, then used arcane tax laws to push them out of the country once they "struck gold." But what, Hoang asks, are the implications of the government's reassertion of sovereignty over its natural resources when the wealthy local officials and entrepreneurs who profit from it are not a nationalist vanguard but a transnational global elite?

In their chapter, Lisa Marie Cacho and Jodi Melamed examine policing as an administrative power that deploys violence work (including killing with impunity) in real time to criminalize, disqualify, and sort people for capitalist care or capitalist destruction, in order to fabricate and maintain specific relations of colonial racial capitalist accumulation in specific geographies. Seeing police work in this way allows us to understand the demands that have emerged from Black, Indigenous, gender-nonconforming, and other racialized and asset-stripped communities in the wake of George Floyd's killing—both the demand to defend oneself from police violence and live and the demand to defend others from the precarity, premature death, and economic violence of counterinsurgency policing—as revolutionary, profoundly loving, and breathtakingly insubordinate. Cacho and Melamed argue that to identify the weaknesses that colonial racial capitalist policing administers, we have to rethink liberalism writ large (private property, separation of powers, law) as a capitalist worlding praxis that relies on organized violence to realize—to make real—its terms of order. Policing must target the enlivening of Black, Indigenous, and people of color when such enlivening targets the stability of colonial racial capitalist modes of accumulation. Using examples of uprisings in the city that settlers named Milwaukee, Cacho and Melamed examine how acts of rebellion from communities that love themselves more than they fear the police, such as unity fires, marches, and a block-party protest in front of the city jail, defeat acts of policing as the street administration of colonial racial capitalism and, in the process, offer alternative ways of living, being, and relating to one another.

Marisol LeBrón also examines police procedures in her analysis of the university administration's deployment of police and private security forces to repress student strikes at the University of Puerto Rico. The strike, a direct challenge to the administration's moves to privatize the flagship campus, offers a striking example of a tipping point at which capital-preserving violence, to which the largely middle- and upper-class students on the flagship campus had been exposed till then, morphs suddenly into capital-positing violence typically reserved for poor and racially marginalized communities. LeBrón's essay focuses on the state's and university administration's responses to the fraught coalitions forged between the student movement and racially and economically marginalized Puerto Ricans during two university strikes. The difficulty that strikers had in maintaining a broader anticapitalist agenda across race and class lines in the face of police violence foregrounds the challenge for students and their supporters in reading the structural relationship between violence and capitalism and formulating a sustainable response to it. LeBrón draws complicated lessons from the strike, pointing to utopian moments of solidarity that emerged when students and security guards embraced and shook hands, but also to the diversion of the second strike from anticapitalist demands to containment of police violence as the coalition expanded. Although the two goals were inherently connected in the minds of many student activists, they became disarticulated as the violence against protesters intensified. Perhaps the twisting course of the strikes and their shifting solidarities, which importantly outlasted the strike and had "lasting transformational effects" on many of those involved, exemplify the potential and difficulty of seeing the link between violence and capitalism in the administrative regimes of financial capitalism. In "Open Secret," Melamed provides a penetrating description of police procedures as "the visible hand of the market," a recognition that undergirds Cacho and Melamed's and LeBrón's chapters, both of which point to the importance of police violence as a key site of study and struggle.[42]

Brian Jordan Jefferson's chapter, "Programming Colonial Racial Capitalism," analyzes how racial and spatial value is encoded in smart city governance through administrative software. In contrast to the overt if routinized violence of police repression, the colonial racial violence of smart technologies is abstracted, opaque, and remote. Smart governance optimizes administrative efficiency and economic growth, thereby reinforcing existing racial and colonial practices of human and geographical valuation, devaluation, expendability, and waste (see also Day). Jefferson analyzes two types of software, one used for property assessment and the other for waste management. If the former administers "the economic values of landscapes," the latter administers "how pollutable they are." The comparison between the two types of software connects the spheres of exchange and ecology to expose how algorithms routinize and rationalize racial and geographical devaluation, as well as ecological and human degradation and destruction. Ironically, as Jefferson notes, both technologies are promoted as "neutral scientifically based" solutions that remedy racially discriminatory decisions rooted in subjective bias. In this way, computerized administration enables "the extension of market control into minority communities inside wealthier Western countries and across economically liberalizing areas of the global South." Such administrative software supports operations on a global scale but delivers lethal violence in localities through operations that are harder to track and resist. The global explosion of property-assessment technology facilitates the subsumption of the cadastral systems of postcolonial countries into global finance markets, whereas waste-management technology enables logistical operations that generate differential "spatial profiles in ways that naturalize the logics of the market and contribute to 'group-differentiated vulnerability to premature death.'" Jefferson points to the urgent need for an "algorithmic abolitionist thinking" that can grapple with the violence of smart urbanization. Indeed, he argues, within these emergent modes of racial colonial governance, built on hierarchies of global space, new possibilities for coalition building between the various devalued populations can emerge.

The third section ("Aesthetics") features two essays, Iyko Day's "Nuclear Antipolitics and the Queer Art of Logistical Failure" and Laura

Pulido's "Erasing Empire: Remembering the Mexican-American War in Los Angeles," which explore the historical erasure of settler colonialism and racial capitalism in public commemoration of two important military events: the atomic bombing of Hiroshima in August 1945 and the Mexican-American War (1846–1848). The century separating the two events shows the recurrence of extra-economic coercion and dispossession in US capitalist development. Yet the liberal ideology of market freedom and democracy requires the disavowal of the deep reliance on lethal force to establish and expand capitalist rule. Both Day and Pulido show how the devastation inflicted by these wars is "aestheticized and anaesthetized" in collective history and memory. These essays explore the various forms of "colonial unknowing" perpetuated by official histories of the Mexican-American War and the Hiroshima bombing.

Iyko Day argues that the global cultural memory of Hiroshima as a cautionary tale of the excesses of technoscientific modernity, espoused in different forms by the US and Japanese state, transmutes the historical exploitation of nuclear modernity into universal stories of suffering that obscure their respective imperial pasts. In contrast to the spectacular violence of the Hiroshima bombing that has preoccupied cultural memory, Day turns to visual representations of nuclear wastelands where radioactive minerals are mined and toxic waste disposed, reading them as the unregarded sites of the slow violence of military and economic domination. From the vantage point of these devastated nuclear wastelands, many of which lie on Indigenous lands and in the global South, "the antipolitical frame of technopolitics reveals the coordinated expansion and technological intensification of imperial state power that is secured through its simultaneous *depoliticization*" (see also Harris and Jefferson on wastelanding). These "radioactive nonsites of nuclear modernity," she argues, locate Hiroshima "in a history of colonial capitalism rooted in energy extraction, from coal and oil to uranium." Day takes up these questions through an analysis of the sculptures in Hiroshima-based artist Takahiro Iwasaki's *Out of Disorder* series. In his table dioramas, Iwasaki uses found materials to represent the energy landscapes of Hiroshima as a literal wasteland. He composes his sculptures from discarded commodities such as toothbrushes, kimonos, and towels, exposing through the arrangement of this human detritus the failure of use values in capitalism and the disruption of capitalist temporality and the commodity form. Thus, Day concludes, Iwasaki's works offer "alternative insights on energy infrastructures in the shadow of nuclear modernity."

Laura Pulido examines how the transition from Mexican to US rule is envisioned and narrated in historical sites and landscapes commemorating the Mexican-American War. She describes how the sites commemorating the US government's seizure of a quarter-million square miles of territory recast the violence of conquest through romantic visions of a bucolic Spanish past that gave way to modernizing US rule. Of two sites that were important battlefields, she notes that the weaponry of domination—cannons and guns—is showcased in decontextualized tributes to their technological sophistication while "the violence of the war is largely evacuated." The Fort Moore Pioneer Memorial lauds the US battalions, pioneers, and Anglo-American settlers as the primary agents responsible for "the evolution of the region from US conquest to the 1950s, when the sculpture was completed." The bas-relief sculpture of pioneers, wagons, cows, houses, and trees provide paeans to modernization, heteropatriarchy, land development, and property ownership and overwrite the violent dispossession and displacement of Indigenous people and Mexicans. To offer a countervision of the Mexican-American War, Pulido examines the visual aesthetics of *Tree of Califas*, which is featured in the underground train stop of the Metropolitan Transit Authority adjacent to the Campo de Cahuenga site. Highlighting the Mexican/Chicanx and Indigenous perspective, the mural embeds the Mexican-American War in the violent transition from Spanish conquest to US conquest. Rather than erasing empire, the installation locates the war in the framework of "inter-imperiality," highlighting and connecting Indigenous dispossession and Mexican racialization between two imperial regimes.[43] The Mexican-American War marks not an entry into capitalist modernity but the recurrence of imperial violence on land seized by multiple empires.

The final section of the book, "Rehearsing for the Future," centers a conversation between Ruth Wilson Gilmore and Michael Dawson that is both a reflection on their careers as legendary scholar-activists and a primer on the work still needed to seize the future away from the structures of dispossessive racial capitalism. As scholar activists who were at the forefront of shaping and cohering racial capitalism as a vitally necessary response to the on-the-ground and on-the-ropes revolutionary movements in California and Chicago that, as Dawson says, "were trying to understand the intersection of white supremacy and capitalism in the United States," Gilmore and Dawson constellate some of the driving forces that centered racial theory within political economy as a way to understand the imperative nows of the present. With remembrances of and stories about Cedric Robinson and Clyde Woods, critiques of the reformist Left, and thoughts on reinvigorating the stakes in understanding that all capitalism is racial, Dawson and Gilmore provide the counternarratives and time lines through which to reimagine how the basic institutions of family, education, work, and care might radically transform away from carcerality, debt peonage, and violence and toward the grassroots collectivities and solidarities that emerge beyond the continual rehearsing and circulation of white supremacist horror on social media.

The year 2020 and the days, months, and year(s) to come may be unprecedented, as many activists, pundits, politicians, and scholars have already said—with the simultaneity of a global pandemic; economic, financial, infrastructural, and housing crises; anti-Black police brutality; social unrest and uprising; authoritarianism; ecological catastrophes; and the competing forces of incarceration, eviction, homelessness, and the vested interests of white supremacy and settler colonialism structuring the logics of access—and we are only just beginning to understand the forces of repression and transformation that have shaped the futures to come. What we can see already is that the logistics of production, policing, health care, and livability are intricately entangled with the structures of property, profit, and security that have been the cornerstones of anti-Black settler colonialism, imperialism, and white supremacy. Incarcerating social-justice workers and anticolonial laborers extracts energy, passion, life, time, knowledge, history, and theory from communities, trying to force interruptions and disruptions in their respective and collective struggles. But this also happens when we lock away the lives of those with less spectacular and less honorable backgrounds as if the complex, difficult choices they made under trying circumstances nullify everything they can offer to their communities and erase all their future brilliant ideas so desperately needed in this society. Resisting itself becomes criminalized and the frame and excuse for death-dealing regimes. In this way, we are all recruited to affirm the logic of colonial racial capitalism by disavowing those whom the carceral state and the authoritarian state have deemed guilty and undeserving. Colonial racial capitalism not only exploits, destroys, extracts, and devalues labor and land but also damages relationships, communities, and the alternative visions and futures that we need to build better lifeworlds. We believe that the chapters included in this collection provide some of the critical tools and frameworks needed to build toward those better lifeworlds that arise from the simultaneous struggles for decolonization and abolition.

NOTES

1. Kelley, "Foreword," xiv. The term *racial capitalism* was used in a pamphlet, *Foreign Investment and the Reproduction of Racial Capitalism in South Africa*, by white South African Marxists Martin Legassick and David Hemson. They were part of a larger group of South African thinkers and activists who used the term to analyze the distinctive nexus of white supremacy, imperialism, and capitalism in apartheid South Africa.

2. Kelley, "Foreword," xiv. See also Milkman, "Apartheid, Economic Growth"; Hudson, "Racial Capitalism"; Clarno, *Neoliberal Apartheid*; Kundnani, "What Is Racial Capitalism?"; Burden-Stelly, Hudson, and Pierre, "Racial Capitalism, Black Liberation."

3. Robinson, *Black Marxism*, 26; Gilmore, "What is the 'Racial'?"

4. Dussel, "Eurocentrism and Modernity," 67.

5. Ferreira da Silva, "Globality," 36.

6. Ferreira da Silva, "Globality," 34.

7. Nast, "'Race' and the Bio(necro)polis," 1458.

8. Prashad, *Poorer Nations*, 10.

9. Jodi A. Byrd, "Indigenomicon," Zoom talk, Digital Democracies Institute, Simon Fraser University, May 5, 2021.

10. Coulthard, *Red Skin, White Masks*, 12.

11. Coulthard, *Red Skin, White Masks*, 7. Coulthard addresses several critiques of "primitive accumulation," among them that Marx and Marxists have narrated primitive accumulation in ways that read the violent dispossession of colonized Indigenous peoples and their lands as a finished moment in the history of modern capitalism, necessary to erect the contemporary relations of exploitation that separate the waged worker from the means of production. This incorrect premise, Coulthard explains, comes from Marx's writings that described primitive accumulation as "the accumulation of capital through violent state dispossession resulting in proletarianization" (10). As Coulthard and others remind us, Indigenous people have also always been laborers and Indigenous dispossession is still ongoing.

12. Coulthard, *Red Skin, White Masks*, 13.

13. Nichols, *Theft Is Property!*, 8, 31, 9.

14. Some scholars, such as Nancy Fraser, see primitive accumulation as always violent because they connect it to racialized expropriation, but as Coulthard reminds us, this is not necessarily the case: state dispossession also works through strategies of accommodation and recognition. Challenges to stagist readings of primitive accumulation have also been made by scholars in Black studies, such as Nikhil Pal

Singh, who critiques the relegation of slavery to a precapitalist or noncapitalist era in Marxist thought.

15. Coulthard, *Red Skin, White Masks*, 13.

16. Coulthard, "Colonialism of the Present."

17. Reddy, "Is Justice a Process or an Outcome?"

18. Melamed, "Racial Capitalism," 77.

19. Barker, "Corporation and the Tribe," 265.

20. See Dawson, "Hidden in Plain Sight"; De Angelis, "Marx's Theory of Primitive Accumulation"; Federici, *Caliban and the Witch*; Federici, "Debt Crisis"; Fraser, "Expropriation and Exploitation in Racialized Capitalism"; Fraser, "Legitimation Crisis?"; Hall, "Primitive Accumulation"; Harvey, *New Imperialism*; Ince, "Between Equal Rights"; Ince, *Colonial Capitalism*; Nichols, "Disaggregating Primitive Accumulation"; Nichols, *Theft Is Property!*; Sassen, *Expulsions*; Sassen, "Savage Sorting"; and Singh, "On Race, Violence, and So-Called Primitive Accumulation."

21. Marx, *Capital*, 899–900.

22. Luxemburg, *Accumulation of Capital*, 364–66, 370–76, 452–54; De Angelis, "Marx's Theory of Primitive Accumulation," 5.

23. See Amin, *Accumulation on a World Scale*; Banaji, *Theory as History*; Coulthard, *Red Skin, White Masks*; Guha, *Dominance without Hegemony*; Guha, *Elementary Aspects*; Mintz, *Sweetness and Power*; Rodney, *How Europe Underdeveloped Africa*; Sanyal, *Rethinking Capitalist Development*; and Williams, *Capitalism and Slavery*.

24. Amin, *Accumulation on a World Scale*, 3.

25. Coulthard, *Red Skin, White Masks*, 14.

26. Ince, "Between Equal Rights," 9, 16–18, 19.

27. Davies, *Left of Karl Marx*; Fuentes, *Dispossessed Lives*; Haley, *No Mercy Here*; McDuffie, *Sojourning for Freedom*; Morgan, *Reproduction and Gender*; Weinbaum, *Afterlife of Reproductive Slavery*.

28. Hong, *Ruptures of American Capital*, xxiv.

29. Gore and LaBaron, "Using Social Reproduction Theory," 563.

30. Moore, *Capitalism in the Web of Life*, 53.

31. Gómez-Barris, *Extractive Zone*, xvi, xix, xvii.

32. Gilmore, "Abolition Geography," 227.

33. Melamed, "Racial Capitalism," 78.

34. Kearney, "Dear Editor—."

35. Gómez-Barris, *Extractive Zone*, xix.

36. Marx, *Capital*, 899.

37. Beckert, *Empire of Cotton*, xv.

38. Melamed and Reddy, "Using Liberal Rights."

39. Vimalassery, Pegues, and Goldstein, "On Colonial Unknowing," 1042; Spivak, *Outside in the Teaching Machine*, 63.

40. Nixon, *Slow Violence*, 2.

41. Gómez-Barris, *Extractive Zone*, xvii.

42. Melamed, "Open Secret."

43. Doyle, "Inter-imperiality," 159.

BIBLIOGRAPHY

Amin, Samir. *Accumulation on a World Scale: A Critique of the Theory of Underdevelopment*. New York: Monthly Review Press, 1974.
Banaji, Jairus. *Theory as History: Essays on Modes of Production and Exploitation*. Leiden, Netherlands: Brill, 2010.
Barker, Joanne. "The Corporation and the Tribe." *American Indian Quarterly* 39, no. 3 (2015): 243–70.
Beckert, Sven. *Empire of Cotton: A Global History*. New York: Alfred A. Knopf, 2015.
Burden-Stelly, Cherisse, Peter James Hudson, and Jemima Pierre. "Racial Capitalism, Black Liberation, and South Africa." *Black Agenda Report*, December 16, 2020. https://blackagendareport.com/racial-capitalism-black-liberation-and-south-africa.
Clarno, Andy. *Neoliberal Apartheid: Palestine, Israel and South Africa after 1994*. Chicago: University of Chicago Press, 2017.
Coulthard, Glen Sean. "The Colonialism of the Present." Interview by Andrew Bard Epstein. *Jacobin*, January 13, 2015. www.jacobinmag.com/2015/01/indigenous-left-glen-coulthard-interview.
Coulthard, Glen Sean. *Red Skin, White Masks: Rejecting the Colonial Politics of Recognition*. Minneapolis: University of Minnesota Press, 2014.
Davies, Carole Boyce. *Left of Karl Marx: The Political Life of Black Communist Claudia Jones*. Durham, NC: Duke University Press, 2007.
Dawson, Michael C. "Hidden in Plain Sight: A Note on Legitimation Crises and the Racial Order." *Critical Historical Studies* 3, no. 1 (Spring 2016): 143–61.
De Angelis, Massimo. "Marx's Theory of Primitive Accumulation: A Suggested Reinterpretation." University of East London, Department of Economics, Working Paper 29, May 2000.
Doyle, Laura. "Inter-imperiality: Dialectics in a Postcolonial World History." *Interventions* 16, no. 2 (2014): 159–96.
Dussel, Enrique. "Eurocentrism and Modernity (Introduction to the Frankfurt Lectures)." *boundary 2* 20, no 3 (Autumn 1993): 65–76.

Federici, Silvia. *Caliban and the Witch: Women, the Body, and Primitive Accumulation.* New York: Autonomedia, 2004.

Federici, Silvia. "The Debt Crisis, Africa and the New Enclosures." In *Midnight Oil: Work, Energy, War, 1973–1992,* edited by Midnight Notes Collective. New York: Autonomedia. 1992.

Ferreira da Silva, Denise. "Globality." *Critical Ethnic Studies* 1, no. 1 (Spring 2015): 33–38.

Fraser, Nancy. "Expropriation and Exploitation in Racialized Capitalism: A Reply to Michael Dawson." *Critical Historical Studies* 3, no. 1 (Spring 2016): 163–78.

Fraser, Nancy. "Legitimation Crisis? On the Political Contradictions of Financialized Capitalism." *Critical Historical Studies* 2, no. 2 (Fall 2015): 157–89.

Fuentes, Marisa J. *Dispossessed Lives: Enslaved Women, Violence, and the Archive.* Philadelphia: University of Pennsylvania Press, 2016.

Gilmore, Ruth Wilson. "Abolition Geography and the Problem of Innocence." In *Futures of Black Radicalism,* edited by Gaye Theresa Johnson and Alex Lubin, 225–40. New York: Verso, 2017.

Gilmore, Ruth Wilson. "What Is the 'Racial' in Racial Capitalism? Magic, Partition, Politics." Keynote lecture presented at the Unit for Criticism and Interpretive Theory Conference on Racial Capitalism, University of Illinois, Urbana-Champaign, March 29, 2019.

Gómez-Barris, Macarena. *The Extractive Zone: Social Ecologies and Decolonial Perspectives.* Durham, NC: Duke University Press, 2017.

Gore, Ellie, and Genevieve LaBaron. "Using Social Reproduction Theory to Understand Unfree Labour." *Capital and Class* 43, no. 4 (2019): 561–80.

Guha, Ranajit. *Dominance without Hegemony.* Cambridge, MA: Harvard University Press, 1998.

Guha, Ranajit. *Elementary Aspects of Peasant Insurgency in Colonial India.* Delhi: Oxford University Press, 1983.

Haley, Sarah. *No Mercy Here: Gender, Punishment, and the Making of Jim Crow Modernity.* Chapel Hill: University of North Carolina Press, 2016.

Hall, Derek. "Primitive Accumulation, Accumulation by Dispossession and the Global Land Grab." *Third World Quarterly* 34, no. 9 (2013): 1582–1604.

Harvey, David. *The New Imperialism.* Oxford: Oxford University Press, 2003.

Hong, Grace Kyungwon. *The Ruptures of American Capital: Women of Color Feminism and the Culture of Immigrant Labor.* Minneapolis: University of Minnesota Press, 2006.

Hudson, Peter James. "Racial Capitalism and the Dark Proletariat." *Boston Review,* February 20, 2018. http://bostonreview.net/forum/remake-world-slavery -racial-capitalism-and-justice/peter-james-hudson-racial-capitalism-and.

Ince, Onur Ulas. "Between Equal Rights: Primitive Accumulation and Capital's Violence." *Political Theory* (2017): 1–30. https://doi.org/10.1177 /0090591717748420.

Ince, Onur Ulas. *Colonial Capitalism and the Dilemmas of Liberalism*. New York: Oxford University Press, 2018.

Kearney, Douglas. "Dear Editor—: An Open Letter from Douglas Kearney." *Cave Canem: A Home for Black Poetry*. https://cavecanempoets.org/an-open-letter-from-douglas-kearney.

Kelley, Robin D. G. "Foreword: Why *Black Marxism*, Why Now?" In Robinson, *Black Marxism*, 3rd ed., xi–xxxiv. Chapel Hill: University of North Carolina Press, 2020.

Kundnani, Arun. "What Is Racial Capitalism?" October 23, 2020. www.kundnani.org/what-is-racial-capitalism.

Legassick, Martin, and David Hemson. *Foreign Investment and the Reproduction of Racial Capitalism in South Africa*. Johannesburg: Foreign Investment in South Africa—A Discussion Series, no. 2, 1976.

Luxemburg, Rosa. *The Accumulation of Capital*. London: Routledge, 1951 (1913).

Marx, Karl. *Capital*. New York: Penguin, 1976 (1867).

McDuffie, Erik. *Sojourning for Freedom: Black Women, American Communism, and the Making of Black Left Feminism*. Durham, NC: Duke University Press, 2011.

Melamed, Jodi. "The Open Secret of Racial Capitalism." Lecture presented for the Unit for Criticism and Interpretive Theory Modern Critical Theory Lecture Series, University of Illinois, Urbana-Champaign, March 27, 2018.

Melamed, Jodi. "Racial Capitalism." *Critical Ethnic Studies* 1, no. 1 (2015): 76–85.

Melamed, Jodi, and Chandan Reddy. "Using Liberal Rights to Enforce Racial Capitalism." *Items*, May 29, 2019. https://items.ssrc.org/race-capitalism/using-liberal-rights-to-enforce-racial-capitalism.

Milkman, Ruth. "Apartheid, Economic Growth, and US Foreign Policy in South Africa." *Berkeley Journal of Sociology* 22 (1977): 45–100.

Mintz, Sidney. *Sweetness and Power: The Place of Sugar in Modern History*. New York: Penguin, 1986.

Moore, Jason. *Capitalism in the Web of Life: Accumulation and the Ecology of Capital*. London: Verso, 2015.

Morgan, Jennifer L. *Reproduction and Gender in New World Slavery*. Philadelphia: University of Pennsylvania Press, 2004.

Nast, Heidi J. "'Race' and the Bio(necro)polis." *Antipode* 43, no. 5 (November 2011): 1457–64.

Nichols, Robert. "Disaggregating Primitive Accumulation." *Radical Philosophy* 194 (2015): 18–28.

Nichols, Robert. *Theft Is Property! Dispossession and Critical Theory*. Durham, NC: Duke University Press, 2020.

Nixon, Rob. *Slow Violence and the Environmentalism of the Poor*. Cambridge, MA: Harvard University Press, 2013.

Prashad, Vijay. *The Poorer Nations: A Possible History of the Global South*. New York: Verso, 2012.

Reddy, Chandan. "Is Justice a Process or an Outcome?" Accessed May 30, 2021. https://bambitchell.henryart.org/is-justice-a-process-or-an-outcome /chandan-reddy.

Robinson, Cedric J. *Black Marxism: The Making of the Black Radical Tradition.* 3rd ed. Chapel Hill: University of North Carolina Press, 2000.

Rodney, Walter. *How Europe Underdeveloped Africa.* London: Bogle-L'Overture, 1972.

Sanyal, Kalyan. *Rethinking Capitalist Development: Primitive Accumulation, Governmentality, and Post-colonial Capitalism.* New Delhi: Routledge, 2007.

Sassen, Saskia. *Expulsions: Brutality and Complexity in the Global Economy.* Cambridge, MA: Harvard University Press, 2014.

Sassen, Saskia. "A Savage Sorting of Winners and Losers: Contemporary Versions of Primitive Accumulation." *Globalizations* 7 (2010): 23–50.

Singh, Nikhil Pal. "On Race, Violence, and So-Called Primitive Accumulation." *Social Text* 34, no. 3 (2016): 27–50.

Spivak, Gayatri Chakravorty. *Outside in the Teaching Machine.* New York: Routledge, 1993.

Vimalassery, Manu, Juliana Hu Pegues, and Alyosha Goldstein. "Introduction: On Colonial Unknowing." *Theory and Event* 19, no. 4 (2016): 1042–54.

Weinbaum, Alys Eve. *The Afterlife of Reproductive Slavery: Biocapitalism and Black Feminism's Philosophy of History.* Durham, NC: Duke University Press, 2019.

Williams, Eric. *Capitalism and Slavery.* Chapel Hill: University of North Carolina Press, 1944.

I Accumulation

DEVELOPMENT BY DISPOSSESSION

The Corporation and the Tribe

The system ain't broke. It was built to be this way.

TOM B. K. GOLDTOOTH (DINÉ/DAKOTA), 2012

A Prologue

This chapter examines how the foundational legal definitions of the "corporation" and the "tribe" between 1790 and 1887 worked together to establish and protect imperialist social relations and conditions in the United States between powerful financial interests, both government and corporate, and Indigenous peoples. Although the analysis is historically focused, I want to frame it by the current political debates and organizing efforts against government and corporate collusion and fraud represented by Occupy Wall Street (ows) and my engagement with Occupy Oakland. I hope this will help us to better understand how the history of the territorial dispossession and collusive fraud enacted by the US government and corporate interests against Indigenous peoples clarifies the kinds of issues of government and corporate collusion and fraud that ows has addressed. To be clear, the 1 percent did not show up in 2008. They have been around all along, targeting Indigenous peoples and their territories over which the US empire was built and continues to operate.

On September 17, 2011, ows began in Zuccotti Park (Liberty Plaza), in Manhattan's financial district, with the goal of "fighting back against the corrosive power of major banks and multinational corporations over the democratic process, and the role of Wall Street in creating an economic collapse that has caused the greatest recession in generations."[1] From my particular viewpoint in Oakland, California, it seemed that ows had swiftly coalesced the demands of a wide array of grassroots-based organizations and individuals for solidarity against and open debate about the more insidious legal protections of government and corporate collusion. For instance, discussions prompted by ows exposed the gross misrepresentations of congressional representatives and energy industry CEOs about job creation and public safety in Canada's Keystone XL Pipeline and its proposed extensions through the United States and then linked these lies to the ongoing struggles of Indigenous peoples for environmental justice.[2] When so many Occupy Oakland participants began showing up in solidarity at Indigenous actions in the Bay Area, such as the Chochenyo Ohlone's Annual Emeryville Shellmound Protest on Black Friday, I genuinely believed that the ows movement had succeeded in opening a critical space for much-needed discussions about the structural, ideological, and social links between the foreclosure of many Black people, Asian Americans, and Latina/os from their homes and the US dispossession of Indigenous peoples from their territorial homelands. I was optimistic—unusually so for me—that these discussions would lead to meaningful solidarity and transformation.

Many things happened that changed my mind and thinking so much that I began the research that informs this chapter. The first occurred on October 27, 2011, when a group of us failed to convince those present at an Occupy Oakland General Assembly to change the name of Occupy Oakland to Decolonize Oakland in recognition of the fact that Oakland is already on occupied lands. Although the assembly did pass a rather non-threatening statement of solidarity with Indigenous peoples, they accused us then and in the Bay Area press of trying to "guilt trip" them into some larger-than-life demand for Indigenous land reparations that went far beyond, they argued, the urgent issues of the foreclosure crisis and the militarized crackdown on ows in Oakland that they cared about. They argued with us more sincerely, and ironically, that changing the name from Occupy to Decolonize would result in them losing "brand recognition" and so their affiliation with the broader movement.[3]

We responded by organizing a series of teach-ins to more carefully work people through the historical, legal, and social connections between the foreclosures on Black, Asian American, and Latina/o homes and the dispossession of Indigenous peoples in the Bay Area. Along with several other mostly Indigenous women, we hosted the teach-ins, just before the Occupy Oakland General Assembly, from mid-December 2011 through early May 2012 at Oscar Grant Plaza and then at community centers within walking distance of the plaza. Initially, the teach-ins gathered a diverse range of individuals. But almost immediately Indigenous peoples—particularly Ohlone—stopped attending. This seemed to be because of the hostile resistance we experienced against the historical links we argued existed between the foreclosure crisis and the dispossession of Ohlone people. The most severe expression of this hostility occurred when a man who identified himself to me as a "member of the Black community" accused me of having a "hidden agenda" to move "Indians" into the "family homes of Black people" that the banks had foreclosed on.

The intergenerational consequences of foreclosure and the pain and frustration of the rampant evictions of Black families from their homes in Oakland were real and vicious. After several such exchanges, I came to believe that those involved in the Occupy movement (including me) had not done so well at fulfilling the core pedagogical mandate of movements like it to provide the historical and social contexts needed for non-Indigenous communities to understand why Indigenous peoples might perceive the foreclosure crisis as merely (though importantly) the most recent representation of a long history of collusive and fraudulent land issues defining the US economy as an imperialist one.

This chapter results from my reflection on the pedagogical approaches and content needed within movements like ows to build lasting solidarities across the very community divides—perceptual, structural, and other—on which the US imperial formation depends. These approaches must be characterized by compassion, generosity, reciprocity, and responsibility and must be historical, social, and legal. Working to reform a bad set of laws that protect Wall Street banking interests from taxation or bringing criminal charges against banking executives will not—on their own—adequately address the needs of our diverse communities. Corrections or amendments or enforcement, in other words, does not demand any real structural change. The kind of social transformations needed can happen only from a place of genuine understanding—compassionate, respectful, and informed—about all of the historical and social complexities of oppression and exploitation that inform the perceptions and experiences of our communities.

An Introduction to "Corporations" and "Indian Tribes"

How does the historical and ongoing dispossession of Indigenous peoples clarify the "corrosive power of major banks and multinational corporations over the democratic process" within the United States? How is "the role of Wall Street in creating an economic collapse that has caused the greatest recession in generations" more effectively understood in relation to ongoing Indigenous struggles against jurisdictional and territorial dispossession than within its more popular frame of reference to the Great Depression?

This chapter, divided into two main sections, considers these questions by examining how the core foundational definitions of the legal status and rights of "corporations" and "Indian tribes" worked in concert to establish and protect imperialist social relations and conditions between powerful financial interests, both government and corporate, and Indigenous peoples. The first part of the chapter examines the limitations of the status and rights of "Indian tribes" to trade—commercially and in lands and resources—by the US Congress through treaties between 1778 and 1871, the six Acts to Regulate Trade and Intercourse with the Indian Tribes between 1790 and 1834, and the pivotal decision of the Supreme Court of the United States (SCOTUS) in *Johnson's Lessee v. McIntosh* of 1823. I compare the consequences of these laws to the SCOTUS decisions regarding corporate rights in *Fletcher v. Peck* of 1810 and *Trustees of Dartmouth College v. Woodward* of 1819. Therein, SCOTUS ruled that the US Constitution provided (1) that states were restricted from invalidating contracts that carried out the sale and acquisition of tribally treatied lands, irrespective of any fraud or the possession of proper title on which those contracts were based, and (2) that corporate charters qualified as contracts between private parties with which states could not interfere.

In the second part of the chapter I examine how the legal status and rights of "Indian tribes" were all but decimated by the US Senate's unilateral suspension of treaty making in 1871 and the terms and administration of the General Allotment Act of 1887. I link the loss of treaty-making powers and territorial dissolution to the SCOTUS decision in *Santa Clara County v. Southern Pacific Railroad Company* (1886). In that decision, SCOTUS ruled that corporations possessed Fourteenth Amendment rights analogous to those of "persons," a stark contrast to the way concurrent law was stripping tribes of any and all legal protections to governance and lands.

Focused historically between 1790 and 1887, this chapter provides a legal analysis of core US statutes and court decisions in the definition and provision of corporate and tribal status and rights. Though focused historically, it anticipates a readership that cares about how this history matters in thinking through the socio-legal importance of the questions raised by ows and movements like it in relation to Indigenous strategies for political coalition and legal revolution. It assumes that the US dispossession of Indigenous peoples clarifies the "corrosive power of major banks and multinational corporations over the democratic process" as well as "the role of Wall Street in creating an economic collapse that has caused the greatest recession in generations" by bringing into sharp relief the collusive and fraudulent relations among the US Congress, the courts, and corporations.[4] In doing so, it does not presume the current system's catastrophes—marked by the 2008 foreclosure crisis—are aberrations or abnormalities of US democracy. Rather, as Tom B. K. Goldtooth (Diné/Dakota), executive director of the Indigenous Environmental Network, said during a 2012 Toronto symposium titled "The Occupy Talks: Indigenous Perspectives on the Occupy Movement," "The system ain't broke. It was built to be this way."[5]

Part 1: Indian Tribes and Corporate Artificiality

THE TRADE IN "INDIAN TRIBES"

The phrase "Indian tribes" appears only once in the US Constitution. Article 1, section 8, enumerates the powers of the US Congress, including jurisdiction over taxation; the national debt and borrowing; naturalization law; bankruptcy and counterfeit law; coinage; post offices and roads; copyright protections; appointment of tribunals; prosecution of crimes on the high seas and offenses against foreign nations; the declaration of war and the commission of armies, naval forces, and militia; and the construction of public buildings. It provides that Congress will "make all laws which shall be necessary and proper for carrying into execution the foregoing powers, and all other powers vested by this Constitution in the government of the United States, or in any department or officer thereof." Clause 3 provides specifically that Congress has the power "to regulate commerce with foreign nations, and among the several states, and with the Indian tribes."

Congressional power to regulate commerce with Indian tribes was enacted in 371 ratified treaties between 1778 and 1871 and six separate statutes in 1790, 1793, 1796, 1799, 1802, and 1834 titled "An Act to Regulate Trade and Intercourse with the Indian Tribes." In ratified treaties, Congress established the boundaries of tribal territories and secured tribal rights to governance within them, excepting jurisdiction over US citizens and slaves or Indians who committed crimes against them. The ratified treaties frequently provided for forms of economic self-sufficiency unique to the tribal signatories, such as protecting hunting and fishing rights in "usual and accustomed places." They often provided for annuities, including payments and goods, in compensation for land cessions. They explicitly guaranteed that no US citizen would be permitted to illegally settle, hunt, or fish within tribal territories. They affirmed congressional authority in tribal trade and protected tribal rights to trade with US citizens.

The 1790 Act to Regulate Trade and Intercourse with the Indian Tribes established a federally regulated licensing system for US citizens wanting to trade with tribes, strict punishments for crimes committed against tribes on tribal lands by US citizens, the prohibition of liquor sales on tribal lands, and restriction against tribal land sales to anyone but Congress by treaty: "That no sale of lands made by any Indians, or any nation or tribe of Indians within the United States, shall be valid to any person or persons, or to any state, whether having the right of pre-emption to such lands or not, unless the same shall be made and duly executed at some public treaty, held under the authority of the United States."[6] In response to rampant treaty violations, the 1793 and 1796 acts provided stricter measures for federal oversight and licensing, stricter measures for horse sales, and an affirmation of treaty provisions respecting tribal boundaries. Anyone attempting to settle on tribal lands was to be expelled, fined up to $1,000, and imprisoned up to one year.[7] These measures were further strengthened in 1799, 1802, and 1834.

Established by the Indian Trade and Intercourse Acts (as they were known), trading houses or posts operated under federal oversight from 1796 to 1822 "to supply the Indians with necessary goods at a fair price and offer a fair price for the furs in exchange" (at the time, furs were the most common trade item). The superintendent of Indian trade, a position established in 1806, and the agents at the posts were appointed through the office of the president, and their accounts were managed by the secretary of the treasury.[8] The posts were closed in 1822, in large part because fur traders had so effectively circumvented the posts' oversight that they became obsolete.[9] In 1824 the secretary of war created the Bureau of Indian Affairs (BIA), in part to oversee trade with the tribes.[10] The BIA was transferred to the Department of the Interior in 1849.

Even while the US Congress recognized and protected the rights of Indian tribes to commerce and trade over/within their territories by ratified treaties and the Indian Trade and Intercourse Acts, it subjected the terms and exercise of those rights to its own plenary authority. This subjugation coalesced in the SCOTUS decision in *Johnson's Lessee v. McIntosh* of 1823.[11] On the surface, the case involved competing claims to the same eleven thousand acres of land in the state of Illinois. The lands fell within the unique territorial boundaries of the Piankeshaw Nation, whose particular borders had been affirmed by 1773 and 1775 treaties with the British. Even SCOTUS argued that the United States inherited the obligations of these treaties from the Crown by the Treaty of Paris in 1783.

The plaintiffs were the legal heirs of Thomas Johnson, who, along with several other British citizens, claimed to have lawfully purchased the acreage and neighboring areas from the Piankeshaw and Illinois nations. The defendant was William McIntosh, who claimed to have acquired a deed to the land in 1818 from the US Department of the Interior. The question before SCOTUS, as Chief Justice John Marshall framed it, was what kind of title the Piankeshaw Nation held in the lands. But before deciding, the Court had to address two facts: (1) the US Congress had acknowledged in its ratified treaties with Indian tribes—as had all European nations before it—that tribes possessed a land title that they could treat upon; and (2) the treaties themselves referred to Indian tribes as sovereign nations with all commensurate jurisdictional rights over and within their territories.

Though not missing the import of treaty language, SCOTUS sided with McIntosh on the grounds that Indian tribes had never been recognized as equal "sovereign, independent states":

> The uniform understanding and practice of European nations, and the settled law, as laid down by the tribunals of civilized states, denied the right of the Indians to be considered as independent communities, having a permanent property in the soil, capable of alienation to private individuals. They remain in a state of nature, and have never been admitted into the general society of nations.

This understanding, SCOTUS maintained, was reflected in the treaties:

> All the treaties and negotiations between the civilized powers of Europe and of this continent . . . have uniformly disregarded their supposed right to the territory included within the jurisdictional limits of those powers. Not only has the practice of all civilized nations been in conformity with this doctrine, but the whole theory of their titles to lands in America, rests upon the hypothesis, that the Indians had no right of soil as sovereign, independent states.

Effectively, SCOTUS rewrote treaty history to find that treaties with Indigenous nations functioned internationally in a way contrary to the precepts of international law. Instead of recognizing Indigenous sovereignty, nationhood, and territorial rights, the Court argued that the treaties had, all along, "disregarded" Indigenous legal status and rights as sovereign nations. The Court argued that the evidence for this fact of disregard was discovery:

> Discovery is the foundation of title, in European nations, and this overlooks all proprietary rights in the natives. The sovereignty and eminent domain thus acquired, necessarily precludes the idea of any other sovereignty existing within the same limits. The subjects of the discovering nation must necessarily be bound by the declared sense of their own government, as to the extent of this sovereignty, and the domain acquired with it. Even if it should be admitted that the Indians were originally an independent people, they have ceased to be so. A nation that has passed under the dominion of another, is no longer a sovereign state. The same treaties and negotiations, before referred to, show their dependent condition.

The Court claimed that by virtue of their relationship to the land as Lockean hunter-gatherers, having always already passed into a Hegelian subservience to dominant sovereigns owing to their need for the master's protection, Indigenous peoples had been made "subject to the sovereignty of the United States." These were well-established facts, the Court contended, of colonial law, which had wisely understood Indigenous people "as an inferior race of people, without the privileges of citizens, and under the perpetual protection and pupilage of the government" on the basis that they were not in full possession of the lands over which they "wandered."

In lieu of full title or property in the lands, SCOTUS offered "aboriginal title" as the kind of title and thus rights that Indigenous people possessed in the lands. Essentially, aboriginal title was the right to use and occupy lands, "a mere right of usufruct and habitation." It was not a right of ownership—with the implied "power of alienation." Consequently, the title could be extinguished if found to be in lack. In other words, tribes not making adequate use or occupation of their lands forfeited all claims to the lands. The *Johnson* decision nullified the rights of Indigenous peoples to own and trade over/within their territories by subjecting the terms and conditions of all commerce in goods and lands to the plenary authority of Congress in evaluating whether or not tribes were properly and adequately using and occupying their lands.

In *Conquest by Law: How the Discovery of America Dispossessed Indigenous Peoples of Their Lands*, Lindsay G. Robertson provides an exceptional analysis of the collusions informing *Johnson's Lessee v. McIntosh*. Johnson's and McIntosh's attorneys were hired by the same land-development company operating out of New England and for decades illegally buying up lands from Indigenous nations all over North America. Even the particular plot of land in question was not in dispute; Johnson and McIntosh held title to lands in Illinois that were fifty miles apart. However, the case served to create the legal fiction that Congress and SCOTUS needed about tribal land title amounting to nothing more than a benefit of federal guardianship, the terms of which were left to the discretion of federal authorities in assessing "use and occupancy" in relation to their own and corporate interests in development.[12]

THE CONTRACT IN "ARTIFICIAL BEINGS"

The unilateral suspension of treaty making, the Indian Trade and Commerce Acts, and the *Johnson's Lessee v. McIntosh* decision are but one cluster of the myriad efforts by US officials to decimate Indigenous territorial rights. Simultaneously, there was a steady centralization and entitlement of corporate rights to buy, lease, develop, and extract from tribal lands and natural resources. In other words, legally contorting Indigenous nations into the function and operation of "Indian tribes" in all matters of trade under congressional authority worked to subject Indigenous peoples and their territories to corporate interests altogether indistinguishable from congressional ones by goal and office.

In the early laws of European kingdoms and nation-states, a king, a parliament, or a pope issued charters to establish institutions such as municipalities, universities, guilds, and churches that were considered self-governing, able to hold property, and enter into contracts. Virtually absent from these early charters were business entities; almost always the charters were aimed at civic bodies that would provide some form of public service. They were called corporations, "from the Latin word corpus, meaning body, because the law recognized that the group of people who formed the corporation could act as one body or one legal person."[13]

By the seventeenth century, charters began to be issued to trading companies that operated as finite partnerships that dissolved at the conclusion of a specifically commissioned job, usually entailing naval exploration and a guaranteed monopoly, such as in the spice trade. Different from earlier chartered entities, these companies did not have the "features of perpetual succession, identifiable persona, and asset separation." Because they proved to be financially risky, they were stabilized by England in 1600 with the charter of the East India Company and by the Netherlands in 1602 with the charter of the Dutch East India Company, both of which were soon granted charters in perpetuity to protect their "building, populating, and governing" of the colonies.[14] In other words, by the early 1600s, chartered corporations were entirely enveloped within the colonial projects of empire building, invested by their respective kingdoms and then nation-states with the powers of government and military.[15] In fact, corporate executive officers were often given state titles (governors) and corresponding authority to purchase land, administer trade, and wage war.

The US Constitution provided that state legislatures take over the responsibility of respecting preconstitutional charters and the task of issuing new ones.[16] The legal veracity of state charters was established by article 1, section 10, clause 1, of the US Constitution, known as the contract clause, which provided that "no State shall enter into any Treaty, Alliance, or Confederation; grant Letters of Marque and Reprisal; coin Money; emit Bills of Credit; make any Thing but gold and silver Coin a Tender in Payment of Debts; pass any Bill of Attainder, ex post facto Law, or Law impairing the Obligation of Contracts, or grant any Title of Nobility."

The first US Supreme Court decision, issued under Chief Justice John Marshall, on the legal import of the contract clause was in *Fletcher v. Peck* of 1810.[17] In *Yazoo: Law and Politics in the New Republic; The Case of Fletcher v. Peck*, C. Peter Magrath provides an important examination of the collusions and fraud that informed the landmark decision and so anticipated those involved in *Johnson's Lessee v. McIntosh*.

In 1789 three land companies formed in Georgia with the purpose of buying land in the Yazoo River area, then included within the treatied boundaries of the Cherokee Nation. The governor signed a deal to sell nearly sixteen million acres of these lands to the companies for $200,000 (1 cent per acre). In 1790 President George Washington issued a stern warning to Georgia regarding the treaty rights of the Cherokee Nation to the lands and the potential of the deal to solicit armed conflict with the Cherokees and their allies among the neighboring Chickasaw, Choctaw, and Creek nations. Undeterred, the state passed a resolution requiring that the payment for the lands be made in gold and silver, which the companies could not accomplish. The deal fell through.[18]

Several years later, four new land companies formed, again with the purpose of buying lands in the Yazoo River area. These companies included speculators from Georgia and Pennsylvania, as well as two senators (one from Georgia and one from Pennsylvania), two members of the House (one from Georgia and one from South Carolina), three judges (including Supreme Court Associate Justice James Wilson), and the Tennessee territorial governor. Between 1794 and 1795, several Georgia legislators received large grants of land in the eastern part of Georgia. In 1795 they passed the Yazoo Land Act. By the act, Georgia claimed fee title to thirty-five million acres of land and sold them to the four companies for $500,000 (1.4 cents per acre). The act likewise directed a resolution to the US president requesting that the necessary treaty be made with the Cherokee Nation securing the extinguishment of the Cherokees' land title and so allowing the sale to proceed.[19]

By this time, the Cherokee Nation had entered into treaties with the United States in 1785 and 1791 that delineated the nation's boundaries in lands within and bordering Georgia. The 1791 boundaries were reaffirmed by treaty in 1794. The boundaries were not redrawn until the treaty of 1798 and then again in treaties of 1804, 1805, 1806, 1816, 1817, and 1819. In each treaty Georgia sought further and further land cessions from the Cherokees. Georgia would achieve its goal for the complete cession of Cherokee land title through the Cherokee removal treaty of 1835.

Meanwhile, the Yazoo Land Act of 1795 was exposed in state politics as a collusion and taken up in debates between Georgian Federalists and Republicans as the 1796 state election approached. The result was felt when Georgia's voters, enraged by the state's creation of large land monopolies, rejected most of the incumbents. The newly elected officials worked quickly to pass a law that repealed the 1795 act, along with the titles issued under its provisions. However, the land companies had already begun selling Yazoo lands throughout the country, in some cases making nearly 650 percent profit on their original investments. One of the most important of these sales was of eleven million acres to the New England Mississippi Land Company, which included wealthy merchants, former elected officials and judges, and land speculators in the New England region. When Georgia legislators repealed the Yazoo Land Act in 1796, the company mobilized its network to challenge the state's repeal law and secure its land claims. Failing to secure passage of a congressional law that would have compensated it for alleged financial losses incurred as a result of the repeal act, the company took its complaints to federal court.[20]

The complaint was orchestrated by the New England Mississippi Land Company in 1803 between land speculator Robert Fletcher (of New Hampshire) and the company's director, John Peck (of Massachusetts). Fletcher alleged that he had bought fifteen thousand acres from Peck and that Peck breached the contract of sale by not having legal title.[21] Peck contended that Georgia's repeal act was invalid. In 1810 the US Supreme Court agreed with Peck.[22]

The Court conceded that there had been fraud underlying the original sale of the Yazoo River lands but rejected Fletcher's argument that Georgia had the power to repeal the 1795 act on the grounds of the fraud. It argued instead that Peck had entered into two valid contracts—one when purchasing the land and one when selling it—and that those contracts operated outside the original fraud: "When a law is in its nature a contract, when absolute rights have vested under that contract, a repeal of the law cannot divest those rights." Fletcher's claim was dismissed, and Georgia's law repealing land titles was nullified.[23]

Although the ruling made frequent passing remarks about "Indian title," it failed in all regards to address the substantive questions of the state's claim to fee title in the lands, the state's rights to sell the lands, the fact that tribal title had not been extinguished by treaty when the claim and sale were enacted by state law, and the fact that the US Congress was not a party to the sale in violation of the Constitution. Instead, SCOTUS sashayed over "Indian title" as if it posed no legal challenge whatsoever to the question of whether or not a state could breach a contract between individuals without violating the Constitution. This fundamentally shifted the significance of the contract clause away from its implication of tribal treaty rights— "No State shall enter into any Treaty . . . or Law impairing the Obligation of Contracts"—and toward service to corporate interests. It allowed, if not outright encouraged, collusive investment practices in land speculation that could be easily legalized by the exchange of money and contractual signatures between those parties committing the fraud.[24]

The second US Supreme Court decision on the legal import of the Constitution's contract clause was in *Trustees of Dartmouth College v. Woodward* (1819). The New Hampshire legislature amended Dartmouth's charter to change it from a private to a public institution, with trustees to be appointed by the governor. The trustees challenged whether or not the state could unilaterally amend the terms of the school's charter.

The suit raised the question about whether or not charters—the mechanism by which corporations were created—fell under constitutional protections. The Court ruled that they did. However, it explained that the entities created by charters—corporations—were created under state authority: "A corporation is an artificial being, invisible, intangible, and existing only in contemplation of law. Being the mere creature of law, it possesses only those properties which the charter of its creation confers upon it either expressly or as incidental to its very existence. These are such as are supposed best calculated to effect the object for which it was created." These "properties" included the right of the individuals making up corporations to "act together as a single person for purposes of holding property, entering into contracts, and suing and being sued in court." The court ruled that charters "enable a corporation to manage its own affairs and to hold property without the perplexing intricacies, the hazardous and endless necessity, of perpetual conveyances for the purpose of transmitting it from hand to hand. It is chiefly for the purpose of clothing bodies of men, in succession, with these qualities and capacities that corporations were invented, and are in use."[25]

The artificiality of chartered entities pretended that corporations were overdetermined by constitutional law and state jurisdiction. It so invested and protected corporate property rights in perpetuity, figuratively clothing male executives in liberties and freedoms from having their corporate-held property and individual investments (and so profits) divided, taxed, or otherwise burdened by regulation.[26] Protected as a constitutional right, corporate property rights trumped tribal territorial claims, even when secured by a treaty, and even when corporations acquired the lands by fraud. *Fletcher* and *Dartmouth* thereby represented the rearticulation of "Indian tribes" into a legal and economic structure predicated on imperialist capitalism without any corporate accountability.

Part 2: Indian Tribes and Persons

The legal status and rights of "Indian tribes" were all but decimated in the Reconstruction period by Congress's unilateral suspension of treaty making in 1871 and the consequences of the General Allotment Act of 1887, which brought about both the privatization of tribal lands and an expansive yet inefficient system of federal administration over remaining tribal lands, natural resources, and financial assets. This virtual obliteration of tribal rights contrasts sharply with the juridical expansion of corporate rights by the SCOTUS decision in *Santa Clara County v. Southern Pacific*

Railroad Company (1886). The Court ruled that corporations possessed Fourteenth Amendment rights analogous to those of "persons," including due process and equal protection. This emboldened, entitled position— and the surrounding rhetoric of the overburdened regulation and taxation borne by corporations—evaded public and federal accountability for the role of railroad and related companies in the dispossession and genocide of Indigenous peoples.

RECONSTRUCTION

During and after the Civil War, Congress enacted a series of laws meant to suspend the secession of the Confederacy, emancipate African slaves, prohibit racial discrimination, and stimulate a free labor economy. The Thirteenth Amendment (1865) and the Fourteenth Amendment (1868) required that southern states, and the tribes that had aligned with them in part or in whole during the war, modify their constitutions and bylaws to abolish slavery and prohibit racial discrimination. For southern states, these requirements were satisfied technically but met with grossly uneven implementation and conflict marked by fiercely contested elections, such as within Georgia over its constitutional revisions in 1865 (when it re-pealed secession and abolished slavery), 1868 (when it extended suffrage to all male citizens), and 1877 (when previous provisions were strengthened). Conflict was also marked more popularly by the formation of the Ku Klux Klan in 1865, initially in Tennessee, and state-sanctioned practices condoning and enabling all manner of racial segregation, including those within education and voting.

For tribes, particularly those that had been removed from the South and into Indian Territory, the requirements of Reconstruction were imposed through treaties, such as those ratified in 1866 with the Cherokee, Choctaw and Chickasaw, Creek, and Seminole nations.[27] The treaties provided that the tribes abolish slavery, enfranchise African freedmen, re-integrate those factions that had fought for the South, and restore property confiscated from those factions during the war. The treaties also provided that tribal territories were to be subjected to the "right of way" of railroads but for the first time required that federally issued licenses to individual and corporate traders be approved by tribal governments (up to then, the BIA issued licenses, often without consulting with tribes). The provisions of abolition and enfranchisement of Blacks were deeply contested in intra- and intertribal politics, including those that denied the existence of Black-Native lineage, property, and voting rights. These provisions also engendered multiple forms of opposition to allotment and statehood, including armed militia and subversive acts of defiance.[28]

The complexities of postwar national politics included many social movements against racial discrimination and segregation and for the enfranchisement of women, as well as intertribal military and unarmed alliances against US treaty violations. At the same time, there was an explosive growth of business-minded corporations: from 7 in 1780, to 335 in 1800, to several thousand in 1850, to over half a million in 1900.[29] Many of these corporations were aimed at the development of tribal territories (railroad tracks, postal routes, townsites, cattle grazing) and the extraction of tribal resources (timber, oil, coal, gold) and were directly or implicitly involved in violence and fraud against non-Indigenous people and Indian tribes that resisted. In an effort to protect their often illegal investment/development schemes against opposition, corporate boards and their attorneys worked to claim constitutional protections, particularly through the Fourteenth Amendment (1868).

The Fourteenth Amendment modified article 1, section 2, clause 3, which enumerated the powers of the House of Representatives and determined the apportionment of representatives and taxes. It is the only appearance of "Indians" in the Constitution: "Representatives shall be apportioned among the several states according to their respective numbers, counting the whole number of persons in each state, excluding Indians not taxed." It provided that "all persons born or naturalized in the United States, and subject to the jurisdiction thereof, are citizens of the United States and of the state wherein they reside. No state shall make or enforce any law which shall abridge the privileges or immunities of citizens of the United States; nor shall any state deprive any person of life, liberty, or property, without due process of law; nor deny to any person within its jurisdiction the equal protection of the laws." In 1870 the Fifteenth Amendment provided that the "right of citizens of the United States to vote shall not be denied or abridged by the United States or by any state on account of race, color, or previous condition of servitude."[30] Together, the amendments attempted to address the social politics of abolition and enfranchisement, as well as to protect the rights of all citizens to be represented fairly in Congress and protected against unlawful government actions or deprivations of "life, liberty, or property, without due process of law."

As the amendments were being debated and passed, so too was Congress assessing its financial obligations to tribes by treaty, no doubt in immediate concern over the nation's economy following the war but also in looking forward to the expansion of its territories into the Pacific and Caribbean. In 1871 the House of Representatives took the initiative by adding a rider to the annual Indian Appropriations Bill before it moved to the Senate: "No Indian nation or tribe within the territory of the United States shall be acknowledged or recognized as an independent nation, tribe, or power with whom the United States may contract by treaty; but no obligation of any treaty lawfully made and ratified with any such Indian nation or tribe prior to March 3, 1871, shall be hereby invalidated or impaired."[31] The Senate agreed. "Indian tribes" were no longer to be recognized as independent authorities with which the United States would "contract by treaty" and so incur any further debt, although existing treaties and financial obligations were to be fulfilled.

The suspension of tribal treaty making invited corporate collusion with federal efforts to subject remaining tribal territorial rights to the goals of capitalist development, coalescing in the perfect socio-legal storm of the privatization of tribal lands and the vast extension of federal administration over remaining lands by the General Allotment Act (1887) and its amendments by the Curtis Act (1898), the Burke Act (1906), and the Omnibus Act (1910).[32] The acts provided for reservations to be broken up in severalty and issued to members as parcels, which ranged from forty to six hundred acres each based on the value of the lands and the members' marital and dependent status. The issuance of title was supposed to be based likewise on assessments of individual "competency." Those deemed incompetent were given trust titles, their property held in trust by the BIA for a period not supposed to exceed twenty-five years, during which time they were to get educated in proper land use. Despite the suspension of trust titles by the Burke Act (1906), 10.6 million acres of individually owned lands are held in trust even now.[33] The gross mismanagement of these lands was addressed by the largest class-action suit in US history, *Cobell v. Salazar* (1996), which was concluded by the Claims Resolution Act (2010). Meanwhile, those who were deemed competent were issued fee titles, awarding them with US citizenship and so subjecting them to property taxes. Almost 60 percent of lands issued in fee were lost within a decade, the majority of them to state property tax foreclosure.[34]

Surplus lands, or lands unassigned to tribal members, were sold to nonmembers. Allotted and surplus lands were divided by the practice of checkerboarding and fractionated heirship. Checkerboarding scattered tribal allotments in between nontribal lands to disrupt tribal governance and collective forms of economic self-sufficiency. It rendered shared-use practices such as collectively operated agriculture and forest conservation impossible. Fractionated heirship divided allotments among heirs who shared an undivided interest in the land. Over time, this has meant that an allotment can have thousands of owners. In most cases, heirs are absentee leaseholders with leases that render them without the ability to use the lands for their own economic self-sufficiency, little financial benefit, and no collateral for developing credit.[35]

Although total tribal and individual landholdings were reduced by about two-thirds through allotment (from 148 to 48 million acres), many of these lands were configured in such a way by checkerboarding and heirship that nonmembers came to dominate the use if not the control of tribal lands. This was furthered by the fact that even before but especially after allotment of a given reservation, corporations secured thousands of leases for grazing and licenses for resource extraction from both reservations and allottees whose titles were held in trust.[36] Allotment's "Indian Tribe" was no match for Santa Clara County's corporate "person." The "Indian Tribe" had suspended rights to treaty making and was left only with an option to agree or not with federal mandates, sometimes but not always negotiated through finite contracts, but both of which were overshadowed by corporate interests in expansive development and figured entirely through an "Indian tribe" that was all but stripped of legal status.

THE EQUAL PROTECTION OF "PERSONS"

In what are known as the *Slaughterhouse* cases (1872), the US Supreme Court issued its first opinion on the legal merits of the Fourteenth Amendment.[37] The cases emerged from three suits in New Orleans, where residents had suffered eleven cholera outbreaks and related ill health as a result of animal matter from slaughterhouses polluting the city's drinking water. In 1869 the state legislature passed a law that allowed New Orleans to charter a single corporation (the Crescent City Livestock Landing and Slaughterhouse Company) with the promise that it would centralize all slaughterhouse operations in the city, confine butchers to areas that kept them away from the city's water supplies, and enable better regulatory oversight. Represented by former Supreme Court justice John A. Campbell (whose Confederate loyalties had forced him to resign from the Court), over four hundred members of the Butchers' Benevolent Association sued to stop the city's takeover of the slaughterhouse industry on the basis of the Fourteenth

Amendment's protections for due process, equal protection, and the privileges and immunities clause (section 1, clause 2: "The Congress shall have power to make all laws which shall be necessary and proper to secure to the citizens of each state all privileges and immunities of citizens in the several states"). In an opinion issued by Justice Samuel Freeman Miller, SCOTUS held to a narrow interpretation of the amendment, arguing that due process applied only to procedure, that equal protection applied only to former slaves ("Freedmen"), and that the privileges and immunities clause applied only to national and not state citizenship rights.

The *Slaughterhouse* decision was overturned in *Santa Clara County v. Southern Pacific Railroad Company* in 1886.[38] In 1879 the California legislature ratified a new state constitution that, among other things, outlined strict rules for the assessment of railroad property values and taxes. In 1882 Santa Clara and Fresno counties assessed the "franchises, road-ways, road-beds, rails, and rolling stock" of the Southern Pacific Railroad Company and the Central Pacific Railroad Company to recover taxes for the previous fiscal year, 1881–1882, under the new rules. The court found that "the state board of equalization, in making the supposed assessment of said roadway of defendant, did knowingly and designedly include in the valuation of said roadway the value of fences erected upon the line between said roadway and the land of coterminous proprietors. Said fences were valued at $300 per mile." The railroad companies appealed, claiming that they were protected from such taxes under a federal statute of 1866, affirmed by an 1870 state law, that established "a right of way over the public domain" and liberal access to "public lands" in order to construct and maintain a continuous railroad line from Missouri to the Pacific, "subject to the use of the United States for postal, military, naval, and all other government service, and to such regulations as congress might impose for restricting the charges for government transportation."

The Supreme Court found that in neither federal law nor state law were fences to be assessed differently from the railroads and adjacent lands and that therefore the state board did not have the power to include the fences in its assessment of the railroads' property values. The Court concluded that "upon such an issue, the law, we think, is for the defendant. An assessment of that kind is invalid, and will not support an action for the recovery of the entire tax so levied."

In framing its conclusion, the Court claimed that corporations were protected against such actions under the Fourteenth Amendment: "One of the points made and discussed at length in the brief of counsel for defendants in error was that 'corporations are persons within the meaning of the Fourteenth Amendment to the Constitution of the United States.' Before argument, Mr. Chief Justice Waite said: The court does not wish to hear argument on the question whether the provision in the Fourteenth Amendment to the Constitution, which forbids a State to deny to any person within its jurisdiction the equal protection of the laws, applies to these corporations. We are all of the opinion that it does." Thereby SCOTUS overturned the strict interpretation of *Slaughterhouse* on the questions of procedural due process and equal protection for "former slaves," not by extending those protections to substantive due process and other racialized groups but by assuming that the protections applied to corporations. This almost dismissive caveat—"We are all of the opinion that it does"—would be the first time SCOTUS ruled that corporations possessed Fourteenth Amendment rights analogous to those of "persons."

Irrespective of the Court's intent, which has been much debated in legal scholarship, the opinion served as precedent for the application of Fourteenth Amendment protections to corporations. So consequential was the decision that it created what has since been referred to as "corporate personhood."[39] The rationale was that the US Constitution upheld the rights of individuals, so their individual guarantees of due process, et cetera, should extend naturally to corporations as mere amalgams of those individuals.[40]

Nowhere within *Santa Clara County* is there any reckoning—even to an imaginary of conquest as a fait accompli—for Indigenous territorial rights, either within the counties suing the railroad for back taxes, more broadly within the state of California, or within the US imperial formation plummeting the nation forward into global capitalism marked by the illegal annexation of Hawaii and the war with Spain over Pacific colonies in 1898. This lack of reckoning underscores the way that "Indian tribes" were perceived to be so thoroughly situated under a federal plenary authority serving corporate interest as to be locally irrelevant. What changes in our understanding of "corporate personhood" if we insist on an account of Indigenous territorial rights within it?

When Spain began its imperial efforts in the region where California was to become a state, it is estimated conservatively that the tribal population was around 300,000. Forced into slavery and starvation by the Spanish military and Catholic Church working in concert to bring about

Spanish-Catholic power, about 100,000 people died between the first mission of 1769 and Spain's cession of the territory to Mexico in 1821. At the close of the US-Mexican War and the acquisition of California as part of the Treaty of Guadalupe Hidalgo of 1848, another 50,000 died as slavery, starvation, and armed conflict characterized tribal-Mexican as they had tribal-Spanish relations. After the gold rush of 1848, US miners, agriculturalists, and railroad workers quickly outnumbered everyone else. Tribes were aggressively removed from their territories in violation of the 1848 treaty, which had provided that the United States would protect tribal land grants. Undeterred, US citizens displaced and outright murdered tribal peoples to gain hold of their lands and coerce survivors into servitude.

California was admitted to the United States as a free state in 1850. In 1851 the legislature passed the Act for the Government and Protection of the Indians, which allowed any "white" to force into work any "Indian" found to be "vagrant." Mexicans were then classified as "whites" in state law, so this enabled the enslavement of tribal peoples by all property owners in the state. Because "Indians" could not testify against "whites" in court, tribal people had no recourse to challenge either their forced removal or enslavement or the physical and sexual violence that often came with it. For despite its status as a free state, California permitted the open sale and indenture of tribal people for labor and sex-trade purposes.[41]

In his 1851 inaugural address to the legislature, Governor Peter H. Burnett promised that "a war of extermination will continue to be waged between the two races until the Indian race becomes extinct."[42] In 1853 the legislature ordered the "extermination" of all Indians. Reimbursed by the federal government, state bounties were paid per Indian scalp or severed head, and all expenses related to the efforts were reimbursed, including the cost of ammunition, guns, and horses. Within two years, California paid out about $1 million to individuals who submitted claims. It was inhumane. Whole tribes, bands, and families were massacred.

Describing this campaign against Native Americans of California and Nevada, Jack D. Forbes emphasizes that it was not merely military or state officials who participated in it: "The sequence of events is all the more distressing since it serves to indict not a group of cruel leaders, or a few squads of rough soldiers, but, in effect, an entire people; for the conquest of the Indigenous Californian was above all else a popular, mass enterprise."[43] By 1860, no more than twenty thousand of the tribal population had survived. Those who did were almost entirely dispossessed of their territories and living in conditions of gross poverty and ill health. Many had begun to identify as Mexican to secure paid work as farmhands, passing into another, analogously complicated status in hopes of survival.

In 1851 the US Congress sent a commission to California to negotiate treaties with tribes for land cession. By 1852, eighteen treaties had been negotiated with more than one hundred tribes. The treaties would have provided the tribes with approximately 8.5 million acres divided into eighteen reservations. However, California's governor and senate actively opposed the treaties, seeing them as excessively generous and cumbersome to the state's goals. They, along with several private citizens (mostly ranchers and miners), lobbied hard to stop the ratification process. As a result, the US Senate put an "injunction of secrecy" on the treaties that held until 1905. But the tribes were never notified that the treaties had not been ratified. Federal and state agents and militia moved many onto smaller reservations (often from several different tribes) under the auspices of carrying out treaty provisions while they purchased the "deserted" lands for themselves.

In his definitive historical study of imperialism, *Violence over the Land: Indians and Empires in the Early American West*, Ned Blackhawk demonstrates how each invading power directly created the economic and social conditions in which the next prospered, and all at Indigenous peoples' expense.[44] Spain and Mexico and then the immigrants who would form California and join the Union in 1850 flourished as a direct result of the genocide and dispossession that they enacted on Indigenous peoples, producing the very conditions through which miners, agriculturalists, and the railroad could lay claim to unfettered access and development of tribal territories and natural resources.

In other words, the "corporate persons" of *Santa Clara County* were able to claim tribal lands, resources, and bodies in California as a result of their involvement in the genocide and dispossession of tribal peoples. *Santa Clara County* legitimated this history and then protected the "persons" involved as corporations with full constitutional rights. *Santa Clara County* was thereby consistent with the historical work of corporations in imperialism and its colonial projects as the entities through which the "building, populating, and governing" of the empire were enabled.[45]

A Conclusion

Got land? Thank an Indian.

JEFF MANARD (PINE CREEK FIRST NATION), 2014

The legal precedent set by the congressional statutes and court rulings described above deeply informed the re-formation of Indigenous governments into corporations of a particular kind. The Hawaiian Homes Commission Act of 1920, the Indian Reorganization Act of 1934, and the Alaska Native Claims Settlement Act of 1971 configured "Native Hawaiian organizations," "American Indian tribes," and "Alaska Native villages" as bodies possessing analogous rights between them to enter contracts. But by the time that these statutes were passed into law, tribes had long since been stripped by SCOTUS of the ability to own and alienate the lands they used and occupied or to enter into contractually binding agreements with each other or other political and economic entities without federal oversight and approval. These serious limitations underscore the core capitalist ideologies and practices that undergird the United States as an imperialist power and social formation. In a state whose capitalism is always already reaching out globally, of course Indigenous peoples cannot have equal or commensurate claims to any lands and resources that might compete with corporate-as-the-government's interests to expand, extract, and profit some more. Of course.

The problematic erasures of the historical contextualization of Indigenous territorial rights within the pedagogical mandates of OWS is not about a forgetting of an imperial-colonial past that can be fixed with a liberalist project of recovery or memorandum of solidarity—as if we just included the facts about the historic wrongs of corporate-federal collusion and fraud in the dispossession and genocide of Indigenous peoples, then all would be righted in radical social justice efforts against "the corrosive power of major banks and multinational corporations over the democratic process."[46]

The erasures of Indigenous territorial rights and historical experiences of corporate-government collusion and fraud are, rather, a politic of epistemology—an ideology and practice of knowledge making—that takes the imperial-colonial narrative for granted in its understanding of US imperialism and in its thinking through strategies of opposition against its injustices. That narrative believes in its own success story—that Indigenous peoples are conquered, disappeared, lost, gone. Tragically but nonetheless as an objective truth, the Indigenous has been eliminated from the lands and resources of the empire and so from relevance to current political debate.

The question for OWS and related movements is why any effort against the US empire needs a scandal of corporate-federal collusion and fraud like that of the Wall Street foreclosure and securities crisis around which to organize. Why OWS so early figured that scandal as a battle of the 1 percent against the 99 percent. Why OWS's resolutions have often been about arrest and redistribution and not a radical transformation of the system. Why Wall Street's current behavior is exceptionalized. As if the US "democratic process" has been merely corrupted and would otherwise not be but for the selfish greed of a few.

It seems that Jean Baudrillard's *Simulacra and Simulation* is important again for understanding that the public performance of scandal is really an act of concealing that there is no scandal at all—that the social relations and conditions registered by the scandal-performed are the norm.[47] This is especially difficult to confront from any political perspective predicated on contrasting the altruism of US democracy with the collusive fraud of Congress and Wall Street. But what if US democracy has only ever been a facade, a mask, a costume? A performance that conceals? That the formative values at work in the US Constitution were not liberty, freedom, and equality as celebrated but were aimed at establishing and protecting government and corporate power of a government invested? What if it is "US democracy" that is "the truth which conceals that there is none"?

This would certainly seem to be the case in the story of the multiple kinds of racialized and gendered inequalities between "artificial entities" and "Indian title," "persons" and distreatied "Indian tribes," that have been articulated historically through corporate, court, and congressional racketeering in Indigenous territorial rights. An epistemological practice that begins with the presumption of the centrality of Indigenous territorial-based claims to sovereignty and self-determination in the constitution of the US political-economic system might more directly expose not only that the "man behind the curtain" has always already been there but that all along there has been a meaningful role of the audience in maintaining the theater of democracy's performance. Leaving behind the goal of trying to fix or correct that which is broken or corrupted, of trying to revenue-share our way into social justice, we might be able to think more productively together about the necessity for meaningful and substantive social reformation if we insisted on the empire's accountability to the territorial rights of Indigenous peoples.

"The Corporation and the Tribe" was originally published in *American Indian Quarterly* 39, no. 3 (Summer 2015): 243–70.

1. Occupy Wall Street, "About." June 2012. http://occupywallst.org/about.

2. See, for example, "Watch: Michael Moore."

3. For a record of the resolution, see "General Assembly Resolutions."

4. "General Assembly Resolutions."

5. Goldtooth, "Occupy Talks."

6. United States, An Act to Regulate Trade, 1 Stat. 137.

7. Prucha, *American Indian Treaties*, 100–102.

8. Cohen, *Handbook of Federal Indian Law*, 10.

9. Prucha, *American Indian Treaties*, 102.

10. Cohen, *Handbook of Federal Indian Law*, 10.

11. Johnson's Lessee v. McIntosh, 21 U.S. 543, 5 L. Ed. 681, 1823 U.S. lexis 293 (1823).

12. See Robertson, *Conquest by Law*. The "Marshall Trilogy," as it has been referred to historically, also included the SCOTUS decisions in The Cherokee Nation v. The State of Georgia (30 U.S. 1, 8 L. Ed. 25, 8 L. Ed. 2d 25, 1831) and Worcester v. Georgia (31 US 515, 8 L. Ed. 483, 8 L. Ed. 2d 483, 1832). Together, these decisions defined "Indian tribes" as having passed under the juridical dominion and so protection of the United States as dependent "wards."

13. Blair, "Corporate Personhood," 788, 789.

14. Blair, "Corporate Personhood," 790, 791.

15. See Deloria, "Self-Determination"; and Anaya, *Indigenous Peoples in International Law*.

16. Blair, "Corporate Personhood," 793.

17. Fletcher v. Peck, 10 U.S. 87, 3 L. Ed. 162, 3 L. Ed. 2d 162 (1810).

18. Magrath, *Yazoo: Law and Politics*, 4–5.

19. Magrath, *Yazoo: Law and Politics*, 6–9.

20. Magrath, *Yazoo: Law and Politics*, 15, 34, 38.

21. Magrath, *Yazoo: Law and Politics*, 54–55, 64–65.

22. See Robertson, *Conquest by Law*, 29–44.

23. It would not be until 1934 that the US Supreme Court would rule that a state could alter the terms of a contract so long as the alteration was rationally tied to protecting the public's welfare (Home Building & Loan Assn. v. Blaisdell, 290 U.S. 398, 54 S. Ct. 231, 78 L. Ed. 413).

24. See Robertson, "Harper," in *Conquest by Law*, 29–44.

25. Dartmouth College v. Woodward, 17 U.S. 250, 4 L. Ed. 629 (1819).

26. For analysis of the impact of gendered ideologies and property rights on Indigenous women, see Berger, "After Pocahontas"; and Perdue, *Cherokee Women*.

27. Treaty with the Cherokee, 14 Stat. 799 (July 19, 1866); Treaty with the Choctaw and Chickasaw, 14 Stat. 769 (April 28, 1866); Treaty with the Creek, 14 Stat. 785 (June 14, 1866); Treaty with the Seminole, 14 Stat. 755 (March 21, 1866).

28. See, for example, Debo, *And Still the Waters Run*; and Harring, *Crow Dog's Case*.

29. Johnson, "Law and Legal Theory," 145.

30. However, it retained this right for men. It would not be until 1920 that the Nineteenth Amendment extended voting rights to women. The Twenty-Sixth Amendment of 1971 would lower the voting age to eighteen.

31. Indian Appropriations Bill, 25 U.S.C., § 71.

32. The collusions were initially conflicted. Some corporations affirmed tribal sovereignty and treaty rights, whereas some argued for their annulment. The differences depended on whether or not, within their respective relations with tribal governments and individuals, they had found success in gaining unfettered access to tribal lands and resources. See Miner, *Corporation and the Indian*; and Bledsoe, *Indian Land Laws*.

33. See US Department of the Interior, "Indian Affairs."

34. Cohen, *Handbook of Federal Indian Law*, 192–94.

35. Cohen, *Handbook of Federal Indian Law*, 216.

36. Cohen, *Handbook of Federal Indian Law*, 214–15.

37. Slaughterhouse Cases, 83 U.S. 36 (1872).

38. Santa Clara County v. Southern Pacific Railroad Company, 118 U.S. 394 (1886).

39. Blair, "Corporate Personhood," 803.

40. See Horwitz, "Santa Clara Revisited"; and Blair, "Corporate Personhood," 804.

41. Chatterjee, *Gold, Greed, and Genocide*.

42. See the California State Library for California governor, Peter Burnett's State of the State Address delivered January 6, 1851. Accessed August 23, 2021. https://governors.library.ca.gov/addresses/s_01-Burnett2.html.

43. Forbes, *Native Americans*, 69.

44. Blackhawk, *Violence over the Land*.

45. Blair, "Corporate Personhood," 791.

46. See especially Bruyneel, "Trouble with Amnesia."

47. Jean Baudrillard, *Simulacra and Simulation*.

Anaya, S. James. *Indigenous Peoples in International Law*. 2nd ed. Oxford: Oxford University Press, 2004.

Baudrillard, Jean. *Simulacra and Simulation*. Ann Arbor: University of Michigan Press, 1994.

Berger, Bethany Ruth. "After Pocahontas: Indian Women and the Law, 1830 to 1934." *American Indian Law Review* (1997): 1–62.

Blackhawk, Ned. *Violence over the Land: Indians and Empires in the Early American West*. Cambridge, MA: Harvard University Press, 2008.

Blair, Margaret M. "Corporate Personhood and the Corporate Persona." *University of Illinois Law Review* no. 3 (2013): 785–820.

Bledsoe, Samuel Thomas. *Indian Land Laws*. Kansas City, MO: Vernon Law Book Company, 1913.

Bruyneel, Kevin. "The Trouble with Amnesia: Collective Memory and Colonial Injustice in the United States." In *Political Creativity: The Mangle of Institutional Order, Agency and Change*, edited by Gerald Berk, Dennis Galvan, and Victoria Hattam. Philadelphia: University of Pennsylvania Press, forthcoming. Abstract available at SSRN: https://ssrn.com/abstract=2272816.

Chatterjee, Pratap. *Gold, Greed, and Genocide: Unmasking the Myth of the '49ers*. Berkeley, CA: Project Underground, 1998.

Cohen, Felix S. *Handbook of Federal Indian Law*. Washington, DC: US Department of the Interior, Office of the Solicitor, 1940.

Debo, Angie. *And Still the Waters Run*. Princeton, NJ: Princeton University Press, 1940.

Deloria, Vine, Jr. "Self-Determination and the Concept of Sovereignty." In *Economic Development in American Indian Reservations*, edited by Roxanne Dunbar Ortiz, 22–28. Albuquerque: University of New Mexico Indigenous American Studies, 1979.

Forbes, Jack D. *Native Americans of California and Nevada*. Happy Camp, CA: Naturegraph, 1982.

"General Assembly Resolutions (Oct 10–Nov 16 Summary)—Occupy Oakland." Occupy Oakland. November 17, 2011. https://occupyoakland.org/2011/11/general-assembly-resolutions.

Goldtooth, Tom B. K. "Occupy Talks: Indigenous Perspectives on the Occupy Movement." Indigenous Environmental Network | Ienearth.org. January 23, 2013. YouTube video. https://www.youtube.com/watch?v=zFWnD5UhbhY (accessed June 10, 2022).

Harring, Sidney L. *Crow Dog's Case: American Indian Sovereignty, Tribal Law, and United States Law in the Nineteenth Century*. Cambridge: Cambridge University Press, 1994.

Horwitz, Morton J. "Santa Clara Revisited: The Development of Corporate Theory." *West Virginia Law Review* 88 (1985): 173–224.

Indian Appropriations Bill, 25 U.S.C., § 71.

Johnson, Lyman. "Law and Legal Theory in the History of Corporate Responsibility: Corporate Personhood." *Seattle University Law Review* 35 (2012): 135–64.

Magrath, C. Peter. *Yazoo: Law and Politics in the New Republic: The Case of Fletcher v. Peck*. Providence, RI: Brown University Press, 1966.

Miner, H. Craig. *The Corporation and the Indian: Tribal Sovereignty and Industrial Civilization in Indian Territory, 1865–1907*. Norman: University of Oklahoma Press, 1989.

Perdue, Theda. *Cherokee Women: Gender and Culture Change, 1700–1835*. Lincoln: University of Nebraska Press, 1998.

Prucha, Francis Paul. *American Indian Treaties: The History of a Political Anomaly*. Berkeley: University of California Press, 1997.

Robertson, Lindsay G. *Conquest by Law: How the Discovery of America Dispossessed Indigenous Peoples of Their Lands*. Oxford: Oxford University Press, 2005.

Treaty with the Cherokee, 7 Stat. 39 (July 2, 1791).

Treaty with the Cherokee, 14 Stat. 799 (July 19, 1866).

Treaty with the Choctaw and Chickasaw, 14 Stat. 769 (April 28, 1866).

Treaty with the Creek, 14 Stat. 785 (June 14, 1866).

Treaty with the Seminole, 14 Stat. 755 (March 21, 1866).

United States. An Act to Regulate Trade and Intercourse with the Indian Tribes. Adopted July 22, 1790. https://www.loc.gov/item/rbpe.21401300.

US Department of the Interior. "Indian Affairs: Frequently Asked Questions." Accessed August 20, 2014. www.BIA.gov/faqs.

"Watch: Michael Moore, Naomi Klein and Others on What's Next for ows." *Nation*, June 29, 2015. www.thenation.com/video/164494/watch-michael-moore-naomi-klein-and-others-owss-possibilities.

"In the Constant Flux of Its Incessant Renewal": The Social Reproduction of Racial Capitalism and Settler Colonial Entitlement

Just as substantive endeavors for decolonization require an analysis of contemporary racial capitalism, a critical understanding of the specificities of racial capitalism in the United States demands confronting Indigenous dispossession and settler colonialism as ongoing in the present. This chapter considers the question of social reproduction as a means of addressing the constitutive triangulation of race, capitalism, and colonialism today. Thinking with Glen Coulthard's call for "reestablishing the colonial relation of dispossession as a co-foundational feature of our understanding of and critical engagement with capitalism,"[1] my intention here is to sketch two possible approaches to the multiply inflected processes of reproduction as a way to apprehend the colonial relation as both integral to the historical development of capitalism and variously articulated with present-day regimes of capitalist accumulation. Attending to the historical significance of racial capitalism and colonialism as distinct and intertwined, this chapter thus asks how and why the conditions and practices of the colonial relation might likewise be remade—be both enduring and mutable—in the context of the historical present.

A focus on the dynamics of social reproduction serves as a way to grapple with colonialism as ongoing, to ask what conception of historicity might be adequate to understanding this sense of "ongoing" in a material, juridical, and political sense that does not minimize disjuncture, discontinuity, and change over time. Attending to social reproduction makes apparent the perpetual *re*making of colonial and capitalist social relations as necessarily volatile, as a tenuous nontotality that capitalist ideology strives to disavow, and as an opening and opportunity for disruption and living otherwise.

In what follows I focus on how property relations, family, and prevailing conceptions of ownership are key sites for the social reproduction of race, capitalism, and the particularities of US settler colonialism. I begin by discussing racial capitalism in relation to reproduction and then consider how debates on "so-called primitive accumulation" matter for understanding the relationship between colonialism and capitalism. I then turn to recent legal challenges to the 1978 Indian Child Welfare Act in the historical context of the removal of Indigenous children through boarding schools, adoption, and foster care, and the broader custodial circuits of poor children of color. Finally, I consider the ongoing fractionation of Native peoples' land in the wake of the 1887 Allotment Act and the attrition of African American land ownership through the partition of tenancy-in-common of heirs' property. I use these examples to show how the racial, colonial, gendered, and generational making of property and the capacity for possession are a consequence of particular historical conditions of dispossession and continue to be reproduced in new ways in the present. Adoption, foster care, and the legal regimes of inheritance— rendered property relations through the emplotment of colonialism and capitalism—in this sense are quite literally a matter of social reproduction and a site of struggle over power and history in the context of the current moment.

The Colonial Pivot of Race, Reproduction, and Accumulation

During the 1970s and early 1980s, scholars and activists introduced the term *racial capitalism* as a means of explicitly naming racial differentiation and racism as inseparable from the capitalist political economy of the settler colonies in southern Africa.[2] Emerging from debates in the Black Consciousness Movement in South Africa during the 1970s, the Manifesto of the Azanian People, presented at the founding conference of the National Forum in 1983, linked socialist anticolonial liberation to the movement against apartheid and racial capitalism: "Our struggle for national liberation is directed against the system of racial capitalism which holds the people of Azania in bondage for the benefit of the small minority of white capitalists and their allies."[3] Asserting that "usage of the land and all that accrues to it shall be aimed at ending all forms and means of exploitation," the manifesto demanded "the abolition of all . . . pass laws" (established in 1952 to constrain and control Black people's movement), "the abolition of all resettlement and group areas removals," and the "reintegration of the 'bantustan' human dumping grounds into a unitary Azania."[4] Neville Alexander, who wrote the draft document of the manifesto based on proposed resolutions deliberated at the conference, insisted that "a non-racial capitalism is impossible in South Africa. . . . Class, colour and nation converge in the national liberation movement."[5]

The analytic of racial capitalism was likewise conceived in terms of social reproduction from the outset. Martin Legassick and David Hemson's 1976 pamphlet *Foreign Investment and the Reproduction of Racial Capitalism in South Africa* not only was among the first publications to use the term *racial capitalism* but also focused on the dynamics of social reproduction to make the argument that colonial spatial politics and racial segregation were constitutive for racial capitalism in South Africa.[6] The authors show how the subsistence economies of the "native reserves" created by the 1913 Native Lands Act, recast as "homelands" or Bantustans in 1959, made segregation and then the formal system of apartheid integral to capitalist social reproduction and the suppression of wages and labor rights. As a counter to those who argue that capitalist modernization eventually leads to the diminished significance of race, they demonstrated how this racial and colonial system expanded with the apartheid regime in partnership with global finance capital. Although Legassick and Hemson were primarily concerned with race and labor, dispossession and the colonial administration of land were indispensable to what they described as racial capitalism. The initial conceptions of racial capitalism were thus articulated with what scholars and activists had begun to name and analyze as *settler colonialism* in the context of southern Africa as well as Palestine during this same time.[7]

Cedric Robinson's theorization of racial capitalism in *Black Marxism* (1983) broadened the temporal and geographic scope of the term to argue that capitalism emerged historically through the already operative logics of racial difference. What Robinson termed "racialism" took shape within Europe under feudalism, gaining further impetus as a means to justify such endeavors as the exploitation of Slavic migrant labor and England's colonization of Ireland. The development of capitalism through enclosure, displacement, and proletarianization across Europe was interdependent with the emergence and subsequent expansion of the Atlantic slave trade. In contrast to variants of Marxist analysis that cast the white male industrial working class of Europe as the privileged agents of historical transformation, Robinson recenters the global contributions and presence of Africa disavowed by European appropriation and erasure, focusing instead on the collective struggle and oppositional consciousness of what he calls the Black Radical Tradition. Robin D. G. Kelley, building on this analysis, specifies that "capitalism developed and operates within a racial system or racial regime. Racism is fundamental for the production and reproduction of violence, and that violence is necessary for creating and maintaining capitalism." Kelley further insists that "race and gender are not incidental or accidental features of the global capitalist order, they are constitutive. Capitalism emerged as a racial and gendered regime. . . . The secret to capitalism's survival is racism, and the racial and patriarchal state."[8] The multifaceted dynamics of reproduction in this sense connect racial capitalism as theorized in the southern African context to the racial and colonial conditions of capitalism more broadly.

A full account of theories of social reproduction is beyond the scope of this chapter but it is nevertheless important to selectively note some of the genealogy of social reproduction as an analytic. According to Karl Marx, "When viewed . . . as a connected whole, and in the constant flux of its incessant renewal, every social process of production is, at the same time, a process of reproduction."[9] As theorized in volumes 1 and 2 of *Capital*, reproduction is divided into simple and expanded reproduction.[10] Simple reproduction "constantly reproduces the capital-relation itself" but without accumulation.[11] Expanded reproduction entails the perpetual renewal or recreation of the means of production (land, raw materials, tools, etc.), of labor power, of the capital relation, and of the conversion of a fraction of the surplus value extracted into capital on behalf of ever-increasing accumulation or so-called economic growth. Rosa Luxemburg critically built upon Marx to emphasize the constitutive spatial dynamics between capitalism and that which is external to capitalism. She argued that "the existence and development of capitalism requires an environment of non-capitalist forms of production," along with a reserve of material and social relations not yet commodified for capitalist market exchange.[12] The capitalist imperative for endless accumulation was thus dependent on continuous so-called primitive accumulation to compel and forcibly appropriate life, labor, and land external to the capitalist system in the process of expanded reproduction. Luxemburg focused on imperialism, international loans, and militarism as principal examples of the means toward such appropriation during the time about which she was writing.

During the mid-1960s, Étienne Balibar usefully situated the question of reproduction as a means of upending the base-superstructure hierarchy and the economic determinism of historical analysis that predominated in Marxist theory at the time. As Balibar notes, "For Marx the conceptual pair of production/reproduction contains the definition of *structure* involved in the analysis of the mode of production. On the plane instituted by the analysis of reproduction, production is not the production of things, it is the production and conservation of social relations."[13] Therefore, social relations are at once the conditions for and consequence of a particular historical mode of production. The link between reproduction and ideology examined by Stuart Hall and others through the work of Louis Althusser and Antonio Gramsci further encouraged an understanding of the primacy of social struggle and how all such struggles engage power "without guarantees" and without being determined in advance by immutable historical determinations. In this way, social relations—including racial formation, colonialism, heteronormativity, and patriarchy—can be understood as always already constitutive of and shaped in relation to the economic in a manner that remains vulnerable to contestation and disruption in their need for perpetual re-creation, reiteration, and reinscription.

Beginning in the 1970s, feminist social reproduction theory critically extended the framework of reproduction in a number of crucial ways.[14] Marxist-feminists focused on the gendered specificities of unwaged reproductive sexual and social labor as central to a materialist analysis of reproduction. Susan Ferguson observes that this analysis demonstrated "the ways in which wider social reproduction of the [capitalist] system—that is the daily and generational reproductive labor that occurs in households, schools, hospitals, prisons, and so on—sustains the drive for accumulation."[15] Where the "wages for housework" movement provided an initial intervention in this regard, subsequent scholarship and organizing have focused on analyzing and challenging hyper-exploitative regimes of racialized domestic labor, the labor of migrant women in the global economy of care work, and the gendered and sexual international division of labor more broadly.[16]

The intellectual labor of Black feminists and women-of-color feminism made clear the necessity of theorizing race in terms of the politics and power relations of biological and social reproduction.[17] For instance, Jennifer Morgan contends that "reproduction functioned foundationally in the development of racialist thinking, the onset of modern slave-ownership, and the experience of enslavement." She points out that "the obscene logic of racial slavery defined reproduction as work, and the work of the colonies—creating wealth out of the wilderness—relied on the appropriation of enslaved women's children by colonial slaveowners."[18] Variations and elaborations on this appropriation remain evident in international economies of biocapitalism today through configurations such as what Alys Eve Weinbaum calls the "surrogacy/slavery nexus."[19] Dorothy Roberts argues that "the criminal regulation of pregnancy . . . today is in some ways unprecedented" but is nonetheless part of the "continuing legacy of the degradation of Black motherhood" and "how the denial of Black reproductive autonomy serves the interests of white supremacy."[20] Yet, here again, attention to the always-contingent politics of reproduction also allows for approaches to interruption, coalitional movement building, and collective living otherwise through practices of radical care and what Jodi Byrd calls "grounded relationalities."[21]

For the purpose of what I am arguing in this chapter, it is important to connect these multifaceted analyses of social reproduction to an understanding of how colonization, both historical and ongoing, continues to be closely aligned with the capitalist imperatives for perpetual expansion and so-called growth (the ever-escalating incorporative intensities of capitalist markets). Therefore, how is it that property relations and possessive capacities require reproduction under historically shifting capitalist modes of accumulation and in ways that constitutively entail differentially racialized value and Indigenous dispossession? Because the social process of reproduction relies on restaging colonial possession and differentially racialized devaluation in order to sustain and extend capitalist social relations, the precise way in which this process occurs—its deliberately racial and dispossessive dynamics—takes on ever greater significance. As the historical circumstances of racial capitalism shifted, Nikhil Singh notes that "the production of race as a method for aggregating and devaluing an entire group has depended on assessing the value of Black social and biological reproduction in terms of capital accumulation and its social reproduction."[22] Silvia Federici contends that capital will always need these nonsubsumed or partially subsumed forms of devalued labor. She argues that capital is "structurally dependent on the free appropriation of immense quantities of labor and resources that must appear as externalities to the market," which are naturalized onto the bodies of those gendered as women and nonwhite people in order not only to expand profit margins but also to pacify, discipline, and divide.[23] In this sense, racialized and gendered relations of appropriation and reproduction have directly to do with the specific questions of property, labor, and possession at work in colonialism and empire.

Marx's formulation of "so-called primitive accumulation"—the coerced incorporation of noncapitalist forms of life, land, and labor into capitalist social relations that separate people from the means of production—continues to serve as a key referent for the analysis of and debate on the intertwining of capitalism, race, colonialism, and imperialism. Disputes over the meaning and scope of so-called primitive accumulation in this respect often focus on whether it is conceived as a foundational moment within the historical development of capitalism or is ongoing and integral to the expanded reproduction of capitalism on a world scale. In Marx's often-quoted phrasing, "The discovery of gold and silver in America, the extirpation, enslavement and entombment in mines of the aboriginal population, the beginning of the conquest and looting of the East Indies, the turning of Africa into a warren for the commercial hunting of black-skins, signaled the rosy dawn of the era of capitalist production. These idyllic proceedings are the chief moments of primitive accumulation."[24] As a counter to the fabulations of classical political economists, in Marx's account the unadulterated violence of primitive accumulation serves as the historical precondition for capitalist value and development. Further exemplified by the enclosure of the commons in England, it is the brutal transformation through which the property relation is consolidated, land is privatized and commodified, and people previously able to live outside capitalist market relations are proletarianized. So-called primitive accumulation is thus the foundational process through which noncapitalist forms of life are forcibly incorporated into capitalist social relations, the ground upon which subsequently, in Marx's phrasing, "the silent compulsion of economic relations" becomes the principal means through which "the domination of the capitalist over the worker" is secured and perpetuated.[25] The violence of modern capitalism, if given teleological inflection, has become primarily immanent and "no longer requires direct applications of coercive force" to maintain the labor relation.[26]

Perhaps the most influential recent reassessment of Marx's thesis has been David Harvey's theorization of "accumulation by dispossession," which, though not focused on the specificities of settler colonialism, is nonetheless concerned with demonstrating how so-called primitive accumulation continues in relation to capital accumulation and figures prominently within the neoliberal era. Harvey's conception of "accumulation by dispossession" jettisons the teleological stagist narrative in order to call attention to the fact that such dynamics persist. Violent dispossession and the silent compulsion of the market coexist and, in fact, are complementary. Rather than a temporal prior, accumulation by dispossession serves as a spatial form prior to capitalist incorporation that is the fodder for imperialist expansion. As with Luxemburg's formulation, the reiterative prior of so-called primitive accumulation in this sense remains external to the capitalist labor relation as the process by which capitalism continues to pursue and appropriate the constitutive outside that is its condition of possibility. Despite the fact that Harvey's conception of "accumulation by dispossession" serves explicitly as a means of theorizing what he calls the "new imperialism," and that the Zapatista uprising figures prominently in his account, he remains largely unconcerned with how the specific conditions of ongoing colonialism or the significance of racialized dispossession might matter for his analysis.[27]

Yet in places such as what is presently called the United States, colonialism and the legacies of racial slavery remain actively constitutive for capitalist accumulation. Colonialism in this context is not or not only a process of expansion and incorporation but is a primary social, economic, and political feature of the United States itself, a retrospective and prospective feature that works in tandem with US imperial exploits globally. It is crucial to address the specific ways in which contemporary capitalism depends on and seeks to reproduce, remake, and repurpose the dynamics of possession and expendability with regard to Indigenous peoples, land, and differentially devalued gendered and racialized labor in the service of the particular political economies, biopolitical orders, and normative sociality of the present conjuncture. Chattel slavery and its afterlives also shape both the historical conditions and present-day dynamics of racialized dispossession. Native and Black dispossession is not a concluded historical moment in a teleology of capitalist development but continues and changes over time in ways that operate in conjunction with other forms of expropriation and subjection and what Lisa Marie Cacho describes as the "differential devaluation of racialized peoples."[28]

Filius Nullius and the White Possessive

For the colonial imaginary of possession and emplacement, the notion of filius nullius ("nobody's child") serves as an indispensable complement to terra nullius and its rationalization of the "doctrine of discovery." These disavowals together appear as alibis for dispossession and reimagine the brutality of removal as discovery and rescue—while seeking to render fully unthought and unconnected the market in African children and children of African descent under chattel slavery. The taking and trafficking of Indigenous children, though varying in emphasis and tactics across time and place, have been a common feature of colonial regimes, initially as an explicit strategy of war and then also as a putatively civilizing process of inculcation and uplift.[29] This is perhaps especially the case in settler projects such as New Zealand, Australia, Canada, and the United States. As Christina Firpo and Margaret Jacobs have noted, "A recognition of the ubiquity of child removal as a colonial tactic offers crucial insights into how colonial authorities gained and sustained power through intervention into the intimate lives of colonial subjects."[30] These were policies that proliferated during the mid-twentieth century, when the United States sought to implement the "termination" of tribal sovereignty and federal treaty responsibilities, Australia promoted "assimilation," Canada advocated "integration," and New Zealand's Adoption Act of 1955 launched closed stranger adoption. Such initiatives were paralleled and compounded by often furtive sterilization campaigns targeting Indigenous women and other poor and colonized women of color.[31] Indigenous peoples' resistance to child removal and sterilization prompted reforms during the latter part of the twentieth century, such as the 1978 Indian Child Welfare Act in the United States, yet adoption and foster care as key social technologies for racial capitalism and settler colonialism persist.

Indeed, not only have the taking and trafficking of Indigenous children continued, but there is now increasing reactionary settler momentum to dismantle established reforms. In the United States these challenges to reformist and protective gains often claim that the extreme harms of earlier policies and practices have been resolved and therefore do not require remediation by contemporary legislation. It is thus useful to briefly review the history that is said to be over and done. During the late nineteenth century, US colonial policy emphasized boarding schools for Indigenous children and then shifted to promoting adoption of and foster care for Native children in non-Native families in the mid-twentieth century.[32] Such assimilative and pedagogical endeavors served as a direct corollary to federal policy for Indian removal, allotment, termination, and relocation. Sarah Deer points out that "although assimilation or indoctrination was the primary goal of the boarding schools, commercialization and profit was a by-product of these boarding school efforts; the local communities often benefited from cheap or free labor as a result of the process. In Phoenix, for example, girls and young women were required to provide domestic services for white families—often with substandard (or no) pay."[33] The schools were designed to inculcate "proper" gender roles, with curriculum for boys focusing on vocational and manual labor and an emphasis for girls on domestic education. Ironically, these conditions also contributed to the pan-Indian consciousness that propelled the emergence of the American Indian Movement and the resurgence of Native American anticolonial activism during the 1960s and 1970s. The number of Native American children in boarding schools continued to grow—as well as the forms of physical, psychological, and sexual abuse endemic to those institutions—until reaching an estimated peak enrollment of sixty thousand in 1973.

During the 1950s and 1960s, adoption initiatives increased significantly as a parallel mechanism for Indian removal.[34] These initiatives also worked in tandem with the termination and relocation policies of the time. Termination became official federal policy in 1953 with the passage of House Concurrent Resolution 108, which closed tribal rolls and began to formally end recognition of tribal nations and the federal supervision through which tribal land was held in protected trust status, and Public Law 280, which extended state criminal jurisdiction over tribal reservation in six states. Tribal assets would be liquidated and distributed among each tribe's members, who would then be encouraged by relocation initiatives to disperse and move to urban centers for work and adaptation to post-tribal life. Placement of Indian children for adoption and foster care by non-Indian families worked in tandem with these policies. The Indian Adoption Project (IAP), a collaborative endeavor between the Bureau of Indian Affairs and the Child Welfare League of America, began in 1958. According to Margaret Jacobs, IAP supporters encouraged the removal of Indian children by disseminating "mutually reinforcing images of unwed Indian mothers, deviant extended families, and hopelessly impoverished and alcoholic parents."[35] By the 1970s, with such state-supported projects as the IAP spin-off Adoption Resource Exchange of North America under way, as many as 35 percent of all Indigenous children in the United States were being taken from their families and placed in foster care or adoptive homes of almost exclusively non-Indigenous families.[36] These were the circumstances to which 1978's Indian Child Welfare Act (ICWA) most directly responded.

More broadly, the national, international, and transracial political economy of adoption has historically relied on a markedly inequitable distribution of resources, vulnerability, and immiseration that is partially a consequence of but is not reducible to relations of colonial dispossession. Laura Briggs points out that within this economic trajectory, it is principally "the children of impoverished or otherwise disenfranchised mothers [who] are transferred to middle-class, wealthy mothers (and fathers)." In the United States "adoptable babies and children became disproportionately black, Latino, and Native, or came from overseas."[37] At the same time, measures such as ICWA and the 1972 statement by the National Association of Black Social Workers responded to the deeply entrenched bias of adoption policies that favored placement with heteronormative white families. The association's resolution affirmed the "inviolable position of black children in black families where they belong." A representative explained that, rather than being a separatist antiwhite position—as it had been depicted by those hostile to considering the issues raised by the resolution—the resolution was "directed at the child welfare system that has systematically separated Black children from their birth families."[38]

From the 1980s onward, neoliberal proponents of so-called colorblind law have attacked ICWA's provision for "preferential placement." The landmark 2013 US Supreme Court ruling in *Adoptive Couple v. Baby Girl* (the so-called Baby Veronica case) similarly cast its decision in post–civil rights terms, condemning racial preference and the alleged "special rights" of tribal nations in order to substantively undermine the defensive measures instituted by ICWA.[39] The Supreme Court opinion overturned a lower-court decision and effectively transferred custody of a young Cherokee girl to adoptive white parents over the opposition of her birth father and the Cherokee Nation. Nonetheless, the Supreme Court decision stopped short of directly challenging the Indian Child Welfare Act. Yet Justice Clarence Thomas's conclusion that the case presented "significant constitutional problems" and Justice Samuel Alito's suggestion that a comparable case could potentially serve to overturn ICWA inspired the subsequent litigation filed by the right-wing Goldwater Institute challenging the constitutionality of ICWA.[40] The institute, working with members of the for-profit adoption industry and religious organizations, has "nearly identical arguments in district and state courts . . . with the hopes that they would eventually find a sympathetic judge."[41]

The *Brackeen v. Bernhardt* suit (2018) was one notable result of this effort. *Brackeen* was an effort to undermine the protective gains of the ICWA by alleging that racial preference and "special rights" have been granted to tribal nations. The lawsuit began with the adoption of a two-year-old

Cherokee and Navajo boy by a white couple in northern Texas. Despite the fact that a Navajo family was willing to adopt the child, the Brackeens won their case. Following the suit, the states of Texas, Louisiana, and Indiana, along with two other adoptive couples, joined the Brackeens to argue that the entirety of ICWA should be declared unconstitutional.

This was the first case in which a state has sued the US Department of the Interior over ICWA's constitutionality. In defense of ICWA, the Cherokee Nation, Morongo Band of Mission Indians, Oneida Nation, and Quinault Indian Nation intervened to join the named defendant. *Brackeen* once again rehashes anti-Native sovereignty arguments that the definition of "Indian child" in ICWA is a racial category and therefore ICWA is "race-based" law. Moreover, presiding judge Reed O'Connor went further, arguing that by recognizing tribal preferences in child welfare proceedings, ICWA represents an illegal grant of power to tribal governments that undermines US national sovereignty. The case thus makes explicit the connection between efforts to undermine the minimal protections in place on behalf of tribal jurisdiction over Native children and a thoroughgoing attack on all manner of Indigenous sovereignty. Judge O'Connor's ruling speaks to both the force and the fragility of settler sovereignty, historically and in the present. Although ultimately *Brackeen* did not challenge the constitutionality of ICWA, it served as yet another juridical step in that direction.

Goldwater Institute attorney Timothy Sandefur states that "American Indian law is fraught with a bloody, tragic, often plainly disgusting history of racism, violence, and even genocide. That history—which played a prominent role in ICWA's origin—must not and cannot be ignored or treated euphemistically." Yet this framing only serves as a rhetorical prelude to Sandefur's contention that "it is tragic that these problems persist to this day—and that ICWA is partly to blame."[42] Alleging that ICWA is racist and claiming to rescue Native children from the supposed tyranny of tribes and failed Indigenous domesticity, the Goldwater Institute insists: "We want federal and state laws to be changed to give abused and neglected Native American children the same protections that are given to all other American children: the right to be placed in a safe home based on their best interests, not based on their race."[43] As is evident with its work to annul antidiscrimination laws, the Goldwater Institute suit aims to make the repeal of ICWA the precedent for extinguishing tribal sovereignty and securing the jurispathic diminution of Indigeneity from a political relation to a minoritized racial difference in the name of "equality" and the defense of individual private property rights.

Much like the framing of attacks on affirmative action, anti-ICWA litigants argue that the law is no longer needed. Yet even with ICWA in place, Native children are still placed in foster care at disproportionate rates. As journalist Rebecca Nagle points out, for example, in South Dakota, Native Americans are less than 15 percent of the state's population, but Native youth represent 50 percent of all children in foster care, with almost 90 percent of them being raised in non-Native homes. In Minnesota, Native Americans are only 1.4 percent of the population, but Native youth represent 23.9 percent of the children in the state foster care system. Indeed, currently more than half of US states are out of compliance with ICWA guidelines.[44] Cases such as *Adoptive Couple* and *Brackeen* are carefully selected to showcase the alleged advantages of adoption by non-Native families rather than to evoke the necropolitical logics of Native disposability that continue to be pervasive.

The intimate forms of appropriation and the reproduction of possessive relations at work in this colonial dynamic make clear some of the ways in which the liberal presupposition of self-ownership and possessive individualism assume an expansive capacity and are reproduced in the taking of Indigenous children. Indeed, the possessive relation of ownership is imagined as extending the domain of the individual. Adoption and foster care of Native children by non-Native parents in this context not only extend a particular affective and proprietary relation to the private sphere of the bourgeois normative family but also perform a preemptory or even eliminatory appropriation that insinuates settler futurity over and against Indigenous life and relations. There is in such colonial practices a biopolitical imperative that accentuates its necropolitical counterpart in the possessive relation and its social reproduction. Crucial in this regard is the question that Aileen Moreton-Robinson poses in the Australian context regarding what the denial of Indigenous sovereignty and the casting of Indigenous people as devoid of both will and the capacity to properly possess do to convey the "constitution, currency and circulation of white possession."[45]

Dispossessive Inheritance

Perhaps less readily apparent than the removal and trafficking of Indigenous people as a means of colonial and racialized dispossession but more overtly as a matter of property and ownership, mechanisms of inheritance in the

United States have served similar or complementary ends. The fraction-ation of landed property for Native peoples in the wake of the allotment policy era (1887–1934) and the partition of heirs' property not limited to but disproportionately affecting African Americans since Reconstruction are significant for the ways in which they link past and present dispossession. For the wealthy, inheritance provides a genealogical distance from conquest, genocide, and colonial slavery that offers a cover of ostensible innocence and launders accumulated fortunes. For Native peoples, the descendants of enslaved Africans, and other racialized peoples dispossessed by coloniza-tion, inheritance endures as struggle and demand. Inherited wealth con-tributes to racially overdetermined economic inequality and advantage far more than present-day income.[46] Thus, as problems arising from pro-tracted dynamics of inheritance, fractionation and the partition of heirs' property have directly to do with the conditions of racial capitalism and colonial calculations of reproducing dispossession. Both participate in the production of property and the reproduction of differential dispos-session today.

In 1887 the General Allotment Act, also known as the Dawes Severalty Act, unilaterally sought to divide the homelands of Native American na-tions into alienable private property and distributed 80- to 160-acre parcels to individual Indian "heads of household." Supposedly designed to protect Native peoples from further genocide and initially placing allotments into trust status until allottees were deemed "competent," allotting tribal lands into individual private properties in fact not only hastened further land loss by direct sale and the appropriation of "surplus" land by the federal government but also accelerated sales to non-Indians by tax forfeiture. Under allotment, Native landholding fell sharply from an already dimin-ished 138 million acres in 1887 to 52 million acres in 1934, when allotment policy officially ended. At the same time, tribal sovereignty was further eroded by the expansion of US federal authority through the administra-tion of allotment.

The allotment act instituted a single regime of private property over and against the heterogeneous forms of property organized through the distinct political authority of each Native nation.[47] The 1900 *Annual Re-port of the Commissioner of Indian Affairs to the Department of the Interior* infamously described the law as "a mighty pulverizing engine for breaking up the tribal mass" and a means through which to "recognize the individ-ual" and "protect the family."[48] Although the law was intended to create "independent" property-owning individuals out of Native peoples, the allotments were conceived as a unique kind of property right over which the federal government continued to act as trustee. As legal scholar Jessica Shoemaker explains,

> While held in trust, allotments were to be subject to complete federal restraints on alienation, which meant that individual Indians could not transfer their property freely nor could tribes effectuate local property norms or apply their common law of descent. In addition to the rigid restrictions during life, allottees were denied the right to devise or otherwise determine the distribution of their allotments at death. Instead, all allotments necessarily passed by the intestacy laws of the state that surrounded them, often to multiple children and relatives. Thus, allotment required sharing of land among an ever-increasing number of heirs, as the original allottees died, and left no means for flexible management, sale, or consolidation at any point in the process.[49]

The immediate and long-term consequence of allotment was the escalating problem of fractionation, the division of property into ever-smaller units through the exponential increase in individual owners as a result of inheritance.[50] Allotment also sought to denationalize tribes and minoritize American Indians as a racial group within the United States.[51] The legal recognition of the right of individual Indians to draft federally approved wills granted in 1910 only amplified logics of liberal individualist "estate planning" that remained anathema to many Indigenous peoples. Despite certain reform initiatives, the dispossessive force of fractionation continues to accelerate today as a direct consequence of allotment policy. Thus, allotment and fractionation are ongoing colonial logics of private property that seek to reproduce normative property and personhood and the deferral of both "proper" possession and self-determination for Native peoples under US rule.

Although fractionation is an especially severe problem for Native peoples as a direct result of US policy and colonization, it is also a substantial issue for other impoverished people of color that remains in some sense an effect of the colonial present.[52] According to a 2016 national Gallup poll, 56 percent of all respondents, 69 percent of respondents identified as poor, and 72 percent of "nonwhite" respondents did not have legal wills.[53] Intestacy, the status of the estate of someone who dies without having made a valid will or other binding declaration, is the basis for tenancy-in-common as the principal form of concurrent real estate ownership in the contemporary United States. Without clear title, tenancy-in-common property cannot be mortgaged or used as a basis of credit, and under default inheritance rules it produces a distinctly unstable form of ownership called heirs' property. Heirs' property is the result of exponential generational transmission wherein the cotenants each have an undivided interest in the entire parcel of land even though their ownership interests remain fractional shares. A real estate speculator seeking to acquire the property can purchase a single heir's share and, with the procurement of this interest, has the right to demand that it be partitioned from the property as a whole. As one legal scholar explains, "If the land cannot be easily subdivided, the court will order a sale of the land and a division of the proceeds. Often, by design, the person triggering the sale will then purchase the entire tract," with the other cotenants frequently not having access to cash or credit to bid for the property.[54] A lawyer in Mississippi thus observed that "the partition action has been greatly abused by land developers. By purchasing the interest of one joint owner, the developer is entitled to sue for partition and have the land sold at auction where he is able to buy the entire tract and force any occupants to vacate the land."[55] With multiple heirs of a single property, tenancy-in-common makes such land particularly vulnerable to such tactics.

Partition sale of heirs' property has directly contributed to significant African American dispossession. In spite of the failed promise of land redistribution during Reconstruction and concerted antiblack laws and violence in the former epicenter of colonial slavery, Black landholding in the US South gained slowly but significantly between 1865 and 1910 to a high of sixteen million acres of farmland. Yet partition sale of heirs' property was part of the precipitous loss of more than ten million acres of Black-owned land between 1910 and 1970. By the 1970s, approximately one-third of all land held by African Americans living in the rural South was held under tenancy-in-common.[56] Moreover, as legal scholar Heather Way observes, "It's most definitely an urban issue too. . . . It's very common to see heirs' property issues in low-income, older neighborhoods, where a house has been in the family and passed down for generations."[57] Way also notes cases in the aftermath of Hurricane Katrina in which Black homeowners affected by the storm were unable to receive disaster-recovery assistance because of title questions arising from heirs' property issues.[58] Such dynamics intensified the disproportionate foreclosure and eviction among impoverished African Americans during the 2006–2008 financial crisis triggered by subprime loan practices.[59] Legislation such as the 2010 Uniform Partition of Heirs Property Act aims to develop due process protections and provide legal recourse for cotenant heirs, but predatory uses of forced partition sale continue to link past and present precarity overdetermined by racism.

Perhaps most significant for the argument that I am making here with regard to reproduction is that both fractionation and the partition of heirs' property simultaneously advance a particular normative relation to ownership while holding the possibility of possession itself in abeyance and presuming the inevitability of loss as part of their instantiation. What is reproduced is at once an individuated possessory relation to private property and the deferral of possession itself. Both are manifest through familial and generational processes that incorporate heteronormative and racial dispositions into their logics and logistics of reproduction, severalty, and property. Furthermore, both are methods of dispossession seemingly detached from the intentions of the state and capital that are nonetheless direct outcomes of historical colonial and racial capitalist dispossession, with significant consequences in the present. Fractionation and heirs' property are not especially exemplary or exceptional instances through which to foreground such practices and circumstances. But considering them together provides a means of acknowledging the conditions of the historical present in this regard, as well as suggesting a particular logic of property and value that emerges in concert with the triangulation of race, capitalism, and colonialism.

Relations Otherwise

The operation of social reproduction is a capacious and always unstable or uncertain process that assembles and co-constitutes social formation. Focusing on social reproduction is a means through which to contend with the specific ways in which contemporary capitalism depends on and seeks to remake and repurpose the dynamics of possession and expendability with regard to Indigenous peoples, land, and differentially devalued gendered and racialized labor in the service of the particular political economies, biopolitical orders, and normative sociality of the present conjuncture. I am suggesting that social reproduction should be understood in such a way that not only complicates but materially and conceptually expands the frame of labor and the labor process, as well as acknowledging relations of land, place, and grounded genealogy. Social reproduction is likewise not only the proposition and production of life itself but also a dialectical relation that distributes attributions of disposability and premature death, organizing the conditions of possibility and impossibility through particular capitalist economies. It does not precede or exceed capitalism but is constitutive of its formation and mutability. The history and present conditions of the foster care and adoption of Indigenous children by non-Indigenous people and the dispossessive force of fractionation and partition of heirs' property in what is at this conjuncture the United States exemplify these dynamics of social reproduction in part because they make apparent the intimate political economies of filiation, attrition, and elimination at work.

Although both racial capitalism and settler colonialism as co-constitutive forms of power and dominion imagine themselves to be in some sense total, inevitable, and in perpetuity, both in fact remain partial, incomplete, and vulnerable to fundamental undoing. Indeed, both racial capitalism and settler colonialism are heterogeneous formations. Both present their logics of expansion as absolute and permanent—ostensibly there is no end to settler colonial occupation, just as there is supposedly no truly feasible alternative to capitalism. Yet attending to the imperative for and work of reproduction not only underscores the unfinished and precarious character of each but might also demonstrate the ongoing prospects for their disruption and disassembly. Most importantly, focusing on social reproduction underscores how both are counter-formations responding to and seeking to contain and subsume such interruption and collective contestation.

NOTES

1. Coulthard, *Red Skin, White Masks*, 14. Early work on settler colonialism that foregrounded its inter-articulation with capitalism includes Emmanuel, "White-Settler Colonialism"; Good, "Settler Colonialism"; Biermann and Kössler, "Settler Mode of Production"; Blaut, "Colonialism and the Rise"; and Denoon, *Settler Capitalism*. For more recent scholarship that theorizes race, capitalism, and colonialism as mutually constitutive, see, especially, Day, *Alien Capital*; Wolfe, *Traces of History*; Ince, *Colonial Capitalism*; Bhandar, *Colonial Lives of Property*; Nichols, *Theft Is Property!*; Estes, *Our History Is the Future*; and Karuka, *Empire's Tracks*.

2. Hudson, "Racial Capitalism"; Kelley, "Why *Black Marxism*?"; Jenkins and Leroy, "Old History of Capitalism."

3. "Azanian Manifesto," 168. See also Alexander, "Illuminating Moment"; and Burden-Stelly, Hudson, and Pierre, "Racial Capitalism, Black Liberation."

4. "Azanian Manifesto," 169.

5. Alexander, "Nation and Ethnicity," 62.

6. Legassick and Hemson, *Foreign Investment*. Legassick and Hemson argue that the "Poverty Datum Line" in South Africa is *"racially* calculated" to encourage "the payment of wage levels at the minimum necessary to secure the reproduction of the workforce. . . . What is judged the minimum necessary for an African family is different from, and substantially lower than, equivalent estimates for the family of a white worker. The Poverty Datum Line concept, in other words, is not only a formula for the reproduction of capitalist relationships in South Africa, but also for the reproduction of *racial* capitalism" (11).

7. Kelley, "Rest of Us"; Clarno, *Neoliberal Apartheid*, 1–23; Veracini, "'Settler Colonialism.'"

8. Kelley, "What Is Racial Capitalism?" See also Melamed, "Racial Capitalism"; Dawson, "Hidden in Plain Sight"; Bhattacharyya, *Rethinking Racial Capitalism*; Burden-Stelly, "Modern US Racial Capitalism"; and Gilmore, *Change Everything*.

9. Marx, *Capital*, 1:35, 1:565.

10. See Marx, *Capital*, vol. 1, parts 7 and 8; Marx, *Capital*, vol. 2, chapters 20 and 21.

11. Marx, *Capital*, 1:575.

12. Luxemburg, *Accumulation of Capital*, 348. Notably, the original subtitle *A Contribution to an Economic Explanation of Imperialism* is unfortunately omitted from the Routledge republication. For a generative collection of engagements with Luxemburg's work, see Cornell and Gordon, eds., *Creolizing Rosa Luxemburg*. For an important contribution that engages Luxemburg while theorizing the "operations" of capital, see Mezzadra and Neilson, *Politics of Operations*.

13. Balibar, "Basic Concepts of Historical Materialism," 437.

14. For example, see Mies, *Patriarchy and Accumulation*; Katz, "Vagabond Capitalism"; Federici, *Caliban and the Witch*; Nadasen, *Household Workers Unite*; Bhattacharya, ed., *Social Reproduction Theory*; and Briggs, *How All Politics Became Reproductive*.

15. Quoted in Bhattacharya, "Mapping Social Reproduction Theory," in *Social Reproduction Theory*, 2.

16. Toupin, *Wages for Housework*; Gutiérrez-Rodríguez, *Migration, Domestic Work and Affect*; Kofman and Raghuram, *Gendered Migrations*; Boris, "Reproduction as Production."

17. Roberts, *Killing the Black Body*; Spillers, "Mama's Baby, Papa's Maybe"; Bridges, *Reproducing Race*; Ross et al., eds., *Radical Reproductive Justice*; Davis, *Reproductive Injustice*; Luna, *Reproductive Rights as Human Rights*; Nash, *Birthing Black Mothers*.

18. Morgan, *Laboring Women*, 144–45. See also Morgan, *Reckoning with Slavery*.

19. Weinbaum, *Afterlife of Reproductive Slavery*; Vora, *Life Support*; Vora, "After the Housewife"; Valdez and Deomampo, eds., "Interrogating the Intersections of Race."

20. Roberts, *Killing the Black Body*, 154, 4.

21. See, for example, Hobart and Kneese, eds., "Radical Care"; Byrd, "What's Normative?"; Spade, *Mutual Aid*.

22. Singh, "Race, Violence, and 'So-Called Primitive Accumulation,'" 57–58.

23. Federici, *Revolution at Point Zero*, 140.

24. Marx, *Capital*, 1:703.

25. Marx, *Capital*, 1:899.

26. Marx, *Capital*, 1:899.

27. Harvey, *New Imperialism*, 137–82. For especially insightful critical engagements with Harvey's conception of "dispossession by accumulation," see Chakravartty and Ferreira da Silva, "Accumulation, Dispossession, and Debt"; and Nichols, *Theft Is Property!*, 52–84.

28. Cacho, *Social Death*, 17. Of course, such dynamics are not limited to Black and Native peoples. See, for instance, Lowe, *Intimacies of Four Continents*; and Kang, *Traffic in Asian Women*.

29. To be clear, I am not talking about adoption and foster care in general but specifically about their use as part of an ensemble of colonial practices that operate in tandem with imperial and white supremacist relations. I am not arguing against the possible legitimacy of adoption or foster care as ways of making family and kinship.

30. Firpo and Jacobs, "Taking Children, Ruling Colonies," 531. See also Briggs, *Taking Children*.

31. Vergès, *Wombs of Women*; Gurr, *Reproductive Justice*; Zavella, *Movement for Reproductive Justice*; Briggs, *Reproducing Empire*.

32. On the history of boarding schools for Indigenous peoples in the United States (and elsewhere), see, for example, Adams, *Education for Extinction*; Lomawaima, *They Called It Prairie Light*; Trafzer, Keller, and Sisquoc, eds., *Boarding School Blues*; and Child and Klopotek, eds., *Indian Subjects*.

33. Deer, *Beginning and End of Rape*, 71.

34. United States Congress, House of Representatives, *Establishing Standards*.

35. Jacobs, "Remembering the 'Forgotten Child,'" 144. See also Jacobs, *Generation Removed*.

36. Palmiste, "From the Indian Adoption Project"; Jacobs, "Remembering the 'Forgotten Child.'"

37. Briggs, *Somebody's Children*, 4, 6.

38. Quoted in Briggs, *Somebody's Children*, 28.

39. Fletcher, Singel, and Fort, eds., *Facing the Future*; Goldstein, "Possessive Investment"; Berger, "In the Name of the Child"; Barker, "Self-Determination"; Beardall, "Adoptive Couple v. Baby Girl"; Rolnick and Pearson, "Racial Anxieties in Adoption."

40. Fort, "Goldwater Institute."

41. Nagle, "Texas Judge Rules."

42. Sandefur, "Escaping the ICWA Penalty Box."

43. Quoted in Dewan and Israel, "Why a Conservative Legal Organization."

44. Nagle, "Texas Judge Rules."

45. Moreton-Robinson, *White Possessive*, 110.

46. Oliver and Shapiro, *Black Wealth/White Wealth*; Strand, "Inheriting Inequality."

47. Justice and O'Brien, eds., *Allotment Stories*; Bobroff, "Retelling Allotment."

48. *Annual Report of the Commissioner of Indian Affairs*, 660, 658. See also Gates, "Next Great Step," 120. Gates also commends the allotment act for having "given a mighty impulse toward family life and the cultivation of home virtues" (120).

49. Shoemaker, "Like Snow," 738.

50. In addition to Shoemaker, "Like Snow," see Shoemaker, "Complexity's Shadow"; McGrath, "Model Tribal Probate Code"; and Royster, "Legacy of Allotment."

51. Barker, *Native Acts*.

52. Mitchell, "From Reconstruction to Deconstruction"; Rivers, "Inequity in Equity"; Mitchell, "Reforming Property Law"; Spivack, "Broken Links."

53. "Majority in US Do Not Have a Will."

54. Graber, "Heirs Property," 277.

55. Quoted in Graber, "Heirs Property," 277.

56. Graber, "Heirs Property," 273.

57. Heather Way, quoted in Persky, "In the Cross-Heirs."

58. Heather Way, quoted in Persky, "In the Cross-Heirs."

59. Nembhard and Otabor, "Great Recession and Land." See also Fields and Raymond, "Racialized Geographies of Housing Financialization." On foreclosure as a technique of racialized colonial dispossession, see Park, "Race, Innovation, and Financial Growth."

Adams, David Wallace. *Education for Extinction: American Indians and the Boarding School Experience, 1875–1928*. Lawrence: University Press of Kansas, 1995.

Alexander, Neville. "An Illuminating Moment: Background to the Azanian Manifesto." In *Biko Lives! Contesting the Legacies of Steve Biko*, edited by Andile Mngxitama, Amanda Alexander, and Nigel C. Gibson, 157–67. New York: Palgrave Macmillan, 2008.

Alexander, Neville. "Nation and Ethnicity in South Africa." In *Sow the Wind: Contemporary Speeches*, 49–64. Johannesburg: Skotaville, 1985.

Annual Report of the Commissioner of Indian Affairs to the Department of the Interior. Washington, DC: Government Printing Office, 1900.

"The Azanian Manifesto." In *Biko Lives! Contesting the Legacies of Steve Biko*, edited by Andile Mngxitama, Amanda Alexander, and Nigel C. Gibson, 168–70. New York: Palgrave Macmillan, 2008.

Balibar, Étienne. "On the Basic Concepts of Historical Materialism." In Louis Althusser, Étienne Balibar, Roger Establet, Pierre Macherey, and Jacques Rancière, *Reading Capital: The Complete Edition*. Translated by Ben Brewster and David Fernbach, 357–480. Brooklyn, NY: Verso, 2015 (1965).

Barker, Joanne. *Native Acts: Law, Recognition, and Cultural Authenticity*. Durham, NC: Duke University Press, 2011.

Barker, Joanne. "Self-Determination." *Critical Ethnic Studies* 1, no. 1 (Spring 2015): 11–26.

Beardall, Theresa Rocha. "*Adoptive Couple v. Baby Girl*: Policing Authenticity, Implicit Racial Bias, and Continued Harm to American Indian Families." *American Indian Culture and Research Journal* 40, no. 1 (2016): 119–40.

Berger, Bethany R. "In the Name of the Child: Race, Gender, and Economics in *Adoptive Couple v. Baby Girl*." *Florida Law Review* 67 (2015): 295–362.

Bhandar, Brenna. *Colonial Lives of Property: Law, Land, and Racial Regimes of Ownership*. Durham, NC: Duke University Press, 2018.

Bhattacharya, Tithi, ed. *Social Reproduction Theory: Remapping Class, Recentering Oppression*. London: Pluto, 2017.

Bhattacharyya, Gargi. *Rethinking Racial Capitalism: Questions of Reproduction and Survival*. New York: Rowman and Littlefield, 2018.

Biermann, Werner, and Reinhart Kössler. "The Settler Mode of Production: The Rhodesian Case." *Review of African Political Economy* 7, no. 18 (1980): 106–16.

Blaut, J. M. "Colonialism and the Rise of Capitalism." *Science and Society* 53, no. 3 (Fall 1989): 260–96.

Bobroff, Kenneth H. "Retelling Allotment: Indian Property Rights and the Myth of Common Ownership." *Vanderbilt Law Review* 54, no. 4 (May 2001): 1559–1623.

Boris, Eileen. "Reproduction as Production: Thinking with the ILO to Move beyond Dichotomy." *Journal of Labor and Society* 22, no. 2 (June 2019): 283–98.

Bridges, Khiara M. *Reproducing Race: An Ethnography of Pregnancy as a Site of Racialization*. Berkeley: University of California Press, 2011.

Briggs, Laura. *How All Politics Became Reproductive Politics: From Welfare Reform to Foreclosure to Trump*. Berkeley: University of California Press, 2017.

Briggs, Laura. *Reproducing Empire: Race, Sex, Science, and US Imperialism in Puerto Rico*. Berkeley: University of California Press, 2002.

Briggs, Laura. *Somebody's Children: The Politics of Transracial and Transnational Adoption*. Durham, NC: Duke University Press, 2012.

Briggs, Laura. *Taking Children: A History of American Terror*. Berkeley: University of California Press, 2020.

Burden-Stelly, Charisse. "Modern US Racial Capitalism." *Monthly Review* 72, no. 3 (July–August 2020): 8–20.

Burden-Stelly, Charisse, Peter James Hudson, and Jemima Pierre. "Racial Capitalism, Black Liberation, and South Africa." *Black Agenda Report*, December 16, 2020. www.blackagendareport.com/racial-capitalism-black-liberation-and-south-africa.

Byrd, Jodi A. "What's Normative Got to Do with It? Toward Indigenous Queer Relationality." *Social Text* 145 (December 2020): 105–23.

Cacho, Lisa Marie. *Social Death: Racialized Rightlessness and the Criminalization of the Unprotected*. New York: NYU Press, 2012.

Chakravartty, Paula, and Denise Ferreira da Silva. "Accumulation, Dispossession, and Debt: The Racial Logic of Global Capitalism—An Introduction." *American Quarterly* 64, no. 3 (2012): 361–85.

Child, Brenda J., and Brian Klopotek, eds. *Indian Subjects: Hemispheric Perspectives on the History of Indigenous Education*. Santa Fe, NM: SAR, 2014.

Clarno, Andy. *Neoliberal Apartheid: Palestine/Israel and South Africa after 1994*. Chicago: University of Chicago Press, 2017.

Cornell, Drucilla, and Jane Anna Gordon, eds. *Creolizing Rosa Luxemburg*. Lanham, MD: Rowman and Littlefield, 2021.

Coulthard, Glen Sean. *Red Skin, White Masks: Rejecting the Colonial Politics of Recognition*. Minneapolis: University of Minnesota Press, 2014.

Davis, Dána-Ain. *Reproductive Injustice: Racism, Pregnancy, and Premature Birth*. New York: NYU Press, 2019.

Dawson, Michael C. "Hidden in Plain Sight: A Note on Legitimation Crises and the Racial Order." *Critical Historical Studies* 3, no. 1 (Spring 2016): 143–61.

Day, Iyko. *Alien Capital: Asian Racialization and the Logic of Settler Colonial Capitalism*. Durham, NC: Duke University Press, 2016.

Deer, Sarah. *The Beginning and End of Rape: Confronting Sexual Violence in Native America*. Minneapolis: University of Minnesota Press, 2015.

Denoon, Daniel. *Settler Capitalism: The Dynamics of Dependent Development in the Southern Hemisphere*. London: Oxford University Press, 1983.

Dewan, Bryan, and Josh Israel. "Why a Conservative Legal Organization Is Desperately Trying to Kill the Indian Child Welfare Act." Think Progress, April 8,

2016. https://archive.thinkprogress.org/why-a-conservative-legal-organization
-is-desperately-trying-to-kill-the-indian-child-welfare-act-762ba8e62d5b.

Emmanuel, Arghiri. "White-Settler Colonialism and the Myth of Investment Imperialism." *New Left Review* 73 (May 1972): 35–57.

Estes, Nick. *Our History Is the Future: Standing Rock versus the Dakota Access Pipeline, and the Long Tradition of Indigenous Resistance*. Brooklyn, NY: Verso, 2019.

Federici, Silvia. *Caliban and the Witch: Women, the Body and Primitive Accumulation*. Brooklyn, NY: Autonomedia, 2004.

Federici, Silvia. *Revolution at Point Zero: Housework, Reproduction, and Feminist Struggle*. Oakland, CA: PM, 2012.

Fields, Desiree, and Elora Lee Raymond. "Racialized Geographies of Housing Financialization." *Progress in Human Geography* (2021): 1–21.

Firpo, Christina, and Margaret Jacobs. "Taking Children, Ruling Colonies: Child Removal and Colonial Subjugation in Australia, Canada, French Indochina, and the United States, 1870–1950s." *Journal of World History* 29, no. 4 (December 2018): 529–63.

Fletcher, Wenona, T. Singel, and Kathryn E. Fort, eds. *Facing the Future: The Indian Child Welfare Act at 30*. East Lansing: Michigan State University Press, 2009.

Fort, Kate. "Goldwater Institute to File a Class Action Lawsuit against ICWA." *Turtle Talk: Indigenous Law and Policy Centre Blog*, July 6, 2015. https://turtletalk .wordpress.com/2015/07/06/goldwater-institute-to-file-a-class-action-lawsuit -against-icwa.

Gates, Merrill E. "The Next Great Step to Break Up Tribal Funds into Individual Holdings." In *Proceedings of the Eighteenth Annual Meeting of the Lake Mohonk Conference of Friends of the Indian*. New York: Lake Mohonk Conference, 1900.

Gilmore, Ruth Wilson. *Change Everything: Racial Capitalism and the Case for Abolition*. Chicago: Haymarket, 2022.

Goldstein, Alyosha. "Possessive Investment: Indian Removals and the Affective Entitlements of Whiteness." *American Quarterly* 66, no. 4 (December 2014): 1077–84.

Good, Kenneth. "Settler Colonialism: Economic Development and Class Formation." *Journal of Modern African Studies* 14, no. 4 (December 1976): 597–620.

Graber, C. Scott. "Heirs Property: The Problems and Possible Solutions." *Clearinghouse Review* 12, no. 5 (September 1978): 273–84.

Gurr, Barbara. *Reproductive Justice: The Politics of Health Care for Native American Women*. New Brunswick, NJ: Rutgers University Press, 2015.

Gutiérrez-Rodríguez, Encarnación. *Migration, Domestic Work and Affect: A Decolonial Approach on Value and the Feminization of Labor*. New York: Routledge, 2011.

Harvey, David. *The New Imperialism*. New York: Oxford University Press, 2003.

Hobart, Hiʻilei Julia Kawehipuaakahaopulani, and Tamara Kneese, eds. "Radical Care." Special issue of *Social Text* 142 (March 2020).

Hudson, Peter James. "Racial Capitalism and the Dark Proletariat." *Boston Review* (Winter 2017): 59–65.

Ince, Onur Ulas. *Colonial Capitalism and the Dilemmas of Liberalism*. New York: Oxford University Press, 2018.

Jacobs, Margaret D. *A Generation Removed: The Fostering and Adoption of Indigenous Children in the Postwar World*. Lincoln: University of Nebraska Press, 2014.

Jacobs, Margaret D. "Remembering the 'Forgotten Child': The American Indian Child Welfare Crisis of the 1960s and 1970s." *American Indian Quarterly* 37, nos. 1–2 (2013): 136–59.

Jenkins, Destin, and Justin Leroy. "The Old History of Capitalism." In *Histories of Racial Capitalism*, edited by Destin Jenkins and Justin Leroy, 1–26. New York: Columbia University Press, 2021.

Justice, Daniel Heath, and Jean M. O'Brien, eds. *Allotment Stories: Indigenous Land Relations under Settler Siege*. Minneapolis: University of Minnesota Press, 2022.

Kang, Laura Hyun Yi. *Traffic in Asian Women*. Durham, NC: Duke University Press, 2020.

Karuka, Manu. *Empire's Tracks: Indigenous Nations, Chinese Workers, and the Transcontinental Railroad*. Berkeley: University of California Press, 2019.

Katz, Cindi. "Vagabond Capitalism and the Necessity of Social Reproduction." *Antipode* 33, no. 4 (September 2001): 709–28.

Kelley, Robin D. G. "The Rest of Us: Rethinking Settler and Native." *American Quarterly* 69, no. 2 (June 2017): 267–76.

Kelley, Robin D. G. "What Is Racial Capitalism and Why Does It Matter?" Simpson Center for the Humanities, University of Washington, November 7, 2017. www.youtube.com/watch?v=REo_gHIpvJc.

Kelley, Robin D. G. "Why *Black Marxism*? Why Now?" In Cedric J. Robinson, *Black Marxism: The Making of the Black Radical Tradition*. 3rd ed., xi–xxxiv. Chapel Hill: University of North Carolina Press, 2021.

Kofman, Eleonore, and Parvati Raghuram. *Gendered Migrations and Global Social Reproduction*. New York: Palgrave Macmillan, 2015.

Legassick, Martin, and David Hemson. *Foreign Investment and the Reproduction of Racial Capitalism in South Africa*. London: Anti-apartheid Movement, September 1976.

Lomawaima, K. Tsianina. *They Called It Prairie Light: The Story of Chilocco Indian School*. Lincoln: University of Nebraska Press, 1995.

Lowe, Lisa. *The Intimacies of Four Continents*. Durham, NC: Duke University Press, 2015.

Luna, Zakiya. *Reproductive Rights as Human Rights: Women of Color and the Fight for Reproductive Justice*. New York: NYU Press, 2020.

Luxemburg, Rosa. *The Accumulation of Capital*. Translated by Agnes Schwarzschild. New York: Routledge, 2003 (1913).

"Majority in US Do Not Have a Will." *Gallup News*, May 8, 2016. http://news.gallup.com/poll/191651/majority-not.aspx.

Marx, Karl. *Capital*, vol. 1, *A Critique of Political Economy*. Edited by Frederick Engels. Translated by Ben Fowkes. New York: Penguin, 1993 (1867).

Marx, Karl. *Capital*, vol. 2, *A Critique of Political Economy*. Edited by Frederick Engels. Translated by David Fernbach. New York: Penguin, 1993 (1893).

McGrath, Daniel. "The Model Tribal Probate Code: An Opportunity to Correct the Problems of Fractionation and the Legacy of the Dawes Act." *Journal of Gender, Race, and Justice* 20, no. 2 (Spring 2017): 403–29.

Melamed, Jodi. "Racial Capitalism." *Critical Ethnic Studies* 1, no. 1 (Spring 2015): 76–85.

Mezzadra, Sandro, and Brett Neilson. *The Politics of Operations: Excavating Contemporary Capitalism*. Durham, NC: Duke University Press, 2019.

Mies, Maria. *Patriarchy and Accumulation on a World Scale: Women in the International Division of Labour*. London: Zed, 1986.

Mitchell, Thomas W. "From Reconstruction to Deconstruction: Undermining Black Landownership, Political Independence, and Community through Partition Sales of Tenancies in Common." *Northwestern University Law Review* 95 (2001): 505–80.

Mitchell, Thomas W. "Reforming Property Law to Address Devastating Land Loss." *Alabama Law Review* 66, no. 1 (2014): 1–61.

Moreton-Robinson, Aileen M. *The White Possessive: Property, Power, and Indigenous Sovereignty*. Minneapolis: University of Minnesota Press, 2015.

Morgan, Jennifer L. *Laboring Women: Reproduction and Gender in New World Slavery*. Philadelphia: University of Pennsylvania Press, 2004.

Morgan, Jennifer L. *Reckoning with Slavery: Gender, Kinship, and Capitalism in the Early Black Atlantic*. Durham, NC: Duke University Press, 2021.

Nadasen, Premilla. *Household Workers Unite: The Untold Story of African American Women Who Built a Movement*. Boston: Beacon, 2016.

Nagle, Rebecca. "Texas Judge Rules Indian Child Welfare Act as Unconstitutional." *Indian Country Today*, October 8, 2018. https://newsmaven.io/indiancountrytoday/news/texas-judge-rules-indian-child-welfare-act-as-unconstitutional-X_4Gx2-IkEKVEYCEdGxSFg.

Nash, Jennifer C. *Birthing Black Mothers*. Durham, NC: Duke University Press, 2021.

Nembhard, Jessica Gordon, and Charlotte Otabor. "The Great Recession and Land and Housing Loss in African American Communities: Case Studies from Alabama, Florida, Louisiana, and Mississippi—Part 2: Heir Property." Working paper, Center on Race and Wealth, Howard University, Washington, DC, July 2012.

Nichols, Robert. *Theft Is Property! Dispossession and Critical Theory*. Durham, NC: Duke University Press, 2019.

Oliver, Melvin L., and Thomas M. Shapiro. *Black Wealth/White Wealth: A New Perspective on Racial Inequality*. 2nd ed. New York: Routledge, 2006.

Palmiste, Claire. "From the Indian Adoption Project to the Indian Child Welfare Act: The Resistance of Native American Communities." *Indigenous Policy Journal* 22, no. 1 (2011): 1–10.

Park, K-Sue. "Race, Innovation, and Financial Growth: The Example of Foreclo-sure." In *Histories of Racial Capitalism*, edited by Destin Jenkins and Justin Leroy, 27–51. New York: Columbia University Press, 2021.

Persky, Anna Stolley. "In the Cross-Heirs." *aba Journal* 95 (May 2009). www .abajournal.com/magazine/article/in_the_cross-heirs.

Rivers, Faith. "Inequity in Equity: The Tragedy of Tenancy in Common for Heirs' Property Owners Facing Partition in Equity." *Temple Political and Civil Rights Law Review* 17 (2007): 1–81.

Roberts, Dorothy. *Killing the Black Body: Race, Reproduction, and the Meaning of Liberty*. New York: Vintage, 1997.

Robinson, Cedric J. *Black Marxism: The Making of the Black Radical Tradition*, 3rd ed. Chapel Hill: University of North Carolina Press, 2021 (1983).

Rolnick, Addie, and Kim Pearson. "Racial Anxieties in Adoption: Reflections on *Adoptive Couple*, White Parenthood, and Constitutional Challenges to the ICWA." *Michigan State Law Review* (2017): 727–54.

Ross, Loretta J., Lynn Roberts, Erika Derkas, Whitney Peoples, and Pamela Bridgewater Toure, eds. *Radical Reproductive Justice: Foundation, Theory, Practice, Critique*. New York: Feminist Press, 2017.

Royster, Judith V. "The Legacy of Allotment." *Arizona State Law Journal* 27, no. 1 (Spring 1995): 1–78.

Sandefur, Timothy. "Escaping the ICWA Penalty Box: In Defense of Equal Protection for Indian Children." *Children's Legal Rights Journal* 37, no. 1 (2017): 6–80.

Shoemaker, Jessica A. "Complexity's Shadow: American Indian Property, Sovereignty, and the Future." *Michigan Law Review* 115, no. 4 (2017).

Shoemaker, Jessica A. "Like Snow in the Spring Time: Allotment, Fractionation, and the Indian Land Tenure Problem." *Wisconsin Law Review* 4 (2003): 729–88.

Singh, Nikhil Pal. "On Race, Violence, and 'So-Called Primitive Accumulation.'" In *Futures of Black Radicalism*, edited by Gaye Theresa Johnson and Alex Lubin, 39–58. New York: Verso, 2017.

Spade, Dean. *Mutual Aid: Building Solidarity during This Crisis (and the Next)*. Brooklyn, NY: Verso, 2020.

Spillers, Hortense J. "Mama's Baby, Papa's Maybe: An American Grammar Book." *Diacritics* 17, no. 2 (1987): 64–81.

Spivack, Carla. "Broken Links: A Critique of Formal Equality in Inheritance Law." *Wisconsin Law Review* 2019, no. 2 (2019): 191–212.

Strand, Palma Joy. "Inheriting Inequality: Wealth, Race, and the Laws of Succession." *Oregon Law Review* 89, no. 2 (2010): 453–504.

Toupin, Louise. *Wages for Housework: A History of an International Feminist Movement, 1972–77*. London: Pluto, 2018.

Trafzer, Clifford E., Jean A. Keller, and Lorene Sisquoc, eds. *Boarding School Blues: Revisiting American Indian Educational Experiences*. Lincoln: University of Nebraska Press, 2006.

United States Congress, House of Representatives. *Establishing Standards for the Placement of Indian Children in Foster or Adoptive Homes, to Prevent the Breakup of Indian Families, and for Other Purposes: Report Together with Dissenting Views* (to accompany H.R. 12533). Report No. 1386, 95th Congress, 2nd session. July 24, 1978.

Valdez, Natali, and Daisy Deomampo, eds. "Interrogating the Intersections of Race and Reproduction in Medicine, Science, and Technology." Special issue of *Medical Anthropology* 38, nos. 7–8 (2019).

Veracini, Lorenzo. "'Settler Colonialism': Career of Concept." *Journal of Imperial and Commonwealth History* 41, no. 2 (2013): 313–33.

Vergès, Françoise. *The Wombs of Women: Race, Capital, Feminism*. Durham, NC: Duke University Press, 2020.

Vora, Kalindi. "After the Housewife: Surrogacy, Labour and Human Reproduction." *Radical Philosophy* 204 (Spring 2019): 42–46.

Vora, Kalindi. *Life Support: Biocapital and the New History of Outsourced Labor*. Minneapolis: University of Minnesota Press, 2015.

Weinbaum, Alys Eve. *The Afterlife of Reproductive Slavery: Biocapitalism and Black Feminism's Philosophy of History*. Durham, NC: Duke University Press, 2019.

Wolfe, Patrick. *Traces of History: Elementary Structures of Race*. Brooklyn, NY: Verso, 2016.

Zavella, Patricia. *The Movement for Reproductive Justice: Empowering Women of Color through Social Activism*. New York: NYU Press, 2020.

The Racial Alchemy of Debt: Dispossession and Accumulation in Afterlives of Slavery

Under our constitution, there can be no such thing as a either a creditor or debtor race. . . . In the eyes of government, we are just one race here. It is American.

ANTONIN SCALIA, CONCURRING OPINION, *ADARAND CONSTRUCTORS, INC. V. PEÑA*, 1995

One hundred years [after Emancipation], the Negro lives on a lonely island of poverty in the midst of a vast ocean of material prosperity. . . . In a sense we have come to our nation's capital to cash a check. When the architects of our republic wrote the magnificent words of the Constitution and the Declaration of Independence, they were signing a promissory note to which every American was to fall heir. This note was a promise that all men, yes, black men as well as white men, would be guaranteed the unalienable rights of life, liberty, and the pursuit of happiness. . . . It is obvious today that America has defaulted on this promissory note. . . . Instead of honoring this sacred obligation, America has given the Negro people a bad check, a check which has come back marked "insufficient funds." . . . But we refuse to believe that the bank of justice is bankrupt. So we have come to cash this check—a check that will give us upon demand the riches of freedom and the security of justice.

MARTIN LUTHER KING JR., "I HAVE A DREAM," 1963

The bondholders are sacred. They cannot be touched. People are not sacred.

CLAIRE MCCLINTON, FLINT DEMOCRACY DEFENSE LEAGUE, QUOTED IN BENJAMIN

J. PAULI, *FLINT FIGHTS BACK*, 2019

Recent work in conceptual art challenges the exemption of art and its production from critiques of racial domination and capitalist exploitation.[1]

These artists expose this omission, not by focusing on the aesthetics of an object but by attending to its modes of production. This radical reorientation seeks to destabilize what is considered art as well as what one considers the function of art to be. Against a notion of art as a unique, stylized object or media, conceptual artists have embraced "the use of any medium, event, or object deemed appropriate to the particular concepts the artist chose to explore."[2] Cameron Rowland's 2016 exhibition, *91020000*, is articulated in this register.[3] The objects for consideration—a desk, a bench, a fireman's suit, a set of giant metal rings—are "ready-made," stubbornly ordinary, unadorned, unembellished, and fungible.[4]

This piece, titled *Leveler (Extension) Rings for Manhole Openings*, consists of large, stacked aluminum rings. *Leveler Rings*, like other works in the exhibition, initially discloses nothing of its origins or function. This opacity is ruptured by Rowland's rigorously researched and elegant notes that reveal how the rings were produced and used, as well as the obscured financial networks in which they circulate.[5] The text fuses with the object; the medium (object/text) expresses a message:[6] "Manhole leveler rings are cast by prisoners in Elmira Correctional Facility. When roads are repaved, they are used to adjust the height of manhole openings and to maintain the smooth surface of the road. Work on public roads, which was

FIGURE 3.1. Cameron Rowland, *91020000*. Installation view, Artists Space, New York, 2016. Courtesy of the artist and Maxwell Graham/Essex Street, New York.

central to the transition from convict leasing to the chain gang, continues within many prison labor programs. The road is a public asset, instrumental to commercial development."[7] As in many other prisons in the state, a plurality if not a majority of the prisoners are Black.[8] The prisoners' labor is compensated at steeply discounted rates—from $0.10 to $1.14 per hour.[9]

Raceless Facades of Capital

The racially banal facade of *Leveler Rings* reflects the presumption of race neutrality that has been the hallmark of the contemporary racial order. Antonin Scalia's declaration that there is no "creditor or debtor race" rejects the very notion of racial subordination and encodes that logic in legal doctrine.[10] Yet the claim to neutrality is fictive both conceptually and materially. As Ruth Wilson Gilmore argues, "Capitalism requires inequality, and racism enshrines it."[11] The racelessness of the capitalist order is and has always been illusory. Likewise, the racelessness of the object is illusory: *Leveler Rings* is freighted with a genealogy that begins with enslavement and extends through its many afterlives to current regimes of state and private power that operate to extract value and manage populations.[12] History is central to understanding how *Leveler Rings* came into being as a condition of Black life.

The modes of production of *Leveler Rings* and the roads built through the use of such rings reflect a refurbished racialized system of incarceration and capitalization that is connected logically and materially to earlier structures. As Rowland explains, when four million formerly enslaved Africans were no longer legally bound to their owners following the end of the Civil War, state power was redeployed to coerce and appropriate freed people's labor through the enactment of laws that "criminalize black life."[13] Without being tethered to a white employer, Black men, women, and children were subject to arrest and conviction for vague and fabricated offenses and were assessed fines and fees through processes that mocked notions of due process. Without the means to pay, the captives were deemed legally indebted to the state, which then leased them to private businesses, where they were subjected to a brutal form of labor extraction as the means of repayment. Through this system the state achieved multiple goals: it increased revenue without raising taxes, avoided expenditures on carceral infrastructure, and satisfied the demand for the cheap labor that was crucial to industrial development. The system was legitimated through law: the imposition of incarceration through debt was deemed to stand outside the proscriptions of the Thirteenth Amendment. That provision abolished both "slavery" as well as "involuntary servitude," but its remaining text, "except as a punishment for crime whereof the party shall have been duly convicted," has been interpreted—arguably misinterpreted—to authorize convict leasing.[14]

Black labor extracted through the carceral regime became a significant feature of the post–Civil War southern economy and was crucial to fueling industrial production and the accumulation of capital. However, profitability was eventually constrained by the lack of transportation infrastructure, which restricted access to distribution networks and markets. Over time, despite ruthless practices to reduce labor costs—wretched housing, insufficient and rancid food, no medical care—leasing prices rose. Rising costs converged with critiques of the brutality of the system and, crucially, its negative impact on the bargaining power of free (white) labor. As the political burdens of the lease system increased, the preferred solution was to remove convicts from the private labor market and return control of coerced labor back to the state. Persons convicted through the same rigged processes were assembled—entrapped, in fact—in chain gangs and were deployed to build roads, bridges, and other state infrastructure.[15] Notably, this reform did not contest and, in fact, legitimated the continued appropriation of Black labor through the carceral system. The demise of convict leasing by the early twentieth century, and of the chain gangs by the 1950s, reflects shifts rather than the elimination of forms of labor control and capital accumulation extracted under carceral threat.[16]

Relations among labor, capital, and race changed as the US carceral regime evolved through different phases. From the early twentieth century to the early 1970s, the percentage of the population subjected to incarceration remained relatively stable, even as imprisonment captured disproportionate numbers of Black people as well as the poor of all races.[17] However, economic, political, and legal changes soon caused explosive growth in prison construction and the rate of incarceration. Invoking Ruth Wilson Gilmore's classic *Golden Gulag*, Rowland identifies mass incarceration as the product of a diachronic interaction between racial ideologies and, citing Gilmore, a crisis of "nonproductive surpluses of 'finance capital, land, labor, and state capacity.'" This led states (California being among the first) to adopt the "prison fix," in which financiers developed "public markets for private capital" tied to carceral projects.[18] As Rowland writes, the result "is an increasing set of capitalizations" that has enmeshed "people in prison . . . [in] a nexus of government economic interests."[19] This includes monopolizing prisoners' consumption of goods and services through private suppliers as well as imposing "pay to stay" fees, in which the state charges people in prison for the costs of their incarceration, creating a debt they carry upon release.

The labor value of prisoners who work is captured for state use in infrastructure improvement and maintenance or is put to use in prison operations.[20] Rowland notes that often the labor of incarcerated people "does not result in publicly traded profit, but rather in savings."[21] Whether a given system produces actual savings is unclear, given decentralized accounting and processes, and shifting definitions of costs, benefits, assets, and liabilities across local, state, and federal carceral institutions.[22] However, as Rowland explains, even without profits in the usual sense, savings is a "form of austerity that may be more efficacious than profit [as] these savings, as absences of costs and information[,] operate as financial and rhetorical instruments of government opacity."[23] In this context Leveler Rings is the product of a form of carceral extraction of value in which racialized labor is managed through state-constructed markets of goods, products, and services that occlude costs and deficits within the broader political economy of mass incarceration.

Whereas race is a construct that inscribes bodies within hierarchies, Leveler Rings also illuminates how race as structure and relation is embedded in things, in objects, even those that appear racially anonymous. The rings, once seen through the text with which they are branded, conjure carceral circuits that trace and retrace one of many afterlives of slavery, evoking a temporal slippage between the time of convict leasing and the chain gang and the present. Simultaneously, the rings mark the transition from these older forms of carceral labor to neoliberal systems in which labor is flexibly deployed and recategorized, at times outside the framework of "work," according to the objectives of capital and changing political and economic contexts. Leveler Rings illustrates the epochal shifts in the nexus of racial regimes, carceral state power, and capitalist accumulation, as well as enduring patterns and logics of racial coercion in which Black bodies and collectivities are perpetually subject to plunder—what critical scholar Clyde Woods termed "asset stripping."[24] Leveler Rings represents an example of how a relation between race and coercion is both repeated and transformed. It is, as law professor Noah Zatz frames, "a site that extends into the present the insights of historiography of slavery and neoslavery[, one] integral to US racial capitalism."[25]

Debt as Essential Structure and Relation

In probing the terrain that *Leveler Rings* illuminates, a persistent feature of these extractive practices, past and present, is debt. Although the concept of debt is as ancient as the concept of money,[26] my reference to debt here does not hark back to classical political economy in the sense of debt as a system of communal exchange. I am concerned more with debt as it currently exists in today's political economy. In this context, debt can be described as "a promise of future reimbursement" that contemplates risk, including both "temporal indeterminacy and unpredictability."[27] The creation of debt involves the issuance of credit—a dialectical relation—in which debt, like credit, is "a mechanism of intertemporal and intrapersonal redistribution."[28] Understanding capitalism to always already encompass racism, I want to consider how debt, as a structure and relation, is implicated in the racial landscape both historically and in the contemporary moment.

One can "read" the racial genealogies unearthed in *Leveler Rings* through debt. Following the Civil War, debt became the principal mechanism through which a system of labor extraction was constructed to replace chattel slavery. The deployment of coerced Black labor was critical to the development of modern economic industries and activities into the twentieth century. Although the value of the Black body as chattel was formally extinguished by abolition, the racial alchemy of debt transformed freed people into assets yet again, "propertizing" and assigning value to Black bodies by virtue of their indebtedness.[29] As Saidiya Hartman has noted so perceptively, emancipation was fabulated as a gift that had been granted, and for which the freedmen were indebted, ensuring their continued availability for extraction through the rights of the liberal subject.[30]

Presently, the labor that produced *Leveler Rings* and that is deployed for state use functions in the shadow of debt. Although earlier estimates suggest that prison industries produce more than $2 billion of annual revenue, prisoners' labor is generally no longer directly leased out to private entities to generate profit for the state.[31] Yet the machinery of incarceration is bound up with race and debt in several crucial ways. First, debt is deeply embedded in policing practices and legal regimes that operate to criminalize Black communities and legitimate racialized surveillance, coercion, violence, and extraction. These abuses were most vividly illustrated in the extrajudicial killing of Michael Brown by police officer Darren Wilson in Ferguson, Missouri. A popular uprising emerged nationally and globally under the banner of Black Lives Matter that condemned routine policing practices as consistently productive of police violence against Black bodies. The BLM-inspired resistance mobilized a critique of policing in Ferguson that exposed the connective tissue between the criminal sanction system, police coercion, and asset stripping. A now-much-cited Department of Justice report as well as litigation brought on behalf of Ferguson's residents documented the experience of Black residents who were aggressively surveilled, repeatedly cited for minor municipal ordinance violations such as "manner of walking in street" and "failure to obey," and fined and assessed a host of fees and penalties used to fund the city's operations.[32] As these onerous "criminal legal obligations" became unpayable, many residents were arrested and incarcerated in city or county jails, where they were required to "sit out their time" in order to discharge their debt.[33] Once incarcerated, they were charged the costs of incarceration and became, literally, captive consumers of essential goods and services sold at highly inflated prices. This extractive infrastructure operated through manufacturing debt and criminalizing nonpayment.

Secondly, debt was central to the expansion of the carceral regime and the explosive increase in the incarceration of Black bodies. Here the institutions of finance capital, public debt, and the bond market incentivized the growth of the carceral state. Again, however, as Gilmore demonstrated, the exponential increase in the prison population was not the consequence of increase in crime. Rather, changes in the political economy drove decisions to funnel surplus capital and people deemed to be surplus labor into carceral institutions, as distinct from other investments in public goods such as education and health.[34]

In this sense, *Leveler Rings* is a provocation to go beyond visual analogies to structural excavations. The rings are material manifestations of recurring patterns of racialized coercion in the extraction of labor and value. These mimetic practices are not uniformly or consistently authorized in law; at times, they tread near or transgress the margins of formal legality. But even when forms of labor coercion are subject to normative and legal condemnation, they do not disappear; they are (re)established through the imposition of debt. Debt peonage, defined as the "voluntary or involuntary service or labor of any persons . . . in liquidation of any debt or obligation," was declared unlawful in 1867.[35] Convict leasing was denounced broadly and declared illegal in many states by 1928.[36] Prison labor is condemned and legally proscribed.[37] Debtors' prisons were declared unlawful as early as the first part of the nineteenth century.[38] Federal constitutional law prohibits incarceration of those lacking resources for failure to pay criminal legal debt,[39] as do many state statutes. Yet incarceration for unpaid fines, fees, and penalties—criminal legal debt—is rampant, as documented in compelling critiques of the "new debtors' prisons."[40] Beyond the criminal context, forms of civil debt creation and debt collection deemed unconscionable and especially burdensome persist, at times despite legal prohibition.[41]

The recurrence of patterns of dispossession and accumulation and the prominent role of debt are prefigured by critiques of neoliberalism that have focused attention on the crucial role of debt in structuring social relations and the political economy more broadly.[42] Critical scholars and activists have documented the oppressive nature of debt for the poor and working class and the link between debt and capitalist accumulation.[43] Many of these accounts have highlighted the use of debt as an asset. Indeed, debt constitutes a highly flexible form of capital that enables the transformation of things—both tangible and intangible—into legally cognizable property and transforms one form of property into another. Through this alchemical process, debt—individual, organizational (corporate), and state—becomes a commodity at the heart of economic activity and is a major preoccupation of state managerial and (de)regulatory policies and practices.

What has been less explored is how, under racial capitalism, the ubiquitous extraction, dispossession, and accumulation through debt are connected to racial and racializing projects. Debt is formally race-neutral, as reflected in neutral financial instruments and rules, but simultaneously debt is also racially constitutive and saturated. Debt functions in racially distinct ways and (re)produces profoundly racially unequal results. It legitimates coercive practices and relations by rendering a racialized system nominally consistent with norms of color blindness. At the same time, debt authorizes forms of extraction that are constructed and concentrated through racial difference but are not limited to specific populations. In this sense as well, debt functions as a form of racial alchemy: it obscures highly racialized processes and racially differentiated burdens, and it normalizes and makes available for generalized application ever-more-rapacious and predatory forms of extraction. Under a racial capitalist order, debt commodifies racial subordination and abstracts systemic racial violence. Through the debtor-creditor relation, racial extraction and dispossession have been tethered to accumulation. Even as accumulation is limited to the capitalist class, the conflation of whiteness and property operates to both entrench and obscure that fact.

Just as property and wealth have been racially differentiated, forms of incurring, valuing, collecting, and leveraging debt have been racially demarcated. Black debtors face limited, if any, access to first-tier financial institutions and products; instead, the debt they accrue is subject to more onerous terms, both in law and in practice.[44] Black debtors are largely foreclosed from using debt as an asset.[45] The racial stratification of debt has been constructed and maintained through the conjoined technologies of racial segregation and Black exclusion from productive credit, and the incorporation or predatory inclusion of Black subjects into extractive credit markets. Drawing from the work of radical scholars, particularly that of Keeanga-Yamahtta Taylor, I understand predatory inclusion to describe an illusory project of racial liberalism that promotes inclusion into the market and existing capitalist structures and institutions as the remedy for Black subordination.[46] The presumption that inclusion of Blacks into mainstream credit markets from which they were previously excluded would ameliorate racial inequity ignores the way that racial hierarchy is intimately entwined in the extraction of value.[47]

Extending this insight, the right to extract payments through extreme forms of coercion is an expectation legitimated by the degraded nature of Black subjectivity. In this sense, Black debtors warrant punishment. At the same time, one could say that Black debt *is* punishment. In other words, not only is debt racially ordered in terms of the consequences and effects of differential burdens and processes: debt further structures and reifies racialized social relations.[48] The racial segregation of debt, which was initially de jure and has now become de facto, has simultaneously devalued Blacks as legitimate subjects to access credit and increased their vulnerability to speculative and asset-stripping debt-creation and debt-collection practices. Yet even the exclusion of Blacks from mainstream credit markets was cast within the narrow legal parameters of "discrimination" that presumed the neutrality of the market but for intentionally biased conduct. This limiting frame rendered most discrimination beyond legal sanction and allowed for experimentation with proxies and technologies that maintained racialized distinctions without explicit reference to race. The realignment materialized in defining risk through opaque processes and discourses of finance that rest on thinly concealed racialized logics. Blacks are constructed as not "creditworthy" and are consigned to subprime credit markets as "risky" borrowers, subject to higher costs and fees.[49] A prominent example is identified by Denise Ferreira da Silva and Paula Chakravartty, who point out that in the context of the 2008 financial crisis, "subprime" became "a racial signifier" as perceived "racial/cultural difference . . . enter[ed] into risk calculations."[50] Thus, the implosion of the mortgage market was ascribed to the borrowers' deficiencies, not the risky and predatory behavior of the finance sector, which generated and financialized the debt for profit. The interpolation of race into risk assessment supports the creation of Black debt on onerous and extractive terms and masks this asset stripping as consensual, contractually governed, rational market exchange. Because Black people have been devalued as economic subjects, deemed forever unstable, subprime, and "high risk," this degraded status (re)authorizes forms of debt formation and collection through coercion and violence, including but not limited to incarceration, that persist in the shadow of law and periodic illegality.

The racialized framework embedded in financial ratings and determinations of creditworthiness has profound implications in a neoliberal social order where debt—individual, corporate, and state debt—is a key commodity at the heart of much economic activity, negotiation, and exchange. Where higher risk is associated with higher returns, Black debt can become a valued commodity.[51] Moreover, if, as has been argued, debt is infinite, this is particularly true for Black debt, which can never be repaid and is rarely if ever forgiven.[52] Thus, although debt is cast as a neutral form of economic exchange, under racial capitalism debt is a racialized structure of extraction and accumulation central to the production and maintenance of (white) property. The liberal concept of property embedded in US law originates in and reifies Indigenous and Black dispossession and labor extraction. Debt bears a similar neutral facade that obscures its racialized histories and its exploitative function. This does not mean that these extractive processes are fixed or that they operate against only one population. Indeed, the processes by which debts are authorized, implemented, and regulated are often highly contingent, contested, and generalizable.[53]

I consider the role of debt as a racialized economic structure and social relation in the context of two examples of extracting value: the first, in the past, involving the (racially) indebted body of the enslaved and formerly enslaved, and the second, in the present, concerning the (racially) indebted community. They illustrate in different ways how debt structures relations among people, capital, and state power; abstracts systemic racial violence; and normalizes racialized extraction and accumulation. I want to complicate and deepen the racial aspect of this account by focusing on the nexus and continuity between forms of labor extraction from Indigenous communities through debt peonage and the post–Civil War labor coercion of freed people through convict leasing. The experiences and histories of Black and Indigenous peoples differ in important ways, but the coercion of Indian labor by colonial and neocolonial regimes through debt normalized these practices and enabled their extension to other populations. Imposing debt peonage on Indigenous peoples was a means of evading a ban on enslavement while authorizing continued racialized dispossession and accumulation through ostensibly raceless forms. The illusion of racelessness not only masks the racial character of capitalism; it also delimits apprehending the complexity of that racial character.[54]

Debt operates on and through collectivities as well as individuals. Thus, Black geographies and spaces as well as Black bodies are similarly subject to being placed under the heel of debt.[55] Black geographies are deemed to be insolvent "waste" lands, "no-go" areas, drowning in debt and in inevitable decay resulting from the deficiencies of their occupants. By virtue of this characterization, Black geographies are transformed into locations to be rescued both through austerity programs and development or "improvement" initiatives that reproduce Black dispossession and capital accumulation through the creation and management of debt.[56] Here I consider the water crisis in Flint, Michigan, as an example of this pattern. The poisoning of Flint is tethered to an economy of race that materialized through the promotion of particular forms of capital-public obligation bonds that the city was compelled to issue to obtain water service. In fact, the city lost safe water service as it accrued more debt—a debt that became literally toxic at the level of everyday life. Unpacking the relationship between debt and water in Flint discloses the way that debt as racialized structure and relation shapes and intensifies the financialization of crucial aspects of Black life and Black geographies. Both then and now, debt's racial alchemy operates to not only legitimate myriad forms of extreme extraction that rest upon and construct Black subordination but to also further concentrate wealth and control in a racialized elite class.

Enslavement and Debt: Black and Red

> No person held to service or labour in one state, under the laws thereof, escaping into another, shall, in consequence of any law or regulation therein, be discharged from such service or labor, but shall be delivered up on claim of the party to whom such service or labour may be due.
>
> FUGITIVE SLAVE CLAUSE, US CONSTITUTION, 1850

> That when a person held to service or labor in any State or Territory of the
> United States, has heretofore or shall hereafter escape into another State or
> Territory of the United States, the person or persons to whom such service
> or labor may be due, or his, her, or their agent or attorney . . . may pursue and
> reclaim such fugitive person . . . either by procuring a warrant . . . or by seiz-
> ing and arresting such fugitive.
>
> FUGITIVE SLAVE ACT OF 1850, CH. 60, 9 STAT. 462

Debt was implicated in chattel slavery and the carceral systems of labor
that replaced enslavement after abolition. Abolition was itself complicated
by the fact that enslavement was so deeply entrenched. Throughout the
colonial period, enslavement was the primordial form of racialized labor
extraction. Chattel slavery was particularly central in the political economy of the North American colonies that ultimately formed the United
States. With the substitution of enslaved African labor for Indigenous
and white indentured labor, chattel slavery also emerged as a system of
property. The racial alchemy of debt "propertized" and securitized Black
bodies as a source of great value. Black bodies were cast as living currency
around which were built valuation systems, insurance, financial products
and institutions, and forms of financialization central to the development
of capitalism.

Indeed, chattel slavery as a system of economic production was central
to the growth of a financial system founded in debt. As historian Calvin
Schermerhorn argues, the slave trade was built on debt as "chains of debt
moved around the Atlantic basin in countermotion to the trajectories of
captives, goods, and commodities." Debt obligations allowed future promises to substitute for immediate payment in circumstances where time and
distance made such payment impossible. Moreover, the expansion of debt
was key: the transatlantic system stretched over continents and encom-
passed a wide range of actors not limited to the immediate purveyors of
captured Africans or to the enterprises that depended upon their stolen
labor. Schermerhorn points out that captives were treated as "debt payments"
by "those who bought, shipped, and sold the survivors to Americans
[, including] shipmasters, merchants, investors, bankers, planters, and
owners of collateral industries."[57]

Debt was not only the mechanism that enabled exchange and commerce; debt was also a means of leveraging value, effectively broadening
the reach of the profits from enslavement through debt markets. Mortgages backed by enslaved persons became paper bonds sold to investors,

thereby generating the capital necessary to fuel the growth of the system of enslavement and the larger economy. Asset securitization expanded profit beyond the interest charged on the debt by abstracting the enslaved Black body encumbered by debt into capital appropriated through racially defined and exclusionary markets. The financialization of the enslaved Black body reflected its value as a commodity that secured dizzying profits that enriched the holdings of financiers and merchants on both sides of the Atlantic.

In a sense, the "slave" was born in debt and embodied debt. As reflected in the Fugitive Slave Clause and the Fugitive Slave Act of 1850, the fugitive was subject to be seized as one who owed a debt to the owner. The fugitive was runaway capital, stolen by herself. Fugitivity was configured as a form of theft in which the enslaved—a "person held to service or labor"[58]—remained indebted to her owner. The concept of compensated emancipation similarly made Black freedom contingent on paying the owner the value of his investment. Indebtedness then was cast as a characteristic of Blackness; the Black body was always already in debt.

Chattel slavery sutured Blackness to debt and capital accumulation in these specific ways, but these systems were also intimately related to Indigenous dispossession.[59] As stolen land is at the heart of the colonial project, critiques of colonialism have rightly focused on Native land dispossession as both a historical and ongoing structure. Yet the system of enslavement of Native peoples by Europeans was another crucial component of the evolution of chattel slavery of Africans and successive regimes of labor coercion. The forms of labor imposed following formal abolition in each case were structured through debt. Indeed, although the system of Indigenous enslavement ended, the coercion and extraction of the labor of Indigenous people continued and relied on debt.

To begin, it is important to recognize the scale of Indian slavery: even though it often operated outside formal legality, that did not diminish its reach or significance. As historian Andrés Reséndez points out, from the inception of European colonization of the Americas in 1492 to the end of the nineteenth century, estimates are that between 2.5 million and 5 million Indigenous people were taken as slaves. This system differed in some ways from the African slave trade, for the majority of Indian slaves were women and children: the latter were ostensibly favored because of their purported ability to adapt, to fit in, to become westernized, whereas a premium was paid for women for their reproductive and domestic labor.[60] Unlike chattel slavery, under Indian slavery, slave status was not formally heritable in all instances, nor were Indigenous enslaved people routinely sold through centralized markets,[61] albeit in some regions there were some intergenerational transfers of slave status and sales between parties.[62]

The enslavement of Indigenous peoples enabled the dispossession of Indigenous land—a process essential to the creation of cash-crop economies later serviced by enslaved African labor. Indian enslavement inflicted massive destruction and precipitated rapid population decline.[63] In addition to overt acts of removal and violence against Indigenous peoples, administrative actions enacted other lethal policies by separating Indigenous peoples from traditional diet and health practices, herding them into toxic conditions, and exposing them to pandemics from European diseases. The resulting depopulation enabled the project of eliminating Indigenous control of native land.

Even though Spain began to limit slavery in the 1500s and prohibited slavery by 1542, this action did not operate to end the practice. Indian slavery endured through other euphemistic forms of servitude—"encomiendas, repartimientos"—and, most relevant here, debt peonage.[64] Apart from the long-standing debate over whether these forms of labor coercion were actual enslavement, crucially, "like a deadly virus, Indian slavery mutated into these strains and became extraordinarily resilient through the centuries."[65] This persistence was particularly evident in the lands that ultimately became part of the western territories controlled by the United States.

After Abolition

A pall of debt hangs over the beautiful land. The merchants are in debt to the wholesalers, the planters are in debt to the merchants, the tenants owe the planters, and the laborers bow and bend beneath the burden of it all.
W. E. B. DU BOIS, *THE SOULS OF BLACK FOLK*, 1903

We do not consider that we own our laborers; we consider they are in debt to us. And we do not consider that we buy and sell them; we consider that we transfer the debt, and the man goes with the debt.
PRESIDENT OF THE AGRICULTURAL CHAMBER OF YUCATAN TO JOHN KENNETH TURNER, 1908

The abolition of slavery in the United States by Emancipation and ultimately the Thirteenth Amendment transformed but did not end racialized dispossession and coerced labor. In slavery's afterlife, systems of extraction were reshaped and reconstituted. A prominent feature of the new regime was the creation and management of Black debt. The convict-lease system, as described previously, was structured around state-created debt arising from criminal legal obligations fraudulently imposed. Black debt was generated through the criminal sanction system and, in the civil arena, through the discourse of contracts. A central feature of the period was the porous line between contractual and criminal debt and the role of debt in manufacturing the illusion of consent. The legal regime of contract, extended to Black people in the transition from chattel to constitutional citizen, became the means by which Blacks were deemed to have consented to their punishment for nonpayment of debt. This, in effect, resembled debt peonage—authorizing a party to compel, under threat of criminal punishment, a person's labor to discharge a debt. In a sense, convict leasing was a state-operated form of peonage.

The convict-leasing system was not a novel form of labor coercion: in the United States, it was first deployed in New York in 1825 and spread through the North and Midwest, where the prisoners were primarily white men; the punishment of enslaved Africans was largely the prerogative of slaveholders.[66] But the expansion of convict leasing in the southern region even after the adoption of the Thirteenth Amendment drew on debt peonage, a form of labor extraction prevalent in the West. Debt peonage had a long lineage: it was imposed on Indigenous peoples in western lands colonized by the Spanish, later governed by Mexico, and subsequently incorporated into the United States at the end of the US-Mexican War in 1848. The persistence of debt peonage after Indian enslavement was formally ended and its emergence and retrofitting in the South reflect the tenacity, flexibility, and adaptability of racial regimes of labor extraction and capital accumulation.

The War for Mexican Independence succeeded in overthrowing Spanish colonial rule in 1822, yet this change in governance did not significantly change the pattern of labor coercion of Indigenous peoples in the region. This was so notwithstanding the fact that the Mexican government extended citizenship to all Indians and formally abolished slavery in 1829. In part this was a result of the persistent influence of a cultural regime that consigned unbaptized Indigenous peoples to the category "gente sin razon" (people without reason) in contrast to "gente de razon" (people with reason): Catholics, Spaniards, criollas (mixed-race people with Spanish ancestry), and others deemed acculturated to Europe.[67] Thus, the demand for labor was articulated through a racialized hierarchy that cast gente sin razon as workers requiring discipline. Formal enslavement was replaced by increased reliance on debt peonage: "In the absence of slavery, the only way for Mexicans to bind workers to their properties and businesses was by extending credit to them." Impoverished and landless peoples were offered loans on predatory terms that virtually guaranteed they could not be repaid. The debtor and his family were thus pressed into indefinite servitude, often further extended by the practice of treating the debts of the father as heritable. Although there were variations across regions in the particular provisions, debt peonage expanded and became entrenched across Mexico.[68]

Equally as significant was the use of the criminal sanction system. The new Mexican government's conferral of universal male citizenship to the multiracial peoples of the region shifted the crucial distinction from citizen/noncitizen to citizen/criminal. As historian Robert Buffington notes, "Criminal *acts* rather than . . . 'natural conditions' . . . provided elite policy makers the flexibility needed to *legally* delimit the all-too-inclusive (if still male) category of citizen."[69] By the 1830s, laws in jurisdictions such as Los Angeles required all Native peoples residing in the area to work or be arrested and fined, and, if unable to pay, to perform forced labor. Over time, the law dispensed with the payment of fines and sentenced Indigenous peoples who were unemployed to work.[70]

Political conflict between the Mexican government and the United States combined with the rise of manifest destiny as the new frame through which colonization and expansion were justified as bestowing a benefit on populations in need of improvement. Although there was opposition to the project of acquiring Mexican lands because that acquisition would also entail the incorporation of the Mexican (nonwhite) populations living there,[71] the Mexican-American War commenced in 1846. It ended in 1848 with the Treaty of Guadalupe Hidalgo, pursuant to which the United States took one-third of Mexico's territory, including Texas, California, and New Mexico, where debt peonage was prominent.

The treaty enabled further legal dispossession of Indigenous lands, effectively eviscerated Mexican land grants, and placed the massive cession lands under control of the US Congress and the designated territorial governments. Each territory confronted fraught questions regarding the pathway to statehood: What would be the status of chattel slavery? And what would be the status of the far more prevalent system of debt peonage? Indeed, there were many debates over whether debt peonage in the West was equivalent to chattel slavery or was distinct, and these questions overlapped with increasing sectional conflict between the North and South, particularly over the question of the expansion of chattel slavery into the territories.[72] Congress adopted the Compromise of 1850, permitting California to enter as a free state, while tightening the Fugitive Slave Act and establishing territorial governments in Utah and New Mexico.

For the elites as well as settlers and would-be elites, it was important that California be both free and securely under white control: the proposed state constitution restricted the franchise to white males, defined *white* to include "white male citizens of Mexico," and banned chattel (Black) slavery. However, rejecting the institution of slavery did not reflect egalitarian sentiment, for the legislature also debated a provision to exclude all Blacks from the state. The opposition to slavery derived from its asserted degrading effect on white workers, but the contempt for slavery extended to contempt for enslaved people as well. Ultimately, the formal ban was abandoned, principally out of fear that it would compromise the state's efforts to enter the union.[73]

At the same time, the subjection of Indians was presumed. In 1850, the year of statehood, the state legislature adopted "An Act for the Government and Protection of Indians"—an Orwellian title for a measure that sought to ensure Indigenous domination. Although the act provided that Indians would be allowed to live in their traditional "homes and villages," they could be removed to another place "at the request of a white person or proprietor."[74] Most significantly, as historian Shirley Ann Moore describes, "Foreshadowing the restrictive work contracts, vagrancy laws, and black codes that would subjugate the freedmen and freedwomen in the post–Civil War South a decade and a half later, the new California law controlled Indian labor, permitting the indenture of Indian children and mandating that all Indians work. On the word of any white person, any Indian deemed to be 'loitering or strolling about' could be arrested and sold to the highest bidder to labor for a period of four months."[75] This law specifically targeted "Indians," but by 1855 it was modified and amended to extend to all "beggars . . . [or] persons who roam about from place to place."[76] This shift proved an influential template for southern states after the Civil War.

Initial efforts to return formerly enslaved people to legal bondage were robust in the form of the Black Codes adopted all across the South by white-controlled state legislatures.[77] One of the first, Mississippi's "Act to Confer Civil Rights on Freedmen," authorized the arrest of any freedman who left his employer by any white person, who, upon returning the freedman to his employer, would then be entitled to receive a fee.[78] The Vagrancy Act required that "all freedmen, free negroes and mulattoes in this State, over the age of eighteen" have written proof of employment at the beginning of the year or face conviction and fines.[79] Congress, under the control of the Republican majority, was angered by these efforts to overturn the result of the war and reinstall slavery, and in response it pushed for the adoption of the Civil Rights Act of 1866 and ultimately the Fourteenth Amendment, which barred states from denying equal protection of the laws. In the wake of these constraints, southern legislatures shifted toward formally race-neutral measures that proved equally effective. Instead of imposing a requirement on "freedmen" or "mulattos," *vagrant* was defined as "any person wandering or strolling about in idleness, who is able to work, and has no property to support him; or any person leading an idle, immoral, profligate life."[80] In so doing, the law conferred virtually unlimited discretion to sanction a person's condition—unemployed, unhoused, unfed—rather than their conduct. Once a person was arrested, conviction followed, as did fines, then transfer, then work, and then—too often—death.

The convict-leasing system was implemented through formally color-blind laws and a ruthlessly targeted system of racialized administration. Replacing the formal racial hierarchy of the Black Codes with the flexibility of vagrancy and other public-order laws allowed for the evolution of a system of labor extraction that thrived for a crucial period in the new political economy of the South. In related time, debt peonage in the West was coming under increasing pressure, and after legal proscription in 1867, it slowly began to decrease in the region. However, important elements of the system, particularly its reliance on debt to control labor, influenced the southern regime. Thus, "the same forms of coercive labor that Congress banned in New Mexico subsequently existed throughout the South into the early twentieth century."[81]

The spectacular violence of the convict-leasing system and free labor's hostility toward it for undermining the power of labor generated pressure for reform and legal restrictions beginning in the late nineteenth century. However, the conflict was resolved by restricting prison labor to state use, replacing convict leasing with the chain gang. Under both regimes, Blackness legitimated predatory extraction through the imposition of debt constructed in color-blind legal forms. In many respects the formal erasure of race has enabled the maintenance and recurrence of predatory forms of debt and coercive collection practices despite the formal demise of debt peonage, the condemnation of debtors' prisons, and restrictions on prison labor.

Debt and Water

Not only do racialized debt regimes extract through individual assignment of obligations and enforcement through criminal sanctions; they also operate through the market of financial products and the structures of state finance under the neoliberal framework. Neoliberalism is heavily reliant on debt as a way of structuring social, political, and economic relations. Neoliberal economies also operate through a process of recycling in which that which is devalued—the throwaway—is monetized. Race is central to this process: the market encodes places and property with present and future valuations while erasing or obscuring the historical patterns of racialized dispossession at its core. Black spaces and geographies are cast as "no man's lands" that are not only forbidding but also trapped in a process of decay from which they must be rescued. The predicate for intervention is often a crisis of debt.

Black geographies are policed through the mechanism of permanent emergency built around debt crises. They are locations that require extra scrutiny—financial racial profiling—ostensibly because they have incurred too much debt and lack the capacity or will to pay. Yet these same Black spaces are prime sites of extraction through debt. Flint exemplifies these phenomena and illustrates how racialized logics function through the structure of debt.

The broad contours of the Flint water crisis are fairly well-known and offer an account of official neglect, mismanagement, and malfeasance of a predominantly Black and poor city. Although this narrative is not wrong, it is incomplete: Flint's water crisis was the outgrowth of a broader set of conflicts and multiple structural crises that involved the manipulation of public finance bonding authority tied to the provision of a public good—access to clean water—and the incentives of the financial market. The net result of the project was the exact opposite of the stated purpose: to obtain clean water at a lower price. Instead, the city and its residents were burdened with more debt and lost access to clean, safe water. The contours of the extraction were shaped through a discourse of improvement and development and were implemented through manipulating the city's debt. The poisoning of Flint is tethered to an economy of race that extracted capital through the city's precarity.

The prevailing narrative regarding Flint begins with its deficits: a majority-Black city (60 percent), a high poverty rate (40 percent), a decaying, debt-burdened wasteland in need of proper fiscal management. Proper management came in the form of an emergency manager appointed by the governor under a law ostensibly intended to relieve fiscally distressed cities and to put their fiscal house in order.[82] On this account, Flint's financial problems resulted from lack of fiscal discipline and the reluctance to implement necessary but politically unpopular decisions. Put another way, as Peter Hammer, a lawyer who has worked closely on the crisis, states, the view was that "municipal distress is the outcome of public mismanagement by groups of people who are incapable of governing themselves."[83]

Still, the emergency manager system was born in controversy. Prior Michigan law authorized the appointment of emergency financial managers to address fiscal problems in local government, but in 2011 Governor Rick Snyder, dissatisfied with the limited authority the law conferred, advocated for the enactment of a new provision that granted sweeping powers to the emergency manager to supplant the authority of elected officials.[84] Public Law 4 was adopted and signed into law. However, the lack of any measure of accountability fueled sustained and broad opposition, leading to a referendum that repealed it. In response, the Republican-led state legislature overrode the electorate and in 2012 enacted a law embodying the same provisions.[85]

Flint became one of several cities or municipal agencies—the majority of them predominantly Black or Latinx—to be deemed a financial disaster in need of rescue.[86] Governor Snyder invoked the act and installed an emergency manager, who superseded the authority of the elected city council. The emergency manager was empowered to negotiate and make all decisions regarding the city's operation—cancel contracts, including collective bargaining agreements, sell public assets, hire and fire city employees—but there was one crucial exception: the manager was foreclosed from challenging any bond contracts and was required to pay the city's debt in full.[87]

In the search for cost savings, the emergency manager turned to the city's water-provision arrangements. Flint had a long-standing contract—since 1967—with the Detroit Water Sewer District (DWSD) to supply Flint's water wholesale. Although there had not been complaints about the water quality, some of the small cities and predominantly white areas of Genesee County complained that they were overpaying Detroit and should seek an alternative water source. A persistent dynamic of white distancing was fueled by conjoining a narrative of cost savings with the depiction of DWSD as dysfunctional and irredeemably fiscally irresponsible. Beginning in the early 2000s, Genesee County began exploring the development of an alternative plan to build a pipeline to Lake Huron. Despite the significant cost—some $600 million—county officials argued that a new system would be more cost-effective. The Karegnondi Regional Water Planning Group was formed in 2007 to begin preliminary studies and was formally incorporated in 2010. The city of Flint was identified as a participant in the project, notwithstanding its prominent status as a too-poor, too-Black space.

As the end of Flint's contract with DWSD approached, there were three options for the water supply: (1) the city could continue to use DWSD water; (2) it could reduce consumption of DWSD water and combine it with Flint River water, treated in Flint's own water treatment plant; or (3) Flint could switch its water source entirely to the Karegnondi Water Authority (KWA) once it was built and, in the interim, could use treated Flint River water. The latter two options required a major upgrade to the Flint water treatment plant at a cost of $25–$60 million.

For a small city already in debt and under emergency management, the prospect of locating that kind of capital was beyond daunting. Nevertheless, the emergency manager selected the KWA option, rejecting the findings of one report that recommended a different choice. He also removed the other, less expensive options from consideration and even rejected an offer from DWSD that potentially provided a 20 percent savings over thirty years when compared to the KWA proposal. By 2013, Flint was still part of the KWA project and was committed to fund 30 percent of the $285 million cost—approximately $85 million. Of course, the core problem was that Flint could not meet this obligation, nor could it have ever done so. The matter became more urgent as KWA prepared to issue bonds in order to fund construction.

The answer came in the form of state intervention to enable the deal. The Michigan Department of Environmental Quality (DEQ) used a procedure for environmental enforcement actions, an "administrative consent order" (ACO), that allows a local government to issue bonds beyond the government's bond limit to repair or mitigate an environmental violation. Correspondence within the DEQ reflects that in this instance staffers searched for a violation that would allow an ACO to be issued, while KWA's bond attorney anxiously warned that construction on the project would have to cease if the ACO were not immediately forthcoming. The violation that was the predicate for the ACO was remediating a small lime-sludge pool. Accordingly, the loan was ultimately issued; it included a stipulation that Flint use Flint River water while waiting for the pipeline to be completed. However, not only was the bulk of the money to be spent on the

KWA pipeline; there was no consideration of financing to repair the city's water treatment plant.

The lack of any plan to provide clean water to the residents of Flint was not legible: the primary focus remained on the financing. On this view, the more salient problem was that, given Flint's fiscal condition, the city would default on repayment. To ensure that the bonds received a high rating and consequently an attractive interest rate, Genesee County promised to backstop Flint's portion of the debt. In exchange, however, should Flint not pay, the county could take a quarter of Flint's state revenue-sharing money and compel Flint to levy a tax to reimburse KWA. According to a member of the Genesee County Board of Commissioners, the reality was that Flint could "lose everything" if it left the KWA project.[88] These terms obligated Flint to gamble its limited finances to pay for a water-supply system that was not yet completed, that it could not yet use, and that could not be accessed without new city infrastructure for which it could not pay. Because this deal was struck with the emergency manager, neither the residents of Flint nor the elected officials who were stripped of decision-making authority had any opportunity for meaningful input. However, the bond deal itself was lauded: it won *Bond Buyer* magazine's "Midwest Region Deal of the Year" award in 2014.

By 2014, the contract with DWSD had ended, the KWA pipeline was not complete, and the city's water treatment plant still had not been repaired. Although the rest of the county continued to get its water from DWSD while construction on the pipeline proceeded, the emergency manager in Flint decided that the city would not continue to purchase DWSD water, and he instead authorized water to be drawn directly from the Flint River. What followed was the silent poisoning of the city's water supply as the untreated water leached lead from the pipes. The consequence was permanent damage to the infrastructure, estimated to cost $1.5 billion to repair.[89]

As the community began to experience persistent and significant health complaints, and the condition of the water visibly deteriorated, residents began to raise concerns, initially to no avail. It took two years of organizing and protest by veteran organizers such as Claire McClinton and Nayyirah Shariff of the Flint Democracy Defense League and Melissa Mays of Water You Fighting For? to break through the wall of denial as officials repeatedly asserted that the water was safe. These organizations, largely led by women of color, persisted in getting the water tested, enlisting the assistance of a few scientists and demanding the provision of alternative supplies of water.

Flint- and Detroit-based organizers marshaled community-based research that not only uncovered the problem with the water but further exposed the multiple structural factors that brought it about. Their analysis first pointed toward the crucial institutional change that enabled the creation of the crisis: the appointment of the emergency manager. After the authority of the mayor, the city council, and the administrative officers had been supplanted, the residents were left without access to information or the means to hold decision makers accountable.

Secondly, although the prevailing view was that Flint's financial distress was caused by "natural" forces of deindustrialization, one proximate cause of its dire straits and debt load was the state's unilateral reduction of Flint's statutory share of revenue reimbursement over several years. The state justified its fiscal decisions to deprive the city of critical resources as needed fiscal discipline, but the foreseeable result, not only for Flint but also for Detroit and other cities, was to make them poorer and more indebted.[90] The stage was set for the fiscal "emergency" that ushered in the emergency management system and provided a rationale for a series of otherwise untenable decisions.

Moreover, as Nayyirah Sharrif explained, the water crisis in Flint was connected to the water crisis in the city of Detroit and the city's bankruptcy. In both instances, debt became the instrumentality and the justification for implementing structural changes in governance and ceding control of the cities' assets and infrastructure to corporate capital. We the People of Detroit, through its Community Research Collective, which included Monica Lewis Patrick, exposed that the financial crisis in DWSD was related to its investment strategy and its integration into the financial markets. In purchasing credit-default swaps and embracing other exotic products and transactions, DWSD lost vast amounts of money when the value of these investments collapsed in the 2008 financial crisis. The deficit placed the agency under severe strain, which it sought to solve on the backs of Detroit's residents by increasing rates and implementing a series of water shutoffs for nonpayment in 2014.[91] This draconian decision did not avert the fiscal problems; the agency faced insolvency. As its financial status deteriorated, so too did the city of Detroit face increasing pressure and scrutiny for its asserted financial decline. Ultimately, Detroit was placed under the control of emergency management. The status of DWSD was implicated in Detroit's bankruptcy petition filed by its emergency manager, but the outcome did not reduce or discharge the agency's debt. Instead, Detroit's bankruptcy settlement created a new entity—the Great Lakes Water

Authority—that took control of DWSD's infrastructure for $50 million per year. Once again, the reorganization reinforced a pattern in which race and debt and dispossession are enmeshed within a logic of development and a discourse of rescue. The consequences were clear to the activists:

NAYYIRAH SHARIFF: One of the consequences that happened is, I mean, I call it, it's a scheme. So what they did, the consequence of that was the city of Flint, which was Detroit's largest customer, water customer, went off the system. It destabilized Detroit's revenue, and it was used as justification, the emergency manager in Detroit used it as justification for them to file bankruptcy. And a consequence of the bankruptcy was that it regionalized the water system.

So really it was taking control away from a majority black community and putting it into the hands of the more wealthy white counterparts. And Flint kind of became collateral damage in the scheme of taking this massively huge water system that's worth billions of dollars and transferring that control into another, another system, probably on this road to privatize the system, and to totally take it away from public hands and transfer it into private corporations. . . .

So right now, like, we're part of a regional authority. Detroit no longer has ownership of their municipal water system. So that was, I would say, like, the overall consequence of this whole thing.[92]

The regionalization of the system was not the only objective of the deal: the reorganization was a prelude to an investment opportunity. Although Flint appeared to lack valuable assets, its indebtedness made it a candidate for another kind of asset stripping: the use of its bonding authority to generate instruments for private investment and capital accumulation. By dispensing with even limited forms of accountability, key elites in the financial sector were able to deploy the city's apparatus to further financialize and extract private profits from public goods and infrastructure. The structure of the bond deal for KWA required the participation of Flint, and the fact that the city was insolvent was not allowed to impede that participation. The object then was not to secure water for Flint but to use Flint to structure the bond deal, producing profits for investors through securing a healthy rate of return and fees for various banking and legal services required in connection with the bond issue.

After the protracted struggle to obtain clean water in Flint in the wake of the water crisis, it did not ultimately come from the KWA. In October 2015 Flint switched back to DWSD, now the Great Lakes Water Authority

(GLWA), and signed a thirty-year contract for its water supply. Yet the city was and is still indebted for its 30 percent ownership share of the KWA pipeline. Although Flint's required payment to GLWA is reduced by the amount that the city pays for debt service, it has not been released from the bond debt, notwithstanding criminal investigations of various parties. The targeting of cities like Flint for these forms of racialized extraction is part of larger processes of accumulation through manufacturing and manipulating debt. As Claire McClinton notes, in contrast to the devaluation of the people of Flint, "the bondholders are sacred."

The struggle over access to water in Flint reveals how dispossession and accumulation are linked and produced through a racial logic that targets Black spaces as useful raw material in public finance, debt production, and financial markets. Examined more closely, it also discloses that under racial capitalism, forms of extraction initiated against particular racialized locations or subjects are rarely limited to one population. Both the problem of manufactured debt and fiscal retrenchment have extended beyond the boundaries of the city.[93] The Flint Democracy League, speaking through McClinton, powerfully illustrates this point: "We are a throwaway class whose lives don't matter. The pretext that was used to even get these emergency managers in motion was that these minority cities are incapable of handling their finances. . . . Let's understand that it was a vehicle to ensnare the whole state before they get through with it. So we have to understand how they use the color question to attack all the people."[94]

Her voice is a reminder. The forms of debt creation and management across societal lines are certain; at the same time, racial hierarchy shapes the contour of these systems and concentrates their effects. The mandate to make Black lives matter is the possibility of altering the necropolitics of racial capitalism, which has required violent extraction and racial domination to sustain itself.

NOTES

Chapter 3 epigraphs: Adarand Constructors, Inc. v. Peña, 515 U.S. 200, 239 (1995); Martin Luther King Jr., "I Have a Dream," March on Washington for Jobs and Freedom, August 28, 1963, Washington, DC; Claire McClinton, Flint Democracy Defense League, quoted in Pauli, *Flint Fights Back*.

1. Analytic philosopher and leading conceptual artist Adrien Piper describes conceptual art as follows:

Most explicitly since [Marcel] Duchamp, the most significant works of art . . . have taken seriously the challenge of heightened cognitive discrimination, i.e., the challenge to compel the viewer to see what he did not see before. . . . [To do so, artists] question and extend the limits of knowledge by offering anomalous objects, innovative in form, content, or both, as an antidote to provincial and conventional habits of thought. . . . The point of presenting geometrically, materially, and formally reductive objects was to draw the viewer's attention away from extrinsic associations and toward the specificity and materiality of the particular object itself. . . . It was even more clearly the intrinsic meaning of the work, and not the cognitive preconceptions the viewer brought to it, that dictated its appropriate conceptualization. In subordinating medium to concept, Conceptual Art not only reaffirmed the conceptual fluidity and inclusiveness of art . . . it also opened the door to the use of any medium, event, or object deemed appropriate to the particular concepts the artist chose to explore. Thus Conceptual Art repudiated all remaining traditional restrictions on content and subject matter as well as on medium. Any such object became a potential locus of original conceptual investigation, and all such objects became potential threats to the conceptual unity of a rigidly or provincially structured self. Piper, "Two Kinds of Discrimination," 41–42.

Piper's work grapples with crucial issues of identity, contesting dominant understandings of race and gender, as well as the structures of the art world and the market. See Piper, "Adrien Piper Research Archive Foundation Berlin."

2. Piper, "Two Kinds of Discrimination," 42.

3. Smith, "Cameron Rowland's '91020000.'" The exhibition was first shown in Artists' Space, New York City, in January 2016.

4. Duchamp, "1959 Interview." Rowland's use of fungible objects upends traditional presumptions that the valuation of art is tied to its rare or unique character, its "pricelessness." Rowland's artistic practice reflects the influence of artists such as Piper and, before her, Marcel Duchamp. Duchamp was a highly influential twentieth-century artist who rejected a conception of art that invested objects with aesthetic value and meaning according to their visual appeal. Instead, Duchamp initiated the use of "readymade" objects, ordinary everyday things, designated as art by the artist. As a result, the focus of the artwork was not "retinal," as Duchamp called it, but the process and the concept that undergirded its presentation.

5. Uri McMillan, email message to author, December 15, 2015. McMillan, a cultural historian, suggests that one might think of this work as "experimenting with the ways that an object might address not only its beholder but the financial networks it circulates within."

6. The text then is (part of) the work itself, conveying a specific and unambiguous message. It is a deeply political project that does not rely on individual perception to determine the work's meaning. As Adrien Piper explains, "The union of the

personal with the political often makes such work seem excessively confrontational or didactic. I think this is because art functions for me as not only a medium of exploration, but also a medium of communication between me and the viewer. The idea that art may actually attempt to communicate something to a viewer is historically a commonsense concept. But it has been lost in a contemporary art context that has been cowed into self-censorship." Piper, *Out of Order*, 1:xxxi.

In this way, Rowland's use of the material form is designed to expose and call attention to structural realities. As he puts it, he is concerned with "how these structural (economic, legal and political) conditions manifest and determine reality. If these realities may be understood through their materiality, then sculpture may be an appropriate form towards an analysis and criticism of such realities. I understand materials to include laws and policies as well as physical matter. The dynamics of privatization, subsistence and criminalization, are central." Cameron Rowland, email message to author, February 25, 2015.

7. Rowland, *91020000*, 5.

8. Weprin, *2018 Annual Report*; Nellis, *Color of Justice*. Blacks also experience the highest rate of incarceration and constitute more than 50 percent of the prison population in twelve states.

9. Rowland, *91020000*, 4.

10. Adarand v. Peña, 515 U.S. 200 (1995).

11. Gilmore, "What Is the 'Racial'?" Crucial to Gilmore's intervention is the reminder that "racial" should not be exclusively or reductively coded as white over Black; see Robinson, *Black Marxism*, 2–4, 25–27. As Cedric Robinson insists, not only can the origins of capitalism not be disaggregated from racism, but from capitalism's inception, its racial character rested on constructed differences among peoples within Europe. Thus, racialist myths were not exclusive to Europe's colonial encounter with Africa but were manifest in, for example, England's earlier colonization and settlement of Ireland—a project justified on the grounds that the Irish were an "inferior race."

12. Hartman, *Lose Your Mother*, 6. Slavery's afterlife is not affect, attitude, or metaphor, nor does it rest on equivalences between current and historical practices. As Saidiya Hartman explains, slavery's afterlife indexes the way that "black lives are still imperiled and devalued by a racial calculus and a political arithmetic that were entrenched centuries ago."

13. Lichtenstein, *Twice the Work*. Although white supremacist ideology had cast Black people as inherently criminal, prior to Emancipation prisons in the South were populated by whites because slave owners were the primary source of punishment of enslaved people. Oshinsky, *"Worse Than Slavery,"* 32. After the war, Black freedom was seen as a threat to "good order," so petty crimes such as theft of food or other essential goods, or "disorderly" behaviors, were magnified as existential threats and invoked to justify the mass incarceration of formerly enslaved persons.

The result was that "Southern prisons turned Black." Oshinsky, *"Worse Than Slavery,"* 34.

14. US Const. amend. XIII, § 1 (1865); Pope, "Mass Incarceration." Legal scholar James Gray Pope argues that the current reading of the amendment as authorizing imprisonment for a crime actually contravenes its original meaning as reflected by the actions taken by the Republican Congress after ratification, including outlawing convict leasing.

15. "Unlike convict leasing, which facilitated private corporations' use of prisoners' labor, the chain gang system restricted the labor of the incarcerated to 'state-use.'. . . . The interwoven economy of road improvement and prison labor expanded on previous stages of industrialization. The development of transport infrastructure and logistics was a precondition for the shipping of slaves across the Atlantic. . . . The transition to chain gang labor extended this genealogy, adapting it to the development of publicly owned infrastructure." Rowland, *91020000*, 2–3.

16. Gorman, "Back on the Chain Gang," 441.

17. Rowland, *91020000*, 3; Scherrer and Shah, "Political Economy of Prison Labour," 32; Delaney et al., *American History, Race, and Prison.*

18. Rowland, *91020000*, 3, citing Gilmore, *Golden Gulag*, 57, 83. That capital investment was routed to prison construction was not inevitable. It was the outcome of a crisis-management strategy in which political consensus was built around a narrative of the "problem" and the characteristics of the "relative surplus population" that was geographically and racially concentrated. See Gilmore, *Golden Gulag*, 107–13.

19. Rowland, *91020000*, 3.

20. Zatz, "Working at the Boundaries," 870. Gilmore notes that even though most states legally require prisoners to work, "the fact is that most prisoners are idle, and that those who work do so for a public agency." Gilmore, *Golden Gulag*, 21. Gilmore's observation is situated in the context of refuting equivalences between contemporary forms of carceral labor and convict leasing, for the latter involved the direct transfer of the value of prisoners' labor to private capital. Nevertheless, carceral institutions are expressly given legal authority to compel incarcerated people to work, and many do, particularly in operating the institutions themselves. Earlier estimates from 2008 are that between 600,000 and 1,000,000 prisoners in jails and prisons work, representing approximately one-half of the total population. Zatz, "Working at the Boundaries," 857. Moreover, given the limits on pay and on the ability to refuse work, or to affect working conditions, "incarcerated . . . workers' labor . . . is the inverse of free waged labor" and can function as a form of punishment. Hatton, "When Work Is Punishment," 175. Prison authorities are not subject to routine mechanisms of accountability or transparency with regard to prisoners' labor. Scherrer and Shah, "Political Economy of Prison Labour," 41. The current value of goods and services produced by prisoners' labor is thus difficult

to accurately access. In 2008, the estimated value was more than $2 billion annually. Zatz, "Working at the Boundaries," 869. In the absence of other rehabilitative options, however, access to work is sometimes cast as a benefit or a privilege for which people in prison compete.

21. Rowland, *91020000*, 4.

22. Gilmore, *Golden Gulag*, 117. Thus, for example, the savings from the reduced price paid for incarcerated labor is not booked as profit but is dispersed as savings. Gilmore notes that the operating budget of the California Department of Corrections, the largest state agency, "is flexible, moving costs among line items," including, for example, paying guards' overtime salaries out of funds allocated for prisoners' medical expenses (119).

23. Rowland, *91020000*, 4.

24. Woods, "Les Misérables of New Orleans."

25. Zatz, "Get to Work," 329. Zatz's project powerfully addresses the undertheorized domain of work requirements enforced through threat of incarceration. His analysis identifies carceral work mandates—policies such as child support and criminal legal debt that require the debtor to "Get to Work, or Go to Jail" as such a location.

26. Graeber, *Debt*, 21.

27. Charbonneau and Hansen, "Debt, Neoliberalism and Crisis," 1042. Lazzarato relies on Friedrich Nietzsche for this formulation.

28. Atkinson, "Rethinking Credit as Social Provision," 1098.

29. One of the main arguments advanced by slaveholders was that abolition destroyed their property without compensation. Indeed, this was the premise of the holding in *Dred Scott* that the Missouri Compromise, which banned slavery in the Northwest territories, operated as an uncompensated taking of private property without due process of law. Dred Scott v. Sandford, 60 U.S. 393 (1857). Although abolition arguably destroyed the value of enslaved persons as assets or wealth, this did not settle the issue of value. Courts decided, often over express legislative provisions to the contrary, that debt obligations secured by enslaved people survived emancipation. Even after the formal end of enslavement, the law legitimated financial transactions tethered to Black bodies through the obligation of contract. In White v. Hart, the Supreme Court held invalid a provision of the post–Civil War Georgia state constitution prohibiting the enforcement of any debt "the consideration for which was a slave," thus permitting such debts to be collected. 80 U.S. 646 (1871). That same year the Court, in *Osborn v. Nicholson*, upheld a debt incurred to purchase a slave notwithstanding Emancipation or the passage of the Thirteenth Amendment. 80 U.S. 654 (1871). Moreover, not only were various compensation schemes for slave owners proposed; ultimately, one was successfully adopted and implemented for slave owners in Washington, DC, who

were paid $300 per enslaved person as part of the District of Columbia Emancipation Act of 1862. Hunter, "When Slaveowners Got Reparations."

30. As Hartman notes, "If the control of blacks was formerly effected by absolute rights of property in the black body, dishonor, and the quotidian routine of violence, these techniques were supplanted by the liberty of contract that spawned debt-peonage, the bestowal of right that engendered indebtedness and obligation and licensed naked forms of domination and coercion, and the cultivation of a work ethic that promoted self-discipline and induced internal forms of policing." She identifies and traces this logic, even in textbooks written for and taught to the freedmen. One passage she cites reads as follows: "With treasure and precious blood your freedom has been purchased. Let these sufferings and sacrifices never be forgotten when you remember that you are not now a slave but a freedman." Hartman, *Scenes of Subjection*, 130, citing Isaac W. Brinckerhoff, *Advice to Freedmen* (New York, 1864). The freedman thus came into being as an indebted subject.

31. Zatz, "Working at the Boundaries," 869–70. Some researchers estimate that a relatively small percentage—perhaps 10 percent—of imprisoned people work in prison industries: private companies that contract for their labor or governmental prison-industry companies that rely on that labor for the production of goods. The majority of incarcerated people who work do so for the operation of the prison itself. Scherrer and Shah, "Political Economy of Prison Labour," 41. Trade-union and small-firm opposition to prison labor has kept the percentage relatively low, as have federal bans on goods produced by compulsory labor. At the same time, there are carve-outs: notably, the federal prohibition does not extend to services provided by prison labor. Zatz, "Working at the Boundaries," 869. There are other provisions that further relax the restriction: the Prison Industry Enhancement Certification Program of 1979 sets parameters for private firms using prison labor; the Percy Amendment authorizes the sale of prison-made goods contingent on meeting specific conditions; and UNICOR, the governmental prison-industry company that produces goods for governmental agencies and, since 2012, for private companies. Scherrer and Shah, "Political Economy of Prison Labour," 40. States have followed suit in creating structures for deploying prison labor to perform services or produce products outside the regulatory framework of employment law regarding wages, hours, or a host of other conditions. Zatz, "Working at the Boundaries," 868–69. The data on the number of hours worked, net wages, and work conditions are not generally collected or published; this is an area in which the state's operations are "opaque." Scherrer and Shah, "Political Economy of Prison Labour," 41. There are signs that convict leasing is once again emerging. Zatz, "Working at the Boundaries," 870. Noteworthy is its reappearance in the agricultural sector, particularly as immigration enforcement has become more draconian. Rice, "How Anti-immigration Policies Are Leading Prisons."

32. United States Department of Justice, *Investigation of the Ferguson Police.*

33. Benns and Strode, "Debtor's Prison"; Harvard Law Review Association, "State Bans on Debtors' Prisons," 1027–30.

34. Gilmore, *Golden Gulag*, 17–20, 125–27. The system of municipal finance is further implicated in buttressing police violence as well as mass incarceration as even difficult-to-obtain judgments or settlements obtained against cities for police brutality are sometimes paid through the issuance of bonds. Goodwin, Shepard, and Sloan, *Police Brutality Bonds*.

35. The Peonage Abolition Act of 1867, U.S. Statutes at Large, 39th Cong. Sess. II. Chap. 187, p. 546 (1867).

36. Mancini, *One Dies, Get Another*, 222. Convict leasing was formally abolished across the South from the 1890s to 1928, while the practice often continued in other forms.

37. Zatz, "Working at the Boundaries," 869. Federal law prohibits the sale of goods produced through prison labor in interstate commerce. However, this prohibition does not apply to goods produced for state use.

38. Hampson, "New American Debtors' Prisons," 19–20. In 1821, Kentucky became the first state to abolish debtors' prisons. "Many other states followed suit in the 1830s and 1840s, and by the 1870s the practice was discontinued by almost all of the states then part of the Union" (21).

39. Federal constitutional law has repeatedly articulated these limitations. Extending a person's jail sentence for inability to pay criminal justice obligation was held to violate equal protection in *Williams v. Illinois*, 399 U.S. 235 (1970). In *Tate v. Short*, the Court held that it was unconstitutional to "impos[e] a fine as a sentence and then automatically [convert] it into a jail term because the defendant is indigent and cannot forthwith pay the fine in full." 401 U.S. 395, 397 (1971). In *Bearden v. Georgia*, the Supreme Court held that it was unconstitutional to revoke a defendant's probation for failure to pay a fine or restitution without determining that the failure is willful. 461 U.S. 660 (1983). However, *Bearden*'s admonition that the state may not "punish a person for his poverty" has largely been observed in the breach. Birckhead, "New Peonage," 1595. In the main, reform efforts have sought to enforce the requirement that the court make an individual assessment of the debtor's ability to pay. Given the localized inquiry and the latitude permitted for judicial discretion, these reforms have been difficult to implement and monitor.

40. The literature is extensive. Some prominent examples include ACLU, *In for a Penny*; Harris, *Pound of Flesh*; and Murch, "Paying for Punishment."

41. Examination of the specific social and political contexts and conditions that triggered legal sanction in each of these instances is beyond the scope of this chapter, although it is important to note that, broadly speaking, dynamics of resistance, reform, and retrenchment are evident, as are changes in political economy and societal ruptures.

42. Political theorist Mauricio Lazzarato has convincingly argued that "neoliberalism has, since its emergence, been founded on a logic of debt." Lazzarato, *Making of the Indebted Man*, 25. As Lazzarato contends, the reality of debt under neoliberalism is that it has become a "highly efficient mechanism of control and capture" as debt has become "infinite." Charbonneau and Hansen, "Debt, Neoliberalism and Crisis," 1042.

43. Lazzarato, *Making of the Indebted Man*; Appel, Whitley, and Kline, *Power of Debt*.

44. Seamster, "Black Debt, White Debt," 31.

45. "Black debt is harder to convert into an asset." See Seamster, "Black Debt, White Debt," 33.

46. In *Race for Profit*, Keeanga-Yamahtta Taylor provides a compelling example of predatory inclusion in post-1960s housing policy that incorporated Black people, and particularly women, into the housing market. As the market was riddled with exploitative patterns and incentives—unfair lending, fraudulent appraisals and disclosures, dilapidated properties—many Black home buyers were left in debt, left in foreclosure, or locked in substandard housing. As Taylor points out, the project of reform was "a classic formulation of postwar racial liberalism" that "posited inclusion as the antidote to the crisis created by exclusion" without contending with the structure of the market under racial capitalism. Taylor, *Race for Profit*, 17.

47. Louise Seamster and Raphaël Charron-Chénier similarly define predatory inclusion as "a process whereby members of a marginalized group are provided with access to a good, service, or opportunity from which they have historically been excluded but under conditions that jeopardize the benefits of this access . . . , reproduc[ing] marginalization for these groups while allowing already-dominant social actors to derive significant profits." Seamster and Charron-Chénier, "Predatory Inclusion and Education Debt," 199.

48. As Miranda Joseph argues, Michel Foucault's "economy of illegalities" under which property crimes of the poor are sanctioned through criminal law while commercial crimes of the capitalist class are managed through systems of mitigation is both a disciplinary project and "a central strategy of racial formation." Joseph, *Debt to Society*, 46.

49. Baradaran, *How the Other Half Banks*. Thus, as Baradaran has documented, the exodus of banking institutions from poor minority communities, facilitated by deregulation, resulted in casting poor people into the market of fringe lenders, such as payday lenders and check-cashing services.

50. Ferreira da Silva and Chakravartty, "Accumulation, Dispossession, and Debt," 363–64.

51. "Black debt is a key industry for generating white wealth." Seamster, "Black Debt, White Debt," 34.

52. Lazzarato, *Making of the Indebted Man*.

53. Though beyond the scope of this chapter, one way of thinking about Black debt is that it marks the outer limits of the coercive and predatory dimensions of debt. This excess provides legitimacy to lesser but still exploitative dimensions of debt creation and collection, with some modifications, extended to other vulnerable populations.

54. Gilmore, "What Is the 'Racial'?"

55. Katherine McKittrick describes Black geographies as follows: "These black geographies, while certainly not solely inhabited by black bodies, are classified as imperiled and dangerous, or spaces 'without'/spaces of exclusion, even as those who have always struggled against racial violence and containment populate them." McKittrick, "On Plantations," 947.

56. In this sense, this observation is consistent with Keeanga-Yamahtta Taylor's description of the "inner-city"—what I describe here as Black geographies—as a place often mistakenly cast as a low-value location: "Far from being a static site of dilapidation and ruin, the urban core was becoming an attractive place of unparalleled opportunity, a new frontier of economic investment and extraction for the real estate and banking industries. The race for profit in the 1970s transformed decaying urban space into what one U.S. Senator described as a 'golden ghetto,' where profits for banks and real estate brokers were never ending." Taylor, *Race for Profit*, 4.

57. Schermerhorn, *Business of Slavery*, 2.

58. Fugitive Slave Clause, US Const. art. IV, § 2, cl. 3; Kish and Leroy, "Bonded Life," 633. Indeed, Jefferson described slaves as "indebted to him."

59. As K-Sue Park has powerfully illustrated, the expansion of mortgage foreclosure as a debt-collection mechanism that included forfeiture of the land was an innovation of the settler colonies in North America. Under English law, a mortgagor could foreclose on a debtor but could not evict him and take the land. This limitation eroded in the colonies. European settlers fraudulently induced Indigenous people to borrow money to purchase goods, securing the loan with the land as collateral. Once the debt was unpaid, the creditors moved to foreclose, and they took the land to discharge the debt. These and related practices were deemed necessary for development to avoid clogging the market. Thus, land became fully commodified in the colonies, enabling the expansion of credit, land acquisition, capitalist accumulation, and concentration of wealth. Park, "Money, Mortgages."

60. Reséndez, *Other Slavery*, 5, 6.

61. Reséndez, *Other Slavery*, 246. Reséndez describes the New Mexico sale of Indigenous slaves as "fragmented," and at times involving negotiations with those subjected to the transaction over the terms of service.

62. Gómez, *Manifest Destinies*, 111–12.

63. Reséndez, *Other Slavery*, 5–6.

64. Reséndez, *Other Slavery*, 10. Notably, even though some of these forms such as encomiendas were constructed to limit the authority of the grant holders by requiring payment of wages, limiting the term of work, and restricting the sale or leasing of the laborers, over time, particularly in the Caribbean and parts of Mexico, these constraints eroded to the point that Indians subjected to this system were effectively enslaved. Reséndez, *Other Slavery*, 36.

65. As Reséndez argues, they shared common characteristics with slavery: "forcible removal . . . , inability to leave, violence or threat of violence to compel work, and nominal or no pay." Reséndez, *Other Slavery*, 10.

66. Freeman and Fraser, "Barbarism and Progress," 2.

67. Moore, "'We Feel the Want,'" 97.

68. Reséndez, *Other Slavery*, 238.

69. Buffington, *Criminal and Citizen in Modern Mexico*, 4.

70. Importantly, Kelly Hernandez's compelling account reveals that this carceral regime was not simply about labor control but also about displacement, dispossession, and Native elimination. Hernandez, *City of Inmates*, 33.

71. Gómez, *Manifest Destinies*, 3–5, 17. Laura Gómez's *Manifest Destinies* includes an illuminating discussion of the debate over manifest destiny, particularly in the context of the American Southwest.

72. Kiser, "'Charming Name,'" 170.

73. Moore, "'We Feel the Want,'" 103, 104.

74. Moore, "'We Feel the Want,'" 105.

75. Moore, "'We Feel the Want,'" 105. As the statute provided,

> Any Indian able to work and support himself in some honest calling, not having wherewithal to maintain himself, who shall be found loitering and strolling about, or frequenting public places where liquors are sold, begging, or leading an immoral or profligate course of life, shall be liable to be arrested on the complaint of any resident citizen of the county, and brought before the Justice of the Peace. . . . And if said Justice . . . shall be satisfied that he is a vagrant . . . he shall make out a warrant under his hand and seal, authorizing and requiring the officer having him in custody, to hire out such vagrant within twenty four hours to the best bidder . . . for the highest price that can be had, for any term not exceeding four months. The Act for the Government and Protection of Indians, ch. 133, Cal. Stat. (April 22, 1850).

76. An Act To Punish Vagrants, Vagabonds, and Dangerous and Suspicious Persons (Cal. 1855), 217.

77. Oshinsky, *"Worse Than Slavery,"* 20–22.

78. An Act to Confer Civil Rights on Freedmen (Miss. 1865), 84.

79. An Act to Amend the Vagrant Laws of the State (Miss. 1866), 9.

80. A vagrant is "any person wandering or strolling about in idleness, who is able to work, and has no property to support him; or any person leading an idle, immoral, profligate life, having no property to support him." An Act to Define and Punish Vagrancy (Ala. 1903), 244.

81. Kiser, "'Charming Name,'" 189.

82. This account draws from Hammer, "Flint Water Crisis," as well as presentations by the Flint Democracy Defense League and We the People of Detroit.

83. Hammer, "Flint Water Crisis," 103, 106.

84. Public Act 101 of 1988 and Public Act 72 of 1990 were passed to give the state some control over governmental bodies facing bankruptcy. Snyder proposed Public Act 4, which in cases of "financial stress" authorized the governor to appoint an emergency manager "to act for and in the place and stead of the governing body and the office of chief administrative officer of the local government." Michigan Public Act 4 (2011). The powers granted were broad: to modify or terminate contracts, including collective-bargaining agreements; to eliminate or consolidate departments; and to privatize and sell public assets. Once the emergency manager was appointed, the governing body and the administrative officer could act only upon his or her approval.

85. Although the law was blocked by popular referendum, it was reimposed in essentially the same form through the state legislature. Michigan Public Act 436 (2012).

86. Because the emergency manager law has been deployed more often against Black cities and municipal agencies, a lawsuit was filed against the state, alleging racially discriminatory administration of the act, in violation of the Fourteenth Amendment equal protection guarantee. The complaint also included a claim under the Voting Rights Act, asserting that the displacement of city government by the emergency manager was a denial of democratic control. In *Phillips, et al. v. Snyder*, the district court dismissed the voting rights claim. 2014 WL 6474344 (E.D.Mich., 2014). The decision was upheld on review. Phillips v. Snyder, 836 F.3d 707 (6th Cir. 2016). The discriminatory administration claim was left standing. In 2017 the petition for review was denied by the US Supreme Court. Bellant v. Snyder, 138 S.Ct. 66 (2017). See also Bosman and Davey, "Anger in Michigan."

87. Stanley, "Emergency Manager," 17.

88. Pauli, *Flint Fights Back*, 89.

89. Hammer, "Flint Water Crisis," 116.

90. As one article describes it, the dire fiscal condition of several Michigan cities was attributable to the state's actions:

> Over the past decade, lawmakers and governors from both political parties have used some $6.2 billion in sales tax collections to fill state budget holes rather than fulfill a statutory revenue sharing promise to local communities, according to the Michigan Municipal League. . . . Detroit, which filed for bankruptcy protection last year, missed out on $732 million between 2003 and 2013, per the report. Flint, under control of an emergency manager, could have had an extra $54.9 million to work with. Cities like Pontiac and Lansing have lost more than $40 million each. The Municipal League says the annual budget "raid" has diverted money that should have been used to maintain city services. It argues that the Legislature has helped caused some of the very financial emergencies that have prompted state takeovers or other forms of intervention.
>
> "It's like somebody stealing your wallet and then coming back hours later and saying, 'What, you have no money?'" said Utica Mayor Jacqueline Noonan, whose small city of 4,700 residents missed out on $1.4 million in the last decade. "It's ridiculous. It's insane." Oosting, "Michigan's Revenue Sharing 'Raid.'"

91. We the People of Detroit, *Mapping the Water Crisis*; Ponder and Omstedt, "Violence of Municipal Debt."

92. Shariff, "Is Flint Michigan's Water Quality Really Restored?"

93. Ponder and Omstedt, "Violence of Municipal Debt," 6.

94. Bailey, "Untold Story of Flint."

BIBLIOGRAPHY

American Civil Liberties Union (ACLU). *In for a Penny: The Rise of America's New Debtors' Prisons*. American Civil Liberties Union, 2010. www.aclu.org/report/penny-rise-americas-new-debtors-prisons.

An Act to Amend the Vagrant Laws of the State. Ch. VI § 2. Laws of the State of Mississippi, Passed at a Regular Session of the Mississippi Legislature, Held in the City of Jackson, October, November and December, 1865. Jackson: J. J. Shannon and Co., State Printers, 1866. https://goo.gl/cJfW5k.

An Act to Confer Civil Rights on Freedmen, and for Other Purposes. Ch. IV § 7. Laws of the State of Mississippi, Passed at a Regular Session of the Mississippi Legislature, Held in the City of Jackson, October, November and December, 1865. Jackson: J. J. Shannon and Co., State Printers, 1866. https://goo.gl/cJfW5k.

An Act to Define and Punish Vagrancy. H. 690, No. 229. General Laws (and Joint Resolutions) of the Legislature of Alabama Passed at the Session of 1903 Held in the Capitol, in the City of Montgomery Commencing Tuesday, January 13th, 1903. Montgomery: Brown Printing Co., Printers and Binders, 1903. https://

play.google.com/store/books/details?id=R81GAQAAMAAJ&rdid=book
-R81GAQAAMAAJ&rdot=1.

An Act to Punish Vagrants, Vagabonds, and Dangerous and Suspicious Persons.
Ch. 175 § 1. The Statutes of California, Passed at the Sixth Session of the
Legislature, Begun on the First Day of January, One Thousand Eight Hun-
dred and Fifty-Five, and Ended on the Seventh Day of May, One Thousand
Eight Hundred and Fifty-Five, at the City of Sacramento. Sacramento: B. B.
Redding, State Printer, 1855. https://babel.hathitrust.org/cgi/pt?id=uc1
.31175020756063&view=1up&seq=239.

Appel, Hannah, Sa Whitley, and Caitlin Kline. *The Power of Debt: Identity and Collective Action in the Age of Finance.* Los Angeles: UCLA Institute on Inequality
and Democracy, April 12, 2019.

Atkinson, Abbye. "Rethinking Credit as Social Provision." *Stanford Law Review*
71, no. 5 (May 2019): 1093–1162. www.stanfordlawreview.org/print/article
/rethinking-credit-as-social-provision.

Bailey, Kristian Davis. "The Untold Story of Flint: The Assault on Democracy for
Poor and Black People." *Black Bottom Archive*, February 28, 2016. http://www
.blackbottomarchives.com/blackpapersocialjustice/the-untold-story-of-flint
-the-assault-on-democracy-for-poor-black-people.

Baradaran, Mehrsa. *How the Other Half Banks: Exclusion, Exploitation and the
Threat to Democracy.* Cambridge, MA: Harvard University Press, 2015.

Benns, Whitney, and Blake Strode. "Debtor's Prison in the 21st Century." *Atlantic*,
February 23, 2016. https://www.theatlantic.com/business/archive/2016/02
/debtors-prison/462378/.

Birckhead, Tamar. "The New Peonage." *Washington and Lee Law Review* 72, no. 4 (Fall
2015): 1595–1678. https://scholarlycommons.law.wlu.edu/wlulr/vol72/iss4/3.

Bosman, J., and Monica Davey. "Anger in Michigan over Appointing Emergency
Managers." *New York Times*, January 22, 2016. https://www.nytimes.com
/2016/01/23/us/anger-in-michigan-over-appointing-emergency-managers.html.

Buffington, Robert. *Criminal and Citizen in Modern Mexico.* Lincoln: University of
Nebraska Press, 2010.

Charbonneau, Mathieu, and Magnus Paulsen Hansen. "Debt, Neoliberalism and
Crisis: Interview with Maurizio Lazzarato on the Indebted Condition." *Sociology* 48, no. 5 (2014): 1039–47. doi:10.1177/0038038514539207.

Delaney, Ruth, Ram Subramanian, Alison Shames, and Nicholas Turner. *American
History, Race, and Prison.* Vera Institute: Reimagining Prison Web Report, October 2018. www.vera.org/reimagining-prison-web-report/american-history
-race-and-prison.

Du Bois, W. E. B. *The Souls of Black Folk.* Chicago: A. C. McClurg, 1903.

Duchamp, Marcel. "A 1959 Interview with Marcel Duchamp: The Fallacy of Art
History and the Death of Art." By Audio Arts. Artspace. February 21, 2018.
https://www.artspace.com/magazine/art_101/qa/a-1959-interview-with
-marcel-duchamp-the-fallacy-of-art-history-and-the-death-of-art-55274.

Ferreira da Silva, Denise, and Paula Chakravartty. "Accumulation, Dispossession, and Debt: The Racial Logic of Global Capitalism—An Introduction." *American Quarterly* 64, no. 3 (September 2012): 361–85. doi:10.1353/
aq.2012.0033.

Flint Democracy Defense League. The National Conference of Black Lawyers
50th Anniversary Conference, Wayne State University School of Law, Detroit,
MI, October 8, 2018.

Freeman, Joshua B., and Steve Fraser. "Barbarism and Progress: The Story of
Convict Labor." *New Labor Forum*, August 1, 2012. https://newlaborforum.cuny
.edu/2012/08/01/in-the-rearview-mirror-barbarism-and-progress-the-story-of
-convict-labor/.

Gilmore, Ruth Wilson. *Golden Gulag: Prisons, Surplus, Crisis and Opposition in
Globalizing California.* Berkeley: University of California Press, 2007.

Gilmore, Ruth Wilson. "What Is the 'Racial' in Racial Capitalism? Magic, Partition,
Politics." Keynote speech at the Racial Capitalism Symposium, University of
Illinois, Urbana-Champaign, March 29, 2019.

Gómez, Laura. *Manifest Destinies: The Making of the American Race.* 2nd ed. New
York: NYU Press, 2018.

Goodwin, Alyxandra, Whitney Shepard, and Carrie Sloan. *Police Brutality Bonds:
How Wall Street Profits from Police Violence.* Action Center on Race and Equal-
ity, 2020. https://acrecampaigns.org/wp-content/uploads/2020/06/ACRE
_PBB_2020_2.pdf.

Gorman, Tessa. "Back on the Chain Gang: Why the Eighth Amendment and the
History of Slavery Proscribe the Resurgence of Chain Gangs." *California Law
Review* 85, no. 2 (March 1997): 441–78. doi:10.2307/3481074.

Graeber, David. *Debt: The First 5000 Years.* Brooklyn: Melville House, 2014.

Hammer, Peter J. "The Flint Water Crisis, the Karegnondi Water Authority
and Strategic-Structural Racism." *Critical Sociology* 45, no. 1 (2019): 103–19.
doi:10.1177/0896920517729193.

Hampson, Christopher D. "The New American Debtors' Prisons." *American Journal of Criminal Law* 44, no. 1 (Fall 2016): 1–48. https://heinonline.org/HOL
/P?h=hein.journals/ajcl44&i=5.

Harris, Alexes. *A Pound of Flesh: Monetary Sanctions as Punishment for the Poor.*
American Sociological Association's Rose Monograph Series. New York: Russell Sage, 2016.

Hartman, Saidiya V. *Lose Your Mother: A Journey along the Atlantic Slave Route.*
New York: Farrar, Straus and Giroux, 2007.

Hartman, Saidiya V. *Scenes of Subjection: Terror, Slavery and Self-Making in Nineteenth Century America.* Oxford: Oxford University Press, 1997.

The Harvard Law Review Association. "State Bans on Debtors' Prisons and Criminal Justice Debt." *Harvard Law Review* 129, no. 4 (2016): 1024–45. https://
harvardlawreview.org/2016/02/state-bans-on-debtors-prisons-and-criminal
-justice-debt.

Hatton, Erin. "When Work Is Punishment: Penal Subjectivities in Punitive Labor Regimes." *Punishment and Society* 20, no. 2 (2017): 174–91. doi:10.1177/1462474517690001.

Hernandez, Kelly Lytle. *City of Inmates: Conquest, Rebellion, and the Rise of Human Caging in Los Angeles, 1771–1965.* Chapel Hill: University of North Carolina Press, 2017.

Hunter, Tera. "When Slaveowners Got Reparations." *New York Times,* April 16, 2019.

Joseph, Miranda. *Debt to Society.* Minneapolis: University of Minnesota Press, 2014.

Kiser, William. "'A Charming Name for a Species of Slavery': Political Debate on Debt Peonage in the Southwest,1840s–1860s." *Western Historical Quarterly* 45, no. 2 (Summer 2014): 169–89. doi:10.2307/westhistquar.45.2.0169.

Kish, Zenia, and Justin Leroy. "Bonded Life." *Cultural Studies* 29, nos. 5–6 (2015): 630–51. doi:10.1080/09502386.2015.1017137.

Lazzarato, Mauricio. *The Making of the Indebted Man.* Amsterdam: Semiotext(e), 2011.

Lichtenstein, Alex. *Twice the Work of Free Labor: The Political Economy of Free Labor in the New South.* New York: Verso, 1996.

Mancini, Matthew J. *One Dies, Get Another: Convict Leasing in the American South, 1866–1928.* Columbia: University of South Carolina Press, 1996.

McKittrick, Katherine. "On Plantations, Prisons and a Black Sense of Place." *Social and Cultural Geography* 12, no. 8 (December 2011): 947–63. doi:10.1080/14649 365.2011.624280.

McMillan, Uri. Email message to author, December 15, 2015.

Michigan Public Act 4. H. 4214, 2011 96th Leg., Reg. Sess. (Mich. 2011).

Michigan Public Act 436. S. 865, 2012 96th Leg., Reg. Sess. (Mich. 2012).

Moore, Shirley Ann Wilson. "'We Feel the Want of Protection': The Politics of Law and Race in California." *California History* 81, no. 3/4 (2003): 96–125. doi:10.2307/25161701.

Murch, Donna. "Paying for Punishment: The New Debtors' Prisons." *Boston Review,* August 1, 2016. https://bostonreview.net/articles/donna-murch-paying -punishment/.

Nellis, Ashley. *The Color of Justice: Racial and Ethnic Disparity in State Prisons.* Washington, DC: Sentencing Project, 2016.

Oosting, Jonathan. "How Michigan's Revenue Sharing 'Raid' Cost Communities Billions for Local Services." *MLive,* January 20, 2019. https://www.mlive.com /lansing-news/2014/03/michigan_revenue_sharing_strug.html.

Oshinsky, David M. *"Worse Than Slavery": Parchman Farm and the Ordeal of Jim Crow Justice.* New York: Simon & Schuster, 1996.

Park, K-Sue. "Money, Mortgages, and the Conquest of America." *Law and Social Inquiry* 41, no. 4 (2016): 1006–35. doi:10.1111/lsi.12222.

Pauli, Benjamin J. *Flint Fights Back: Environmental Justice and Democracy in the Flint Water Crisis.* Cambridge, MA: MIT Press, 2019.

The Peonage Abolition Act of 1867, U.S. Statutes at Large, 39th Cong. Sess. II. Ch. 187, p. 546 (1867).

Piper, Adrian. "Adrian Piper Research Archive Foundation Berlin." Accessed June 1, 2020. www.adrianpiper.com.

Piper, Adrien. *Out of Order, Out of Sight*, vol. I, *Selected Writings in Meta-Art 1968–1992*. Cambridge, MA: MIT Press, 1999.

Piper, Adrien. "Two Kinds of Discrimination." *Yale Journal of Criticism* 6, no. 1 (1993): 25–75. https://philpapers.org/rec/PIPTKO.

Ponder, C. S., and Mikael Omstedt. "The Violence of Municipal Debt: From Interest Rates Swaps to Racialized Harm in the Detroit Water Crisis." *Geoforum* 132 (July 26, 2019): 271–80.

Pope, James Gray. "Mass Incarceration, Convict Leasing, and the Thirteenth Amendment: A Revisionist Account." *New York University Law Review* 94 (2019): 1465–1554. www.nyulawreview.org/issues/volume-94-number-6/mass -incarceration-convict-leasing-and-the-thirteenth-amendment-a-revisionist -account.

Reséndez, Andrés. *The Other Slavery: The Uncovered Story of Indian Enslavement in America*. New York: Houghton Mifflin Harcourt, 2016.

Rice, Stian. "How Anti-immigration Policies Are Leading Prisons to Lease Convicts as Field Laborers." *Pacific Standard*, June 7, 2019. https://psmag.com /social-justice/anti-immigrant-policies-are-returning-prisoners-to-the-fields.

Robinson, Cedric. *Black Marxism: The Making of the Black Radical Tradition*. 2nd ed. Chapel Hill: University of North Carolina Press, 2000.

Rowland, Cameron. *91020000* exhibition booklet. New York: Artists Space Books and Talks, 2016.

Scalia, Antonin. Concurring opinion, Adarand Constructors, Inc. v. Peña (1995) 515 U.S. 200, at 239 (1995).

Schermerhorn, Calvin. *The Business of Slavery and the Rise of American Capitalism 1815–1860*. New Haven, CT: Yale University Press, 2015.

Scherrer, Christoph, and Anil Shah. "The Political Economy of Prison Labour: From Penal Welfarism to the Penal State." *Global Labour Journal* 8, no. 1 (2017): 32–48. doi:10.15173/glj.v8i1.2774.

Seamster, Louise. "Black Debt, White Debt." *Contexts* 18, no. 1 (2019): 30–35. https://journals.sagepub.com/doi/10.1177/1536504219830674.

Seamster, Louise, and Raphaël Charron-Chénier. "Predatory Inclusion and Education Debt: Rethinking the Racial Wealth Gap." *Social Currents* 4, no. 3 (2017): 199–207. doi:10.1177/2329496516686620.

Shariff, Nayyirah. "Is Flint Michigan's Water Quality Really Restored?" Interview by Eddie Conway. Real News Network, June 26, 2018.

Smith, Roberta. "In Cameron Rowland's '91020000,' Disquieting Sculptures." *New York Times*, January 28, 2016. https://www.nytimes.com/2016/01/29/arts /design/in-cameron-rowlands-91020000-disquieting-sculptures.html.

Stanley, Jason. "The Emergency Manager: Strategic Racism, Technocracy, and the Poisoning of Flint's Children." *The Good Society* 25, no. 1 (2016): 1–45. doi:10.5325/goodsociety.25.1.0001.

Taylor, Keeanga-Yamahtta. *Race for Profit: How Banks and the Real Estate Industry Undermined Black Homeownership.* Chapel Hill: University of North Carolina Press, 2020.

United States Department of Justice, Civil Rights Division. *Investigation of the Ferguson Police Department,* March 4, 2015.

U.S. Const. amend. XIII, § 1 (1865).

U.S. Const. art. IV, § 2, cl. 3. Vagrancy. Ch. 144, § 5055. The Mississippi Code of 1906 of the Public Statute Laws of The State of Mississippi, prepared and annotated by A. H. Whitfield, T. C. Catchings, and W. H. Hardy. Nashville: Brandon Printing Company, 1906.

We the People of Detroit. *Mapping the Water Crisis: The Dismantling of African-American Neighborhoods in Detroit,* 2016. www.wethepeopleofdetroit.com /water.

We the People of Detroit. The National Conference of Black Lawyers 50th Anniversary Conference, Wayne State University School of Law, Detroit, MI, October 8, 2018.

Weprin, David I. *2018 Annual Report, Standing Committee on Correction.* New York State Assembly: Standing Committee on Correction, 2018. https://nyassembly .gov/write/upload/postings/2019/pdfs/20190319_0085751.pdf.

Woods, Clyde. "Les Misérables of New Orleans: Trap Economics and the Asset Stripping Blues, Part 1." *American Quarterly* 61, no. 3 (2009): 769–96. www .jstor.org/stable/27735018.

Zatz, Noah. "Get to Work or Go to Jail: State Violence and the Racialized Production of Precarious Work." *Law and Social Inquiry* 45, no. 2 (2019): 304–38. doi:10.1017/lsi.2019.56.

Zatz, Noah. "Working at the Boundaries of Markets: Prison Labor and the Economic Dimension of Employment Relationships." *Vanderbilt Law Review* 61, no. 3 (2008): 857–958. doi:https://scholarship.law.vanderbilt.edu/vlr/vol61 /iss3/3.

II Administration

THE OPEN SECRET OF COLONIAL
RACIAL CAPITALIST VIOLENCE

In Search of the Next El Dorado: Mining for Capital in a Frontier Market with Colonial Legacies

Over the last fifteen years we have witnessed the simultaneous economic rise of East Asia economies and the decline of Western economies. As of 2012, according to the World Bank, Asia's stock markets accounted for 32 percent of global market capitalization, ahead of the United States at 30 percent and Europe at 25 percent.[1] In this context, categories like First World and Third World or global North and global South are no longer useful concepts for thinking about the world economy. The world is now divided between a global elite of ultra-high-net-worth individuals and poor folks in developed and emerging markets around the world[2] or, as Chandra Mohanty previously conceptualized this division, the one-third world and the two-thirds world, respectively.[3]

With their rapid growth, emerging and frontier markets are poised to become the most important markets of the twenty-first century.[4] Found in developing countries with rapid industrialization and increasing integration into the global economy, emerging and frontier markets are experiencing growth rates more than double those of advanced economies.[5] Despite the centrality of emerging markets in the global economy, these markets have attracted more attention from managers and investors than from scholars in the social sciences or humanities.[6]

Social scientists who examine emerging markets focus their work primarily on how institutions—or the formal and informal "rules of the game"—affect economic activity.[7] For example, economic sociologists focus on the conditions for investment, such as levels of corruption, stability of the legal regime, and types of accountability.[8] Political scientists develop typologies of state regimes through cross-country comparisons.[9] Humanities researchers tend to focus overwhelmingly on the devastating consequences of dispossession that result from these capital flows.[10] The majority of this work analyzes capitalism through a problematic binary of wealthy, white, foreign capitalists and a group of dispossessed, local poor people of color.[11] Virtually no one studies the capitalists themselves and the tensions that exist at the top between foreign and local elites who cooperate and compete to profit off national resources.

This chapter is motivated by one basic question: how do foreign investors move money from around the world into emerging and frontier markets (a) with histories of colonialism and imperialism and (b) where local elite government officials strongly resist new forms of neo-economic colonialism from foreign investors? This chapter brings together insights from the humanities and social sciences to examine how the broader social, historical, and colonial contexts set the stage for contemporary investment relations between foreign investors and postcolonial/imperial government officials in highly regulated and protected sectors of the economy that might be perceived as particularly nationalistic, such as mining, oil, gas, natural resources, and real estate.

Drawing inspiration from scholars of postcolonialism and racial capitalism, this chapter makes two important contributions to the study of global elites. First, it employs Michael Burawoy's extended case method by applying "reflexive science to ethnography in order to extract the general from the unique, to move from 'micro' to the 'macro,' and to connect the present to the past in anticipation of the future, all by building on preexisting theory." In doing so, this chapter works to analyze contemporary investment flows through a postcolonial lens by "dig[ging] beneath the political binaries of colonizer and colonized . . . metropolis and periphery," East and West, and capital and state, to uncover the multiple processes and tensions in negotiating control of a country's natural resources.[12] Second, working through a framework of racial capitalism, this chapter disrupts the current scholarship that focuses on the ultra-wealthy with assumptions that they all come from Western nations. The emergence of new wealth made in Russia, East and Southeast Asia, and the Middle East unsettles previous assumptions that wealth is associated with Western nations and by proxy with whiteness. As I illustrate, a new global elite that makes up part of the one-third world has become extremely wealthy as a result of the fortunes amassed in emerging and frontier markets. Pushing the analysis one step further, this chapter advances a *colonial racial capitalist* framework that accounts for the fact that elites of any color can exploit the poor of color.[13] At the same time, power struggles among global elites occur between groups of people who are not all white. In fact, local elites operate with anticolonial frames that are often caught in a power struggle with foreign investors over who gets to profit off the national resources.

The country that I focus on in this chapter is Vietnam; however, as the chapter will detail, capital investment into this market comes from all over the world. I trace the movement of global capital from offshore companies in places like the British Virgin Islands to special-purpose vehicles or holding companies in Singapore or Thailand before being invested onshore in Vietnam. The sector of the economy that this chapter focuses on is mining.[14] Because this sector is so small, however, this chapter develops a composite case by merging investments into three different mines to better anonymize my data sources. The case illustrates how mining for capital led to a showdown between investors and the government that left each entity feeling slighted by the other and ultimately led to the demise of a $140 million investment project. This created a cascade effect of losses for both institutional investors and small mom-and-pop shop investors from all over the world.

Vietnam: Legacies of Colonialism

Vietnam endured more than a thousand years of Chinese colonialism. The Han Chinese Empire led a conquest of Vietnam in 111 BCE, which was followed by a revolt against Chinese occupation by the Trung sisters in 39 CE. After the Vietnamese gained independence in 939 CE, they continued to adopt Chinese political institutions and social values while creating their own distinct cultural world. During its early conquest in 111 BCE, the Han Dynasty forced Vietnam to adopt the Chinese writing system, their native language and culture, and Confucianism. Through a series of dynasties (Ly, Ngo, Dinh, Le, Ly Tran, and Ho) and after a thousand years of on-and-off rule, Vietnam gained its independence from China following a Vietnamese rebellion and Le Loi's defeat in 1427. Between 1427 and the early 1600s, Vietnam was led by the Le and Mac dynasties.

In the early 1600s, Alexandre de Rhodes, a French Jesuit missionary, first arrived in Hanoi. France obtained control over northern Vietnam following victory over China in the Sino-French War in 1884. Between

1844 and 1873, the French captured various parts of Vietnam, starting with Da Nang, followed by Saigon, and then finally Hanoi. French Indochina, which was established in 1887, brought together Annam (Da La), Tonkin (Hanoi), and Cochinchina (Saigon), Cambodia, and Laos. For nearly a century the French colonized modern-day Vietnam, Cambodia, and Laos, which were officially known collectively as the French Indochinese Union in 1877. France colonized Vietnam for nearly sixty years before it came under Japanese occupation in 1945 during World War II. Between 1946 and 1954, the Viet Minh engaged in an anti-French resistance war, led by Ho Chi Minh and the People's Army of Vietnam's Vo Nguyen Giap. In 1954 Ho Chi Minh declared the independent Democratic Republic of Vietnam after the Viet Minh won the war with France in the Battle of Dien Bien Phu. This led to the partition of Vietnam into two parts: the Democratic Republic of Vietnam in the North, under the control of the Viet Minh, and the State of Vietnam in the South. Following the Geneva Accord of 1954, the French left Vietnam, bringing an end to French Indochina.

The Tonkin Gulf incident of 1964, which involved the USS *Maddox* and North Vietnamese boats in an international confrontation, eventually led to the US involvement in the Vietnam War. This war, also referred to as the Second Indochina War, was officially fought between North Vietnam and South Vietnam. The North was backed by the Soviet Union and China, and the South was supported primarily by the United States, with allies from South Korea, Thailand, the Philippines, and Australia. United States involvement in South Vietnam dramatically transformed the local political economy, for the US military fought alongside the South Vietnamese republican forces against northern Vietnamese communist fighters. Between 1962 and 1975, the United States spent more than $169 billion on the Vietnam War, which was more than the total economic aid given to all other developing countries during those years.[15] The capture of South Vietnam in Saigon by the People's Army of Vietnam led to the fall of Saigon in 1975, marking the end of the Vietnam War and the reunification of North and South Vietnam.

After the fall of Saigon, Vietnam was closed off from other nations, but "the Vietnamese were no longer hesitant to assert their territorial claims against China, nor were the Cambodians reluctant to press theirs against Vietnam."[16] During 1978–1979, Vietnam found itself in an armed conflict with Cambodia to remove Pol Pot from power. In China, however, Mao fully endorsed Pol Pot's plans for Cambodia. At the same time, the Sino-Vietnamese War, also known as the Third Indochina War, involved a border conflict as China reacted to Vietnam's invasion of Cambodia. In addition, Vietnam began to lay claim to the islands in the Spratly group in the South China Sea, which led to a series of naval conflicts with China that lasted for a decade.

During the postwar period, "Vietnam was in need of massive aid in order to rebuild and while the leadership in Hanoi was attracted to Western aid which would have come with more advanced technologies, they wanted to strengthen their relationships with the Soviet Bloc and China who would provide half of the aid and Western Europe, the United States, Japan, and Canada would provide the other half."[17] The Soviet Union was richer at the time and provided much more aid than China did, and in exchange the Soviet Union expected Vietnam to support Soviet policies, which made Vietnamese leaders anxious about getting caught in the middle of a Sino-Soviet conflict. The White House perspective on this conflict was that the Vietnam-Cambodia conflict represented the war between China and Russia.

In 1978 Zbigniew Brzezinski—President Jimmy Carter's national security adviser at the time—went on a trip to China, where he declared US support for China against "regional hegemony," which was in reference to Vietnam's preparation to invade Cambodia. Brzezinski pressed Carter to develop a relationship with China as part of a long-term strategy to oppose regional hegemony by any single power, thereby signaling to China that Washington was sympathetic to its troubles with the Soviet Union and Vietnam. To the United States, Vietnam was just a puppet for the Soviet Union, and the fact that China was worried about Vietnam becoming a Soviet base at the time was important for US strategic influence in the region.[18]

Meanwhile, Vietnam effectively closed its doors to foreign relations (except for the Soviet Bloc) and established a communist property market where the state owned and controlled the land. Vietnam's socialist project then began to collapse under conditions of extreme poverty. Vietnam continued to suffer from economic stagnation, lagging productivity, and rapid inflation. During the time that the newly independent country negotiated its conflicts and strategic relations with China, Russia, and Cambodia, citizens in the country were living in an environment of widespread poverty, heavily subsidized production, and postwar infrastructural instability as the country worked to rebuild itself.

Vietnam's Postwar Market Economy: Opening Its Doors to Foreign Trade and Investment

In 1986, after a decade of lagging productivity and rapid inflation in the context of communist reform and other worldwide transformations (glasnost and perestroika in the Soviet Union and the Deng Xiaoping reforms in China), Vietnam introduced the Doi Moi program of economic liberalization, which effectively transitioned Vietnam into a socialist-oriented market economy in which the Communist Party maintained a political monopoly. These reforms opened Vietnam to foreign trade, investment, and large-scale tourism, setting off a prolonged and continuing period of economic growth and development.[19] In a "market economy with a socialist transition," foreign investors were allowed to enter the market, and the government encouraged private businesses via free trade, free markets, and profits for some and wages for others.[20] After 2000, economic changes accelerated, and the political balance shifted as the country managed pressure from foreign investors to open its economy. Vietnam approved the sale of its state-owned companies.

Between 1986 and 2005, most of the foreign capital entering Vietnam came primarily from Western nations, including the United States, Canada, and Australia. In this culturally defined socialist market, which was characterized by "fuzzy property boundaries,"[21] there were no clear boundaries between state and society and no clear rules about private property.[22] In addition, the state had to manage its disparagement of private property in order to organize relations that encouraged investment, thereby shaping a new relational and cultural constitution of foreign and local capital. Until 2005, foreign direct investment (FDI) in Vietnam went primarily into export-oriented manufacturing industries, such as garments and textiles, footwear, furniture, wood, and automobiles, which accounted for 42 percent of the cumulative approved FDI in 2005.[23] However, the mining industry has grown by a factor of ten, from $2.13 million in 2000 to $20.58 million in 2013. This is capital brought onshore and does not account for the capital sitting in offshore bank accounts designated for the exploration and development of these mines.[24] However, there are no official statistics on the flow of capital that went into the privatization and sale of state-owned enterprises.

In 2007 Vietnam officially joined the World Trade Organization (WTO) as the 150th member and established both bilateral and multilateral trade agreements, further strengthening its relationship with other member nations. Following its membership in the WTO, Vietnam's economy experienced an annual economic growth of 8 percent per year. This growth served as a magnet for investment: FDI increased dramatically each year between 2006 and 2014 (see figure 4.1). The amounts shown in figure 4.1 represent reported capital that had been registered and disbursed. Totals for committed or promised capital are higher. For example, at the peak of the 2008 financial crisis, committed capital reached nearly $71 billion.

Furthermore, the persistent weakness of Western economies in the wake of the 2008 global economic crisis enabled countries in the region to play a major role in structuring Vietnam's economy. Between 1995 and 2005, Australia, Canada, and the United States were the largest providers of FDI to Vietnam. By 2010, however, the five leading contributors were South Korea, Japan, Singapore, Taiwan, and the British Virgin Islands (see figure 4.2).[25] These shifting capital sources overpowered both Western investments and overseas remittances, putting an Asian face to wealth in Vietnam through new inter-Asian circuits of global capital.[26]

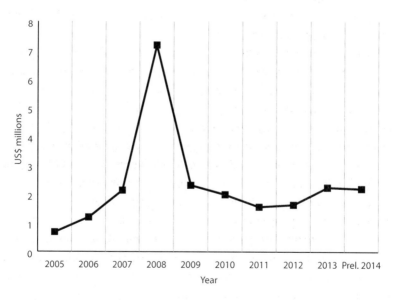

FIGURE 4.1. Disbursed Foreign Direct Investment in Vietnam, 2005–2014. Source: General Statistics Office (GSO) Vietnam 2014.

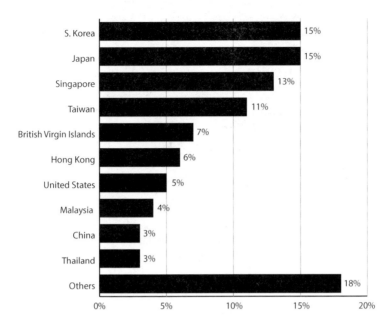

FIGURE 4.2. Vietnam Foreign Direct Investment by Source Country, 2015. Source: *Vietnam Economic Times* and General Statistics Office (GSO) of Vietnam; see Nguyen (2015).

Rivalry between the United States and China in Contemporary Vietnam

In recent years, China and the United States have been competing to gain a foothold in the region. In 2015 Chinese leaders established the Asia Infrastructure Investment Bank (AIIB). In a responsive effort to moderate China's influence in the region, several Western nations (the United States, Canada, and Australia) came together to establish the Trans-Pacific Partnership (TPP). The rivalry between the United States and China is transparent. As the TPP website literally states, "The rules of the road are up for grabs in Asia. If we don't pass this [Trans-Pacific Trade Partnership] agreement and *write those rules*, competitors [i.e., China] will set weak rules of the road . . . undermining US leadership in Asia."[27]

When President Donald Trump took office, he denounced the TPP because of its ties to the Obama legacy, leaving the other countries to renegotiate a trade agreement without the United States. Even though the United States is no longer part of that trade agreement, the first Southeast Asian leader to visit the White House under the Trump administration came from Vietnam (even though the United States had stronger strategic relations with the Philippines and Thailand). This is because Vietnam had hired the Podesta Group of brothers—one of whom was formerly the campaign director for Hillary Clinton—to lobby for the Vietnamese prime minister's visit to the White House. This was part of an ongoing effort to maintain trade relations and moderate China's influence in the region. Shortly after that, Trump and Canadian Prime Minister Justin Trudeau both made stops in Vietnam, making similar efforts to maintain a foothold in the region.

After President Trump pulled out of the TPP, China began negotiating more than a dozen trade agreements, collectively called the Regional Comprehensive Economic Partnership, in an effort to build alternatives to the World Bank and the International Monetary Fund, which are Western institutions. In this context, "America's status as the linchpin of the global economic order is now endangered. The trading system China dominates has reduced the long dependency of Latin American and sub-Saharan African countries on American and European markets. China is now . . . in the process of making East Asia the center of the new world economy."[28] In this context, smaller countries such as Vietnam pivoted toward China after Trump's election, enabling them to take a much more aggressive stance against foreign investors that originate in Western nations, thereby contesting Western forms of hegemony but drawing on alternative regional investment relations.

A Protectionist Anticolonial State

With complex histories of Chinese colonialism, French colonialism, and US imperialism, as well as relations with the Soviet Bloc, Vietnam has gone to great lengths to ensure that foreigners do not become new economic colonialists and that local resources, land, and commodities remain owned and controlled internally by local Vietnamese. Therefore, state banks are the main source of internal capital allocation, which is based on long-term *relationships with the state*; local business networks gain access to the best market sites through personal ties to the Communist Party.[29] Several scholars who examine Vietnamese state-society relations show that the relationships between private and public sectors are often murky and highly contentious: state-society relationships involve entrepreneurial practices where public officials and private investors provide networking services while simultaneously lining their pockets.[30] As Tu Nguyen asserts, "In a political climate in which administrative power is decentralised and diffused, the growth of non-conventional interests and new modes of mass mobilisation convolutes the power hierarchies and blurs the line separating public and private interests."[31] Importantly, Vietnam's decentralized government has led to much internal variation related to state-market-society. Edmund Malesky, Neil McCulloch, and Nguyen Duc Nhat point out that it is important to look at the internal variation of governance within countries. In their view, "Most business/government interactions [are] decentralized to the provincial level, including business registration, environmental and safety inspections, labour oversight, local government procurement, and land allocation. . . . As a result, many studies have documented that the provincial government, more than the central government, is the relevant level of government when analyzing the institutional climate facing firms."[32] Their findings point to the possibility that multiple state-market relations can exist within the same state, depending on the investment project's provincial location and the relationship that both local and foreign investors have with their local state officials. The varied relationships that investors have with state officials are crucial because Vietnam does not have strong legal institutions and the law is open to interpretation at the provincial level.

Hun Kim's and my qualitative research on inter-Asian circulations of capital in Ho Chi Minh City's property market further reveals that the city is being remade through different circuits of foreign capital.[33] The rise of East Asian financial centers dramatically altered intraregional investment, transforming less developed countries in Southeast Asia into a lucrative new frontier, thus increasing inter-Asian circulations of capital.[34] Political elites in less developed countries must now find ways to appeal to local entrepreneurs, Western (US, Canadian, and Western European) investors, and Japanese investors, as well as investors from other parts of East/Southeast Asia.[35] At the same time, recent global economic transformations have produced a newly competitive landscape for Western and East/Southeast Asian investors looking to invest in emerging markets.[36]

The competing circuits of FDI are "grounded in state experimentation with variegated governing techniques and competing regulatory modes that drive the city's development."[37] Importantly, Kim shows how opaque and transparent modalities of reform coexist in the same market. Developing the concept of *regulatory opacity*, Kim describes the practices of state agencies and urban developers as they negotiate a multitude of urban development regulations at both urban and national levels. Kim's concept of *regulatory transparency* highlights the work of the state, in concert with multilateral institutions, to address the problem of state corruption in urban development. These two contradictory modes of governance—

opacity and transparency—coexist in the same space. Advancing Kim's work by looking at this relationship from the perspective of market actors, I argue that the varying degrees of legal transparency and opacity, coupled with a decentralized government, enable local and state officials to keep profits generated through resource extraction in the hands of local elites.[38]

Research Methods

Data collected for my larger book project map a global network of financial elites throughout the world.[39] Overall, I conducted twenty-six months of ethnographic- and interview-based research in three main phases: 2009–2010, 2012–2015, and eighteen continuous months during 2016–2017. During 2016–2017 I traveled more than 350,000 miles, following the movement of global capital from offshore accounts in such places as the British Virgin Islands, the Cayman Islands, Samoa, and Panama to special-purpose vehicles or holding companies in Singapore and Hong Kong before being invested onshore in Vietnam and Myanmar. I also conducted follow-up interviews on shorter research trips during 2017–2019. In total, I interviewed more than three hundred respondents, including private wealth managers, fund managers, chairpersons, local entrepreneurs, C-suite executives, lawyers, bankers, auditors, and company secretaries. The investment deals I have studied range between $200,000 and $450 million and include such sectors as real estate, manufacturing, mining, technology, the service sector, and trade. I had the generous help of thirteen research assistants who spent a great deal of time with me helping to recruit research subjects, accompanying me on interviews, writing field notes, transcribing, coding the data, writing narrative summaries, and helping me comb the internet for news articles, legal proceedings, and press releases in order to triangulate our case studies.

Overall, only 52 percent of my interview subjects gave me permission to audio-record. For those who did not allow me to record their interviews, I took extensive field notes; if a student accompanied me, he or she did the same so that I had two sets of notes for each interview.

This chapter focuses on a small subset of interviews in the mining sector. To anonymize my research subjects, I do not use the real names of the people, firms, or natural resources in this chapter. In addition, I created a composite case by merging three cases with similar investors into one in order to anonymize all of the people with whom I spoke. The reason for this is that there are only two or three major mining projects in the country; the same is true for oil and gas companies. Therefore, naming the strategic resource would make it impossible to anonymize my research subjects. In addition, I triangulate interview data with legal documents, press releases, and media interviews to gain some perspective outside of the protagonist who leads the story from the interview. I focus on a natural resource in a highly protected sector of the economy that has heavy state involvement.

Mining for Capital: A Showdown between Foreign Investors and the Government

VIETNAM AS THE MODERN "EL DORADO"

George began his relationship with Vietnam after his first trip in 1989, when a small group of investors came to Vietnam, all in search of "an El Dorado," as he called it. At that time he told me, "Your typical mining areas are often very well developed and tightly controlled and tightly owned. So you are always looking for something where the chances of finding something are better and the chances of finding something bigger are better." He was then working in Australia, where it was difficult to find good ground because all the major mines had already been explored with advanced technologies.

The logics of colonial racial capitalism are evident in George's motives to go to Vietnam in search of a new frontier, or "El Dorado," as he called it. Vietnam was attractive to George and his team because it was just beginning to open up and had not been explored with modern technologies. George told me that in their own research, a look back in time showed that Vietnam was once a place that had been mined by explorers from all around the world. In one of their corporate presentations, which they used to raise capital, they had a slide that detailed the history that dates back to 1850, when Chinese miners first discovered *Vietranium* in Vietnam (*Vietranium* is the pseudonym for the real mineral). Then in the early 1900s, a major British development company mined small shallow pits with limited tunnels. Sometime between 1950 and 2000, a group from an unidentified country (possibly Thailand, based on our interview) dug a couple of tunnels and ended its development after concluding that the price of the mineral was too low and not worth the exploration, development, and extraction efforts. By the time George began poking around, he said: "Historically we always knew that Vietnam was a good *Vietranium* producer. There were some well-known mines that the French had mined, the Portuguese mined, and geologically when you look at it from space and all of the records, it looked like a very good area to be in, and it was just opening up. It was a country [where] we felt we could acquire good land packages that were a reasonable size and productive." This history allowed George and his team to generate a great deal of buzz around the mine in order to raise capital based purely on speculation. Using a speculative logic of potential, George was able to raise money from global financial institutions and small mom-and-pop investors interested in entering this highly speculative new frontier.

When I asked him about the risks going in, he told me that some of their major concerns were that there was a lack of "good working mining legislation and a lack of any international mining infrastructure in terms of knowledge, administration, and modern commercial economics." In their initial discussions with government officials, they spent four to five years negotiating between their tax rate and what the government wanted. From George's perspective, they wanted certainty up front, and their idea of what would be an acceptable profit was different from the government's. They believed that the investment came with great risks that the government did not understand because officials could not comprehend the modern business structure or technology that would be required in the research and exploration phase.

At the same time, these officials believed that it would not be fair if George and his team took charge, had a great commercial success, and made a fortune because *Vietranium* was inherently a product of Vietnam; therefore, any profits belonged to the Vietnamese people. After years of not being able to negotiate a "sound business agreement with the government and what the [Communist] Party put forward," they ended up buying into a project where all of that had already been negotiated and the existing partner was looking for an opportunity to exit.

COWBOY DAYS OF VIETNAM

Once George and his partners got the license, they had to do a lot of work before they were comfortable putting money into the production process of the mine. As George explained, "There were a whole lot of cowboys around Vietnam in that time, and a lot of promises were made in that time just so they could get the documentation in place." In a postcolonial/imperial state it was difficult for them to figure out who were the important political power players or who had access to the key government officials who could help move their project along. In the beginning they relied a great deal on middlemen, otherwise known as brokers or fixers. George stated: "They were a lot of carpetbaggers walking around. They were guys promising that they could get you deals and were asking for money up front to do it, and in the end it was almost impossible for anyone to give you a deal. There were a lot of guys saying they had relationships that could get you a deal like they knew the daughter or wife of this person, and you would just have to pay the money, [but] you wouldn't get anywhere."

Over the course of nearly thirty years in Vietnam, the one lesson George learned was that negotiations with government officials were a "full-time dynamic and ever-changing process," as he described it. This regulatory opacity—the lack of clarity with regard to regulations and legislation—meant that every step of the process had to be negotiated. Moreover, because the people in positions of political power shift every couple of years, all of these relationships had to be renegotiated with every new election, making it exceptionally difficult to develop long-term projections. Given the sheer number of years that George had spent in Vietnam, it seemed like he might feel very confident about knowing how to navigate government relations. In fact, several other interviewees who had made investments in very different sectors of the economy told me that George was someone to whom they often went to seek advice on how to manage government relations. When I asked him to reflect on how his strategies for dealing with government relations had evolved over the years, he said:

> This is the puzzle of Vietnam. I don't think you ever quite solve the puzzle, because the puzzle is constantly changing, because Vietnam doesn't seem to have one strong man or one strong woman or a strong entity. It's a difference between being designed that way—it's as if the communist system has been designed [so] that no one ever truly gets full decision making. It will always need the support of someone else. Those political alliances or allegiances are constantly changing, and they all have different political capital that they are using for different projects, and it is a constantly changing wind. You are constantly at a stage of wondering if you have enough support to keep a project moving.

George went on to describe how state officials are constantly shifting positions every four to five years with each new election cycle in the party:

There always seems to be someone retiring in the next twelve to eighteen months, and they are aggressive. I've got to make as much money as possible, so I am not signing or doing anything unless there is a lot of money on the table. It always seems to be someone that you need. . . . [With] natural resources, there is a lot more control [because] the Vietnamese treat their oil, coal, and gold resources as theirs. When I think of property, I think you have the owner of land on one side and the rest of the bureaucracy you have to find your way through. . . . But the owner of our land is typically the government. . . . I spend 70 percent of my time dealing with government relations.

For George and his partners, one of the greatest risks and areas of uncertainty had less to do with the actual processes of exploration, extraction, and production in the mine and much more to do with managing the dynamic relations with government officials. With every new election cycle, they had to deal with a new set of personalities and demands that were much less predictable under a system without a clear set of written state policies and legislation.

Ironically, the move to Vietnam turned out to be a double-edged sword. On the one hand, because it was a country that was just opening up, with a lack of clear legislation, it had a frontier "El Dorado" feel, where George and his partners could gamble and cash in on the "gold rush." On the other hand, the lack of clear legislation also meant that they were constantly beholden to the different people who occupied various positions of power. This tug-of-war could eventually be the demise of their entire investment.

THE "BACK TAX": NAVIGATING MURKY RELATIONSHIPS WITH VIETNAMESE GOVERNMENT OFFICIALS

In negotiating the tension between navigating an unpredictable bureaucracy and trying to move forward with their investment, George and his partners did a lot of "front running" in the early stages of development, when they moved forward on investments without the proper licenses in place at the start of a project. He said:

We are a little bit like property people; you have to front run quite a lot, to the extent you can. But more and more now, it is difficult for us to do anything without approvals and licensing first. In the early days, [government officials] pushed us to get into production . . . before it was commercially viable. Then it seemed once you do get into production and you are making money—for a while the process worked. You got approvals when you needed them because money was flowing, people were getting paid, taxes were being paid. And then we fell afoul with the tax department, and life became impossible. You didn't get anything. That was really hard because we spent $140 million while the government was trying to shut us down, and we had to find a way to keep going.

What George described was pressure from the government to raise money and begin the production phase in the mine. The project had raised over $140 million through a variety of different sources, from institutional investors to small mom-and-pop investors, who, according to the court documents, had invested as little as $2,500. When things were going well, he explained, "they were flush with investment money, and everyone was getting paid."

Then one day the government effectively shut them down by issuing them a back-tax bill once it discovered that the mine was commercially viable; this was a strategy to push the investors out. George said:

What happened was one day we woke up, and the tax department said we owed them $15 million without any basis. They had done a similar thing to [a large company that George was acquainted with], and I think there was another motor vehicle company, and it was just a shakedown. The grossly inefficient government departments are told by the Ministry of Finance that they need to raise more money, and just like in the old days when businesses were government owned, government business had to find more money and satisfy the state budget. . . .

It is hard to know when to involve lawyers, because . . . law firms are not well established. The law is totally different. It's not strength-based law, where the government is constantly putting out directives. . . . It's mainly negotiation. You have to work behind the department and work one department off of another one. For example, . . . we had to go to the Ministry of Science and show what the *Vietranium* processing was, and they said that it was obvious that we had processed the ore into some sort of state, and the tax department would say they disagree and determine the tax. That took us years. In the meantime, we had this $15 million back tax hanging over our heads, and there was no way we could pay the $15 million because we would never get it back. So we then came under *tax coercion*, which means they were constantly taking away our invoice book, constantly trying to shut us down, and made an administrative nightmare for us. . . . We tried all sorts of lobbying groups and law firms, and none of them would take the case because we were dealing with the [highest level of government], and they are very corrupt. They didn't want to use their political capital representing us. Their only suggestion was that we owed $15 million and we probably [would] just have to pay 10 percent of that in bribes, but there is no way we can pay a $1.5 million bribe. I am listed on global securities in Canada and Australia. I know where I would end up [implying jail].

From George's perspective, the lack of a clear rule of law with respect to taxes meant that the government could arbitrarily levy a $15 million back tax, which would place the investment in a status of noncompliance and affect its listing on the US, Canadian, and Australian stock exchanges. This status could force them into bankruptcy, effectively pushing George and his partners out of the country.

George also described how challenging it had been to get proper media attention to portray their side of the story. He compared Vietnam to Korea: "There are a smaller number of really powerful Vietnamese businessmen who are also politicians, who are trying to collect the full sweep of investments in the Korean way. The political interests and the media would always work against the foreign investor because the Vietnamese [politicians and bureaucrats] are incredibly nationalistic and patriotic, almost xenophobic. They hate to see foreigners come in and mine natural resources and take profits out of the country." George was describing a tension that resonates with Vietnam's history of colonialism, anticolonialism, and imperialism. As a foreign investor, he saw government relations deteriorate as the government tried to push them out after discovering that the mine had valuable resources. In this way, George's efforts to bring "modern technologies" to a new frontier backfired as the government took the mine back after the most risky and speculative stage of investment. However, from the government's perspective, those resources belonged to the country and were not something they would allow a foreign investor to easily exploit.

THE VIETNAMESE GOVERNMENT'S PERSPECTIVE

Although I was not able to formally interview the government officials linked to this specific project, several interviews and reports by journalists helped me to triangulate this case from the government's perspective.

In an interview the director of the Department of Taxation told the press that "there were signs that these companies had sold their mineral to parent companies at less than market prices while materials were imported at higher prices to evade taxes." In the same report, the deputy prime minister told local authorities that "tax debts must be collected or guaranteed before the two *Vietranium* mining companies are issued new licenses."[40] This back tax was assessed after the mining company reported cumulative losses of $30 million in 2014. What government officials are referring to here is the process through which investors book their liabilities onshore in Vietnam while declaring their profits offshore in another country. These tax-avoidance strategies have long been attributed to foreign investors.

I read the government officials' public statements, and then I searched through the court filings to find a detailed chart of the mining company's tax default as the company worked to declare bankruptcy. The court documents revealed the complex ownership structure of the companies, which led the government to conclude that George and his team were trying to evade taxes onshore. Figure 4.3 shows the legal offshore structures George and his team set up all around the world. The Vietnamese entities are subsidiaries of companies in Thailand and the British Virgin Islands, and the latter two are a subsidiary of a company incorporated in North America. Given the setup of this structure, it not difficult to see why the government might conclude that George and his group were not being honest about their earnings.

After two years of unsuccessful negotiations over their tax bill, the Vietnamese government revoked their business registration certificate, forcing the mining company to stop all operations. Public reports stated that at the time of losing its business license, the mine had already racked up over $145 million in losses. In 2017 George and his firm announced its withdrawal from Vietnam and stated that the companies would be sold to get money in order to repay their debts. Following this announcement, several people in Vietnam commented on what they felt were problems with the mine and its relationship to the government.

However, the buyers of the companies were two of the firm's former executives. As local advisers to the government began investigating, they told the press, "The biggest question is why a heavily indebted company can be sold. The buyers understand the problems with the companies and therefore, it is a mystery why they bought such bad companies. Maybe the buyers have found the solutions to the companies' problems *or* it is just a game played by foreign investors?" (emphasis added).

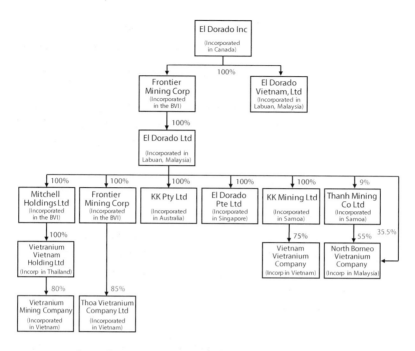

FIGURE 4.3. El Dorado Mining Company ownership structure. Source: author composite.

In my conversations with George, he insisted that all of this was a calculated ploy by the Vietnamese government to smear the company's image in the country. He insisted that they were honest with their reporting and that they were good guys caught in a bad system, where everyone is believed to be underreporting their earnings. He said:

> We responded to [those reports by] saying that we are an international company, and we are listed on reputable stock exchanges; we are audited by international auditors, and we can't do that. But they had a mindset at the time—they weren't worldly and they thought, "*We know auditors can be bought, everyone can be bought,*" and they didn't trust us. I don't know whether it was if they truly believed that or not or if there was a plan to squeeze us out, but the effect was that the pressure came from all directions, and very few people were willing to stand behind us.
>
> Quite frankly we cannot pay huge bribes; we cannot pay $200,000 here, $500,000 there, and $1 million over there. We can't do it.

In some respects, I believe most of the wealth created in Vietnam is through corruption and comes from internal contracts . . . the building of infrastructure, roads, bridges, courts, airports. This is why with the TPP, they really insisted on private investors being able to sue the government. Americans had a similar problem in China because 97 percent of the economy was the government. . . .

In our case, when it came to a problem of renewing licenses . . . they said openly in the People's Committee when they met us [that] "you will not be able to renew this license until you bring a Vietnamese partner up to a certain percent ownership, and we want the Vietnamese partner to be in control and we want them to be in control of the money."

The press is controlled. When we said to the [People's Committee] that if you keep up the royalty, then we will shut down. Their response was "Don't threaten us." . . . We are not threatening you; it's a fact! We cannot afford to pay it, and they would say we are cheap. . . . We are captive. No one will buy this project; Vietnam is a pariah. . . . No one will put in more money.

What George was describing is a showdown between El Dorado Mining and the Vietnamese government. Neither party trusted the other, and both felt that they were fundamentally being cheated somehow. The tension escalated as El Dorado Mining solicited help from foreign embassies and governments, but Vietnam's unwillingness to back down led George and his group to begin financially engineering the sale and transfer of the company within the same group of people. After over two years of being in a standoff with the government, however, George sold their stake in the firm to a group of other executives. Shortly after that, they declared bankruptcy and left Vietnam for good. In my last follow-up conversation with him, they were pursuing legal advice and public relations consulting in London but did not feel hopeful that they would reach any kind of resolution with the government.

In the end, the truth probably lies somewhere in between what the government claims to be an underreporting of earnings and what George and his firm believed was a hostage takeover of a business that was just beginning to generate profits as a result of its refusal to pay out bribes. Vietnam's resistance to new forms of economic colonialism has greatly affected both parties, for George and his team are now mired in a whole slew of lawsuits from their investors, seeking to collect the debt owed to them, while the government manages a mine that once employed more than two thousand people and now is boarded up and completely empty. This kind of loss that George described is one where it is very difficult to see light at the end of a tunnel because nearly thirty years of nonstop negotiations led to a government takeover of their business.

Resisting Neocolonialism

In the foreword to Frantz Fanon's *The Wretched of the Earth*, Homi Bhabha writes,

> It must seem ironic, even absurd at first, to search for associations and intersections between decolonization and globalization—parallels would be pushing the analogy—when decolonization had the dream of a "Third World" of free, postcolonial nations firmly on its horizon, whereas globalization gazes at the nation through the back mirror, as it speeds toward the strategic denationalization of state sovereignty. . . . While it is the primary purpose of decolonization to repossess land and territoriality in order to ensure the security of the national polity and global equity . . . in what way, then can the once colonized . . . become figures of instruction for our global century?[41]

At the time of Bhabha's writing, the humanities and social sciences were fixated on the divide between First World nations and Third World nations that had emerged as a consequence of colonialism.

Today, that very world order has become less stable. The rise of China and other East and Southeast Asian nations has given smaller countries like Vietnam a platform not only to resist new forms of neo-economic colonialism from Western nationals but also to test the limits of their economic relations with Western investors by allowing them to pour money into a country, asking them to assume a great deal of risk in the early stages of mining for capital and raising capital, and then effectively pushing investors out of the country once they have struck gold in the "El Dorado." For Fanon and Bhabha, this very act serves the purpose of decolonization, but what does that mean, and how do we theorize that in a postcolonial context?

From the perspective of foreign investors, this case study illustrates the ways that colonial relations of the past helped investors legitimize the project by speculating that *Vietranium* was in fact there and that all they needed was money to bring modern technologies to Vietnam. From the perspective of Vietnamese state officials, however, pushing investors out after they had effectively mined the area serves as a model for how other nations might still be able to hold on to what is theirs. But in an increasingly global world where the top 1 to 10 percent of the global elite are effectively citizens of many places, who even benefits from resistance struggles between global and local elites?

In a postcolonial and postwar context, after the Vietnamese effectively fought off the Chinese, the French, and the Americans, for years they were dependent on these very countries for both public aid and private investment. As several countries vied for economic influence in the country, this provided Vietnam with the power to pit powerful nations against each other. The new competition between China and the United States has enabled Vietnam to turn away from Western capital and toward East and Southeast Asian investors, thereby resisting the "peremptory and polarizing choices that superpowers impose on their 'client' states."[42] But does resisting one form of colonialism come with the pressure to accept another form? In pushing Western investors out of the country, Vietnamese state officials now have the power to choose between two "varieties of capital": (a) state capital, which comes from many different countries, such as China, and serves the interests of the state; and (b) global private capital, which serves the interests of shareholders.[43] Given the rise of non-Western nations, are we beginning to see one form of domination replacing another?

The colonial racial capitalism framework in this chapter examines the case of a communist postcolonial/post-imperial state and analyzes how that state relies on neoliberal policies to expand global capitalism while also privileging state ownership and control over important natural resources in the mines. It is this tension between foreign investors and local anticolonialists that interrupts the transfer of wealth from Vietnam to foreign capitalists. Therefore, a racial framework here must take into account the fact that "race" looks different not just in different countries but in different governments and different investment narratives that are not easily collapsed as working only in the interests of global capitalists. We must think about the multiple layers involved in a context of colonial racial capitalism that allows global elites to capitalize on inside access to deals and resources. At the heart of this chapter is a story of how Vietnamese state actors actively push back against neo-economic colonialism. Local state elites adopt a strategy of allowing foreigners to come in to explore and develop the mines and then pushing out foreigners after they have been able to mine valuable resources. At the same time, because these investments are so risky, foreigners use offshore vehicles that allow for high levels of financial speculation to capture capital offshore and to protect their investments from full state capture. This is not a simple story of exploiter/exploited, colonizer/dispossessed, but rather a new tension that is possible only in the aftermath of colonialism and imperialism.

This changing global economic order opens the door for a new set of questions about how to theorize and conceptualize colonialism outside of overused binaries like East/West, global North/global South, or First World/Third World. New South–South relations, coupled with the persistent weakening of Western power, have fundamentally shifted the political economic landscape and require new theories of postcolonialism as new insurgent economic groups test the limits of Western power.

Directions for Future Research

In an effort to study capitalists and the flow of capital, this chapter focuses primarily on the friction between local and global elites. However, underneath this tension is an important land and labor story. Future research would benefit from an analysis of how these relations of colonial racial capitalism affect the miners and the communities located around the mining industries. The view that I had was a view from above: looking at investment sites through the eyes of local elites and foreign investors. The view from above highlights a story of capital, investment, and nation. However, a view from below would focus on a labor story that is a consequence of these elite power struggles. No one triangulates the view from above with the view from below, but there is an important body of work in the area of racial capitalism that zooms in to focus on the consequences of foreign investment and development for local communities. For example, a critical view offered by Macarena Gómez-Barris is one that highlights how the extractive nature of capitalism in mining often involves a search for "undeveloped" Indigenous people's land.[44]

These neocolonial power struggles at the top have two possible effects. On the one hand, mining will likely have an effect on the land and communities most vulnerable to exploitation, as so many others have described. On the other hand, Nhi Ba Nguyen and colleagues have found that mining is one of the drivers of socioeconomic well-being at the national level.[45] These findings seem to leave open the possibility that the local government's adoption of a protectionist stance might be the key mechanism to the redistribution of wealth locally by drawing on investors at a global scale. Hence, a focus on the people embedded in these mining communities in the contexts of a power struggle between foreign capitalists and local elites might address a much larger question of who ultimately wins and loses in a context of colonial racial capitalism.

NOTES

1. World Bank, "Global Financial Development."

2. Freeland, *Plutocrats*.

3. Mohanty, " 'Under Western Eyes Revisited,' " 505–6. Mohanty borrows the terms *One-Third World* and *Two-Thirds World* from Gustavo Esteva and Madhu Suri Prakash, who use them to refer to social minorities and social majorities in both the North and the South that are differentiated by their quality of life (Esteva and Prakash, *Grassroots Post-modernism*, 16–17). The terms avoid the geographical and ideological binarism of terms like *First World* and *Third World* and highlight uneven development within and across affluent and postcolonial nations under global capitalism.

4. O'Neill, *Growth Map*, x.

5. Hoskisson et al., "Strategy in Emerging Economies"; Gray, "World's Fastest Growing Economies."

6. Davis and Marquis, "Prospects for Organizational Theory."

7. North, *Institutions, Institutional Change*.

8. Fligstein, *Architecture of Markets*; Gereffi, "Global Economy"; Storz et al., "Bringing Asia"; Witt and Redding, "Asian Business Systems."

9. Kang, *Crony Capitalism*.

10. Krippner, "Unbounding the Economy."

11. Byrd et al., "Predatory Value."

12. Burawoy, "Extended Case Method," 5, 6.

13. This colonial racial capitalism framework emerged through feedback given to me by Lisa Cacho as she engaged with my public lecture at the Race and Capitalism Conference held at the University of Illinois, Urbana-Champaign, in 2019 and from her feedback on the working draft of this chapter. I would also like to thank my research assistant, Brian Fenaughty, for his critical engagement with the ideas here.

14. To date, most of the research on mining in Vietnam has looked primarily on the role that mining has played with respect to economic development and its ability to influence the livelihoods of local communities. See, for example, N. Nguyen, Boruff, and Tonts, "Mining, Development, and Well-Being."

15. Wood, "Basic Needs."

16. Chanda, *Brother Enemy*, 11.

17. Chanda, *Brother Enemy*, 180–81.

18. Chanda, *Brother Enemy*, 181.

19. Hoang, *Dealing in Desire*.

20. Davies, "Vietnam 40 Years On."

21. Stark and Bruszt, *Postsocialist Pathways*, 130.

22. Hoang, "Risky Investments."

23. T. N. Nguyen, "Foreign Direct Investment."

24. N. Nguyen, Boruff, and Tonts, "Mining, Development and Well-Being."

25. GSO of Vietnam, *Foreign Direct Investment Projects*.

26. Hoang, *Dealing in Desire*; Hoang, Cobb, and Lei, "Guest Editors' Introduction."

27. USTR, "Trans-Pacific Partnership."

28. Mishra, "Rise of China."

29. Witt and Redding, "Asian Business Systems."

30. See, for example, Beresford, "*Doi Moi* in Review"; and Gillen, "Examination of Entrepreneurial Relationships."

31. T. P. Nguyen, "Rethinking State-Society Relations in Vietnam," 100.

32. Malesky, McCulloch, and Nhat, "Impact of Governance and Transparency," 681.

33. Kim, "Capturing World-Class Urbanism"; Hoang, "Risky Investments."

34. Koolhaas, "Beijing Manifesto."

35. Hoang, "Risky Investments."

36. Nam, "Phnom Penh."

37. Kim, "Capturing World Class Urbanism."

38. Hoang, "Risky Investments."

39. Hoang, *Spiderweb Capitalism*.

40. *Vietnam Economic Times* article from 2016, not described here to maintain anonymity of research subjects.

41. Bhabha, Foreword, xi.

42. Bhabha, Foreword, xiv.

43. Lee, *Specter of Global China*.

44. Gómez-Barris, "Mapuche Mnemonics."

45. N. Nguyen, Boruff, and Tonts, "Mining, Development and Well-Being."

Beresford, Melanie. "*Doi Moi* in Review: The Challenges of Building Market Socialism in Vietnam." *Journal of Contemporary Asia* 38 (2008): 221–43.

Bhabha, Homi K. Foreword to *The Wretched of the Earth*, by Frantz Fanon, vii–xli. New York: Grove, 2004.

Burawoy, Michael. "The Extended Case Method." *Sociological Theory* 16, no. 1 (1998): 4–33.

Byrd, Jodi, Alyosha Goldstein, Jodi Melamed, and Chandan Reddy. "Predatory Value: Economies of Dispossession and Disturbed Relationalities." *Social Text* 36, no. 2 (2018): 1–18.

Chanda, Nayan. *Brother Enemy: The War after the War—A History of Indochina since the Fall of Saigon*. New York: Macmillan, 1986.

Davies, Nick. "Vietnam 40 Years On: How a Communist Victory Gave Way to Capitalist Corruption." *Guardian*, April 22, 2015. https://www.theguardian.com/news/2015/apr/22/vietnam-40-years-on-how-communist-victory-gave-way-to-capitalist-corruption.

Davis, Gerald, and Christopher Marquis. "Prospects for Organizational Theory in the Early 21st Century: Institutional Fields and Mechanisms." *Organizational Science* 16, no. 4 (2005): 332–43.

Esteva, Gustavo, and Madhu Suri Prakash. *Grassroots Post-modernism: Remaking the Soil of Cultures*. London: Zed, 1998.

Fligstein, Neil. *The Architecture of Markets: An Economic Sociology of Capitalist Societies*. Princeton, NJ: Princeton University Press, 2001.

Freeland, Chrystia. *Plutocrats: The Rise of the New Global Super-Rich and the Fall of Everyone Else*. New York: Penguin, 2012.

General Statistics Office (GSO) of Vietnam. *Foreign Direct Investment Projects Licensed in Period 1988–2010*. Ministry of Planning and Investment, 2011.

Gereffi, Gary. "The Global Economy: Organziation, Governance, and Development." In *The Handbook of Economic Sociology*, 2nd ed., edited by Neil J. Smelser and Richard Swedberg, 160–82. Princeton, NJ: Princeton University Press, 2005.

Gillen, Jamie. "An Examination of Entrepreneurial Relationships between the State and Nonstate in Ho Chi Minh City, Vietnam." *Urban Geography* 31, no. 1 (2010): 90–113.

Gómez-Barris, Macarena. "Mapuche Mnemonics: Reversing the Colonial Gaze through New Visualities of Extractive Capitalism." *Radical History Review* 124 (2016): 90–101.

Gray, Alex. "These Are the World's Fastest-Growing Economies in 2017." 2017 World Economic Forum. www.weforum.org/agenda/2017/06/these-are-the-world-s-fastest-growing-economies-in-2017-2.

Hoang, Kimberly Kay. *Dealing in Desire: Asian Ascendancy, Western Decline, and the Hidden Currencies of Global Sex Work*. Oakland: University of California Press, 2015.

Hoang, Kimberly Kay. "Risky Investments: How Local and Foreign Investors Finesse Corruption-Rife Emerging Markets." *American Sociological Review* 83, no. 4 (2018): 657–85.

Hoang, Kimberly Kay. *Spiderweb Capitalism: How Global Elites Exploit Frontier Markets*. Princeton, NJ: Princeton University Press, forthcoming.

Hoang, Kimberly Kay, Jessica Cobb, and Ya-Wen Lei. "Guest Editors' Introduction: Inter-Asian Capital Circulations, Cultural Transformations, and Methodological Positions." *positions: asia critique* 25, no. 4 (2017): 633–44.

Hoskisson, Robert, Lorraine Eden, Chung Ming Lau, and Mike Wright. "Strategy in Emerging Economies." *Academy of Management Journal* 43, no. 3 (2000): 249–67.

Kang, David. *Crony Capitalism: Corruption and Development in South Korea and the Philippines*. New York: Cambridge University Press, 2002.

Kim, Hun. "Capturing World Class Urbanism through Modal Governance in Saigon." *positions* 25, no. 4 (2017): 669–92.

Koolhaas, Rem. "Beijing Manifesto." *Wired*, August 1, 2004.

Krippner, Greta. "Unbounding the Economy." *Socio-Economic Review* 15, no. 3 (2017): 679–90.

Lee, Ching Kwan. *The Specter of Global China: Politics, Labor, and Foreign Investment in Africa*. Chicago: University of Chicago Press, 2017.

Malesky, Edmund, Neil McCulloch, and Nguyen Duc Nhat. "The Impact of Governance and Transparency on Firm Investment in Vietnam." *Economics of Transition* 23, no. 4 (2015): 677–715.

Mishra, Pankaj. "The Rise of China and the Fall of the 'Free Trade' Myth." *New York Times Magazine*, February 7, 2018. https://www.nytimes.com/2018/02/07/magazine/the-rise-of-china-and-the-fall-of-the-free-trade-myth.html.

Mohanty, Chandra. "'Under Western Eyes' Revisited: Feminist Solidarity through Anticapitalist Struggles." *Signs: Journal of Women in Culture and Society* 28, no. 2 (2002): 499–535.

Nam, Sylvia. "Phnom Penh: From the Politics of Ruin to the Possibilities of Return." *Traditional Dwellings and Settlements Review* 22, no. 1 (2011): 55–68.

Nguyen, Hung. 2015. "Seminar Held on Fdi Impact." *Vietnam Economic Times*, October 4, 2015. http://vneconomictimes.com:8081/article/vietnam-today/seminar-held-on-fdi-impact.

Nguyen, Nhi Ba, Bryan Boruff, and Matthew Tonts. "Mining, Development and Well-Being in Vietnam: A Comparative Analysis." *Extractive Industries and Society* 4 (2017): 564–75.

Nguyen, Thanh Nga. "Foreign Direct Investment in Real Estate Projects and Macroeconomic Instability." ASEAN *Economic Bulletin* 28, no. 1 (2011): 74–96.

Nguyen, Tu Phuong. "Rethinking State-Society Relations in Vietnam: The Case of Business Associations in Ho Chi Minh City." *Asian Studies Review* 38, no. 1 (2014): 87–106.

North, Douglass. *Institutions, Institutional Change and Economic Performance.* Cambridge: Cambridge University Press, 1990.

O'Neill, Jim. *The Growth Map: Economic Opportunity in the BRICs and Beyond.* London: Penguin, 2013.

Stark, David, and Laszlo Bruszt. *Postsocialist Pathways: Transforming Politics and Property in East Central Europe.* New York: Cambridge University Press, 1998.

Storz, Cornelia, Bruno Amable, Steven Casper, and Sebastien Lechevalier. "Bringing Asia into the Comparative Capitalism Perspective." *Socio-Economic Review* 11, no. 2 (2011): 217–32.

USTR (Office of the United States Trade Representative). 2016. "The Trans-Pacific Partnership." https://ustr.gov/sites/default/files/TPP-Strategic-Importance -of-TPP-Fact-Sheet.pdf.

Witt, Michael, and Gordon Redding. "Asian Business Systems: Institutional Comparison, Clusters and Implications for Varieties of Capitalism and Business Systems Theory." *Socio-Economic Review* 11, no. 2 (2011): 265–300.

Wood, Robert. "Basic Needs and the Limits of Regime Change." In *From Marshall Aid to Debt Crisis: Foreign Aid and Development Choices in the World Economy,* edited by Robert E. Wood, 195–231. Berkeley: University of California Press, 1986.

World Bank. "Global Financial Development." Policy Research Working Paper 6175, *Benchmarking Financial Systems around the World.* Washington, DC: World Bank, 2012.

"Don't Arrest Me, Arrest the Police": Policing as the Street Administration of Colonial Racial Capitalist Orders

As Black-led marches took to the streets of Milwaukee night after night in May, June, July, and August of 2020, long-time Indigenous community defenders lit a ceremonial fire, calling it a unity fire. There would be many more unity fires in the coming months, but this particular fire burned for four days.[1] When the fire was lit, Mark Denning, the unity fire's first firekeeper, described it as a gathering for Milwaukee's Indigenous community to come together in a time of illness, isolation, and unrest. They enacted Indigenous sovereignty and governance by listening and thinking together in ceremony and preparing for diplomacy with elected settler city officials.[2] As uprisings against police violence continued to hold the streets of Milwaukee, Indigenous community defenders invited Black march leaders, various religious groups, students, social justice organizations, and everyone else to participate in the unity fires. As Denning explained, the fire was for reflection, not congregation or rally.[3] Yet as the fire burned, it was clear that reflection can be collective and that collective reflection can itself become a ceremony for uniting consciousness and creating grounded relations.

The fire brought together people participating in Black radical uprisings with people participating in ongoing Indigenous existence-as-resistance, both experiencing the present, both respecting and honoring the land on which the fire had been lit and continued to burn. They shared stories about police violence, stories about the central role of police violence within long histories of anti-Blackness and eternities of anti-Indianism. They talked with one another about what matters, deep epistemes of Indigenous knowing and Black knowing, of knowing Milwaukee as Black liberator land despite premature death, of knowing Wisconsin as Indigenous homeland despite ongoing settler wars of conquest to diminish Native resurgence. These small but powerful sparks were co-enlivening Black and Indigenous lives, undoing the performative power of criminalization and undermining the ways in which criminalization devalues Black and Native lives to justify the many kinds of violences that colonial racial capitalisms require. Because it promoted collective reflection and intense, reciprocal listening, the unity fire opened possibilities, such as becoming relatives in a grounded relation with land as agential or enacting abolition and decolonization. The unity fire itself is about possibility. During some of the ceremonies, precious, life-giving medicines are burned. To explain why, Denning says, "One of our young people asked, if that medicine is so beautiful and so clean and wonderful, and you sing to it to help create it, to help someone out, why is it that you would destroy it? That to me kind of comes to the end of why this was done was because when those kinds of things come crashing down around a person, when destruction is present, sometimes, and not all the time, but sometimes creation can happen for something more beautiful."[4] As Denning explains, they lit a unity fire not to guarantee change but to create possibility for change, to light the sparks.

Unity fires continue to be lit in the city settlers call Milwaukee on Potawatomi, Ho-Chunk, and Menominee homeland because the sparks are needed and necessary, not only in this settler city but in all settler cities across the nation. George Floyd was Minneapolis police officer Derek Chauvin's second murder and fifth death. In 2005 Chauvin and another officer were chasing a vehicle that then hit another, causing two people to die on impact and a third passenger to die a few days later from the injuries. And in 2006 he murdered Wayne Reyes, a member of the Leech Lake Ojibwe Nation.[5] Indeed, we must credit seventeen-year-old Darnella Frazier, who filmed George Floyd's last moments, and the bystanders who were doing all they could, for saving countless lives that the four officers in Minneapolis would surely have taken throughout their careers. This scared, brave, traumatized teenager filmed the murder that became a movement not just against police violence but against what police violence is purposed to fabricate and defend: colonial racial capitalism.

In "Why *Black Marxism*, Why Now?" Robin D. G. Kelley describes 26 million people taking to the streets in the wake of the police murder of George Floyd as an uprising against racial capitalism.[6] Here we follow Kelley's thread and what the movement itself teaches us. In this chapter, we examine why the demand to live in the face of police violence—to defend *yourself* from the police while Black and/or Indigenous—is revolutionary and why the collective demand to defend *others* from the violences of colonial racial capitalisms (including police violence *and* the conditions of precarity, unlivability, and premature death that it secures) is also revolutionary. These acts are revolutionary because they know and denounce the purpose of police "violence work" to be the real-time, on-the-street administration of counterinsurgency for colonial racial capitalism.[7] They know that at the end of the day the police target the enlivening of BIPOC, queer, two-spirit, trans, and poor (or, more accurately, economically immiserated) lives when such enlivening (often and inevitably) targets the stability of colonial racial capitalist modes of accumulation by threatening relations of accumulation in a specific, political geography (i.e., real estate capitalisms that produce profits through racialized segregation) or by threatening its boundary conditions (seeing land as kin, rather than private property; demanding collective well-being that threatens capitalist modes of profiting from social reproduction by commodifying housing, health, food, and education).

To ground our thinking, we examine the summer 2020 uprisings against policing on the southwest shores of Michigami, where the Milwaukee, Menominee, and Kinnickinnic rivers meet on Potawatomi, Ho-Chunk, and Menominee homeland in the city that settlers call Milwaukee, which remains a meeting place for diasporic Indigenous people from throughout Turtle Island and has hosted Black liberators from the beginning of ongoing wars of conquest and occupation. Milwaukee, like every other settler city, is "a spatialized expression of settler violence."[8] In Milwaukee it is primarily the police, as the visible hand of collective settler violence, who target Indigenous empowerment—that is, the enlivening of Indigenous lives and the relatives and relations (human and more-than-human) that co-sustain Indigenous worldings. Undeniably, the target of policing is BIPOC empowerment: the enlivening of Black and Indigenous lives. Empowerment takes several forms. We see it in the basic form of a will to live, to save oneself and others from being killed by police, *and* in the determination to save others from the violences of colonial racial capitalism that require police violence. And we see it in collective empowerment, such as Indigenous unity fires and Black protest parties. The targets of policing are all those ways of living that portend the abolition of "deliberately propagated fatalities and forms and patterns that coalesce into premature death" that colonial racial capitalisms require.[9]

Policing is an administrative power that deploys violence work in real time to criminalize, disqualify, and sort people for capitalist care or capitalist destruction in order to fabricate and maintain specific relations of colonial racial capitalist accumulation in specific geographies.[10] Acts of resisting police power constitute threats to the colonial racial capitalist order, which is why such acts are revolutionary and hence so thoroughly criminalized. We argue that attempts to save your life and/or the lives of others from police violence or police-maintained organized abandonment while Black, brown, Asian, Indigenous, asset-stripped, and/or gender-nonconforming are not only powerful acts but also profoundly loving and breathtakingly insubordinate. To paraphrase Ruth Nicole Brown, defending yourself from or trying to evade police violence means that you love yourself more than you fear the police.[11] If you love yourself more than you fear the police, you defy the devaluing logics of colonial racial capitalism and the administrative powers that work to sustain it. If you love yourself more than you fear the police, then you repudiate police authority by affirming your right to be treated with dignity. If you love yourself more than you fear the police, you run or you resist arrest the moment you recognize that the officers are taking away the precious life you built for yourself. And if you love others more than you fear the police, then you risk your safety, your freedom, even your own life to protect others from harm. Decriminalizing saving one's life and others' lives from counterinsurgency policing is thus, at once, a pragmatic and revolutionary act.

Policing as Administrative Power: Killing with Impunity

In order to understand policing as the street administration of colonial racial capitalism, we have to understand the world system of liberal capitalist democracies, constitutively and continually structured by colonialism, racial domination, and heteropatriarchy, to be a mode of governance that irreducibly deploys criminalization, such that whole populations of people can be strategically—sometimes more or less permanently, sometimes "at will"—subject to rule by coercion, even as they exist within a capitalist world system that uses liberal freedoms (with violence)[12] as realizing praxis concepts to manifest and stabilize conditions of capital accumulation. Operationalized with and as racialization (usually but not necessarily along color lines), criminalization "sorts humans for capitalist care or destruction."[13] Criminalization reserves the capacity to exercise liberal "freedoms," to be governed by "consent," to participate in capitalist "democracy" (always limited, racialized, and settler/colonial) for privileged groups whose "consent" can be aligned with dominant capitalist classes.[14]

Developed over long histories of correlating liberalism, capitalism, race making, gender making, and colonialism, liberal capitalist democracies continually place the violence required by dominant capitalist arrangements (always racial, always colonial) outside the realm of the political by combining the materializing effects of liberalism's praxis concepts— property, deed, ownership—and the tool of criminalization to performatively constitute populations that can be left out of liberal rights for strategic purposes and to represent other nonliberal rights demands (collective, Indigenous) to be irrational, illegal, and immoral. Thus, for US capitalist democracy and elsewhere in the transnational order it helps articulate, criminalization is always our mode of governance, constitutively with liberal (always capitalist) rights.[15]

To understand police as administrators who criminalize as they do violence work for colonial racial capitalist orders in the United States (and other settler colonial and colonizing Western "democracies"), we have to leave behind a lot of stories that *liberalism writ large* (liberalism conceived as a thick episteme that organizes an enduring common sense) tells about itself: about the economy (free markets), the state (consent by the governed), and civil society. More to the point, we have to *stop thinking about liberalism in liberal terms*—that is, we have to stop thinking about it as primarily an economic, moral, or political philosophy that upholds individual rights, civil liberties, and economic freedoms. Instead, we should think of liberalism as a capitalist worlding praxis, as a realizing, onto-epistemological power, as a power that enables the ways in which capitalism not only tries to dictate how we exist in the world but also structures how we make sense of the world in which we live. In other words, to think of liberalism as a capitalist worlding praxis means to understand we cannot rely on liberal solutions (better laws and political rights) to colonial racial capitalism because colonial racial capitalism does not exist without liberalism.

Liberalism is founded in and continues to work through colonial administration, racial and gendered slavery, Indigenous dispossession, and the management of racial difference.[16] These liberal narratives of individual rights, civil liberties, and economic freedoms shape how we interpret our relations to one another, to land, and to all social and ecological life through a capitalist value-making system that reduces land to property, plants and animals to extractable resources, and human beings to their labor power as productive, reproductive, or unproductive. To think of liberalism as a capitalist worlding praxis means to understand that liberal narratives are schemas that colonial racial capitalists use to continually divide people, practices, domains, and situations into the political (hegemony) and the administrative (coercion). The work of the administrative is to ensure circulations of colonial racial capitalist accumulation and to manage the "ungovernable" through policing and bureaucracy.[17]

In order to understand how power—including police power—really works to secure and reproduce conditions for capital accumulation, we must again *think outside liberal epistemes*. If we use a colonial racial capitalist framework of analysis, we see that accumulation is operationalized through liberal onto-epistemes that are capitalist-worlding praxis concepts, always conjoined with specific formations of organized (police-military-privatized) physical violence, always targeting groups that are marked by the dominant as permitted to be violated through intersecting processes of racialization, gendering, heteropatriarchy, ethno-nationalism, and more. We also see that liberal modes of understanding separate "kinds" of power (political versus economic power, legal power versus police power, etc.) are useful subterfuges that disguise and deploy a more fundamental, operationalizing power for colonial racial capitalist orders that we call *administrative power*.

According to liberalism as a thick, enduring episteme, power is not located in what it defines as the "administrative"; rather, it is located in law, economy, politics, and popular will. For liberal epistemes, administration is just neutral procedures or technical routines that provide efficiency and ensure against bias—not a power itself. In contrast, the historical and lived experiences of much of humanity—sorted into groups through racialized, heteropatriarchal, settler colonial, and criminalizing schemes endemic to racial capitalist modernity and marked off for administrative (not political) governance—encounter "administrative power" as constitutive to and required for colonial racial capitalism, allowing us to see liberalism as a theory and practice of administration backed up by police-military-physical force.

Rather than power exercised merely as laws getting passed, technological progress, or political processes responding to the will of the people, liberal praxis concepts (politics, law, progress) can be understood as part of a kind of "it-gets-done (if-it-can-get-done)" administrative power. Under various kinds of duress and out of a moving base of forces (competitive, oppositional, alternative, residual, or emergent), specific dominating colonial racial capitalist class assemblages determine social processes as much as possible to realize accumulation, then recursively assemble law, political rationales, and technological fixes accordingly.

Far from being the handmaid to rule according to a "separation of powers," administrative power is at once legislative, adjudicating, and executive. It tries—and happily often fails—to arrange things in a way that appears apolitical so that day to day the empirical, accumulative goals of the reigning colonial racial capitalist bloc are achieved by hook or by crook. Police power, as a kind of administrative power, works this way. Rather than being a purely executive power or enforcement power, it operates recursively along a law-administration-force continuum, doing violence work that has already been justified as necessary to sustain reigning relations of accumulation (hyperbolized as "law and order"), then assembling legal, moral, standard operating protocol, and even using after-the-fact medical ("excited delirium," "sickle cell trait") justifications for acts of police violence.

In reality, this very logic was the foundation for the Uniform Arrest Act, first proposed in 1942. At the time, the vast majority of arrests by police officers were technically illegal. The Uniform Arrest Act proposed that states change their criminal laws so that officers' mostly illegal actions in practice would become legal on the books. To reconcile police officers' actions with the law on the books, the writer of the act, Sam B. Warner, spent months with officers to observe how they arrested people in practice. With the input of a committee consisting of police officers, judges, prosecutors, law professors, defense attorneys, and attorneys general, Warner drafted the act so that arrest laws would match officers' arresting, detaining, searching, and questioning procedures—essentially legalizing officers' illegal policing practices. For instance, in some states it was not legal for officers to use deadly force unless they were arresting someone who had committed a felony with violence. It was also a person's right to resist an illegal arrest with force; it was even within people's rights to kill an officer to protect themselves against death or great injury if they were resisting an illegal arrest.[18] By criminalizing resistance to an illegal arrest, as legal scholars Craig Hemmens and Daniel Levin comment, officers' authority could "follow the badge rather than the law."[19] In addition to permitting officers the use of deadly force against people suspected of committing misdemeanors and criminalizing civilian efforts to resist illegal arrests, the Uniform Arrest Act also advocated changes that made it easier to detain people (who had not been arrested) for longer, to frisk any potential suspect for weapons irrespective of reasonable suspicion and without an arrest, and to arrest people suspected of committing misdemeanors without a warrant even if the officer did not witness the crime committed.[20]

Many believe that the criminal justice system is able to keep law enforcement in check, but in actuality these powers are not separate at all. People believe that law is supposed to check police power to make sure that police authority is not abused, but in actuality police do what they want first and then find the law, policies, or procedures to justify their actions after the fact. People believe that prosecutors are supposed to use the law to rein in and discipline police abuse of power, but in actuality they cite the law as the reason why officers cannot be prosecuted at all for killing civilians, not just enabling but empowering officers to continue criminalizing, terrorizing, abusing, and murdering those most vulnerable. This recursivity (the meaning of law is the effect of police violence work) shows us how policing is an administrative power that is "above the law" because its actual work is to criminalize groups of people whose vulnerability, disposability, and precarity are value making for others within specific circulations of colonial racial capitalism (i.e., by generating fines and fees through policing) or to secure the conditions of possibility for these circulations (i.e., by valuing private property over BIPOC lives).

To put it plainly, criminalization operationalizes colonial racial capitalisms. By "operationalize," we mean that criminalization provides a "how" for circulations of colonial racial capitalism in process; it is a procedure that shapes and conditions relations of accumulation. In the words of Ruth Wilson Gilmore, "Criminalization remains a complicated means and process to achieve a simple thing: To enclose people in situations where they are expected, and in many ways compelled, to sicken and to die. . . . [Carceral geographies] reveal real human sacrifice as an organizing principle, or perhaps more precisely as an unprincipled form of organizing, which returns us to racial capitalism and the role of criminalization in it."[21] And as Robert Nichols writes,

> The extension of criminal jurisdiction has long been central to the subjugation and displacement of indigenous polities. . . . What has changed is that unlike previous eras (unlike even, the 1970s, e.g., Pine Ridge), the incarceration of indigenous peoples is increasingly dehistoricized—and thus depoliticized—through its representation as the general extension of racialized criminality. . . . [Criminalization] functions to erect a strict separation between *criminal control* and *conquest* despite indigenous

societies' continued insistence that externally imposed coercive control over their members (for whatever reason) is an affront to the inherent right to self-government.[22]

In other words, police criminalize Indigenous people for colonial racial capitalisms by depoliticizing and severing their relations to the land that "contradictorily provides the material and spiritual sustenance of Indigenous societies on the one hand, and the foundation of colonial state-formation, settlement and capitalist development on the other."[23]

Police are administrators who criminalize in real time as they do the violence work that colonial racial capitalism requires. From the beginning of colonial racial capitalist modernity, criminalizing processes and repertories have sorted people, geographies, and socialities into the political and the administrative, yet these have arguably taken on a specific, central function in the United States in the era of official antiracism because they enable the ways of anti-Blackness and other racial and settler colonial oppressions to appear compatible with versions of multiculturalism that differentiate BIPOC people marked as law-abiding or assimilable from those who are criminalized and therefore marked as disposable and excludable.[24] Policing is only one of many processes and apparatuses that fabricate, manage, and organize criminalization. It exists in a specific continuum with "therapeutic" apparatuses of public administration—education, housing, health care, social-service management, and other apparatuses—which, like policing, continually fabricate and operationalize dividing lines between the respectable poor and the lumpen rabble, between those worthy of state care and the unworthy, between people marked as victims and those marked as threats. Like policing, these administrative apparatuses criminalize to legitimate social violence (hunger, political exclusion, denial of health care, sexual exploitation) that is already built into schemes of colonial racial capitalist accumulation.

What is singular about policing and criminalization is that *the specific activity of policing* (as opposed to other criminalizing processes) is to enforce colonial racial capitalist conditions *on the street* and *in real time* through violence work. Policing is an activity that *makes criminal* in real time to justify officers' physical violence that has already been authorized in the name of "law and order"—that is, in the name of fabricating and maintaining a colonial racial capitalist order of value making and accumulation that circulates and produces group-differentiated (BIPOC, the asset-stripped) premature death.[25]

Gilmore gives us a sense of policing as *the* activity that criminalizes in order to enforce racial capitalist orders *to the point of real-time killing*. In an interview published in the *Guardian* after the Baltimore uprisings in response to the police murder of Freddie Gray in 2015, Gilmore asks us to rethink the idea that police kill Black people because society sees them as criminals. Instead, Gilmore asserts, racialized criminalization is the effect or the consequence of police power to kill Black people with impunity: "I think many people respond to these high-profile police killings by thinking: 'They can kill us because they can lock us up.' But I think it goes the other way: they can lock us up because they know they can kill us, because they can kill with impunity."[26] The difference is not insignificant: if the police can murder BIPOC people because they can turn them into criminals, then it means all our attention should focus on making laws fairer and officers less racist. But if it is the other way around, if police can criminalize BIPOC people because they can kill them with impunity, then we have to change everything. It's crucial to recognize that the reason why police can kill BIPOC people with impunity is because colonial racial capitalism renders asset-stripped, racialized, vulnerable people disposable. This power to kill those deemed disposable with impunity is the basis of police power. In other words, as Gilmore suggests, behind the police power to criminalize is the police power to kill in real time on the street in order to preserve and defend prevailing colonial racial capitalist arrangements.

Because people who are *in reality* ruled by domination and coercion, not hegemony (people marked for capitalist destruction, not capitalist care), *resist* this order of things all the time, they are marked as counterinsurgent even when only living their lives. Living their lives is a form of resistance both individually and collectively; making their lives more livable and more enjoyable is about resisting colonial racial capitalism by taking up space on public or, rather, stolen land denied to them and the land's Indigenous kin.

For instance, during the post–World War II era in Milwaukee, as in much of the nation, law enforcement harassed Black residents frequently, extensively, cruelly, brutally, and indiscriminately. The constant, oppressive presence of police in Black neighborhoods was not about keeping Black people safe; it was not about protecting Black residents. It was about exerting control over every aspect of Black social life, criminalizing African Americans' relationships to one another and to their own neighborhoods. As Simon Ezra Balto writes, "Officers working the beat in black Milwaukee racked up significant numbers of arrests for vagrancy, public consumption of alcohol, and loitering—charges directly related to people's presence in and uses of public space."[27] These charges were explicitly about criminalizing all the parts of Black life that were not about working for someone else—criminalizing all the activities Black people did with one another after work was over. It also tells us that police harassment was not just about enforcing segregation; it was also about criminalizing Black presence in *public* space on *stolen* land. In other words, law enforcement did not just criminalize Blacks' relationships with white people and white spaces; they also criminalized Blacks' social relationships with one another, Blacks' leisure and recreational (noneconomic) activities, and Blacks' relationships to the public spaces they shared.

This situation continues today, and it is the same policing that is intrinsic to ongoing settler colonial occupation, to violence work for colonization, on land that settlers call Milwaukee. Settler colonial occupation requires the persistent policing of Indigenous relations, presence, and bodies (especially unsheltered and poor people) because the persistence of Indigenous life itself threatens the (always incomplete) territorialization of settler command and control. In other words, it threatens US nation-state sovereignty, which, Manu Karuka reminds us, is always a counter-sovereignty.[28] As the authors of *Red Nation Rising* explain, US settler capitalist democracy requires a commitment to collective violence in order to keep Indigenous people off the land, to hinder Indigenous practices and relations based on land, and to repress Indigenous sovereignty. In Milwaukee this commitment to collective violence is mostly contracted out to police, whose enduring function for settler society is "Indian killers."[29] Milwaukee police are able to criminalize Black and Indigenous people because they do violence work as the infliction of administrative power—that is, they are tasked to use lethal violence to maintain relations of colonial racial capitalist accumulation such as racial segregation, settler occupation, migrant precarity produced through border-organized matrices of oppression, and "carceral regimes of private property" that alienate, cage, and commodify human relations with land and other life-affirming material beings and caretaking activities.[30]

How Police Use Discretion to Criminalize

Counterinsurgent policing on the street and in real time must be constant. It must also be flexible in terms of its operations and targets because (1) colonial racial capitalist strategies of accumulation are always changing (through and because of competition and opposition) and (2) many contemporary strategies enmeshed with neoliberal multiculturalism require the momentary rehabilitation of criminalized groups (e.g., "redevelopment" strategies for real estate capital, "rehabilitation" strategies for therapeutic carceral economies, "human resource" strategies for education corporations). Thus, police as street administrators of colonial racial capitalist orders require operational flexibility. Police must continually and flexibly fabricate and enforce dividing lines (enduringly racialized) between people marked as moral, legitimate, worthy of investment, and innocent and those marked as immoral, suspicious, disposable, and threatening—in short, criminalizable—in accordance with specific colonial racial capitalist strategies of accumulation.

Today, police criminalize in real time BIPOC movement through city space to maintain the territorialized whiteness that drives real-estate profits, and police criminalize BIPOC immobility when neighborhoods are targeted for redevelopment. Police criminalize to produce benefits and profits for criminal justice economies and technologies, including prison, weapon, and surveillance industries. They criminalize in real time, on the street, for financial capitalism: to anchor municipal finance and bond schemes, to boost payday lenders, to prepare places for investment, and to produce fines and fees for city budgets. They criminalize in real time informal economic activities that are the survival work of the asset-stripped yet also criminalize activities of leisure, recreation, and sociality that embody self-determination and nurture liberatory existence that threatens colonial, racial orders.

When we see that police criminalize in real time to fabricate and maintain colonial racial capitalist orders, we can see instances or acts of policing as administrative (or as enactments of administrative power) and recognize that police activities are not "responses" to individual actions; rather, the violence work they inflict has already been "decided upon" (not intentionally) by the requirements of strategic colonial racial capitalist arrangements and the necessity to defend police power. Criminalizing, enacted with and through acts of policing, does the deed *and* is the cover-up.

Key to criminalization is an indispensable procedure of police power that is often perceived as being only about what individual police officers do (rather than an anchor for policing as acts of administrative power) and thus preoccupies reformers: police discretion. Discretion is necessary for policing as administering colonial racial capitalist orders in real time and on the street pervasively and flexibly, as an "it-gets-done" kind of administrative sorting, ordering, disqualifying, and marking of people through violence work for accumulation. Discretion also, counterinsurgently, lets police inflict sanctioned violence day to day to make sure that the social relations defined as legal by the capitalist state (private property, eminent domain, the commodification of health, housing, land) define the material conditions of daily life, thus repressing Indigenous, Black radical, socialist, and other anticapitalist, grounded modes of relationality.[31] Discretion gives police the operational power to structure every single encounter: to look the other way or pursue, to warn or arrest, to insert someone into the criminal justice apparatus of human sacrifice and impoverishment or not.

Liberal law-and-order proposals often point to discretion as the weak point in policing—police act in a biased way, they make bad decisions, they go after the wrong person—but discretion is not a weakness in policing. Police discretion is the *source* of its operational strength. Discretion is a way of fixing the structures of social domination durably in the experiential and lived dispositions of police as violence workers who are socialized to act in accord with background conditions structured by toxic masculinity, anti-Blackness, settler colonialism, and heteropatriarchy. This means that the administering police do on the fly—surveilling, informing, repressing, arranging things on the street, drawing the line between the worthy poor and disposable lumpen—can be done "with discretion" in accord with all these background conditions. In fact, as Andrea Ritchie reminds us, police discretion is the foundation for policing the everyday living of BIPOC communities:

> Police officers are afforded almost unlimited discretion when determining who and what conduct is deemed disorderly or unlawful. More specific regulations, such as those criminalizing sleeping, consuming food or alcohol, or urinating in public spaces, *criminalize activities so common they can't be enforced at all times against all people*. As a result, both vague and specific quality-of-life offenses are selectively enforced in particular neighborhoods and communities, or against particular people, including people who, due to poverty and homelessness, have no choice but to engage in such activities in public spaces.[32]

A prime example of discretion in Wisconsin (as in much of the nation) is traffic stops. Police routinely target cars with tribal license places as well as cars with feathers or dream catchers hanging from visors or rearview mirrors.[33] Because it is illegal to hang anything that might obstruct a driver's view, police use their discretion to decide whether or not something hanging from a rearview mirror obstructs a driver's view. Police also don't need a reason to pull someone over—they can easily argue that a traffic violation might be occurring, which can be premised on how a person drives, a "broken" taillight, the color and make of the vehicle, registration stickers, and so forth. Mary Annette Pember recounts a terrifying incident when an officer pulled her over in northern Wisconsin as she was driving off the reservation after attending a ceremony. After she answered the officer's questions—"What are you doing here? Where are you from? Where are you going? Where are you staying?"—he asked for her license and registration. Trying to be helpful, Pember's autistic daughter opened the glove box. In response, the officer put his hand on his gun and shone his flashlight toward her daughter and the glove box, which made her daughter scream. Fortunately, Pember was able to defuse the situation. He told her that he pulled her over because she ran a stop sign, but he didn't give her a ticket. She writes that "I'm pretty sure I had stopped at the sign, but I sure wasn't going to argue with him."[34] The incident, extremely common for Indigenous drivers, reveals the extent of police discretion; there is essentially no limit. He could pull her over whether or not she actually stopped at the sign.

Pulling someone over provides officers the opportunity to find a reason to arrest by, for instance, conducting a test for driving under the influence or searching for drugs, contraband, or "weapons" (which are themselves defined according to officers' discretion). In Native nations where police have jurisdiction due to Public Law 280, Indigenous persons are overrepresented in jails by as much as five times. In Vilas County, Wisconsin, where the Lac du Flambeau Band of Lake Superior Chippewa Indians live, half of the incarcerated population is Indigenous, but Natives represent only 11 percent of the county's residents. In 2018 data reported that the rate of Indigenous people incarcerated in Wisconsin was second only to that of African Americans.[35] The experience of being pulled over for a traffic stop is so common that Natives refer to it as a DWI crime: "driving while Indian."[36] Police discretion enables officers to essentially pull anyone over at any time because officers' feelings and beliefs—not reality—found the premise for discretion.

When the practice of officers using their discretion to pull over people who were not engaging in traffic violations was challenged in the Milwaukee court system as a violation of a person's rights, it was simply converted into law by *State v. Houghton* (2015). In *State v. Houghton*, the Wisconsin Supreme Court determined that a reasonable suspicion of a traffic violation is enough evidence to conduct a traffic stop and any subsequent searches; hence, an officer's "objectively reasonable mistake of law may form the basis for a finding of reasonable suspicion."[37] In other words, officers can argue that they suspected someone was maybe engaging in a traffic violation; if it turns out that their suspicion was groundless, they can still reasonably suspect that you may be engaged in criminal activity, which provides them the legal justification to search your person or your car, and whatever they find can send you to jail or prison. This happens often with drivers who hang decorative items from rearview mirrors—it is obvious that such trinkets do not obstruct a driver's view, but the court determined that even when such cases are obviously not violations, police officers' actions should still be considered "reasonable mistakes." It did not matter if Pember stopped at the sign or didn't. If the officer decided to search her car, any evidence he found could be the basis for an arrest because his "reasonable mistake" can still be the basis for someone's arrest and subsequent incarceration. Police discretion does the deed and is the cover-up.

So-called reasonable mistakes do not need to be legal or legalized; even discretionary police conduct found to be unconstitutional continues unabated, underlining that police discretion is the source of its operational strength. In 2017 the American Civil Liberties Union (ACLU) of Wisconsin, representing six Milwaukee residents, sued the city of Milwaukee over its police department's racially discriminatory, unconstitutional stop-and-frisk program.[38] The plaintiffs were all Black and Latinx and included a seventeen-year-old Black teenager who had already been stopped three times (the first time when he was eleven) and a Latinx grandmother. *Collins v. City of Milwaukee* (2017) exposed that from 2010 to 2017, the Milwaukee Police Department (MPD) conducted hundreds of thousands of pedestrian and traffic stops without reasonable suspicion—in other words, officers conducted stops and sometimes searches for no justifiable reason at all.[39]

The former chief of police, Edward Flynn, denied that such a stop-and-frisk program existed. However, he did share Milwaukee's policies as an example of "best practices" for the report *Stop and Frisk: Balancing Crime Control with Community Relations*.[40] In this report the MPD's policy is clearly about the hyper-policing of Black and brown people and the places they live: "We operate under the belief that when we focus on the right person or persons responsible for crime and disorder, we will see results. Our interaction with the community and enforcement of laws and ordinances are not random, instead it is a purposeful linkage of enforcement and gives proper attention to areas prone to violent crime and disorder."[41]

As the ACLU documented, the MPD's "not random" policies and directives essentially constituted a stop-and-frisk program conducted in predominantly Black and Latinx neighborhoods. As the suit asserted, "The strategy includes blanketing certain geographic areas in which residents are predominantly people of color with 'saturation patrols' by MPD officers, who conduct high-volume, *suspicionless* stops and frisks throughout the area. Over time, the MPD's program has developed into a formal and informal quota system that requires patrol officers to meet numerical targets for stops on a regular basis."[42] In fact, the de facto stop-and-frisk program was so punishing that it was difficult for officers to execute at the level expected. Therefore, the president of the Milwaukee police union brought it to the attention of the Milwaukee Fire and Police Commission in 2016. As he complained, "Police officers were clearly directed that the norm, *or average*, was two traffic stops per day. The requirement therefore moving forward, was that everyone would be required to produce two stops every day. For those that did not comply, they could expect progressive discipline up to and including termination. . . ."[43]

The ACLU did win the case. Nusrat Choudhury, deputy director of the ACLU Racial Justice Program, wrote a hopeful blog post, citing Milwaukee as an example for the rest of the nation to follow:

> The settlement mandates reforms that are expansive and profound. It requires the overhaul of how police conduct and report stops and frisks in Milwaukee. The settlement also compels the city to take concrete steps to ensure that police stops and frisks are supervised and monitored and that officers who conduct unlawful encounters are counseled, retrained, or disciplined. And the City must sustain the Community Collaborative Committee, a group of community members who will meet regularly with Milwaukee police and the City's Fire and Police Commission to provide input on policing strategies and their impact on the public.
>
> Cities and towns across the United States should do what Milwaukee is now *required* by the settlement to do—conduct internal and external audits to ensure that stops and frisks are supported by the reasonable suspicion required by the Fourth Amendment. If stops and frisks do not meet this standard, officers must be disciplined for violating the Constitution. Only a true embrace of evidence-based policing and accountability measures can guard against policing based on bias in violation of the 14th Amendment's basic guarantee of equal protection of the law. And to work for all of us, policing depends on law enforcement efforts based on evidence, not stereotypes or bias.[44]

The most recent data reveal that the changes "required" of the MPD over the last three years have not been implemented in meaningful ways. The MPD complies with sharing its data (although many records are still incomplete), yet officers continue to stop and frisk primarily Black and Latinx residents without justification at alarming rates, *which should serve as evidence that police reform through law is completely untenable.* Among several stipulations, the MPD was supposed to show that 15 percent of no-action encounters were conducted without reasonable suspicion, but police officers actually regressed, showing that 63.2 percent were conducted without reasonable suspicion, up from 50 percent in the previous report.[45] More than half of all discretionary police encounters without reasonable suspicion involved Black people, so we can assume that this number disproportionately affects African Americans.[46] The MPD was also supposed to demonstrate that fewer than 15 percent of frisks were conducted without reasonable suspicion that the person stopped was armed and dangerous, but 87.2 percent of frisks were not justified. Of those frisked, 86 percent were Black and 7.9 percent were Latinx, together totaling 93.9 percent of all those frisked in Milwaukee. This has had dire consequences for those targeted: 70.6 percent of the contraband found was discovered during unjustified frisks.[47]

Police saturate Black and brown neighborhoods and decide who is suspicious and who is not. The fact that a neighborhood has a heavy police presence means that more people will be arrested. Discretion is indispensable for policing, and it is kept in play by making sure that so many life activities are criminalized that *they can't be enforced at all times against all people.* Whether police discretion is legalized or disciplined, nothing happens to curtail it or check it because the violence work of police discretion maintains colonial racial capitalist relations of accumulation. It does not matter whether police actions are legal, illegal, or a "reasonable mistake" because their violence work is not about enforcing the law; it is about preserving colonial racial capitalist relations of accumulation—keeping entire Black, Indigenous, and Latinx communities unreasonably vulnerable to capitalist exploitation, violence, and policing itself.

In Milwaukee, stop-and-frisk, discretionary policing keeps the city racially segregated (by making it dangerous for BIPOC working-class people to live or travel through white areas), and racial segregation works for racial capital accumulation by structuring a development strategy in which city officials and real estate capitalists use the banality of "two Milwaukees"—one white, one Black, one rich, one poor—to justify financing downtown projects (stadiums, condominiums, office buildings) and withholding public and private money from Black and brown neighborhoods.[48]

Stop-and-frisk, discretionary policing in Milwaukee is also part of a colonial racial capitalist economy that profits from border imperialism. People who were set on the move by US-backed capitalist violence in Mexico and Central and South America are coerced into extractive housing and labor conditions by a matrix of oppressions that pervasive on-the-street, stop-and-frisk policing maintains in Milwaukee.[49] Discretionary policing also maintains settler capitalism through constant potential violence against Indigenous presence in the city of Milwaukee, making Indigenous stewardship and relations with the land, water, plants, medicines, and other life-sustaining material beings difficult while instead turning these into private property, investments, and fixed capital.[50] Overall, the discretionary policing of BIPOC and asset-stripped Milwaukeeans functions as counterinsurgency for colonial racial capitalism by wielding the threat of violence (the impunity to kill) constantly and pervasively against those whose disposability, domination, or premature death enables capital accumulation for elites and allies.

Criminalizing Self-Defense from and Activism against Police Violence

With Milwaukee's Black and brown neighborhoods saturated by police who are able to stop and frisk anyone they want despite the finding that their practices are unconstitutional, despite the settlement requiring the department to change, and despite grumblings from police officers themselves, it should come as no surprise that more arrests will be made in "not random" areas. These circumstances are created because police's right to kill "the right person or persons" with impunity has already been "decided upon." Because they can kill anyone in entire communities deemed disposable, it does not matter whether their use of "not random" discretion is accurate, legal, or constitutional. Hence, more people will be caught in dangerous and/or compromising situations not just because police face no consequences when they conduct unconstitutional frisks without reasonable suspicion but also because of the sheer number of officers patrolling these neighborhoods.

The structure of the criminal justice system itself makes it extremely difficult to hold officers accountable and makes it impossible to provide all criminally accused a jury trial, so using the court system to address not only officers' misconduct but also officers' mistakes or inaccurate charges is extremely burdensome for the criminally accused.[51] Somil Trivedi and Nicole Gonzalez Van Cleve argue that prosecutors' reliance on police to win their cases has created a "persistent, codependent relationship between police and prosecutors [that] exacerbates police misconduct and violence and is aided by prosecutors in both legal and extralegal ways."[52] When accused people don't have the time and money to go to court, they may be pressured to take a deal and plead guilty or no contest to crimes they did not commit because it is expensive, time-consuming, and emotionally exhausting to go to court even for petty crimes. As Malcolm M. Feeley says in *The Process Is the Punishment*, "Pretrial detention, bail, repeated court appearances, and forfeited wages all exact their toll on the criminally accused."[53] It's understandable, then that people sometimes resist arrest or run away. They know that the police do not have to arrest them and that the cases themselves may even fall apart in court, so they might run away or resist arrest to be able to work the next day, to be able to go home that night, to escape costly court and lawyer fees, to hold on to dignity, to bypass further humiliation, or to avoid having to take a plea because a plea would be more convenient and cheaper than fighting the charge in court. It makes sense that with so many very public cases about police brutality and killings, some people would try to defend themselves against the possibility of police violence by resisting arrest or running away. These actions of BIPOC people loving themselves more than they fear the police are not just about self-defense; they are also forms of resistance that undermine police power itself.

In order for policing to administer colonial racial capitalist orders on the street and in real time through violence work, policing's prime directive—and where the administrative character of policing is readily graspable—is the defense of police power as such. Through charges such as "failure to obey" or "resisting arrest," police criminalize people who threaten in real time exercises of racialized colonial capitalist police power. Such charges defend police power by making every act of resistance to police activities criminalizable. Importantly, police criminalize BIPOC and asset-stripped people who threaten police power in real time (for example, by not responding to a police command or just seeming not to respond) as intolerable threats who can be killed for *this one act alone*. This is because such acts of refusal embody challenges to police power writ large, not merely resistance to an individual officer's will.

In this way the act of self-defense against acts of police violence in real time, on the street, performatively diminishes police power because it embodies a refusal to submit to illegitimate authority, and it epitomizes loving oneself over fearing the police. When uprisings against police violence mourn and honor people whose revolutionary acts of self-defense against police power were not able to save their lives, the empowering chants of protesters are not only angry and sad but also insightful, genius, and revolutionary. They discredit the power of police to criminalize those they kill with impunity by saying the names of loved ones over and over and over again, etching their names in art, media, public policy, law, public debates, movements, hearts, and minds, reminding everyone that those deemed disposable are never ever that, that these loved ones are absolutely irreplaceable, desperately missed, and fiercely loved. When marchers proceed to #sayhername or when they imbue George Floyd's name with preciousness and power, they identify and resist criminalization as a mode of governance, a fulcrum of US multicultural white supremacist settler capitalist democracy. They make us attend to the role of criminalization in colonial racial capitalism and policing as counterinsurgency violence work, essential for a system that relies constitutively on organized premature death. Marchers know that in the eyes of the state, Black, Indigenous, Latinx, Asian, Arab, queer, trans, two-spirit men, women, children, and teenagers become criminals in death *precisely for defending their lives from the police*. Imbuing their names with incalculable worth and immeasurable value, with soul-deep mourning and bone-aching anger, with preciousness and power activates an epistemological imperative, a Black radical imperative, a queer-of-color imperative, an Indigenous decolonial imperative: these lives lost are irreplaceable.

"Don't Arrest Me, Arrest the Police" is a crystallized expression of the collective, embodied knowledge that police brutalize BIPOC people precisely for their will to live and to defend themselves against police as administrators of a social order predicated on the insecurity and violability of BIPOC lives and the lives of poor people. The chants rehearse a legal-social order that judges the need of those killed to defend themselves from police as imminently reasonable and condemns police power for its genocidal license to kill. By stripping away the recursive procedure of criminalizing people for trying to save their lives from police, they help us see that evasive actions taken to defy the racialized death-dealing powers of police should be legible as revolutionary acts.

For example, when people in Milwaukee began marching after the police murder of George Floyd in 2020 (they are still marching), they chanted, along with Floyd's name, the names of Black, brown, and Indigenous people killed in Milwaukee for the "crime" of trying to save their lives from officers fully committed to their job of maintaining racialized social control in the hyper-segregated city. Protesters said the name "Dontre Hamilton," a young man with schizophrenia who was sleeping on a downtown park bench outside a Starbucks. He was shot fourteen times by Darren Wilson after he grabbed the baton that Wilson was using to beat him. He was killed when he exercised his legal right to self-defense against an officer's use of excessive force. They say "Jay Anderson" for a young father and cook at Ruby Tuesday's who was awakened by police while sleeping in his car in a park and killed for having his hands below the officer's line of sight. He was killed because lethal force was used first, making self-defense impossible. They say "Antonio Gonzales" for a twenty-nine-year-old queer Indigenous-Latinx lover of Emo-music who was killed outside his front door by the same officer who would later kill Anderson because he held on to a sword he clutched (but did not wield threateningly), perhaps as a talisman of protection. And they say "Sylville Smith" for a neighborhood-famous, much-loved "soft soul" who was chased by a police officer he knew disliked him and was killed as he threw his legally possessed gun on the ground to give the officer no excuse to shoot him. He was exercising a duty to retreat, was engaged in an act of self-preservation, and was doing everything he could to not be read as "resisting arrest" or as "threatening." He was trying to save his life. As Sylville's father said to marchers in Milwaukee, "He was running away from the problem. How can he be the problem?"

After each killing, the police officer involved claimed self-defense while using each young man's own self-defensive actions—trying to stop the blows raining down, throwing away a gun he was legally allowed to carry while running for his life—as "proof" of criminality. After each killing, community members turned their names into shibboleths of pain and protection, saying them again and again. Their names have become revolutionary commitments, rehearsals for freedom, promises to remain alive and thus insurgent, to exist and resist, to decriminalize the murdered and condemn their killing. Their names defy the logic of disposability, of interchangeability, of surplus. Saying their names is not only about the refusal to forget and the refusal to be forgotten; it is also a demand for a reckoning with *irreplaceable* lives stolen: saying their names is a first pragmatic step to change everything.[54]

Movements against police violence decriminalize people who died trying to save their lives from the police. Because movements politicize police violence, demand responses from elected officials, encourage people to stay on the streets, and win some definitional authority over police encounters for the policed, movements against police violence also threaten police power. They create relations where people collectively commit to watch police, to stand up for one another during police encounters, to film and spread warnings and community intelligence about police actions. Movements against police violence turn criminalizing procedures on their heads because they enliven infrastructures of radical consciousness of police violence work as itself criminal. When peaceful marchers are met with armored tactical vehicles, tear gas, tasers, riot shields, batons, and police aligned in military formation, it demonstrates how this kind of extreme lethality is always there in ordinary (which is always counterinsurgent) policing, always just one mayoral declaration of "civil disturbance" away, on permanent, settler colonial standby. In short, it lets us know that policing's function is gendered racial and colonial oppression.[55]

Because of the far-reaching and radical power of movements against police violence, state-legal-police assemblages target these movements for special kinds of repression and especially repress those who gather the marches, who are known as community defenders, who motivate people to march together to demand that police stop killing Black, brown, Native, poor, and gender-nonconforming people. In fact, the charge of "resisting arrest," though now banal and used for daily repressive policing, was first used to target the Black Panthers, the Young Lords, and the American Indian Movement and other revolutionary movements crystallized from commitments to collective self-defense against police violence. Such charges were used to criminalize activism and provide law enforcement the legal reasoning they needed to use violence to suppress community leaders. Representing Black, brown, and Indigenous activists as violent criminals who resisted arrest diverted attention away from movement demands, discredited the community work that activists did, and in some cases even delegitimated the activists' organizations. The charge of "resisting arrest" is important in narrating these stories because Black, brown, and Indigenous activists were often not criminals who resisted arrest but "criminals" *because* they "resisted arrest," according to police.

Historian and activist Yohuru Williams details a violent confrontation between members of the Milwaukee Black Panther Party (BPP) and the police in Milwaukee in 1969.[56] The event that ignited this controversy occurred when police charged Black Panthers Jesse Lee White, Earl Walter Leverette, and Booker Collins for resisting arrest. According to the officers, the BPP members were pulled over because their car matched the description of another that had allegedly shot at a patrolman. As Officer Thomas Lelinski arrested the men, Lieutenant Raymond Beste pointed a shotgun at them. Lelinski claimed that White shoved him and tried to escape, encouraging Collins and Leverette to enter the struggle at the exact same time that police backup arrived. The officers claim they used appropriate force and quickly squashed the conflict.

White, Leverette, and Collins told a different version of the event. According to these targeted BPP members, when the rest of the police arrived, they had already been handcuffed by the arresting officers. All the officers—those that arrested them as well as the more than twenty officers who arrived as backup—proceeded to beat the already handcuffed men with "fists, firearm butts, and blackjacks."[57] White, Leverette, and Collins were charged with the misdemeanor of resisting arrest. Williams explains that this confrontation and the legal trial and appeal that followed exhausted the chapter's resources and energy, which then decimated its membership and soon resulted in the local party's disbandment by the national offices of the BPP. Although it's possible that Lelinski and Beste had reasonable suspicion to arrest White, Leverette, and Collins, it's also clear that there was no evidence to connect them to the alleged shots fired from a car that supposedly looked like theirs. The only "crime" that White, Leverette, and Collins were charged with and ultimately convicted of after losing their appeal was "resisting arrest." This was the illegal activity that turned these community leaders into criminals. When the supposed crime that led to the arrest cannot be proven in court, we need to consider that the arrest itself that the men resisted may have been completely unwarranted and perhaps even illegal. Officers can easily claim "reasonable suspicion" (isn't their car the same color as one we suspect?), which places the law on their side, but this "suspicion" did not lead to any convictions. Instead, this suspicion led to more than twenty officers violently beating three handcuffed men for a crime they did not commit. The law reads this suspicion as "reasonable," giving law enforcement officers the benefit of the doubt, the ability to use their judgment, their discretion. But police discretion and the laws, policies, and procedures that empower and protect officers' decisions to arrest or not, to tase or not, to shoot or not, are not at all reasonable but were in all likelihood simply a policing tactic to humiliate and intimidate prominent activists, to bankrupt their cash reserves, and to discredit the Milwaukee chapter of the Black Panther Party by turning their leaders into "criminals."

Recently, "resisting arrest" has been taken out of the bag of tricks again in Milwaukee. In the first days of the new 2020 march on Milwaukee, the police tried to use "resisting arrest" tactics to threaten and suppress activists, as they had historically toward the Milwaukee Black Panthers. This time, their primary target was community defender Frank Sensabaugh, better known as Frank Nitty II, who has demonstrated the capacity to move large numbers of Black, white, brown, and Native residents to peaceful protest. As he marched with hundreds across a downtown bridge, officers with the Milwaukee County Sheriff's Department tear-gassed and violently arrested him while he was live-streaming. According to Nitty, the police were threatening to charge him with felony resisting arrest.[58] Apparently, the officers, dressed in riot gear and body armor, hurt themselves while slamming Nitty's prone and complying body to the ground. Nitty's body itself, all by itself, is narrated as an automated weapon that is somehow able to "assault" officers while lying on the ground, motionless.[59] As with Kayla Moore, Mike Brown, Tanisha Anderson, Carlos Ingram-Lopez, Tony McDade, Mario Gonzalez, George Floyd, Jonathan Tubby, Davinian Darnell Williams, Eric Garner, Adam Toledo, Delmar Espejo, Jason Ike Pero, and far too many others, Nitty's Black body was literally criminalized for its mere existence and potential to move, justifying the charge of "resisting arrest." In this case, as in others, Nitty was not charged with anything, but he was made aware that the Milwaukee County Sheriff's office was not just considering the charge but circulating the narrative that he "resisted arrest" to the mainstream media to give a reason for injuring him so badly that he was taken to a hospital.[60]

Because uprisings have the power to interrupt policing as administering colonial racial capitalisms in real time and the power to politicize violence that police depoliticize through criminalizing procedures (such as using resisting arrest or self-defense to justify and depoliticize killing with impunity), state legislatures have accelerated the passage of laws to defend police power in advance. Since the Ferguson, Standing Rock, and George Floyd uprisings, state legislatures have been proposing laws that make people who protest the violences of colonial racial capitalism, administrative power, and/or the policing agencies vulnerable to repressive police violence, incarceration, and/or heavy fines. Such laws have a counterinsurgent function: to criminalize people occupying space (in the streets, on the land) to defend themselves and all kin from police and capitalist exploitation (furthering Black liberation, enacting Indigenous sovereignty, demanding livable lives where they are) *before they gather* so that all the violence deployed on them in defense of police power can be represented as depoliticized counterviolence.[61]

Since the 2016 Standing Rock uprisings, there have been more than 226 initiatives at the state and federal level to suppress, criminalize, and punish peaceful assembly. According to the International Center for Not-for-Profit Law, which tracks legislation limiting the right to protest, seventeen states have enacted harsh penalties for protests near gas and oil pipelines and other "critical infrastructure," a category that most of these laws expand to include any place or equipment associated with existing or planned oil, gas, electric, water, telecommunications, railroad, and other projects and facilities.[62] In West Virginia a law was passed eliminating police liability for injuries and deaths while dispersing "riots and unlawful assemblies." Many states have added criminal and civil penalties for protesters who block traffic, sit in, or stand in, thus redefining core strategies of "peaceful civil disobedience" as "rioting." Conversely, white supremacists are being protected by law for engaging in acts of violence. Oklahoma and Iowa have granted immunity to drivers who run over protesters, redefining hit-and-run as noncriminal if motivated by the driver's support for "law and order," rendering BIPOC activists and their allies disposable when they destabilize and delegitimate the power of police to kill with impunity. Since the spring and summer 2020 uprisings, a torrent of laws have been passed that redefine the smallest gathering of people as riots, even when literally nothing has happened. Police (or their white settler counterparts/vigilantes) need only to fear that a gathering of BIPOC people in public is a prelude to something happening. For example, in April 2021 Arkansas passed a law that redefines *rioting* as engaging with two or more persons in "tumultuous" conduct that creates a "substantial risk" of "public alarm." Other pending legislation would prohibit people convicted of lawful protesting from receiving student loans, unemployment assistance, or housing benefits (Indiana) and bars anyone convicted of unlawful protesting from holding state employment (Minnesota).[63]

Florida's HB-1 bill (which became law in April 2021), "Combating Public Disorder," typifies the current tactic of layering multiple punishments for people who protest police violence and its ideological and financial supports: it makes it a felony to participate in a riot, defined as three or more people acting in common to "assist each other in violent and disorderly conduct"; it makes pulling down or otherwise damaging a historical (Confederate) monument a second-degree felony with a fifteen-year prison sentence; it provides draconian mandatory sentences for assaults on law enforcement officers during protests and forbids protesters from being released on bail before seeing a judge; it allows residents or elected officials to appeal to the state should a municipality seek to cut police budgets; and it frees from civil liability people who deliberately injure protesters. Such legislation plays defense for police power; it hyper-criminalizes, in advance, people who protest police violence while cloaking police and nonpolice agents of the settler racial capitalist state (i.e., white settlers who run over protesters) with legal protections to encourage them to hurt protesters—to defend police power with extreme violence.

These contemporary laws, which criminalize BIPOC activists and allies before they decide to protest, basically make BIPOC protest itself illegal, not only discrediting activism before it starts but also justifying police repression of activists before they organize as a way of upholding the law. By further criminalizing protests, marches, and uprisings through these new laws, state legislatures are attempting to depoliticize police repression similar to the ways in which "resisting arrest" justifies and depoliticizes police killings for much of the US public.[64] This is why we have to think outside of liberal terms. We name the law-administration-force continuum *administrative power* in part to emphasize that laws are not politically neutral: they are used to violently repress and criminalize BIPOC communities, activisms, teachings, and everyday living. We cannot rely on the law or policy changes to prevent police violence when the very purpose of these is to preauthorize, manage, and extend it. Consider how often more police training is offered as the solution to police violence, which merely increases police budgets and infrastructure without actually lessening police violence or officer-caused deaths.[65]

Although it's incredibly disheartening to witness so many laws passing so quickly to criminalize protesters before they gather, it's important to remember that this is another example of the recursivity of police violence work. There are so many uprisings around the nation precisely because officers are so rarely charged or prosecuted for injuring or killing BIPOC—whether they are protesting, lawbreaking, or just living their lives—because state statutes and the codependent relationship of police and prosecutors make it incredibly difficult to use the law to hold officers accountable. People who run over protesters are already not charged with hit-and-run crimes.[66] Efforts to defund the police are already undermined by rerouting police budgets to other institutions' budgets for policing, such as moving New York Police Department (NYPD) money to the department of education, which hires the NYPD as school safety agents.[67] Indigenous land and water protectors are already arrested for trespass and rioting when they try to block pipelines, mines, and other harmful settler intrusions on treaty lands and waters, unceded lands and waters, or Indigenous homelands and waters (all of Turtle Island). Criminalizing "trespassing" and criminalizing land and water protectors are themselves examples of the capitalist worlding praxis that turns land into private property and water into an extractable natural resource. And as we've been arguing, in cities such as Milwaukee, police regard economically immiserated Black, Indigenous, Asian, and Latinx people and the neighborhoods they live in as if they are disposable, as if the police are able to kill them with impunity and therefore are able to use their "discretion" to criminalize these people on the street in real time, extracting them from their communities through incarceration, detention, and all the consequences that come with these, such as losing wages or employment. This new rash of laws is not "new"—in the sense that there are already laws on the books that criminalize BIPOC protesters—but rather these current anti-protest laws are responding to new forms of organizing, contemporary methods of publicizing local uprisings through social media, present-day strategies for acquiring allies, and, of course, all the violence work of white supremacist counterprotesters. Just as with the Uniform Arrest Act, discussed above, laws are being written to legalize the violence work that police are already doing. These new laws are the effect of police violence work that has already been happening on the street in real time against protesters as they are protesting, publicizing, and undermining police violence.

Police, of course, exert special effort to surveil, harass, and target for criminalization activists known to defend the community from the police or who expose policing as intrinsic to gendered racial capitalist domination and settler occupation in their community activism. We often think of this as COINTELPRO (Counter Intelligence Program) repression, which in the era of US President Donald Trump appeared under the sign of the FBI-fabricated category of "Black Identity Extremists." That the purpose of the category was to organize, stoke, and aim police power at activists whose commitments to Black community defense were articulated as defense from police violence is obvious from the title of a 2018 FBI intelligence assessment—"Black Identity Extremists Likely Motivated to Target Law Enforcement"—which was disseminated to eighteen thousand law enforcement agencies across the country.[68] Eventually, the Trump administration dropped the category for a facile substitute, "Racially or Ethnically Motivated Violent Extremists." The administration of US President Joseph Biden has retained this designation with the stated intention of using it to identify, deter, and prosecute white supremacists, but its lineage speaks to the ease with which it can enable and disguise government action against politically targeted Black activists.

Yet, as we see from the example of the Milwaukee Black Panthers, politically motivated police persecution of activists doesn't have to be organized by the FBI. Police departments on their own initiative regularly subject known activists to pervasive and saturating policing that wields the threat of criminalization and punishment in escalating intensities. Such policing of community defenders is sometimes the charge of "special operations" or "special investigations" units, but more often police harass activists under the cover of "suspected criminal activities" of all types (drug dealing, burglary, gang activity, attempted murder, etc.).

Black Milwaukee activist Vaun Mayes was arrested in 2018 to criminalize him for his leadership during the Sherman Park 2016 uprising, which honored and remembered Sylville Smith, who was killed by police officer Dominique Heaggan-Brown. Mayes was arrested for allegedly planning to firebomb a police station and intimidating a witness, crimes that never did occur.[69] The so-called evidence that led to Mayes's arrest—the makings of Molotov cocktails—was found not in Mayes's possession or in his home but in dumpsters near Sherman Park. The federal raid of Mayes's home turned up only empty juice bottles.[70] In addition to the lack of evidence and Mayes's role as a prominent activist, what makes this arrest so clearly about punishing and criminalizing his activism is that he was also charged under specific sections of the Civil Obedience Act, which was designed to repress activism in the 1960s. The federal statute criminalizes any conduct that might interfere with police officers carrying out their duties during "civil disorder" (i.e., protests, riots, rebellions, and uprisings). Recently, the law has been used against protesters in major cities, such as Portland, Oregon, and Philadelphia. Mayes is one of only two people in the Eastern District of Wisconsin ever charged under this law since the 1970s. (The other person charged hurt a police officer during the August 2020 protests in Kenosha, Wisconsin, honoring Jacob Blake, a Black man left paralyzed after being shot seven times in the back by police officer Rusten Sheskey. Sheskey's actions were found lawful; he was not charged or disciplined.)[71]

Arresting Mayes criminalizes him. In real time and on the streets, police officers arrested him in 2018. Because he is facing pending federal charges, he has been unduly vulnerable to police abuse, harassment, humiliation, and intimidation since then. He is reminded daily of his vulnerability to police violence. He is constantly harassed and pulled over in officers' attempts to remind him that he is vulnerable, in their attempts to curtail all the community work he does. And because of the pending charges, he never resists; he is always compliant, no matter the affronts to his dignity. Because he is criminalized, everything they do to him is already legally justified, preauthorized as maintaining law and order. Officers know Mayes because he is so involved in protesting police shootings, and officers also know that Mayes's pending federal charges make him always reasonably suspicious. They know and Mayes knows that because he is criminalized, all and any of his actions can be read as giving the police probable cause. Criminalizing Mayes does the deed and is the cover-up.

Criminalizing Community Defenders and Those They Defend from Premature Death

Although Mayes's prior arrest renders him incredibly vulnerable to police harassment, it does not stop him from protesting police power or from defending others against the violences of colonial racial capitalism that require the violence work of policing. In Milwaukee, capital accumulation circuits through legal and illegal economies (capital doesn't care; criminalization allows for intensive kinds of capital extraction and exploitation), and it works through racialized and gendered violences that include hyper-segregation and organized abandonment, hedge-fund-driven housing (eviction) markets, poverty-wage service work, the subsidizing of white leisure and work environments, "therapeutic" economies of (for-profit, nonprofit, municipal) carceral management, and the hyper-extraction of sex work from the commodified bodies of women, girls, and boys made disposable through racialized criminalization inflicted by policing. In Milwaukee, called "the Harvard of pimp schools," defending Black women, girls, and boys from the violence of human-trafficking economies subtended by criminalizing policing often falls to community defenders such as Vaun Mayes.

When Mayes was arrested again in June 2020, he was at Fortieth and Lloyd Streets, trying to calm a rightfully angry crowd.[72] After two young Black girls went missing, dozens gathered in front of a home suspected to be involved in sex trafficking. They had been missing for days, but the police never issued an Amber Alert, claiming that the girls were not eligible. The community took it upon themselves to find the young girls and other Black children who had gone missing. They went to the suspicious house on their own. The police then arrived outfitted in riot gear, yet their presence did not make anything or anyone safer. Even though the police stationed themselves outside the house, it was still somehow set on fire. The house was burned along with any evidence of sex trafficking that officers claimed did not exist.[73] Some members of the crowd tried to enter the home—perhaps to confront the people inside, look for missing children, or get evidence to confirm that children were being sexually exploited. Some may have feared that evidence was being destroyed. Mayes was arrested in this context, although it is not clear from the video released by the MPD to Fox6 Milwaukee that Mayes was among those who entered the house. (He is seen only walking up the steps.)[74] The police blotter listed his charge as burglary, and the statement put out by former Milwaukee Police Chief Alfonso Morales said Mayes's arrest was "in connection with the civil unrest" on Fortieth and Lloyd Streets, in particular for a "felony charge related to his alleged involvement in criminal activities."[75]

The MPD's statement, found in several news articles, also commented on the missing girls' experiences: "MPD interviewed both teenagers who denied going to or being at the residence and denied meeting or knowing anyone who lived at that residence. There is also no evidence to substantiate that human trafficking occurred at that location."[76] Much of online crime reporting today publishes police statements word for word yet prefaces them with a journalistic title which suggests that investigative reporting was conducted. Fox6 Milwaukee did not even acknowledge that it was using the MPD's statement in its article titled "4 Sought in Arson, Shots Fired Near 40th and Lloyd; Police Say No Evidence to Suggest Missing Girls Were There."[77] In this article, "written" by Angélica Sánchez and Ashley Sears, exact sentences and phrases from the MPD statement are used throughout but not acknowledged as such, thereby providing police statements the guise of objectivity and neutrality. The MPD statement on the arrest of Mayes and its use by mainstream media criminalize and discredit the people involved in the protest while dismissing the girls' traumatic experiences, representing Mayes's arrest as necessary for maintaining law and order.

This is policing on the streets and in real time—Mayes, community defender and respected activist, is criminalized, arrested for a crime that he did not commit. He was at the scene, trying to deescalate the crowd and help the mothers find their missing girls. He was trying to protect young Black teenagers who he knew were vulnerable to the violences of an informal economy that profited from the sex work of those most socially and politically marginalized, those inordinately immiserated. The violence work of police—willfully not conducting a thorough investigation when the girls were reported missing, neglectfully letting people's homes and any potential evidence burn, intimidating community members who took it upon themselves to find missing children, and arresting a prominent activist who live-streamed the events—ensured that people profiting from the informal economy would continue to profit while those exploited by it and those trying to challenge it would be further criminalized.

It would be irresponsible to take the MPD's words at face value and dismiss the residents' anger and fears because sex trafficking in Milwaukee is a thriving industry; the city is known as the "Harvard of pimp schools," and Wisconsin is known as "the hub of human-trafficking."[78] And importantly, what makes Black, Latinx, and Indigenous women, girls, boys, and LGBTQ youths so intensely vulnerable to human trafficking in Milwaukee is policing. A 2018 report confirmed that victims of sex trafficking in Milwaukee were not just overwhelmingly young, Black women and girls—they were also young, Black women and girls who had previous interactions with the Milwaukee Police Department.[79] In other words, criminalization was key to making young Black women and girls, already economically immiserated, immensely vulnerable to sexual exploitation and commodification. Their interactions with police evidence both their vulnerability to violent situations (domestic violence, child abuse, and sexual assault) and their vulnerability to policing itself (drug crimes, homelessness, stealing, missing person reports, prostitution, and prior experience of trafficking). Both these vulnerabilities create conditions of possibility for sex-trade economies, a mode of gendered racial colonial capitalist accumulation.

The missing girls' confusing, disoriented statements should be read in this context. When the community found the girls 3.5 miles from the suspicious house, a mother of one of the missing girls, Selcy Perkins, along with Mayes, addressed concerned community members and the press. As she told reporters, "My daughter said she walked a lot of places. She's saying she's been in this house, she's saying she wasn't in this house. She said she laid down, she woke up and now she's saying she was never at this address. . . . So to be honest with you I don't know what is going on with this address, but what I do know is there are a lot of children and a lot of parents affiliated with missing children at this same address. This address was not just pulled up out of the air."[80] If the girls were earning money for sex, this would complicate how they answered questions and how their statements would be represented and received. Perkins's daughter is likely not easily read as an "innocent" victim. The false dichotomy between victimization and agency informs how people assign blame and confer compassion. If children and teens are choosing sex work, they will be seen as at least partially culpable for the abuses they face, which can obscure the fact that trafficked minors, who earn money for sex, are extremely vulnerable to sexual exploitation and violence.

Both Mayes and Perkins told reporters that "the house is just one of many in the area that have kids coming and going."[81] If kids are choosing to come and go, it is likely that children and teens are not just coerced but are also choosing this work, whether for money, out of fear, or through necessity. They may be choosing to come and go because they are being manipulated or threatened by someone in the industry, but it's also possible that sex work gives them a sense of autonomy. And because they are complicated young people, their reasons may change from day to day. Yet regardless of whether children are engaging in sex acts for money of their own accord, it is the act of criminalization that makes them so very vulnerable to exploitation and abuse.

Because minors cannot legally consent to sex, under Wisconsin and federal law any sex act with a minor for money is considered trafficking.[82] However, many states, such as Wisconsin, allow minors who are trafficked to also be arrested for prostitution. Perkins's daughter told her mom that she saw MPD officers ten times and spoke to them once while she was missing. Seeing MPD officers and receiving no help can have several interpretations—officers could be actually involved in trafficking or simply did not care, and/or Perkins's daughter could have feared that interacting with the officers would lead only to sexual exploitation, abuse, and arrest. Because she was missing, we know that even if she had been coming and going before, something terrible happened to her that made it impossible for her to go home. She needed members of the community to care, to look for her, to find her, to put it out there that she was loved.

In her work critiquing the ways in which anti-trafficking advocates fail to consider Black girls' specific vulnerabilities to criminalization and sex work, Jasmine Phillips asserts that "the dominant exploiter-victim narrative obscures the economic and social realities that serve as pathways into sex work . . . [because it] assumes that a majority of girls involved in sex work are doing so under the authority and control of an exploiter."[83] Young Black women and girls involved in sex work cannot be represented as completely and easily victimized; they are more likely to be criminalized and/ or arrested for prostitution rather than aided by laws like the Trafficking Victims Protection Act (2000).

Young people were returned because community members took it upon themselves to look for them. If these children had been found by police, they would likely have been arrested for prostitution, starting or adding to a criminal record, which would make them even more vulnerable to sexual exploitation, abuse, and violence. Doing little to nothing when these young Black children and teens go missing for days, weeks, and more is essentially killing them with impunity: informal economies, such as human trafficking, are often highly exploitative, extracting labor from those deemed disposable by turning their bodies into commodities. The power of police lies in its organized abandonment of the neighborhood's most vulnerable children, leaving them for dead when they are missing, arresting them if they are found. The MPD narrated its actions as legitimate and sent the statement to mainstream media to be written up, word for word, under the guise of journalistic objectivity. Mayes critiqued the MPD: "You call it vigilantism, but I call it three almost four young people returning home in a matter of hours versus them being missing for days and weeks with you all handling it."[84] He cared about the young, criminalized Black girls and boys that the MPD was not looking for. He was part of the reason that the children were found, and he was arrested because of it.

A Block-Party Protest on the County Jail Lawn

Part of the force of administrative power lies in the very narratives we weave to explain how it works because it appears to operate so thoroughly, so pervasively, so ubiquitously, and with such devastating effects and deadly consequences. And we have explicated only one small aspect of administrative power: policing. In doing that we have explained how police discretion is not an aberration or a weak link in a fair system of law and order, but a factor necessary for the system to operate efficiently and dangerously to do the sorting on the street and in real time that criminalizes people and actions that threaten colonial racial capitalist arrangements. Additionally, we've examined how liberalism as a capitalist worlding praxis preauthorizes police killings of those whom colonial racial capitalism deems disposable. Indeed, to explain how administrative power works requires that we refuse the narrative it tells about itself: that it is incredibly overwhelming, touching everything and everyone.

But it is absolutely crucial that we remember several vitally important aspects of this form of colonial, racial violence that disguises itself as the benign race-neutral business-as-usual work of institutions. First, no form of power is absolute. Second, what makes administrative power appear absolute and totalizing is also what makes it so incredibly fragile. Administrative power seems to touch all and everything; it appears to require the cooperation and complicity of millions of people to either do the violence work of business as usual or to ignore it. In fact, a lot of ideological work goes into representing administrative power as too overwhelming to overcome, too dangerous to defeat, and too big to bother trying. But, in fact, the opposite is true. The larger the reach, the deeper the entrenchment, and the more people involved, the more fragile this power actually is. It is a power like glass—glass is quite durable and strong, but the thinner the glass, the more prone it is to cracking, breaking, or shattering, which brings us to the third point we need to keep in mind. Movements that undo administrative power do not need to have an overwhelming reach, intensity, or number of people in order to effectively interrupt its devastating consequences and delegitimate its reasons for enacting violence. The common question "What do we do now?" assumes that resistance to oppression needs to match or be more forceful than oppressive power structures in order to effect meaningful change. We believe this is the wrong question because all acts of resistance (no matter how small) to colonial racial capitalism and the administrative violences that sustain it work not only to undermine and discredit colonial racial capitalism but also to offer, in the process, alternative ways of living, being, and relating to one another. They are, as Gilmore says, "rehearsals for freedom."[85] Therefore, a better question to ask is "How can we support and join the work that activists and community defenders are already doing?" Like very thin glass, administrative power can be shattered by the smallest acts of rebellion—by communities that love themselves more than they fear the police.

So we end with community members who love themselves and one another more than they fear the police to illustrate how administrative power, though deadly and devastating, is also so very fragile. It is so fragile that it can shatter when Black people hold a party. When Vaun Mayes was arrested on June 29, 2020, Frank Nitty II organized Black community members and their allies. They gathered outside the Milwaukee County Courthouse and County Jail, where Mayes was detained, demanding that he be set free. They chanted, "Don't arrest me, arrest the police!" and "Free Vaun Mayes!"[86] They set up a DJ and played songs to dance to, including Kendrick Lamar's "Alright" and Marcia Griffith's "Electric Boogie." They grilled food. They played spades. They set up video games and a bounce house for children. Someone did henna tattoos. They set up tents and air mattresses and camped out, waiting. For two days, they set up a twenty-four-hour celebration of Black social life, taking up space, using land not as property but as a partner in doing revolutionary work. They repurposed this land by using it as a site for life, love, music, games, dancing, building relationships, relaxing, self-care. In chalk, they scrawled "Black Lives Matter" on the concrete, reclaiming and renaming the land itself so that for these days this land was used not solely as the foundation for the courthouse and the jail, as the foundation for institutions that did the not-at-all benign business-as-usual work of disrupting Black, brown, and Indigenous lives and relationships. For these two days this space was about Black people enjoying their lives and one another; for these two days this space enabled the protesters to make not just "peaceful" but loving demands.

The protesters were caring for one another in front of the county courthouse and jail. As they waited for their demand that Vaun Mayes be set free to be realized, they became examples of alternatives to unpaid reproductive labor. Care work was not just collective at the party; it was also no longer "work." Care work was central to celebrating Black life. People were feeding each other, watching over everyone's children, playing cards and board games, having a good time, enjoying one another's company while they waited. They supported each other, nervous, anxious, excited, and confident. Colonial racial capitalism could not make a profit from the people who decided to party at the courthouse instead of working at their jobs. And even those who went to work first or after or even during the protest party interrupted the usual work/rest pattern of colonial racial capitalism. Instead of collapsing and falling asleep in front of a mind-numbing television show at the end of a long, exhausting workday, they went to 949 North Ninth Street to a twenty-four-hour protest party where rest and dancing and friendship were energizing, creative, necessary, and revolutionary.

The protesters were doing the hardest but most rewarding work of all, visioning and living in the world they wanted, enacting and putting into practice their collective "freedom dreams."[87] We might read them as working against the ways in which Black life has so often been portrayed as one-dimensional, as only the struggle against racism, as only pain and disappointment. Because liberalism assumes that white empathy is the only path to Black liberation, liberals and liberal media too often showcase and exploit Black suffering because this is the assumed way to encourage white people to demand that Black people's individual rights need to be protected in the name of democracy. We might read the partygoers as working against this portrayal, but of course they are not thinking at all about the people who don't support them; they are not worrying about whether coverage of their protest party will encourage not-yet-allies to be supportive. They don't care about the branding of their revolutionary work.

They are just living their complex lives, loving one another, spending time with one another, enjoying one another, and working very hard to create a welcoming place for Vaun Mayes to join when he is released. They make sure there is food for him to eat, people to talk to and love him, children to play with and music to dance to. They make sure they are witnesses to the trauma of his arrest and detainment, and they make sure they are participants in and witnesses to the triumph of his release.

Vaun was released, as they knew he would be. A bounce house and a buffet shattered administrative power. A DJ and a Sony PlayStation undid all the purposeful violence work that police officers, using their "discretion," put in to arrest Mayes. The partying protesters shattered administrative power with food, music, community, love, and time. And this shattering was so much more powerful than the arrests and detainments. The arrest ignited anger and frustration. But the release touched the protesters down deep, where feelings really matter. When Vaun was freed, it wasn't just the protesters who felt euphoric, ecstatic, and energized; it was also everyone who watched their live feeds, anticipating their success. On one post Marquita Hartfield wrote, "I can't even Lie this is very touching! We need more of this and less of the bullshit! Salute to all y'all! This is what you call a good ol time!"[88] With so much of this chapter focusing on all the terrible ways that administrative power weaves itself into Black social life, some might think that all anyone would be able to feel would be resentment, anger, despair, and paralysis. But administrative power, no matter how overwhelming it seems to be, is just nowhere near as powerful as a good time. As Eva Welch posted, "They were down there with a DJ, a buffet, a damn bouncy house, a dance party! OMG This has to go down as the BEST protest ever!!!! I LOVE MILWAUKEE!"[89] The best protest ever was so very touching—touching everyone down deep and so powerfully that all they felt was love, and this love was felt so profoundly that they could not contain it, could not be embarrassed by the intensity of their emotions. Antwann McBride took footage of Vaun's release; in his filming he took us to Frank Nitty II. Antwann was overcome with emotion. You can hear it in his voice. He speaks slowly with so much intention, every word emphasized: "This [camera on Frank Nitty] the real GOAT [greatest of all time], Bro. I love you, man, love you. My mom love you, my family love you, my nieces love you. The world love you! We all love you, Frank!" He takes the camera to scan the party and Vaun being embraced and says, "Look at this, man, just so beautiful. Vaun free! Vaun free, Baby!"[90]

The thing with glass is that with just one tiny crack, it is only a matter of time before the rest of it shatters. All the partygoers knew this, and they felt the shattering. Vaun is released, but they don't go home. They are energized now, still euphoric, still ecstatic, filled with so much love for Frank Nitty, for Vaun Mayes, for themselves, for one another, for the city and the land it's built on. They stay, party more, demand the release of activist Demetrius Griffin, who live-streamed the police overseeing people leaving the home on Fortieth and Lloyd.[91] Griffin is also freed.

We can't lie. The euphoria and the love of the protest partygoers are so very touching that it touches us too even a year later (and for one of us, more than eight hundred miles away). It touches us more deeply than administrative power, no matter how extensive, ever could. We feel it too, this energizing, contagious, uncontainable love, able to shatter administrative power with a bounce house, able to replace fear of the police with freedom dreams, able to rehearse freedom in front of the county jail, just so beautiful.

NOTES

1. Repairing Together, "Unity Fire MKE."

2. "When we want to hear from the community, we're going four days for 24 hours. That's an entirely different mindset than the public servants that are elected into positions that are supposed to [represent] us." Mark Denning, quoted by Erin Bloodgood in "Mark Denning Lifts Native Voices."

3. Repairing Together, "Unity Fire MKE."

4. Repairing Together, "Unity Fire MKE."

5. Read, "Derek Chauvin."

6. Kelley, "Why *Black Marxism*, Why Now?"

7. With the term *violence work* we follow Micol Seigel, who describes police as agents of violence who "realize—they *make real*—the core power of the state" (10) and differ from other agents of multiple kinds of structural violence (psychic, epistemic, discursive, etc.) in that they are authorized by the state to use physical force on the bodies of human beings. In Seigel's words, police are violence workers "whose labors are enabled by the fact that at some point they are entitled to bring out the handcuffs" (11).

8. Bordertown Violence Working Group, *Red Nation Rising*, 6.

9. Gilmore, "Abolition Geography," 229.

10. On policing as the fabrication and maintenance of social orders structured in dominance, see Neocleous, *Fabrication of Social Order*. On policing—in the United States and as a US export to allied nations across the globe—as a means for "suppressing civil unrest and securing the conditions for the smooth operation of capitalism," see Schrader, *Badges without Borders*. On the function of police in fabricating neoliberalism and functioning as counterinsurgency to Black and brown freedom struggles from during and after the Watts rebellion in 1965 to post-Katrina uprisings in New Orleans in 2005, see Camp, *Incarcerating the Crisis*.

11. Ruth Nicole Brown, personal communication with Lisa Marie Cacho, December 2018.

12. See Reddy, *Freedom with Violence*.

13. Million, "Resurgent Kinships," 399.

14. Historically, these privileged groups align with configurations of "whiteness as property" and the "the white possessive," yet they are always dynamic, with "multicultural white supremacy" and "neoliberal multiculturalism" naming two distinct "membership" groups included in US political hegemony today. Dylan Rodríguez articulates this rethinking of hegemony as a subset of governance reserved for privileged (white) subjects this way: "Given the various genealogies and long historical continuities of coercive power that persistently puncture and disrupt the possibilities for constructing consensual relations of state authority and popular consent to a modern social order—including but not limited to land displacement and conquest, settler colonial occupation, ecological and cultural genocide, chattel enslavement, legal non-personhood, and violently enforced gender normativity— the consensual basis of 'hegemony' has *always* been overwhelmingly reserved for the geographies, publics, and privileged collective subjectivities of White Being, including non-citizen, immigrant, and even 'undocumented' white Europeans." Rodríguez, *White Reconstruction*, 20.

15. On liberalism writ large as a set of praxis concepts (private property, the nation-state, and possessive individualism, etc.) developed historically to manage colonialism, settler colonialism, and global circuits of capitalist accumulation, see Lowe, *Intimacies of Four Continents*; Nichols, *Theft Is Property!*; Ince, *Colonial Capitalism*; and Bhandar, *Colonial Lives of Property*.

16. See Lowe, *Intimacies of Four Continents*.

17. The authors would like to thank Chandan Reddy for this formulation of the division of humanity into the political and the administrative. Moreover, wherever "administrative power" is theorized in this chapter, it should be understood as bearing the imprint of Reddy's thoughts and interventions. This chapter is in conversation with other works on "administrative power" coauthored with Reddy, such as the paper presented by Melamed and Reddy, "Administrating Today's Racial Capitalism." See also Melamed and Reddy, "Using Liberal Rights."

18. Warner, "Uniform Arrest Act," 329, 330.

19. Hemmens and Levin, "Resistance Is Futile," 492.

20. Other proposed changes were the following: to have discretion in giving summons to appear in court instead of arresting for misdemeanors, to release arrested persons without their having to go before a magistrate, to keep suspects in detention as long as necessary with a judge's orders, and to permit officers to require witnesses to identify themselves by name and address (he identified the last suggestion as optional). See Warner, "Uniform Arrest Act."

21. Gilmore, "Abolition Geography," 228, 229.

22. Nichols, "Colonialism of Incarceration," 446, 448–49. For more on how the Indian Civil Rights Act of 1968 and court cases undermine Indigenous sovereignty through criminalization, see also Cacho, "Civil Rights, Commerce."

23. Coulthard, *Red Skin, White Masks*, 7.

24. See Melamed, *Represent and Destroy*.

25. See Cacho, *Social Death*.

26. Gilmore, quoted by Vulliamy, "Rebellion in Baltimore."

27. Balto, "'Occupied Territory,'" 235.

28. See Karuka, *Empire's Tracks*.

29. Bordertown Violence Working Group, *Red Nation Rising*, 40.

30. Red Nation, "Communism Is the Horizon," 23.

31. On "grounded relationality," see Byrd et al., "Predatory Value," 14.

32. Ritchie, *Invisible No More*, 55 (emphasis added).

33. Vaisvilas, "American Indians Incarcerated."

34. Pember, "Driving While Indian."

35. Vaisvilas, "American Indians Incarcerated."

36. Pember, "Driving While Indian"; Pember, "Another Reality."

37. State v. Richard E. Houghton, Jr., 2013AP001581-CR (Wis. 2015).

38. ACLU, Collins et al. v. City of Milwaukee et al.

39. Choudhury, "Stop-and-Frisk Settlement."

40. Many of the "best practices" in this report, such as data collection on pedestrian and traffic stops, were not actually happening in the MPD, according to the ACLU lawsuit.

41. La Vigne et al., *Stop and Frisk*, 47.

42. ACLU, Collins et al. v. City of Milwaukee et al. (emphasis added).

43. Crivello, letter to Fire and Police Commission.

44. Choudhury, "Stop-and-Frisk Settlement."

45. Crime and Justice Institute, *City of Milwaukee Settlement Agreement,* 20.

46. Crime and Justice Institute, *City of Milwaukee Settlement Agreement,* 7, 9.

47. The settlement also stipulated that not more than 15 percent of traffic stops, field interviews, and no-action encounters should be conducted without reasonable suspicion. Crime and Justice Institute, *City of Milwaukee Settlement Agreement,* 13–15, 20.

48. Hashimoto, "Tale of Two Milwaukees."

49. See Walia, *Undoing Border Imperialism.*

50. In the greater Milwaukee region, settlers continue to violate the treaty rights and sovereignty of Wisconsin's Native nations, even when it comes down again to desecrating and removing Indigenous burial mounds to make way for golf courses. This is the case with the ancestors of the Ho-Chunk Nation illegally disinterred in the building of a third golf course at the Kohler Resort. See Malewitz, "Discovery of Ancient Human Remains."

51. For example, in the Illinois Cook County courthouse, almost 95 percent of cases are resolved through plea bargains rather than trials. Van Cleve, *Crook County,* 72.

52. Trivedi and Van Cleve, "To Serve and Protect," 933.

53. Feeley, *Process Is the Punishment,* 15.

54. Gordon, *Ghostly Matters,* 201–8.

55. We must contextualize white obsessions with "looting" with how powerfully movements against police violence delegitimize police power by revealing its repressive, counterinsurgent function. One answer to "Why are white people so obsessed with looting?" is that the obsession itself stabilizes police legitimacy with an anti-Black criminalization fix while suppressing white group complicity with oppressive policing and racial/settler dominations in general. It also fixes looting in a criminal framework, setting up a good protester/bad protester dichotomy to legitimize and normalize policing the uprisings, marches, etc. (And let's not forget that looting is a redistribution of wealth.)

56. Williams, "'Give Them a Cause.'"

57. Williams, "'Give Them a Cause,'" 250.

58. Glauber, "'This Is Organized Chaos.'"

59. At the time of this writing, Nitty has filed a lawsuit against several Milwaukee sheriff's officers for targeting him during the protest. TMJ4.com, "Milwaukee Activist Frank Nitty."

60. TMJ4.com, "Milwaukee Activist Frank Nitty."

61. On how the US state always represents its excessively cruel violence (police and military) against racialized groups to be a counterviolence, see Reddy, *Freedom with Violence*.

62. International Center for Not-for-Profit Law, "US Protest Law Tracker."

63. Epstein and Mazzei, "GOP Bill Targets Protestors."

64. Cacho and Melamed, "How Police Abuse the Charge."

65. Brenes, "Police Reform Doesn't Work."

66. One of the authors has firsthand knowledge about how people who run over protesters are not charged with crimes and how journalistic accounts take police statements as facts. Like the articles on Van Mayes at Fortieth and Lloyd, this news article that misreports an incident when she was hit by a driver at a protest is the actual police statement but is not acknowledged as such. See Danbeck, "Police."

67. Jorgensen, "Student Activists Ask Mayor"; Anuta, "School Safety Agents." Supposedly, the full transition to getting the NYPD out of the schools will be accomplished by 2022. In the meantime, the NYPD will receive more "training" to redefine its duties.

68. ACLU and Media Justice, Request to Federal Bureau of Investigation.

69. Vielmetti, "Law Targets Rights Activists."

70. Holmes, "Questions Surround Vaun Mayes' Arrest."

71. Vielmetti, "Law Targets Rights Activists."

72. Jannene, "Protest Organizer Vaun Mayes Arrested."

73. Jannene, "Mother Connected"; WTMJ News, "More Than 10 Injured."

74. Fox6 Now Milwaukee, "Police Share Video.'"

75. Milwaukee Police (@MilwaukeePolice), Twitter, June 29, 2020, 5:45 p.m. https://twitter.com/MilwaukeePolice/status/1277719873955782663.

76. Milwaukee Police (@MilwaukeePolice), Twitter, June 29, 2020, 5:45 p.m.

77. Sánchez and Sears, "4 Sought in Arson." Another such account was posted by WTMJ News, which posted the MPD's statement but titled it "More Than 10 Injured Including Officers, Firefighter after Shooting, House Fire following Demonstrations on Milwaukee's North Side."

78. Sullivan, "Hub of Human Trafficking"; Holmes, "Harvard of Pimp Schools."

79. Milwaukee Homicide Review Commission et al., *Estimating the Magnitude*.

80. Jannene, "Mother Connected."

81. Jannene, "Mother Connected."

82. Sullivan, "Hub of Human Trafficking."

83. Phillips, "Black Girls and the (Im)Possibilities," 1656.

84. Chernéy Amhara, "Vaun Mayes Holding Press Conference after Unrest near 40th and Lloyd," recorded live. Facebook, June 25, 2020. www.facebook.com /watch/live/?v=326935238311357&ref=watch_permalink.

85. Ruth Wilson Gilmore, personal communication with Jodi Melamed, March 2019. Gilmore also spoke about "rehearsals for freedom" in her keynote address for the Racial Capitalism Symposium for the Unit for Criticism and Interpretive Theory at the University of Illinois, Urbana-Champaign, March 29, 2019. See Gilmore, "What Is the 'Racial' in Racial Capitalism?"

86. Carson, Vielmetti, and Spicuzza, "Community Activist Vaun Mayes Arrested."

87. Kelley, *Freedom Dreams.*

88. Marquita Hartfield, comment on Antwann McBride's Livestream Facebook, 45:46. Facebook, June 30, 2020. www.facebook.com/comediansipsippi/videos /3603887212969415.

89. Eva Welch, "For years I have watched." Facebook, June 30, 2020. www.facebook .com/eva.deva.52/posts/10157907998966785.

90. Antwann McBride, Livestream Facebook, June 30, 2020. www.facebook.com /comediansipsippi/videos/3603887212969415.

91. Jannene, "Activists Clean Up."

BIBLIOGRAPHY

American Civil Liberties Union (ACLU). *Collins et al. v. The City of Milwaukee et al.* July 16, 2019. www.aclu.org/cases/collins-et-al-v-city-milwaukee-et-al.
American Civil Liberties Union (ACLU) and Media Justice. Request to Federal Bureau of Investigation, Under the Freedom of Information Act. June 11, 2020. www.aclu.org/sites/default/files/field_document/2020.06.11_racially _motivated_extremism_foia.pdf.
Anuta, Joe. "School Safety Agents Will Stay Under NYPD This Year, despite City's Claims of $1B Cut." *Politico New York*, July 2, 2020. www.politico.com/states /new-york/albany/story/2020/07/02/school-safety-agents-will-stay-under -nypd-this-year-despite-citys-claims-of-1b-cut-1296868.
Balto, Simon Ezra. "'Occupied Territory': Police Repression and Black Resistance in Postwar Milwaukee, 1950–1968." *Journal of African American History* 98, no. 2 (2013): 229–52.
Bhandar, Brenna. *Colonial Lives of Property: Law, Land, and Racial Regimes of Ownership.* Durham, NC: Duke University Press, 2018.
Bloodgood, Erin. "Mark Denning Lifts Native Voices with a Traditional Fire Ceremony." *Shepherd Express*, September 17, 2020. https://shepherdexpress .com/news/hero-of-the-week/mark-denning-speaks-out-on-behalf-of-native -americans/#/questions.

Bordertown Violence Working Group. *Red Nation Rising: From Bordertown Violence to Native Liberation*. Oakland: PM, 2021.

Brenes, Michael. "Police Reform Doesn't Work." *Boston Review*, April 26, 2021. http://bostonreview.net/race/michael-brenes-police-reform-doesnt-work.

Byrd, Jodi, Alyosha Goldstein, Jodi Melamed, and Chandan Reddy. "Predatory Value: Economies of Dispossession and Disturbed Relationalities." *Social Text* 36, no. 2 (135) (2018): 1–18.

Cacho, Lisa Marie. "Civil Rights, Commerce, and US Colonialism." *Social Text* 36, no. 2 (135) (2018): 63–82.

Cacho, Lisa Marie. *Social Death: Racialized Rightlessness and the Criminalization of the Unprotected*. New York: New York University Press, 2012.

Cacho, Lisa, and Jodi Melamed. "How Police Abuse the Charge of Resisting Arrest." *Boston Review*, June 29, 2020. www.bostonreview.net/race-law-justice/lisa-cacho-jodi-melamed-how-police-abuse-charge-resisting-arrest.

Camp, Jordan. *Incarcerating the Crisis: Freedom Struggles and the Rise of the Neoliberal State*. Oakland: University of California Press, 2016.

Carson, Sophie, Bruce Vielmetti, and Mary Spicuzza. "Community Activist Vaun Mayes Arrested on Allegations of Burglary as a Party to a Crime." *Milwaukee Journal Sentinel*, June 29, 2020. https://www.jsonline.com/story/news/local/2020/06/29/milwaukee-activist-vaun-mayes-arrested-burglary-charge/3280476001/.

Choudhury, Nusrat. "Stop-and-Frisk Settlement in Milwaukee Lawsuit Is a Wakeup Call for Police Nationwide." *ACLU Blog*, July 13, 2018. www.aclu.org/blog/criminal-law-reform/reforming-police/stop-and-frisk-settlement-milwaukee-lawsuit-wakeup-call.

Coulthard, Glen. *Red Skin, White Masks: Rejecting the Colonial Politics of Recognition*. Minneapolis: University of Minnesota Press, 2014.

Crime and Justice Institute. *City of Milwaukee Settlement Agreement: Semi Annual Analysis of Traffic Stops, Field Interviews, No-Action Encounters, and Frisks*, April 2021. https://city.milwaukee.gov/ImageLibrary/Groups/cityFPC/Reports/Crime-and-Justice-Institute/CJISemiannualAnalysisApril2021.pdf.

Crivello, Michael V. Letter to Fire and Police Commission, May 5, 2016. http://www.city.milwaukee.gov/ImageLibrary/Groups/cityFPC/agendas5/160728_III_D.pdf.

Danbeck, Jackson. "Police: Driver Accidentally Hits Milwaukee Bicyclist Attending Protest." *TMJ4.com*, September 25, 2020. www.tmj4.com/news/local-news/police-driver-accidently-hits-milwaukee-protester-who-was-a-riding-bike.

Epstein, Reid J., and Patricia Mazzei. "GOP Bill Targets Protestors (and Absolves Motorists Who Hit Them)." *New York Times*, April 22, 2021. https://www.nytimes.com/2021/04/21/us/politics/republican-anti-protest-laws.html.

Feeley, Malcolm M. *The Process Is the Punishment: Handling Cases in a Lower Criminal Court*. New York: Russell Sage Foundation, 1992 (1979).

Fox6 Now Milwaukee. "Police Share Video of 'Multiple Suspects' Wanted for Removing Property from 40th and Lloyd." *Fox6now.com*, June 30, 2020. www .fox6now.com/news/police-share-video-of-multiple-suspects-wanted-for -removing-property-from-home-near-40th-and-lloyd.

Gilmore, Ruth Wilson. "Abolition Geography and the Problem of Innocence." In *Futures of Black Radicalism*, edited by Gaye Theresa Johnson and Alex Lubin, 225–40. London: Verso, 2017.

Gilmore, Ruth Wilson. "What Is the 'Racial' in Racial Capitalism? Magic, Partition, Politics." Keynote address for the Racial Capitalism Symposium for the Unit for Criticism and Interpretive Theory at the University of Illinois, Urbana-Champaign, March 29, 2019.

Glauber, Bill. "'This Is Organized Chaos': How Activists Frank Nitty and Khalil Coleman Have Kept Milwaukee Marching for More Than 2 Weeks." *Milwaukee Journal Sentinel*, June 15, 2020. https://www.jsonline.com/story/news/2020 /06/15/milwaukee-protests-how-frank-nitty-khalil-coleman-became-leaders -george-floyd-march-police-brutality/5345133002/.

Gordon, Avery F. *Ghostly Matters: Haunting and the Sociological Imagination*. Minneapolis: University of Minnesota Press, 1997.

Hashimoto, Yui. "The Tale of Two Milwaukees." *Urban Milwaukee*, July 12, 2020. https://urbanmilwaukee.com/2020/07/12/op-ed-the-tale-of-two-milwaukees/.

Hemmens, Craig, and Daniel Levin. "Resistance Is Futile: The Right to Resist Unlawful Arrest in an Era of Aggressive Policing." *Crime and Delinquency* 46, no. 4 (2000): 472–96. doi.org/10.1177/0011128700046004004.

Holmes, Isiah. "The Harvard of Pimp Schools." *Urban Milwaukee*, February 28, 2018. https://urbanmilwaukee.com/2020/07/12/op-ed-the-tale-of-two-milwaukees/.

Holmes, Isiah. "Questions Surround Vaun Mayes' Arrest." *Urban Milwaukee*, February 6, 2019. https://urbanmilwaukee.com/2019/02/06/questions-surround -vaun-mayes-arrest/.

Ince, Onur Ulas. *Colonial Capitalism and the Dilemmas of Liberalism*. New York: Oxford University Press, 2018.

International Center for Not-for-Profit Law. "US Protest Law Tracker." May 17, 2021. www.icnl.org/usprotestlawtracker/?location=&status=enacted&issue =&date=&type =legislative.

Jannene, Jeramey. "Activists Clean Up around Burned House as Questions Remain." *Urban Milwaukee*, June 24, 2020. https://urbanmilwaukee.com /2020/06/24/activists-clean-up-around-burned-house-as-questions-remain /nggallery/image/2120-n-40th-st-4/.

Jannene, Jeramey. "Mother Connected to '40th and Lloyd' Incident Speaks Out." *Urban Milwaukee*, June 26, 2020. https://urbanmilwaukee.com/2020/06/26 /mother-connected-to-40th-and-lloyd-incident-speaks-out/.

Jannene, Jeramey. "Protest Organizer Vaun Mayes Arrested." *Urban Milwaukee*, June 29, 2020. https://urbanmilwaukee.com/2020/06/29/protest-organizer -vaun-mayes-arrested/.

Jorgensen, Jillian. "Student Activists Ask Mayor Not to Hire More NYPD School
Safety Agents." *Spectrum News*, April 24, 2021. https://www.ny1.com/nyc/all
-boroughs/education/2021/04/24/student-activists-ask-mayor-not-to-hire
-more-nypd-school-safety-agents.

Karuka, Manu. *Empire's Tracks: Indigenous Nations, Chinese Workers, and the Transcontinental Railroad*. Oakland: University of California Press, 2019.

Kelley, Robin D. G. *Freedom Dreams: The Black Radical Imagination*. Boston:
Beacon, 2002.

Kelley, Robin D. G. "Why *Black Marxism*, Why Now?" *Boston Review*, February 1,
2021. http://bostonreview.net/race-philosophy-religion/robin-d-g-kelley-why
-black-marxism-why-now.

La Vigne, Nancy G., Pamela Lachman, Shebani Rao, and Andrea Matthews. *Stop
and Frisk: Balancing Crime Control with Community Relations*. Washington,
DC: Office of Community Oriented Policing Services, 2014.

Lowe, Lisa. *The Intimacies of Four Continents*. Durham, NC: Duke University Press,
2015.

Malewitz, Jim. "Discovery of Ancient Human Remains Complicates Plans for Golf
Course in Sheybogan." *Sheybogan Press*, May 25, 2021. www.sheboyganpress
.com/story/news/2021/05/25/kohler-sheboygan-golf-course-hits-snag-after
-ancient-remains-found/5243156001.

Melamed, Jodi. *Represent and Destroy: Rationalizing Violence in the New Racial
Capitalism*. Minneapolis: University of Minnesota Press, 2011.

Melamed, Jodi, and Chandan Reddy. "Administrating Today's Racial Capitalism
through Differential Rights." Paper presented at the Racial Capitalism Symposium for the Unit for Criticism and Interpretive Theory at the University of
Illinois, Urbana-Champaign, March 29–30, 2019.

Melamed, Jodi, and Chandan Reddy. "Using Liberal Rights to Enforce Racial
Capitalism." Social Science Research Council, July 30, 2019. https://items.ssrc
.org/race-capitalism/using-liberal-rights-to-enforce-racial-capitalism.

Million, Dian. "Resurgent Kinships: Indigenous Relations of Well-Being vs. Hu-
manitarian Health Economies." In *Routledge Handbook of Critical Indigenous
Studies*, edited by Brendan Hokowhitu, Aileen Moreton-Robison, Linda
Tuhiwai-Smith, Chris Andersen, and Steve Larkin, 392–404. New York:
Routledge, 2021.

Milwaukee Homicide Review Commission, Rethink Resources, Medical College
of Wisconsin Institute for Health and Equity, Milwaukee Sexual Assault
Review, and Milwaukee Police Department—Sensitive Crimes Division.
*Estimating the Magnitude of Sex Trafficking Risk and Victimization of Juveniles
and Young Adults City of Milwaukee January 1 2013 through December 31, 2016*,
March 1, 2018. www.doj.state.wi.us/sites/default/files/ocvs/human%20traf-
ficking/sextraffickingreportfinal03012018.pdf.

Neocleous, Mark. *The Fabrication of Social Order: A Critical Theory of Police Power*.
London: Pluto, 2000.

Nichols, Robert. "The Colonialism of Incarceration." *Radical Philosophy Review* 17, no. 2 (2014): 435–55.

Nichols, Robert. *Theft Is Property! Dispossession and Critical Theory.* Durham, NC: Duke University Press, 2019.

Pember, Mary Annette. "Speak Your Piece: Another Reality." *Daily Yonder: Keep It Rural,* April 27, 2015. https://dailyyonder.com/speak-your-piece-another -reality/2015/04/27.

Pember, Mary Annette. "Speak Your Piece: Driving While Indian." *Daily Yonder: Keep It Rural,* March 9, 2015. https://dailyyonder.com/speak-your-piece -driving-while-indian/2015/03/09.

Phillips, Jasmine. "Black Girls and the (Im)Possibilities of a Victim Trope: The Intersectional Failures of Legal and Advocacy Interventions in the Commercial Sexual Exploitation of Minors in the United States." UCLA *Law Review* 62 (2015): 1642–75.

Read, Richard. "Derek Chauvin, Officer Arrested in George Floyd's Death, Has a Record of Shootings and Complaints." *Los Angeles Times,* May 29, 2020. https://www.latimes.com/world-nation/story/2020-05-29/chauvin -shootings-complaints-minneapolis-floyd.

Reddy, Chandan. *Freedom with Violence: Race, Sexuality, and the US State.* Durham, NC: Duke University Press, 2011.

The Red Nation. "Communism Is the Horizon; Queer Indigenous Feminism Is the Way." *The rednation.org,* September 21, 2020. http://therednation.org/wp -content/uploads/2020/09/TRN-pamphlet-final.pdf.

Repairing Together. "Unity Fire MKE." Accessed May 25, 2021. https:// repairingtogether.org/unity-fire-mke.

Ritchie, Andrea J. *Invisible No More: Police Violence against Black Women and Women of Color.* Boston: Beacon, 2017.

Rodríguez, Dylan. *White Reconstruction: Domestic Warfare and the Logics of Genocide.* New York: Fordham University Press, 2021.

Sánchez, Angélica, and Ashley Sears. "4 Sought in Arson, Shots Fired Near 40th and Lloyd; Police Say No Evidence to Suggest Missing Girls Were There." *Fox6now.com,* June 26, 2020. www.fox6now.com/news/4-sought-in-arson -shots-fired-near-40th-and-lloyd-police-say-no-evidence-to-suggest-missing -girls-were-there.

Schrader, Stuart. *Badges without Borders: How Global Counterinsurgency Transformed American Policing.* Oakland: University of California Press, 2019.

Seigel, Micol. *Violence Work: State Power and the Limits of Police.* Durham, NC: Duke University Press, 2018.

Sullivan, Zoe. "Hub of Human Trafficking: Underground Sex Trade Thrives in Milwaukee." *Guardian,* November 2, 2015. www.theguardian.com/us-news /2015/nov/02/hub-human-trafficking-underground-sex-trade-milwaukee.

TMJ4.com. "Milwaukee Activist Frank Nitty Files Lawsuit against Milwaukee County Sheriff's Office." *TMJ4.com,* August 28, 2020. www.tmj4.com

/news/local-news/milwaukee-activist-frank-nitty-files-lawsuit-against-the
-milwaukee-county-sheriffs-office.

Trivedi, Somil, and Nicole Gonzalez Van Cleve. "To Serve and Protect Each
Other: How Police-Prosecutor Codependence Enables Police Misconduct."
Boston University Law Review 100 (2020): 895–933.

Vaisvilas, Frank. "American Indians Incarcerated at among Highest Rates in Wisconsin, as Many as Half the Inmates in Some Jails." *Green Bay Press Gazette*,
March 17, 2021. https://www.greenbaypressgazette.com/story/news/native
-american-issues/2021/03/17/native-americans-incarcerated-among-highest
-rates-wisconsin/6841084002/.

Van Cleve, Nicole Gonzalez. *Crook County: Racism and Injustice in America's Largest Criminal Court.* Stanford, CA: Stanford Law Books, 2016.

Vielmetti, Bruce. "Law Targets Rights Activists." *Milwaukee Journal Sentinel*, May 9,
2021: A4.

Vulliamy, Ed. "The Rebellion in Baltimore Is an Uprising against Austerity, Claims
Top US Academic." *Guardian*, May 2, 2015. www.theguardian.com/us-news
/2015/may/02/baltimore-rebellion-is-uprising-against-austerity-freddie-gray.

Walia, Harsha. *Undoing Border Imperialism.* Chico, CA: AK, 2013.

Warner, Sam B. "The Uniform Arrest Act." *Virginia Law Review* 28, no. 3 (1942):
315–47.

Williams, Yohuru. "'Give Them a Cause to Die For': The Black Panther Party in
Milwaukee 1969–77." In *Liberated Territory: Untold Local Perspectives on the
Black Panther Party*, edited by Yohuru Williams and Jama Lazerow, 249–51.
Durham, NC: Duke University Press, 2008.

WTMJ News. "More Than 10 Injured Including Officers, Firefighter after Shootings,
HouseFire following Demonstrations on Milwaukee's North Side." *WTMJ
.com*, June 23, 2020. https://wtmj.com/news/2020/06/23/house-catches-fire
-after-demonstrations-on-milwaukees-north-side/.

Policing Solidarity: Race, Violence, and the University of Puerto Rico

On February 9, 2011, in the midst of an ongoing student-led strike against state and university officials' efforts to shrink and privatize the University of Puerto Rico (UPR) system, students at the university's flagship campus in Río Piedras organized a "pintata," or paint-in, as an artistic protest against administrators' attempts to silence them with police intervention. An event in which students planned to spend the afternoon painting messages of resistance on the street in front of the university library ended unexpectedly as one of the most violent moments of the strike.

With the pintata under way, students became outraged when they spotted a police officer videotaping the activity. A group of students approached the officer and asked why they were being recorded when they were not doing anything wrong and demanded to know what the police planned to do with the video.[1] Almost immediately the situation grew tense, as the students insisted on answers and more police arrived on the scene. Eventually, one of the students attempted to take the camera from the officer, and the situation turned violent. Metal-tipped batons, boots, and fists rained down upon the protesters, some of whom responded by throwing paint at the police, turning their dark-blue riot gear white. As students ran to try to escape the violence, police officers tore through campus trying to catch them, swinging their batons wildly and hitting anyone in their path. That afternoon, both blood and paint stained the pavement in front of the university library. Video and photographic footage shows police officers using excessive force, deploying pepper spray and other chemical irritants, unrelentingly beating students with batons, and applying illegal choke holds and pressure techniques on students.[2]

The shocking spectacle of police violence that students endured during the pintata flashed across television and computer screens all over Puerto Rico. By the time of the pintata, there was already a pervasive sense that many Puerto Ricans had grown tired of the violence that seemed to be steadily engulfing the campus since the police had been stationed there in early December. After the violence of the pintata, the police presence on campus became dangerous and unacceptable. For instance, an editorial that appeared in the *Puerto Rico Daily Sun*, the local English-language newspaper, the following day compared the police attack on students to "the acts of the dictatorships we all denounce and reject." The editorial asked readers, "Is this to be the new institutional order? Police every 100 feet? The right to free speech reduced to the 100 square feet between police officers? Has the UPR become the testing grounds for a new institutional order?"[3]

The pintata and the other moments of state violence that punctuated the two student strikes at the UPR—which occurred from April 21, 2010, to June 21, 2010, and from December 7, 2010, to March 7, 2011, respectively—were certainly worthy of outrage and condemnation. However, the violence unleashed on students did not evidence new contours of policing and state repression, as the editorial team at the *Puerto Rico Daily Sun* and others suggested. Instead, both the violence of the state during the UPR strikes and the range of reactions that it provoked revealed much about where, under what circumstances, and against whom violence had been rendered acceptable within contemporary Puerto Rican society. What happened during the UPR strikes provided many relatively racially and economically privileged Puerto Ricans a glimpse into forms of state violence that had become routine in the archipelago's predominantly Black, low-income, and Dominican im/migrant communities over the course of the 1990s and early 2000s. In this way, observers perceived patterns of police brutality, harassment, and surveillance as "new" when enacted against UPR students, particularly those at the Río Piedras campus, who tended to come from the middle and upper classes. This unwillingness to see an expansive trajectory of violent policing in Puerto Rico demonstrates the extent to which much of the public had normalized police violence against racially and economically marginalized Puerto Ricans.

The strikes at the UPR put on full display forms of police repression and violence that had been long tested, deployed, and confined within public housing and other low-income areas around Puerto Rico. This chapter explores how police violence against student protesters and their supporters

drew upon strategies of containment solidified, in part, through the policing of racially and economically marginalized populations during the
mano dura era. "Mano dura contra el crimen" refers to a series of crime-
reduction measures introduced by Governor Pedro Rosselló in 1993, when
he deployed police and military forces within public housing and other
low-income spaces around the archipelago, but primarily across the big
island, during the 1990s in an effort to eliminate drug trafficking. This
chapter also carefully charts how UPR students' exposure to state violence
and repression created moments of solidarity with racially and economically marginalized communities that had been criminalized. At the same
time, I detail moments when students sought to leverage their privileged
positions to assert that they were "students, not criminals," and thus *undeserving* of state violence. Students responded to their own experiences of
brutality and repression by either undermining or reifying the structures
of anti-Black racism, segregation, and classism that had animated policing
throughout the archipelago. The strikes at the UPR illuminate how punitive
policing, and mano dura contra el crimen in particular, have created a complicated legacy that young Puerto Ricans are forced to negotiate as they
weigh the benefits of forging solidarity across race and class differences or
adhering to hierarchies of belonging and exclusion that mark criminalized
populations as disposable.

The Radical Opposition from the Streets

The battle for accessible and affordable public education that occurred
at the UPR in 2010 and 2011 emerged within a context of intense neoliberal
reform, marked by the dismantling of the public-employment sector, the
privatization of public resources, a protracted economic recession, and a
seemingly hard right turn in Puerto Rican politics. In the spring of 2009
Wall Street credit houses threatened to demote Puerto Rico's credit rating
to junk status. Against this backdrop, on March 9, 2009, Puerto Rico's republican and pro-statehood governor, Luis Fortuño, introduced Ley 7, or
Public Law 7, a "special law declaring a state of emergency and establishing
a plan for fiscal stabilization to save the credit of Puerto Rico."[4] Scholars
Yarimar Bonilla and Rafael Boglio Martínez note that Ley 7 enabled Fortuño to "'restructure' public employment in ways that would otherwise be
illegal: unilaterally suspending union contracts, overriding labor laws in
order to dismiss public-service workers, and denying those who remain

employed the job protections guaranteed in their union contracts."[5] This law was particularly devastating in its targeting of the public sector, which had emerged as the largest employer in Puerto Rico following the collapse of the industrial economy during the 1970s.

In early September 2009 the Fortuño administration announced that it would be laying off more than seventeen thousand public-sector workers in an attempt to stabilize the economy. Puerto Ricans took to the streets throughout the month of September to protest the decision. On October 15, 2009, an estimated 200,000 demonstrators flooded the streets of San Juan as part of a one-day general strike protesting the economic and political agenda of the Fortuño administration. The one-day Paro Nacional del Pueblo (People's National Stoppage) was a manifestation of the widespread discontent with Fortuño's so-called economic recovery plan and the annexationist governor's attempts to further integrate Puerto Rico into the US economy despite clear negative consequences for the working class.

Students mobilized against Ley 7 not only in solidarity with public-sector laborers but also because the law slashed university funding. The government used Ley 7 to alter the formula used to allocate funds to the university, with UPR's percentage of the state budget dropping from 9.6 percent to approximately 8.1 percent. To make up for the shortfall in funding, university administrators announced that they would be increasing tuition, decreasing scholastic and athletic scholarships, and doing away with fee exemptions for university employees and their families.[6] Students argued that these actions by university administrators would make it significantly harder for many low-income and working-class families, which were already underrepresented in the student body, to send their children to study at the UPR. For student activists, Ley 7 and the budgetary cuts at the UPR were asking the poor and working classes to disproportionately shoulder the costs of the economic crisis at the same time that engines of upward social mobility, such as public-sector employment and public education, were being destroyed.

After the Paro Nacional, students, especially those who would become active participants in the UPR strikes, lamented the lack of sustained action and coordination on the part of the labor unions that had helped organize the massive one-day stoppage. According to student activist Abner Y. Dennis Zayas, "After the Paro Nacional the labor movement threw in the towel. . . . They did absolutely nothing. That, of course, has a series of explanations, but, in that sense, the radical opposition from the streets against the policies of the government fell to the student movement."[7] A number of student activists also understood the university to be a potential catalyst for a renewed, broad-based social movement against the neoliberal agenda of the state. Ricardo Olivero Lora, a UPR law student, summed up this perspective during the first transmission of Radio Huelga, or Strike Radio, a student-run radio broadcast: "These times are crucial for society because the current government, in an abusive manner, has launched an offensive against the working class, to the point that many are in a state of hopelessness. We want to make this a place where we can return that hope."[8] Understanding and positioning themselves as a vanguard, students felt that the struggle at the UPR had the potential to spark larger mobilizations against the agenda of the Fortuño administration across Puerto Rican society.[9]

In addition, for student activists the university seemed to be an ideal site to discuss how the crises affecting Puerto Rico hit youths especially hard. Student activists at the UPR hoped that they could help respond to the challenges that Puerto Rican youths faced as they navigated Puerto Rico's anemic economy: limited upward mobility, rising personal indebtedness, and a continued reliance on outward migration for decent employment options. In this vein the student movement posited a reinvigorated public university as a possible path toward personal and community empowerment. However, contradictions would emerge over the course of the strikes as it became apparent that a more affordable UPR would not necessarily correspond to an accessible and welcoming public university system for racially and economically marginalized youths.

The Threat of Confrontation

Months of organizing preceding and following the Paro Nacional eventually culminated in students at the University of Puerto Rico Río Piedras (UPR-RP) campus calling a forty-eight-hour strike on April 21, 2010. Students asked the administration to stop tuition hikes, reinstate fee waivers, and guarantee that none of the UPR campuses would be privatized. The students told administrators that if university officials failed to meet their demands, they would go on a strike of indefinite duration. The administration failed to take the students' demands seriously, and as a result students at the UPR-RP announced a strike on April 23 to force the administration into negotiations. The Association of Puerto Rican University Professors and the Brotherhood of Non-Teaching Employees of the University of Puerto Rico both urged their members to respect the picket line. By May 4, ten out of eleven campuses, which are spread out across the big island, had joined the indefinite strike. Only the Recinto de Ciencias Medicas, the University of Puerto Rico's medical school, did not join the indefinite strike, which was a result of the time-sensitive nature of its scientific investigations and its work with patients. However, the medical school did hold a brief work stoppage in solidarity with the other campuses.

The Fortuño administration stationed police on the perimeter of the UPR-RP campus immediately following the announcement of the strike. The police remained at the perimeter and did not enter the campus due to the política de no confrontación, or nonconfrontation policy, an informal agreement between university administrators and the Puerto Rico Police Department (PRPD) that prohibited police from intervening in campus affairs. The nonconfrontation policy had emerged from a long history of state violence and repression directed at the student movement. Although the nonconfrontation policy was firmly in place during the 2010 strike, the threat of police brutality and harassment remained real in the minds of many students and their supporters. Immediately after the strike was announced, heavily armed riot police became regular fixtures outside the campus's perimeter gates. Police officers looked on as UPR-RP students created encampments at each of the seven portones, or entrance gates, controlling access to the university campus. Meanwhile, university administrators called in additional private security guards to monitor and control the protesters. Then, on May 13, 2010, during a campus assembly, students voted to continue the strike. With the strike's ratification, state officials and university administrators grew increasingly concerned, and police became more aggressive in their approach to the strikers and their supporters.

On May 20, 2010, students took their demands beyond the portones and joined union leaders, public employees, and others in protesting a political fund-raiser at the Sheraton Hotel that Governor Fortuño was attending. As the students had moved beyond the campus grounds, they were beyond the reach of the nonconfrontation policy. When students and labor activists attempted to disrupt the fund-raiser, police responded by unleashing tremendous violence upon the protesters. Images and videos from the Sheraton showed police punching, kicking, clubbing, and applying illegal choke holds to students and other protesters. A particularly shocking image showed the PRPD's second-in-command, José A. Rosa Carrasquillo, kicking UPR student José "Osito" Pérez Reisler in the genitals as he lay restrained and defenseless on the floor.[10]

Status updates from PRPD officers' Facebook pages seemed to confirm that the police went to the Sheraton looking to harm protesters in general, and UPR students specifically. As Facebook user Alexander Luina, who identified himself as a member of the PRPD, wrote, "Finally, after 12 days I can use my baton in this damn strike."[11] Perhaps most disturbing, Facebook user William Concepcion, who identified himself as a member of the Fuerza de Choque (the PRPD's antiriot squad), wrote that "I finally clubbed somebody today. Fuck, I hope things get crazy so I can empty out this rifle."[12] After a variety of Puerto Rican news outlets publicized the Facebook accounts and posts, Police Superintendent Jose Figueroa Sancha ordered an investigation to determine the legitimacy of the cited Facebook accounts and status updates. He stood by the actions of the police at the Sheraton, calling the police "heroes" and denouncing the students for provoking them.[13]

Although university and government officials attempted to paint the student movement as violent and dangerous following the incident at the Sheraton, the violent words and deeds of the police led a growing number of Puerto Ricans to come out to the portones to provide support and protection. The scores of people joining the strikers in solidarity with their demands forced university administrators to meet students at the negotiating table. After two months of protests and with ten of the UPR's eleven campuses shut down, the strike came to an end on June 21, 2010. Administrators met many of the students' basic demands, including reinstating canceled tuition waivers, delaying the imposition of tuition hikes and fees, and protecting student leaders from reprisals.[14] The student movement, and much of the public, regarded the agreement between strikers and the university as a historic victory for the student movement and a serious blow to the Fortuño administration's neoliberal agenda. However, the victory was short-lived as state and university officials quickly began to reverse the hard-won achievements of the student movement.

Proxy Violence

In the aftermath of the successful strike, state officials and administrators quickly took steps to reverse the gains of the movement. The legislature added four new appointees to the UPR's board of trustees in an attempt to stack the board in favor of the then-current administration and to neutralize opposition.[15] The new board of trustees lost no time imposing an $800 student fee, which would go into effect in January 2011. The university administration also made substantive cuts to faculty benefits and eliminated or put on "pause" a number of academic programs across the university system. Students responded to the university and state officials' duplicity with threats that they would once again paralyze the university system with a strike.

Students at the UPR-RP began a forty-eight-hour stoppage on December 7, 2010, demanding that the administration overturn the imposition of the new $800 student fee. If the administration did not comply with the students' demand to repeal the fee, they vowed to once again go on indefinite strike. In response to the stoppage and a looming second, indefinite strike, university administrators contracted the private security firm Capitol Security for approximately $1.5 million.[16] On the evening before the forty-eight-hour stoppage, the firm, on orders from university administrators, demolished the iconic entrance gates to the Río Piedras campus in an attempt to prevent student strikers from once again shutting down the university.

Students did not anticipate the removal of the gates, but they were even more surprised by the individuals who showed up wearing T-shirts with the word SECURITY emblazoned in yellow letters on the front. Capitol Security had hired young, inexperienced men and women from Villa Cañona in Loíza, a predominantly Black and low-income barrio in a predominantly Black and low-income municipality, to tear down the portones and act as security personnel during the stoppage and potential strike. According to some of the youths recruited to work security at the university, a municipal employee approached local young people, offering them ten dollars an hour to "work" at the UPR.[17] "They told us: 'get in the van, we have work for you.' No one trained us for that," remarked a twenty-five-year-old from Villa Cañona who worked security during the stoppage.[18] On an archipelago with official unemployment statistics hovering above 16 percent and where the federal minimum wage was $7.25 an hour, it is not surprising that youths from one of the poorest municipalities in Puerto Rico jumped at the opportunity that Capitol Security presented.[19]

Youths from Loíza, untrained and without much information about what exactly they would be doing on the university campus, were brought in, in lieu of police, to subdue the students. The youths from Loíza represented a way around the university's nonconfrontation policy that would allow state and university officials to violently repress the student movement and reestablish control without formal police intervention. Although

Capitol did not provide the youths with any form of training for the situation they were about to encounter at the university, some reported being explicitly told to use violence against the protesters to maintain order.[20] Shortly after the destruction of the portones, the youths contracted by Capitol Security were seen "patrolling" the campus, some armed with wooden two-by-fours, metal pipes, and knives, and getting into verbal and physical confrontations with protesters. Videos also began to circulate that showed confrontations between guards and students, which worked to reinscribe the youths working for Capitol Security as alien and threatening to the UPR community. These videos often circulated on social media along with a narrative that a gang of violent thugs hired by the university was threatening students, which played into a history of racialized and classed representational practice directed at low-income youths, particularly those from spaces like Loíza.

Some students understood the young men around campus to be merely performing toughness because they were actually scared by the situation; however, other students and members of the public saw their performance as a very real indicator of the kind of violent pathology allegedly endemic to spaces like Loíza. These assumptions about poor Black and dark-skinned youths had been historically solidified through the spectacle of almost two decades of intensified, targeted police raids in public-housing complexes and low-income barrios such as Villa Cañona. The enclosure and militarized policing of economically and racially marginalized communities marked these spaces as hot zones of violence, or zonas calientes, characterized by deviance and immorality, which needed to be controlled and contained through state intervention.

Student activist Giovanni Roberto, himself a young Black man from a low-income family, heard fellow students using racist and classist language to describe the youths sent by Capitol. According to Roberto, "In the Fine Arts *porton* the interaction between the students and the people contracted by Capitol Security began to turn increasingly tense. There were people who wanted to prevent them from removing the *portones*, and with much indignation they shouted; they shouted at 'those people.' That same night I started to hear one or another racist or classist comment. 'Where did they find these murderers?' or more blatantly 'What slum or project did they get them from?'"[21] The violent antagonism that emerged between the student protesters and the youths from Loíza unleashed responses that played upon prejudices about Loíza, Blackness, and poverty that had long been a feature of the Puerto Rican popular imagination.

Such responses reproduced the state's justification for disproportionate police intervention, like mano dura, in low-income and predominantly Black areas, which rendered these areas and populations as dangerous and threatening with a natural propensity toward violence and even the enjoyment of it. According to Roberto José Thomas Ramírez, the administration tried to create "an animosity" among UPR students and "the expectation that they [the youths contracted by Capitol] came to kill."[22] Thomas explained that this narrative would in turn make the student movement act aggressively toward these low-income youths in a way that would undercut the movement's claim of inclusivity and solidarity with the poor and working classes. The university administration, acting on behalf of the state, exploited existing prejudices against these young people from Loíza, based on their racial, spatial, and economic background, and pitted them against university students in the hopes of frustrating any form of alliance or solidarity between them.

Students' and their supporters' race- and class-based prejudices toward the young people contracted by Capitol allowed the machinations of the state and its security apparatus to remain hidden. The racist and classist interpretations of these tensions functioned to occlude the ways in which the state was enacting, or at least attempting to enact, violence by proxy. Because the state could not send the police into the university without violating the nonconfrontation policy and threatening its legitimacy, it instead subcontracted security functions to young people from Loíza, many of whom were themselves intimately familiar with state violence. It is no mistake that the state conscripted the youths of Villa Cañona and expected them to mimic the routine violence that they had experienced or witnessed during police raids in their communities. In 2007 police had occupied Villa Cañona under the auspices of dismantling the drug points that operated there. Rather than reducing drug dealing and drug-related violence, the police occupation of Villa Cañona resulted in dozens of reports of police brutality and misconduct, prompting investigations from the Puerto Rican Civil Rights Commission and the local branch of the American Civil Liberties Union.[23]

Disturbingly, Benjamin Rodríguez, a supervisor at Capitol Security who helped to recruit the youths from Villa Cañona as guards during the UPR stoppage, had played a central part in the occupation and raids that occurred in Villa Cañona as the PRPD's then-assistant superintendent of field operations. According to Villa Cañona community leader Maricruz Rivera Clemente, Rodríguez "takes the Black people of Loíza like all they're good for is to beat people up and they don't recruit us for other work." Rivera Clemente added, "They take them to give the students at the university a beating. Instead of giving them scholarships so they can be students, they want them to reproduce the suffering of their communities of origin."[24] Through their recruitment by Capitol Security on behalf of the state, these youths from Villa Cañona were in some respects made victims of police violence twice over: first by witnessing and experiencing rampant police brutality in their community and second through the dehumanizing expectation that they would enact a similar violence against others as police proxies. Furthermore, these youths were subjected to the psychologically violent realization that the only way they would be allowed to set foot on the UPR campus was as violence workers.[25] Many of the young loiceños reported that the first time they had visited the Río Piedras campus was when they showed up to take down the portones. This narrative of the foreclosed space of the university speaks to the incredible inaccessibility of UPR-RP to many racially and economically marginalized young people.[26]

Leaders within the student movement struggled with how to respond to the young guards recruited by Capitol and the racist and classist responses that their presence on campus generated among some students. Student leader Giovanni Roberto was incredibly troubled by the racist and classist sentiments he heard within the student movement. At the same time, he was disgusted by what he saw as an overt attempt on the part of the administration to play on racial, spatial, and class cleavages to prevent solidarity between young people who were experiencing different manifestations of Puerto Rico's ongoing economic and social crisis. One moment in particular crystallized for Roberto the need for the student movement to reach out to the young people from Loíza in a sincere and earnest way. On the evening of December 7, at the end of the first day of the forty-eight-hour paro, or stoppage, while watching coverage on the local news Roberto spotted a former student of his from the school where he worked as a teacher in Loíza in 2008: "One of the students from that school was there, on the other side, on behalf of the administration and the government. I was disheartened seeing him on the television. I felt rage and sadness, but I confess that I had no idea how to deal with the situation."[27]

Later that night, troubled by what he had seen, Roberto had a long conversation with fellow student activist Xiomara Caro about how to respond to the situation. According to Roberto, he and Caro debated whether one had to be full of "hate—*desprecio*—toward the system, towards capitalism, towards what capitalism is, what capitalist systems do all the time to people" in order to be an activist and effect change or if a movement needed "a feeling of love, to be united, to have human connection" to be successful. Roberto notes that in his conversation with Caro they came to an understanding that a hatred of capitalism and inequality alone cannot fuel social transformation; rather, social movements must be driven by solidarity and connection with others feeling the effects of an oppressive system.[28]

This recognition of the importance of love and solidarity in social movements informed Roberto's subsequent approach to the youths contracted by Capitol Security. Roberto added that the racial composition of the student movement also made him conscious of the need to respond to the situation with love and understanding for the young people from Loíza rather than with the class and racial hostilities that university and state officials hoped to exploit. According to Roberto, "The fact that part of the movement were white boys" who hadn't "lived the life that young Black, mostly male, people live" created an inability for many within the student movement to identify with the young guards and caused them to instead react with contempt. He continued, "So when they saw Black people, the way they were dressing, the way they were acting and talking, I felt that a lot of people were rejecting them in a negative way. I heard comments and I felt bad. I felt angry. I'm part of a movement that does not understand this situation. The situation that causes those young people to be scapegoats, in a way. Or be divided against other young people."[29]

Recognizing his commitment to the student movement and simultaneously having an intimate understanding of its blind spots regarding race and class, Roberto worked to conceive of ways to connect both groups of youths subjected, albeit in radically different ways, to the violence of the state. At 7:45 on the morning of December 8, after a night of altercations and vandalism on campus, Roberto addressed the young people contracted by Capitol in front of students, supporters, and the press. He began his address to the guards by letting them know that he and the student movement did not consider them enemies. He said he wanted to clarify for the guards what exactly the student movement was struggling for and against. Roberto related to the guards, saying, "Part of my personal story, and what explains why I am so convinced of what we are doing here, is that I am also from a poor barrio and I am also Black just like you all. When I was young, my parents couldn't find work, just like you all who don't find work now. And I lived for many years on cupones [federal assistance]. I lived until I was sixteen years old on cupones. Until I was sixteen. Almost my whole life." Roberto explained that he was on strike in part because ever since he was a small child, his mother had taught him that everyone has a right and should aspire to be equal. Continuing, he asked the guards: "But what's wrong? In this world we are not all equal. Why is Loíza un pueblo de negros [a Black town]? Why is Carolina un pueblo de negros? Why are Dorado and Condado considered pueblos de blanquitos [towns full of rich whites]? It's called racism. It's called institutionalized racism. It's been called racism for many years. Decades. They don't want us to leave. Those born in Loíza stay in Loíza. Those born in Carolina stay in Carolina. When we come here to fight every day, it's so that all of you also have an opportunity to break that cycle." Roberto urged the young guards to leave their posts and join the students in struggling for a more accessible educational system, and by extension a more equitable society. Students had in fact taken up a collection offering to pay the youths from Loíza their day's wages if they left their security posts and joined them in protest. "I think that all of you, who today are standing on that side, tomorrow should be on this side. *On this side.* Know that what we want is for you all to have an opportunity to study here. That is what we are fighting for," he said before extending his hand to one of the young security guards.[30] When the young guard refused to shake Roberto's hand, another guard approached him to shake his hand and then hugged him. After a night of violence between students and guards, Roberto's speech to the guards ended with a remarkable sight: students and guards shaking hands and hugging one another.

The embraces and words exchanged between the guards and students represented a utopian moment in which the student movement challenged the racism and classism within its ranks and constructed connections with youths whom both the university administration and its students often excluded from the elite space of the UPR-RP campus. It also represented a moment when young people who were being pitted against one another could come together, if only for a brief moment and only symbolically, and express solidarity. This was all the more impressive when the segregation that structured these young people's lives had typically made that incredibly difficult. The UPR reproduces hierarchies of power and privilege within Puerto Rican society and as a result places limits on meaningful connections across race and class differences both on campus and beyond. The segregation perpetuated by the university, as well as that which marks Puerto Rican society more generally, makes this display of solidarity between students and the young loiceños important. On the morning of December 8, Giovanni Roberto succeeded in cogently outlining for both students in the movement and the young guards the ways in which the state benefited from the antagonism between them. Simultaneously, Roberto challenged UPR students to confront their own racism and classism, which caused them to lash out against the youths contracted by Capitol. For Roberto, the student movement needed to shift in order to make itself relevant in the lives of the economically and racially marginalized youths who had often been excluded from spaces of privilege such as the UPR.

When I asked student activists about this moment and the decision to reach out to the young people working for Capitol, they noted that it was in large part Roberto who pushed the need for the student movement to express solidarity with young people from Loíza and consider what it would mean to bring their concerns into the student struggle. Many of these same students also noted that that moment was possible *only* because of Roberto's own embodiment and experience. A few times, I heard some version of the remark, "Well, it *had* to be Giovanni who spoke to the young people working for Capitol." Such comments highlight the burden placed on Roberto to act as a liaison between the student movement and the youths working for Capitol. Roberto was expected to act as a "bridge leader" because so few self-identified Black and low-income students were involved in the student movement as leaders.[31] The general makeup of both the student body and the student movement at the UPR, especially the UPR-RP campus, helps to explain why student activists may have had difficulty recognizing their own racial and class privileges and biases as they interacted with the young people working for Capitol. Roberto's leadership during this moment and his willingness to act as a bridge between these two groups of young people challenged the student movement to consider the gulf between its rhetoric of inclusivity and its actual exclusivity when confronted with race and class differences.

However, Roberto's utopian gesture of solidarity was short-lived. Capitol's management personnel replaced the young guards he had addressed a short while later with a group of older guards in the hopes of short-circuiting any potential identification or solidarity with the student movement. According to an executive from Capitol Security, the company replaced the guards "because they suffered from Stockholm Syndrome," implying that the students were somehow the guards' captors.[32] State and university officials immediately prepared to implement a new security regime on campus. For the first time in the thirty years since the implementation of the nonconfrontation policy, police could officially enter the Río Piedras campus to "reestablish order." The violence experienced by students following the installation of the police on campus, and the circulation of images of that violence via both traditional and social media, provided for many Puerto Ricans a glimpse of police power and practice that had long occurred, largely out of public sight, in low-income barrios and public-housing residenciales.

"In the Flesh"

University administrators and government officials positioned the conflicts between students and guards, and the acts of vandalism that occurred on the evening of December 7, as evidence of the need for police to enter the UPR-RP campus. According to Governor Fortuño, the police would provide necessary protection for the faculty and students being threatened by a small, radical fringe terrorizing the campus. In a press conference announcing the installation of police personnel on campus, Fortuño said, "The acts of violence and vandalism that all of us witnessed early on Tuesday were the last straw. The people of Puerto Rico have been more than patient and university officials more than lenient during this conflict. Enough is enough." Attempting to minimize the support that the student movement had garnered within and outside of the university, Fortuño added, "The instances of terrorism perpetrated over the past forty-eight hours have clearly shown that the violent actions of a small minority of individuals claiming to represent students are promoting an agenda that really is alien to the vast majority of students at the UPR and has nothing to do with the issue of the cuota [$800 fee], which they are using as an excuse."[33]

Suddenly, the police officers in riot gear who had been outside the portones during the first strike and the forty-eight-hour stoppage were inside the gates to ensure "order." As has often been the case in Puerto Rico when police forces occupied a space under the auspices of guaranteeing public safety, their presence generated greater fear and violence. Police officers harassed, abused, and arrested students participating in strike-related activities. The administration placed a ban on political protest on campus immediately following the stoppage, and as a result police were able to arrest students for small acts of resistance such as handing out pro-strike pamphlets on campus.

On December 10, 2010, a group of community leaders representing a number of barrios and public-housing complexes issued a statement denouncing the police presence on the UPR campus. These community leaders, who were active in a number of residents' councils and community organizations in low-income communities around the big island, called for an end to police aggression and announced their solidarity with the student movement and its goals.[34] The statement read, in part: "They've cornered them, they imposed a fee that they can't pay, they prevent them from protesting anywhere, they surveil them, they deny them dialogue and solutions. The police and University administration treat our young people like animals, like lesser humans, without rights. These students are our children, our grandchildren, neighbors in our community; they are people who do not have the money to pay this fee and are seeking a decent public education for all Puerto Ricans. We're going to support them, there is no doubt." In the statement, organizers linked the brutality experienced by the student movement to the police repression of their communities, creating connections and solidarity between their two struggles. They highlighted the ways in which violent and discriminatory policing, which had been perfected in low-income communities, was now on full display at the university, noting that "our communities are familiar with police brutality. We have experienced in the flesh the discrimination and violation of the rights of our residents on multiple occasions. In a country where the state disproportionately abuses its power, there is no choice but to mobilize, university and community, to address these abuses that are now daily."[35] This expression of solidarity not only condemned the state's violence against student protesters but also reminded a public that may have been sympathetic to the plight of UPR students that such rampant abuse was quotidian in low-income and racially marginalized communities. In this way, their expression of solidarity both supported the student movement and called for an end to police violence on campus, while also drawing attention to the routine violence experienced in marginalized communities that often garnered little outrage or solidarity.

For their part, student activists attempted to draw attention to the state's use of police violence as a blunt instrument of repression at the UPR and in public housing in order to connect struggles that were often viewed in isolation from one another. For instance, following attempts by university and government officials to paint students and protesters as responsible for the violence taking place on campus, José García, a student and spokesperson for the Organización Socialista Internacional (International Socialist Organization), issued the following call for solidarity to public-housing residents: "You know who the violent ones are who come to club people. You know it's the police. We must remind the country who the violent ones are."[36] Although students at times glossed over the differences in power and privilege between themselves and the residents of marginalized communities, their attempts at solidarity revealed important parallels with the potential to result in coalitions against state abuse. Students also looked to the long-standing resistance against the repressive agenda of the state in public housing and low-income barrios as a source of inspiration and strength in their own organizing. As Xiomara Caro put it, "Resistance, where you see it most, is in the caseríos [public housing] . . . and what we did in la iupi [UPR] was a resistance. . . . So there's a parallel there because we're both, in a way, trying to resist what the system is trying to turn us into."[37]

As the second strike progressed, state and university officials attempted to deepen racial and economic animosities and prevent cross-coalitional organizing. To do so, they employed the physical infrastructure the state had created while policing public-housing communities. Following the administration's ban on on-campus protests, police took students arrested for violating the ban to minicuarteles in nearby public-housing complexes. One of the lasting features of mano dura contra el crimen is an archipelago of mini-police stations and holding cells built in public-housing complexes. These minicuarteles were built, much like the perimeter fences around public-housing complexes, to discourage drug trafficking and ensure a permanent police presence within public housing. During the second strike, police arrested students, separated them by gender, and took the men to the station in the Monte Hatillo public-housing complex and the women to the station in the Manuel A. Pérez public-housing complex.

The sheer number of arrests taking place at the UPR-RP campus as a result of the protest ban ensured a steady stream of police, students, and supporters entering and disrupting the lives of these public-housing communities. Pedro Lugo, a student activist and reporter for Radio Huelga, suggested that the police brought arrested students to Monte Hatillo and Manuel A. Pérez to create conflict and resentment between students and residents: "The police took them to the project jails because they thought that the community would reject the solidarity of the supporters that would show up to support the jailed students." The presence of community outsiders entering public housing to support arrested students, along with the increased police presence, resulted in tensions among students, their supporters, and community residents. According to Lugo, at one point some residents threw rocks at students and their supporters to express their resentment against the growing police presence in their community. Following the incident, student activists approached residents and discussed the ways in which police forces were trying to create conflict between them and asked for their support: "Some people talked to them and they understood the problem. A couple of days passed without any incidents with the community, so the police decided not to take them [there] anymore. The police said that they moved them [to new locations] because those headquarters have the biggest cells."[38]

The communities of Monte Hatillo and Manuel A. Pérez had been subject to ongoing raids by police forces since the early 1990s; therefore, it is no surprise that a sudden influx of increased police forces in addition to community outsiders would lead to tensions and resentment. Knowing this, it does not take much of a stretch of the imagination to see it as a deliberate tactic on the part of the police to create conflict between UPR students and public-housing residents. Did police hope that this tactic of placing university students in holding cells in public-housing complexes would make arrested students feel even more isolated, under the assumption that these two populations were disconnected from and even hostile toward each other? Did police purposefully attempt to disrupt the lives of public-housing residents by bringing arrested students, and subsequently their supporters, to Monte Hatillo and Manuel A. Pérez in order to breed resentment between these groups? The fact that the police stopped bringing arrested students to Monte Hatillo and Manuel A. Pérez once residents, students, and activists were able to reach an agreement with one another suggests that the state had a vested interest in exploiting and exacerbating racial and class cleavages in order to once again prevent solidarity between low-income communities and the student movement. The use of public-housing minicuarteles, alongside the employment of young men and women from Loíza to act as police proxies, highlights the vulgar and intentional ways in which the state has attempted to manage populations through difference.

"¡Fuera, Fuera, Fuera Policía!"

Despite the attempts of state and university officials to use heavily racialized and classed police violence to prevent cross-coalitional solidarity with the student movement and its demands, the state's violence against the student movement eventually moved thousands of Puerto Ricans to align themselves with the students and demand an end to the police occupation of the university. Interactions between students and police at the university became increasingly violent and frequent as the strike went on. These incidents of regular police brutality, harassment, and arrest peaked with the pintata on February 9, 2011, that began this chapter. Immediately following the pintata, professors and employees of the UPR announced a twenty-four-hour work stoppage in solidarity with the students in light of recent events.[39] Then, on February 12, 2011, approximately ten thousand Puerto Ricans marched through the streets of Río Piedras in solidarity with the students, calling for a complete withdrawal of the police from campus. A constant refrain shouted throughout the march was "¡Fuera policía, fuera!" (Get out, police, get out!) and "¡Fuera, fuera, fuera, policía!" (Out, out, out, police!). On February 14, heeding these calls, the Fortuño administration ordered the police removed from campus.

Although the second strike did not officially end until March, many Puerto Ricans outside the student movement understood the removal of the police from campus to be the effective end of the strike at the UPR.[40] As students and their supporters worked to force the government and university to reinstate the nonconfrontation policy and get the police to leave campus, the student movement suddenly became reduced to a movement against police brutality. In this way, victory for the student movement, in the eyes of many supporters, became contingent upon the removal of police from campus rather than the protection of the university against privatization or the cultivation of efforts to create a public education system accessible to all Puerto Ricans.

For some student activists, the focus on removing the police from campus, though necessary, inadvertently resulted in their larger questions of economic and social justice losing urgency in the face of immediate bodily danger and harm. Thus, when the police left campus, the strike was considered over despite the fact that students found themselves, in many ways, in a similar position to the one they had been in when the strike began. Reflecting on how the second strike ended, Xiomara Caro noted, "In retrospect, one of the criticisms, . . . at least internally, is that it became an issue of police brutality. We sold out to everyone else."[41] According to Waldemiro Vélez Soto, this shift in attention fragmented the student movement and confused the public about the demands of the strike: "It was a mistake. For example, if the demands were accessibility, a university open to the people, the poor, workers, etcetera . . . then victimizing ourselves because of police abuse is moving us on to another issue. It gives emphasis or impetus to that issue when that was never the primary issue when we started this struggle. You confuse the people because suddenly it becomes a principal demand. Then, when the police leave, then the strike is considered over, no?"[42] Giovanni Roberto made a similar point: "I think one of the problems was [that] one of the main goals was to get the police out of campus, which was never the main goal for us [in the student movement]. But for the people who supported us, in some way, they established that as the main topic. And that was a mistake in my opinion." According to Roberto, the shifted focus onto police violence allowed for the subject of the student movement's initial concern—a shrinking and increasingly inaccessible public university system—to continue unaddressed as long as overt physical violence ceased: "We should reject the whole politic that the administration was doing in the university. If we [just] concentrate on the security policy, the whole thing is going to continue."[43]

In this way, although police brutality became a rallying point of solidarity for Puerto Ricans in the archipelago and diaspora, some students within the movement saw this emphasis on ending police brutality as foreclosing or displacing what they understood as more important conversations about austerity, public resources, and social access. That police violence was perceived as a distraction from the "real" issues of the student movement highlights the difficulty students had at times decentering narrow student concerns in favor of broader issues affecting nonstudent populations, especially those living in racially and economically marginalized communities. For Puerto Ricans who found themselves under assault almost daily by police repression, standing up against the violence aimed at UPR students could have represented a point of connection and solidarity, even if they might not have identified with issues such as halting tuition and fee hikes. Including an end to police brutality and repression as a central plank of the second student strike, especially given the students' expressed desire to build a more expansive and inclusive student movement following the interactions with the young guards working for Capitol, could have had the potential to bring el barrio and la iupi together across racial, spatial, and classed divides to challenge the agenda of the state.

Violent criminalization by the state represented a point of commonality between UPR students and Puerto Ricans who lived in so-called zonas calientes. However, at times students attempted to challenge their criminalization without also challenging the underlying logics of criminalization that ensnared so many beyond the university's gates. Perhaps one of the most common refrains heard during protests and seen written on signs was "Somos estudiantes, no somos criminales" (We are students, we are not criminals). Another common slogan was "Luchar por una educación pública de excelencia no es un delito" (Fighting for a quality public education is not a crime). These slogans rejected the state and university administration's attempts to criminalize protest and dissent, yet they also reinforced the idea that students, unlike "real" criminals, are undeserving of violence at the hands of the state. In formulations like these, students were undeserving of violence *because* they were students and not common criminals, which implicitly sanctioned state violence against those involved, either by choice or by lack of choices, in the informal economy.

Appealing to hierarchal notions of belonging and worth within Puerto Rican society, students missed opportunities to make connections with other populations experiencing criminalization and to challenge the implicit understanding that people who are designated criminal are violable and expendable. As Latina scholar Martha Escobar points out in another context, such "decriminalizing motions turn into violent acts themselves" as the innocence of some is secured at the expense of others. In other words, appeals to tropes of innocence and merit reinforce the idea that there are real criminals who are deserving of the violence visited upon them at the hands of the state and their fellow citizens.[44] By dismissing the centrality of challenging police violence to the student movement and appealing to privileged notions of students' inherent "goodness," student activists missed an important opportunity to build a coalition around mutual experiences of criminalization. This kind of coalition building might have allowed the student movement to make stronger and more lasting connections to racially and economically marginalized communities.

Building Coalitions in the Shadow of the State

Although students struggled with how to express and forge solidarity across difference, the strikes of 2010 and 2011 nonetheless enabled necessary connections between the student movement and residents of economically and racially marginalized communities, who are often excluded from the UPR. During my discussions with a number of the individuals who had participated in the 2010 and 2011 student strikes, many of them expressed a genuine desire for the UPR to become a more inclusive and accessible space that did not reproduce the pernicious forms of segregation that mark Puerto Rican society more generally. This was particularly true for those students who themselves hailed from low-income and lower-middle-income neighborhoods. The elite status ascribed to the UPR, as well as students' own desires for economic security through upward mobility, sometimes made meaningful and lasting coalitions with the communities that regularly experienced police violence difficult. And sometimes these displays of solidarity on the part of students did not resonate with racially and economically marginalized communities, nor were they always reciprocated. Nonetheless, the fleeting displays and expressions of solidarity between students and low-income communities that occurred during the strikes had lasting transformational effects on many of the individuals involved and challenged the scope of the student movement and its demands. These moments of tension and solidarity, though fraught, illuminated a common struggle against various spatial, racial, economic, and political inequalities endemic to state violence and the state-sanctioned use of policing as a solution to crisis.

NOTES

1. In "Carpeteo Redux" I discuss this moment in relation to the long history of targeted political repression and harassment of political dissidents in Puerto Rico.

2. Video footage of police intervention and brutality during the pintata can be seen in this two-part video report for *Diálogo*, the UPR student newspaper: Editores Diálogo, "9 de febrero motín en UPR-RP," and "Motín en UPR-RP—9 de febrero de 2011 (2da parte)."

3. "Editorial: The Police Must Leave Campus."

4. "Ley especial declarando estado de emergencia fiscal." Translation by author.

5. Bonilla and Boglio Martínez, "Puerto Rico in Crisis."

6. Bonilla, "Caribbean Youth Battle."

7. Abner Y. Dennis Zayas, interview by the author, Río Piedras, Puerto Rico, March 8, 2012. Translation by author.

8. "Radio Huelga: Conéctate a la resistencia." Translation by author.

9. José Laguarta Ramírez makes a similar point when he notes that, following the Paro Nacional, "widespread discontent and vocal protest failed to materialize into significant resistance, in part as a result of the weakness, fragmentation, or cooptation of the leadership of the traditional labor movement (itself a result of ongoing neoliberalization since the 1980s). In this context, UPR students were increasingly seen as (and imagined themselves to be) the last redoubt of popular opposition." See Ramírez, "Struggling to Learn," 34.

10. For footage from the protest at the Sheraton, see "Motín en actividad de fortuño por huelga en la UPR—parte 1" and "Motín en actividad de fortuño por huelga en la UPR—parte 2." For more on José "Osito" Pérez Reisler, see Serrano, "Demanda por patada testicular."

11. Quoted in Sepúlveda, "Inundan Facebook las expresiones de supuestos policías." Translation by author.

12. Quoted in Sepúlveda, "Inundan Facebook las expresiones de supuestos policías."

13. Sepúlveda and Bauza, "Superintendente ordena investigación."

14. Stanchich, "University of Puerto Rico Student Strike Victory."

15. Stanchich, "University of Puerto Rico Student Strike Victory."

16. Stanchich, "More Violence in Puerto Rico."

17. See Cobián, "Los recogen en Loíza y los meten de guardias"; and Roberto, "De cuando el barrio entró a la UPR."

18. Quoted in Cobián, "Los recogen en Loíza y los meten de guardias." Translation by author.

19. Giovanni Roberto makes this point clear in "De cuando el barrio entró a la UPR."

20. Cobián, "Los recogen en Loíza y los meten de guardias"; Roberto, "De cuando el barrio entró a la UPR."

21. Roberto, "De cuando el barrio entró a la UPR."

22. Roberto José Thomas Ramírez, interview by the author, Río Piedras, Puerto Rico, March 2, 2012. Translation by author.

23. For more information on the police occupation of Villa Cañona and the violence that followed, see the short documentary "El color de la justicia [2008]."

24. Quoted in Cobián, "Los recogen en Loíza y los meten de guardias." Translation by author.

25. Huggins, Haritos-Fatouros, and Zimbardo, *Violence Workers*.

26. Cobián, "Los recogen en Loíza y los meten de guardias."

27. Roberto, "De cuando el barrio entró a la UPR." Translation by author.

28. Giovanni Roberto, interview by the author, Río Piedras, Puerto Rico, January 31, 2012.

29. Roberto interview, January 31, 2012.

30. "Giovanni Roberto—Discurso a Guardias Capitol—UPR 2010." Translation by author.

31. Historian Lauren Araiza defines *bridge leaders* as individuals within organizations or groups who cross divides to build coalitions that did not occur spontaneously with other organizations or groups. As she notes, "But even with all of the

necessary ingredients in place, individuals were needed to serve as catalysts. Bridge leaders had to recognize the potential in forming a coalition and convince their colleagues of its merits." For more, see Araiza, *To March for Others*, 9, 170.

32. Hernández, "Police Takes Over Campus."

33. "Fortuño Afirma Policía Restableció Orden en la UPR." Translation by author.

34. The leaders represented Cantera in Santurce, the Luis Llorens Torres public-housing residence, Sonadora in Aguas Buenas, Piñones in Loíza, Mariana in Humacao, San Antonio in Caugas, and Los Filtros in Guaynabo.

35. Del Mar Quiles, "Condena unánime"; translated by the author.

36. Quoted in Bauza, Díaz, and Cobián, "Calma en la UPR." Translation by author.

37. Xiomara Caro, interview by the author, Río Piedras, Puerto Rico, March 7, 2012.

38. Pedro Lugo, personal correspondence with the author, December 9, 2013.

39. Diaz Alcaide, "Se van a paro los profesores de la UPR."

40. The end date of the second strike is debatable. Some suggest that the strike did not end until May 2011; however, for many the end of the strike was marked by an incident in which UPR-RP chancellor Ana Guadalupe and the chief of campus security were assaulted by protesters on March 7, 2011. Although many students claim that the individuals who assaulted the chancellor and chief of campus security were not actually affiliated with the student movement and were police operatives, this moment soured the public's support, and the movement had difficulty mobilizing in the assault's wake.

41. Caro interview, March 7, 2012.

42. Waldemiro Vélez Soto, interview by the author, Río Piedras, Puerto Rico, April 26, 2012. Translation by author.

43. Roberto interview, January 31, 2012.

44. Escobar, *Captivity beyond Prisons*, 63.

BIBLIOGRAPHY

Araiza, Lauren. *To March for Others: The Black Freedom Struggle and the United Farm Workers*. Philadelphia: University of Pennsylvania Press, 2014.
Bauza, Nydia, Maritza Díaz, and Mariana Cobián. "Calma en la UPR—Minuto a minuto." *Primera Hora*, December 17, 2010. www.primerahora.com/noticias /gobierno-politica/nota/calmaenlaupr-minutoaminuto-454555.
Bonilla, Yarimar. "Caribbean Youth Battle for the Future of Public Education: General Strike at the University of Puerto Rico Goes into Its Fourth Week." *Stabroek News*, May 17, 2010. www.stabroeknews.com/2010/05/16/features

/caribbean-youth-battle-for-the-future-of-public-education-general-strike-at
-the-university-of-puerto-rico-goes-into-its-fourth-week-2.

Bonilla, Yarimar, and Rafael Boglio Martínez. "Puerto Rico in Crisis: Government
Workers Battle Neoliberal Reform." NACLA Report on the Americas 43, no. 1
(2010): 6–8.

Cobián, Mariana. "Los recogen en Loíza y los meten de guardias en la UPR sin
explicaciones." Primera Hora, December 13, 2010. www.primerahora.com
/noticias/gobierno-politica/nota/losrecogenenloizaylosmetendeguardiasenla
uprsinexplicaciones-452612.

"El color de la justicia [2008]." YouTube, March 24, 2011. http://youtu.be
/H3CiyzJjSC0.

Del Mar Quiles, Cristina. "Condena unánime a represión policiaca contra estudiantes UPR." InterNewsService, December 10, 2010. www.claridadpuertorico
.com/content.html?news=0AEA6E32304856266FA474702F02DE32.

Diaz Alcaide, Maritza. "Se van a paro los profesores de la UPR." Primera Hora,
February 10, 2011. www.primerahora.com/noticias/gobierno-politica/nota
/sevanaparolosprofesoresdelaupr-472401.

Editores Diálogo. "Motín en UPR-RP—9 de febrero de 2011 (2da parte)." YouTube,
February 9, 2011. http://youtu.be/LjBaWESdTjg.

Editores Diálogo. "9 de febrero motín en UPR-RP." YouTube, February 9, 2011.
http://youtu.be/_DVtAd5avqo.

"Editorial: The Police Must Leave Campus." Puerto Rico Daily Sun, February 10,
2011.

Escobar, Martha D. Captivity beyond Prisons: Criminalization Experiences of Latina
(Im)migrants. Austin: University of Texas Press, 2016.

"Fortuño Afirma Policía Restableció Orden en la UPR y Se Quedará Mientras Sea
Necesario." Primera Hora, December 9, 2010. www.primerahora.com/noticias
/gobierno-politica/notas/fortuno-afirma-policia-restablecio-orden-en-la-upr
-y-se-quedara-mientras-sea-necesario.

"Giovanni Roberto—Discurso a Guardias Capitol—UPR 2010." YouTube, December 10, 2010. http://youtu.be/xXzpbYB7Ndo.

Hernández, Juan A. "Police Takes Over Campus after Stoppage." Puerto Rico Daily
Sun, December 9, 2010. https://www.prdailysun.com/news/Police-takes-over
-campus-after-stoppage (no longer available).

Huggins, Martha K., Mika Haritos-Fatouros, and Philip G. Zimbardo. Violence
Workers: Police Torturers and Murderers Reconstruct Brazilian Atrocities. Berkeley: University of California Press, 2002.

LeBrón, Marisol. "Carpeteo Redux: Surveillance and Subversion against the
Puerto Rican Student Movement." Radical History Review 128 (2017):
147–72.

"Ley especial declarando estado de emergencia fiscal y estableciendo plan integral
de estabilización fiscal para salvar el crédito de Puerto Rico." Ley Núm. 7 del
año 2009 (P. de la C. 1326).

"Motín en actividad de fortuño por huelga en la UPR—parte 1." primerahoravideos, YouTube, May 21, 2010. www.youtube.com/watch?v=04TIgF6Cj_U.

"Motín en actividad de fortuño por huelga en la UPR—parte 2." primerahoravideos, YouTube, May 21, 2010. www.youtube.com/watch?v=XSimXwuJWfA.

"Radio Huelga: Conéctate a la resistencia." *Desde Adentro*, May 2, 2010. http://rojogallito.blogspot.com/2010/05/radio-huelga-conectate-la-resistencia.html.

Ramírez, José Laguarta. "Struggling to Learn, Learning to Struggle: Strategy and Structure in the 2010–11 University of Puerto Rico Student Strike." PhD diss., City University of New York, 2016.

Roberto, Giovanni. "De cuando el barrio entró a la UPR." *Socialismo Internacional*, October 26, 2013. https://latrincheraobrera.wordpress.com/2013/10/26/de-cuando-el-barrio-entro-a-la-upr.

Sepúlveda, Karol Joselyn. "Inundan Facebook las expresiones de supuestos policías 'orgullosos' de macanear estudiantes de la UPR." *Primera Hora*, May 21, 2010. www.primerahora.com/noticias/gobierno-politica/nota/inundanfacebooklasexpresionesdesupuestospoliciasorgullososdemacanearestudiantesdelaupr-388928.

Sepúlveda, Karol Joselyn, and Nydia Bauza. "Superintendente ordena investigación por expresiones desacertadas de policías." *Primera Hora*, May 22, 2012. http://www.primerahora.com/noticias/gobierno-politica/nota/superintendenteordenainvestigacionporexpresionesdesacertadasdepolicias-388999.

Serrano, Oscar J. "Demanda por patada testicular." *Noticel*, May 16, 2011. www.noticel.com/noticia/104753/1346977531000.

Stanchich, Maritza. "More Violence in Puerto Rico as University Student Fee Is Imposed." *Huffington Post*, December 15, 2010. www.huffingtonpost.com/maritza-stanchich-phd/more-violence-in-puerto-r_b_810628.html.

Stanchich, Maritza. "University of Puerto Rico Student Strike Victory Unleashes Brutal Civil Rights Backlash." *Huffington Post*, July 7, 2010. www.huffingtonpost.com/maritza-stanchich-phd/university-of-puerto-rico_b_635090.html.

SEVEN · Brian Jordan Jefferson

Programming Colonial Racial Capitalism: Encoding Human Value in Smart Cities

Forms of humanity are separated (made "distinct") so that they may be inter-connected in terms that feed capital. [Ruth Wilson] Gilmore elsewhere names this process "partition" and identifies it as the base algorithm for capitalism.
JODI MELAMED, "RACIAL CAPITALISM," 2015

The so-called smart city has been touted by technology firms, urban of-ficials, and academics as a means of making property assessment, public health, sanitation, and security more efficient. Although city spokespeople and tech companies hail the trend as the coming of urban utopias, an in-creasing number of urbanists are drawing attention to the inequalities gen-erated through smart governance.[1] However, in most of these works racial inequities are viewed as effects of the process. Here, the deepening impov-erishment and marginalization of minority populations are cast as a func-tion of cities replacing low-wage, minority labor with the global technical elite. The lens of colonial racial capitalism helps reveal how these inequities might not be mere surface effects but rather are operational logics written in the very source code of smart governance.

This chapter explores how racial difference is encoded in smart city software, which is increasingly extended to indigenous hinterlands. It turns attention to academics, administrative officials, international specialty groups, and technology firms that design software to assess the value of geographic locations and the groups that populate them. Two technologies are examined—property-assessment software and waste-management software—through academic studies, government reports, international organizations' white papers, and private-sector publications.[2] The chapter shows how the differential valuation of nonwhite people and places is not only a result of smart governance but also a constitutive logic. It illustrates how smart governance not only results in racial inequality but is literally programmed to produce it.

The first section of this chapter reviews how racial inequities are often understood in smart urbanization literature. It directs attention to how inequalities in these works are explained mostly as consequences of economic restructuring. The section then considers how recent works on racial capitalism can expand this explanation, namely by viewing racial nonequivalence as an *input* in the production of social space, not just an output. Sections two and three analyze computerized property-assessment software and waste-management software, respectively. These cases show how cities use these tools to assign specific populations and areas different levels of value in ways commensurate with racial and colonial logics. It also explores the central role of on-ground struggles in the spread of smart technology. In each case, the chapter investigates how opposition to the proliferation of these tools generates new avenues for abolitionist mobilization.

Smart Tech and Racial Inequality

Toward the end of the last millennium, a rising chorus of city officials praised self-monitoring and reporting technology (SMART) as a means of managing economic, political, and social issues arising from urban mutations.[3] There is an extensive body of work in urban theory on such issues, especially those arising from urban amassments of global corporate power, environmental degradation, intensifications of economic inequality, and overpopulation. These studies show the vast repertoire of smart tech that has been embraced by city officials as remedies for these problems.[4] Other scholars trace the inequalities engendered by these technological solutions, including the new forms of excluding and profiling already-marginal urban groups.[5] Some in this vein highlight how post-Fordist modes of urban accumulation rely on relocating the manufacturing industries that black and Latina/o workers historically depended upon. The new geographies of flexible production, unthinkable without IT infrastructures, have thus left entire communities functionally obsolete. Critics warn that inequality will be an unavoidable consequence of smart city policy and administration.[6] But what if these deepening inequalities were not merely effects but also the *means* of urban transformation? What if uneven redistributions of wealth, power, and poverty were necessary conditions for IT-driven forms of capital accumulation?

Colonial racial capitalism provides conceptual resources to answer these questions. The framework is fine-tuned to magnify how the state and tech companies combine to reproduce racial divisions and exploitation under auspices of smarter governance. As various scholars working within the tradition of racial capitalism have shown, the state has been fundamental in securing nonwhite land, labor, and lives for the benefit of agricultural, mercantile, industrial, and real estate capitalists. Exploring state-capital relations in the context of smart cities offers a window into the IT sector's position within this wider history, thus opening new vistas for future research from the colonial racial capitalist perspective.

Redlining Software

"If the accumulation of capital," Marxist geographer Neil Smith argues, "entails geographical development and if the direction of this development is guided by the rate of profit, then we can think of the world as a 'profit surface' produced by capital itself."[7] Although Aihwa Ong has shown how the image of capitalism as a global undifferentiated surface is a chimera of political economic metatheory, the desire to establish such a surface nevertheless persists and has literally materialized in a number of property technologies.[8] Widely popularized in the 1970s, computer-assisted mass-appraisal software (CAMA) analyzes property market data to determine values for landed property markets. This software is promoted by city spokespeople and technology firms as an example of technology's ability to produce neutral, scientifically based assessments of land in both urban and rural settings. It generates simulations of cities in which buildings, facilities, and land lots are depicted as pure exchange values. Sometimes their use values are coded according to predefined land uses. In China, CAMA has recently been merged with geographic-information systems to create three-dimensional models of properties for users to explore values as if they were in an open-world video game. Since the 1980s, major cities across the world have adopted some version of this software.

The global explosion of property-assessment technology over the past three decades has been propelled to a large extent by US-based firms such as Cisco Systems, Environmental Systems Research Institute, PropertyInfo Corporation, and Tyler Technologies. Many of these firms have combined forces in the International Association of Assessing Officers (IAAO), which provides consultation, software packages, and technical assistance to government agencies for CAMA-related matters. The spread of the software has also been reinforced by the United Nations (UN), which has encouraged cities to adopt the software to accommodate transnational real estate markets.[9] But whereas urban decision makers are embracing the technology as a way to circumvent prejudicial valuations, property submarkets are always already structured by long-standing group-based inequalities.[10] Therefore, the architects and promoters of CAMA have had to navigate the uneven terrain of property markets lest they disturb entrenched power relations.

Public officials, international organizations, and technology firms each publicize CAMA as a way for cities to maximize administrative efficiency and economic growth. This is especially evident in cities in postcolonial countries, where the software is promoted as a means of modernizing cadastral systems to join global property-finance markets. The software is also often touted as a way to address market volatility born of extraordinary population growth in such countries. The UN has been one catalyst behind CAMA's global spread, praising its ability to forge worldwide "valuation standards [that] define the matters to be taken into account in valuation practice primarily when dealing with valuations for private sector activities such as mortgages, investment and accounting. Such standards are increasingly international in character reflecting the growing awareness of the strong links between valuation standards and [real estate] financial markets, and globalisation."[11]

Real estate professionals have also embraced CAMA as a response to the planetary detonation of real estate capital. Only through the software, according to many, can professionals capitalize on "economic globalization [that] creates new opportunities in real estate market, product and service. . . . Real estate professionals have to re-orientate themselves so that they can move up the service value-ladder and avoid being marginalized under intense competition in a global market."[12]

Whether through government officials, international organizations, or the private sector, efforts to circulate property-appraisal software appear to be a matter of adapting to the vicissitudes of the global marketplace. In fact, some CAMA packages analyze market data to generate dynamic models of property markets. For residential properties, the most common data pertain to a property's condition, cost of construction, internal features, land use, land value, location, type of construction, quality of materials, and size. Market-activity data are also analyzed to determine a type of property's cost value. For instance, the average selling price of a category of property and its number of sales over a defined period of time are coded in most early CAMA programs as value determinant.[13] There is no lack of variety when it comes to CAMA products. Some estimate the selling price of properties by analyzing sales transactions over time; others analyze past events in property markets to solve current problems; others mimic the reasoning of human assessors to make their own value determinations.

For the past decade, these types of software have been promoted by tech firms working in postcolonial countries as a means of generating public revenue to manage urban growth. In many South and Southeast Asian cities, assessment software is used to manage problems spawned by issues such as residential market volatility caused by rapid population increases.[14] Singaporean experts have devised valuation algorithms for similar purposes.[15] In Malaysia, assessment software is promoted to value commercial properties for tax-levying purposes in order to repair and expand overburdened infrastructure.[16] Computerized valuation has been advertised in similar ways in Latin America, which economists are quick to point out often lacks revenue-productive property-tax systems.[17] This has become especially problematic given the continued expansion of megacities and their corresponding public-service needs. Associations and firms based in the United States, such as the Appraisal Institute, Fugro Geospatial, and O'Connor Consulting, and the Russian-based Top Systems, have spearheaded efforts to introduce algorithmic property valuation throughout the region. It has also been pushed in Mexico as a way of generating property-tax revenue to address strains on public services incurred by urban sprawl.[18]

Property, Tech, and Social Differentiation

Although computerized valuation represents urban environments as grids of exchange value, it would be shortsighted to assume that physical properties are the only things that function as value determinant. Most CAMA applications encode traditional metrics as indicators of value: average rent, home-ownership rates, median family size, median household income, and/or population density. In such instances, group-based characteristics are independent variables, whereas cost values are dependent. In some Asian and Latin American cities, computer-based cadastres are linked to drones to identify and monitor economic, physical, legal, environmental, and social characteristics of land parcels and the people who occupy them.[19] Therefore, such appraisals do not determine exchange value in a sociological vacuum; they inherit and reproduce social differentiations.

The link between social difference and property appraisals in CAMA is obscured by the technology's staunchest promoters. In fact, ethnoracial inequalities have been sold by city officials as *reasons* for embracing computerized property valuation. In New York City, CAMA's rise was spurred by coalitions looking to combat discriminatory property assessments in the early 1980s. Before the rent gap was achievable, residential properties in the "poorer, more debilitated boroughs" were assessed up to 250 percent more than those in the wealthier districts.[20] City officials explain how these overassessments increased property taxes for low-income minorities, which in turn decreased their eligibility for public aid.[21] This prompted the Department of Finance into a "computer crusade to eradicate the discrimination" against minority home owners perpetuated by human assessors. The department teamed with the Appraisal Institute to design a location value response surface model that, in addition to typical assessment variables (e.g., age, cost of construction, size), also coded "value influence centers" such as businesses, high-end shopping districts, and other amenities as positive values.[22] The absence of these amenities in poor communities led to lower property values. Many companies pitched the software as a corrective to the subjective biases of assessors.[23] Such uses of difference to legitimize the marketplace enact what Melamed terms "multicultural neoliberalism,"[24] for it codes free markets as *mediums* of ethnic and racial inclusion. In this discourse, multiculturalism and economic freedom are positively correlated. As such, the extension of market control into minority communities inside wealthier Western countries and across economically liberalizing areas of the global South is construed as a means to increase intragroup equality.

More recently, the nexus of race, property, and information tech has been identified in "platform urbanization" rhetoric. Sara Safransky explores a Detroit-based community development investment fund's use of market-value assessment (MVA) software in efforts to slash public services.[25] Ostensibly designed to combat redlining, MVA identified "risky" areas primed for disinvestment. Safransky details the factors used to determine risk built into the software: building code violations, credit scores, education, employment, housing vacancies, presence of subsidized housing, prime/subprime loans, and racial makeup, among others.

Thus, MVA, employed in the 2010 Detroit Works initiative, generated dis/investment maps that remarkably resembled the Home Owners' Loan Corporation's infamous residential security maps from the 1930s. In San Francisco, Erin McElroy illustrates how proptech enables racial dispossession via automated landlordism, planning, property management, and zoning. She specifically illustrates how computer-driven evictions, speculation, and residential surveillance abet larger gentrification processes that displace and geographically marginalize poor, black San Franciscans. McElroy also notes how the dispossessed appropriate similar technology to develop community-based housing-justice strategies.[26]

In addition to social difference, its corollary, regional difference, was a key theme used to legitimize CAMA's rapid spread. In these cases, indigenous groups find themselves subjected to the ever-encroaching specter of private landed property, which is defined over and against their material well-being. Cities in Australia, British Columbia, Canada, New Zealand, and Queensland adopted CAMA to value agricultural lands being absorbed into urban sprawls. AGJD Consulting, ESRI, and IAAO have all advocated strongly for municipalities in Canada, Namibia, Sierra Leone, and South Africa to embrace CAMA to value rural lands outside of cadastralized urban centers. The implementation of CAMA in many similar cases proceeded through developmentalist discourses that cast rural and indigenous landscapes as backward. To assuage the indigenous groups in these farmlands, government officials have characterized appraisals as a way to help them "grow and develop towards the goals of self-sufficiency and economic development."[27]

But the absorption of indigenous lands into global property markets is no mere equalizing process. On the contrary, it thrives on differentiation. Many critics of the algorithmic assessment of indigenous farmlands argue that it reflects efforts by metropolitan governances to shift tax burdens from urban centers to rural farmlands.[28] This claim stems from the fact that, thanks to intercity competition over foreign investment, most tax-exempted land uses are commonly located in urban centers. Population density is often coded as having the strongest correlation with value; high density means high value, and vice versa. Moreover, critics argue that the assessments reinforce the rural's subordinate relation to the urban. By coding farming as a taxable land use on the one hand and urban characteristics as a tax-exempted land use on the other, the former's value to the latter is activated anew. Indeed, proponents of CAMA routinely emphasize the need to generate revenues by taxing these farmlands to fund programs associated with urban growth.[29] This highlights the ongoing nature of accumulation by indigenous dispossession, which works in part through the illusion that indigenous lands are outside the capitalist system.[30]

In terms of global regions, algorithmic valuation is similarly publicized by international investors, nongovernment organizations, and public officials as a means of modernizing the global South. Through administrative software, advocates frame entrance into global markets as a "predetermined route" for all nation-states and thereby reproduce colonial relations.[31] Such arguments have been made for implementing CAMA in central European, east African, eastern European, and Latin American cities and rural areas to avoid being left behind in the rapidly changing global economy.[32] This narrative also extends to countries that were never colonized. The introduction of CAMA in Chinese cities was praised as instancing one more example of China "starting from behind, absorbing knowledge from more advanced economies, [and] adapting to local needs."[33] Smart tech therefore *feeds* on global South/North differentiations, if only in the rhetoric of its salespersons.

Automated Wastelands

Smart governance does not only play a part in determining the economic values of landscapes; it also plays a part in determining how pollutable they are. Since the late 1960s, municipal authorities across the world have slowly embraced computer-aided forms of waste-disposal optimization and landfill site selection to manage explosions of waste in expanding cities.[34] In 2006, 619 million tons of solid waste were produced in cities in Organization for Economic Cooperation and Development (OECD) countries, with US cities producing more waste than all European Union (EU) cities combined. Software designed to determine ideal locations and sizes of landfills, waste-to-energy plants, and trash incinerators has been one way of addressing this "global epidemic of urban waste."[35] But these locations were partially determined through colonial understandings of social and regional difference, which influenced the design and deployment of waste-optimization software.

It may seem fitting to interpret the spread of algorithmic waste management simply as a technical response to population growth. In the 1990s many municipal agencies in Western cities began turning to database management, decision support, geographic information, and spatial statistics software to cut costs of waste management. During this time, US-based companies such as Computer Support, Ivy Computer (now Trash Flow), and Soft-Pak were key vendors. Another key player was the Irish-based firm AMCS, which provided waste-management software throughout Australasia. According to experts, a key innovation in these applications was the way that they applied principles of private property and economic growth to municipal solid waste (MSW) management.[36] Early MSW management applications were designed to minimize waste collection, transport costs, disposal costs, and waste-truck routes using economic evaluations.[37] Inventory cost, the number of required vehicles, and transport times were analyzed to determine the route's efficiency and suggest optimal pickup crew sizes, landfill destinations, pickup frequency, and truck sizes.

Early MSW management software was designed to find ideal locations for new waste facilities based on exclusively economic variables.[38] Most waste-optimization software is used to evaluate scenarios exclusively through the lens of cost-benefit analysis.[39] Many proponents of the software place emphasis on economic efficiency over environmental and social considerations. For some models, the profit of developers, investor dividends, and the economic impact on surrounding areas are among the most heavily weighted variables.[40] Newly industrializing countries across sub-Saharan Africa, South America, and Asia have turned to software firms such as the Chinese-based EdgMachine and the Spanish-based Repsol for MSW management software. In Chinese municipalities, for instance, solid-waste software and wastewater-management software have been developed using methods from pollution-loss theories originally made to evaluate economic losses.[41] Here cost of disposal, loss of production, and traveling expenditures are identified by officials as the most important considerations. In India, state officials recently launched the Smartnet initiative, which enables relations between IT firms and more than a hundred special-purpose vehicles that oversee smart-city development. Through this public-private exchange, dozens of municipalities have assigned MSW disposal to private contractors, which determine waste-facility construction based on economic impact, cost-effectiveness, and land use, among other factors.[42]

Beyond city settings, waste-management software has been extended to nonurban landscapes. Focusing on rural villages in northern Egypt, S. Anwar and colleagues prescribe a model which suggests that transporting MSW from cities to remote rural areas is far more cost-effective than removing it from remote areas.[43] And in addition to disincentivizing MSW transport, algorithmic waste disposal can enroll nonurban territories as "operational landscapes" for urban waste outputs, making them into dumping grounds for conspicuous urban consumption. This is the typical result in waste-disposal applications that code distance from cities as positive values in waste-facility siting.[44] In both examples, the function of waste tech is to differentiate the pollutability of areas based on their economic significance, thereby exposing low-value landscapes to hazardous waste in a differential manner.

Waste Tech and Social Differentiation

Cost-effectiveness is not the only consideration in the software-aided management of urban waste. The environmental racism endemic to industrialization continues to manifest in different ways.[45] Waste-management tech arrived in US cities around the time of various exposés of environmental racism. During the late 1980s, when Computer Solutions, GEOWARE, and Trux Software began selling MSW management software to municipal agencies throughout the United States, several reports brought to light the extraordinary higher rates at which low-income minorities were exposed to toxic-waste facilities.[46] The category of race was confirmed as the strongest predictor of exposure to abandoned toxic-waste sites, lead poisoning, and municipal toxic-waste facilities in US cities. Activists attributed this to the fact that these groups resided in areas with low property values, which made it acceptable to pollute them from an economic point of view. Poor nonwhites' lack of political power to resist toxic siting near their homes was also emphasized as a contributing factor. But what was often overlooked is the fact that distance from toxic facilities is a racialized privilege that would be reproduced through various tools, including software.[47]

Close analysis of several landfill-siting software applications reveals their function in unevenly distributing exposure to waste. For starters, low levels of home ownership, household median income, and residential property values are coded as positive indicators for facility siting.[48] Waste-facility-siting models use risk-benefit analysis to determine "acceptable levels" of hazardous exposure in poor, predominantly minority communities.[49] Furthermore, when determining waste siting according to profitability, working-class black, immigrant, and indigenous communities are invariably in disadvantageous positions to voice their grievances.[50] These conditions combine instrumental rationalities of the state with industrial forms of death and dehumanization. Placed into its political context, the software used to determine who gets exposed to such harms performs what we might call *necrocomputation*.

Such a failure to incorporate considerations for differential toxic exposure also characterizes software for assessing the so-called social costs of waste facilities. Instead of coding group-based inequality as a social cost, these typically measure a facility's effects on land uses.[51] By coding social costs as such, group-differentiated exposure to waste is blocked from measurement. The US federal government has redacted studies using geographic-information systems to map group-based disparities in hazardous-waste exposure.[52] The software can therefore help reinforce the "history of excluding people of color from the mainstream environmental groups, decision-making boards, commissions, and regulatory bodies."[53]

The many "Not in My Backyard" movements that have coalesced in cities that have adopted the software applications should therefore come as no surprise.[54] This is far from unexpected given that racialization, Nikhil Pal Singh observes, is always accompanied by "spatial and signifying systems that stigmatize and depreciate one form of humanity for the purposes of another's health, development, safety, [or] profit."[55] Were MSW management software to include data on group-based differentials, it would run the risk of disrupting the privilege of not being exposed to toxic waste. Indeed, clashes between the spread of computerized waste management and minority populations have coalesced in several European cities. Critics of data-driven waste management in cities of the European Union direct attention to a general lack of consideration of environmental discrimination.[56] Discussions about the ways that immigrants are disproportionately exposed to incinerators, industrial and nuclear sites, and waste-management facilities are consistently absent at international conferences and in academic research and corporate literature.[57] This is despite the growing preponderance of "waste markets" in the heavily minoritized urban fringe and in rural areas.

In addition to racial differentiation, the spread of waste tech is differentiated geographically, most notably through socio-spatial categories established through colonial doctrines. Much like computerized appraisal, computerized waste management exhibits a consistent tendency to devalorize rural areas to the benefit of urban centers of accumulation. So where the appraisal algorithms off-load tax burdens onto rural territories, optimization algorithms off-load garbage. This is pronounced in cities in rapidly urbanizing East Asian countries looking to disentangle urban-rural land uses on the grounds that Western planning theory deems mixed areas ineffective.[58] To compound matters, beyond issues of land use the centrality of cost-benefit analysis often leads to conclusions that in areas with "dispersed, small populations, the collection and transport of recyclate to processing centers presents potentially important environmental and cost disincentives—it may be that direct landfilling of waste with minimal recycling is the [best option]."[59]

Global regional difference has also worked as a selling point for technology firms in postcolonial countries. As Denise Ferreira da Silva has shown, differentiating global regions on the grounds that they are categorically outside of and behind Western Europe/United States civilization helps justify extensions of Western power.[60] Firms such as TransAct Energy Corporation, Veolia Environnement, and WRATE have thus touted waste-management software throughout the global South as a means of catching up to the global North in refuse-disposal practices. Public and private advocates of waste-management software working in the global South insist that these countries do so to "learn from the experience of industrialized countries to solve serious pollution problems."[61] As Ayona Datta demonstrates, smart-city rhetoric is the latest iteration of colonial powers trying to remake global South governances in the image of the West by using technoscientific modernization as a pretext.[62] Indeed, the World Bank has rigorously promoted waste-management technologies in the global South as a way of increasing private-sector activity in state decision making such as in the West.[63] Intergovernmental support for these firms was codified in the UN's 1992 Rio Declaration of Environment and Development, which articulated a vision for mobilizing commercialized technology to achieve low-cost disposal services in poor countries.[64] Advocates for waste tech in poorer global South countries also emphasize the fact that these nations rely heavily on the informal sector, which is argued to be irregular and inefficient, thus desperately in need of technological upgrade.[65]

Programming Racial Difference

> The tendency of European civilization through capitalism was thus not to homogenize but to differentiate—to exaggerate regional, subcultural, and dialectical differences.
>
> CEDRIC ROBINSON, *BLACK MARXISM*, 1983

Like any mode of capital accumulation, accumulation through smart governance proceeds in part through positing social, hence geographic, nonequivalencies. The implementation of computerized property and waste tech moves through long-standing structures of group-based inequalities, extending them in time and space, transforming them, creating in the process novel contradictions and forms of resistance. The centrality of profiling is made clear in computer-assisted property appraisal. Trevor Ngwane illustrates how property regimes have long served as mechanisms for racializing space, expressed in submarket differentiations.[66] CAMA software reproduces these submarkets under the heading of putative finer districts, comprising high levels of home ownership, median household incomes, and proximity to amenities, among other factors, on one hand and "inner-city" submarkets determined by the preponderance of old buildings, residences with low square footage, and low home sale values on the other.[67] The profiles, which map onto residential segregation, are then used as rationalizations for placed-based (dis)investment and tax abatement. This preserves existing disparities in property value, thus ensuring that minority neighborhoods maintain their relative valuelessness. In fact, lowering the values of minority submarkets, which always precedes gentrification, was the point of establishing algorithmic appraisal in New York, which was legitimized through multicultural rhetoric.

Computer-assisted waste management similarly generates spatial profiles in ways that naturalize the logics of the market and contribute to "group-differentiated vulnerability to premature death," given its toxic import.[68] And it can do so only by encoding spatial and hence social differences. Municipalities also attempt to raise revenues from rural areas by coding them as distinct from cities in order to fund urban projects. This casts the rural as a resource for dealing with urban growth, though only through reproducing the nonurban. Technology firms similarly benefit from the production of regional difference by casting its commodity as a medium through which postcolonial hinterlands can close the development gap with Western countries.

Smart governance reflects the extent to which forms of capitalist governance, computerized or not, rely on establishing notions of group-based inequality prior to and through the accumulation process. As Adam Bledsoe and Willie Wright argue, the enshrinement of racial inequality is one of several tactics of justifying the racialized effects of this process.[69] And the tactic is deployed on a global scale. It is therefore important to stress that the planetary profusion of smart governance encounters, organizes, and disposes of humans and environments in ways that are prefigured by colonial racial classifications. This adds another dimension to the observation that contemporary urbanization is "variegated, uneven, volatile, contradictory, and emergent[and] assumes specific forms across divergent spatiotemporal contexts."[70] Specifically, we see that differentiation is not only an output of urban transformations but also an *input*, which offers deeper insights into where, why, and how economies of space are changing alongside socio-technological mutation.

Beyond the Algorithm

Scrutinizing smart governance from the perspective of racial capitalism reveals the extent to which it is prefigured by and creates new forms of racial dispossession and disparity. These findings highlight the need for algorithmic abolitionist thinking that calls the types of norms and values behind smart governance to the fore. Such a point of view maintains that it is not enough to chronicle the unequal effects of the rise and spread of technologically administered populations. Such inattention to the *social forces* at work behind smart governance has led to some theoretical missteps. For one, in addition to chronicling how the spread of the smart city can reproduce established social inequalities, one must also scrutinize it in terms of whether or not the reproduction of long-standing social inequalities is one of its driving objectives.[71] One thing that smart urbanization shows is that data-driven governance is employed in many instances to preserve if not expand inequity. This is most obvious in the way that racial taxonomies prefigure algorithmic practices in border patrol, law enforcement, and/or national security. The slow and uneven rolling out of smart technologies of governance does not signify the birth of a fully automated mode of statecraft, operating beyond the grasp of human control. Such phantom-like agency is an ideological mirage that renders invisible those who benefit from the application of computing technology to governance. Nor does it signify, as Zuboff suggests, the end of racial supremacy as an organizing principle of political and economic power.[72] On the contrary, from the standpoint of racial capitalism, algorithmic governance is the *latest vector* of white supremacist political economy.

It is therefore vital to understand the constitutive function that racial differentiation performs in creating conditions for smart modes of governance. As the cases explored above demonstrate, the algorithmic apparatuses of such cities are specifically designed such that they devalue specific areas and make them unequally susceptible to disinvestment and despoilment. In many instances, the key function is to legitimize the harmful practices required to increase profit rates, which are to begin with already ethno-racialized, gendered, nationalized, regionalized, and sexualized. An abolitionist view would direct attention to the extent to which such deployments of software technology permeate society. Moreover, the perspective is sensitive to the fact that the use of algorithms to differentiate populations and places according to their value can potentially generate new solidarities and ways of producing social space. The people and places that are identified by algorithms as economically devalued or exposed to pollution are revealed to share one common characteristic—they are relatively valueless from the vantage point of current configurations of global accumulation. This is not merely an issue of class: some of these groups are proletarianized; others are not. But what they all hold in common is that they have been differentiated by governances as less valuable, however defined. Acknowledging this provides a basis for coalition building between the various algorithmically devalued populations, which offers new opportunities for resisting the racial violence so central to the evolution of the capitalist mode of production.

NOTES

1. Kitchin, "Continuous Geosurveillance"; Luque-Ayala and Marvin, "Maintenance of Urban Circulation."

2. This essay relies on extensive analysis of four types of documents to understand and cross-verify these dynamics. The academic studies analyzed here were taken from journals where experts design mathematical models for property assessment and waste management for the expressed purpose of encoding them in software. The essay also analyzes reports on such software from international organizations. Technical reports and promotional material from technology firms that design and sell property evaluation software are also examined. Finally, conference papers and white papers from professional property-assessment and waste-management associations are also subjected to discourse analysis.

3. Townsend, *Smart Cities*, 93–114.

4. Graham and Marvin, *Telecommunications and the City*; Amin and Thrift, *Cities*.

5. Graham, "Software-Sorted Geographies," 570; Cardullo and Kitchin, "Being a 'Citizen,'" 1–5.

6. Vanolo, "Is There Anybody Out There?" See also Brenner and Schmid, "Towards a New Epistemology?," 151–58.

7. Smith, *New Urban Frontier*, 157.

8. Ong, *Neoliberalism as Exception*.

9. "Rural Property Tax Systems."

10. Ranganathan, "Thinking with Flint," 17–19; Bonds, "Race and Ethnicity I," 1–5.

11. "Rural Property Tax Systems," 39.

12. Liu et al., "What We Do," 470.

13. McCluskey, "A Critical Review," 5.

14. Erbam and Piumetto, *Making Land Legible*.

15. Leng, "Mass Appraisal."

16. Kamarudin and Daud, "CAMA Application."

17. Sepulveda and Martinez-Vazquez, "Explaining Property Tax Collections."

18. Peña et al., "Planning Support Systems," 30.

19. Erbam and Piumetto, *Making Land Legible*.

20. Laberis, "Property Appraisal System."

21. DePalma, "Reassessments Hit Homeowners Hard," 10.

22. The city later entered into a four-million-dollar contract with Vision Appraisal Technology in 2007 and a twenty-million-dollar contract with Tyler Technologies a decade later.

23. McCluskey and Franzsen, "Land Value Taxation"; Harris, "'Assessing' Discrimination," 1–10; "Guidance on International Mass Appraisal," 1–5.

24. Melamed, *Represent and Destroy*.

25. Safransky, "Geographies of Algorithmic Violence," 200–205.

26. McElroy, "Property as Technology," 16–18.

27. "First Nations Agriculture Needs Assessment."

28. Bahl and Linn, *Urban Public Finance*.

29. Peña et al., "Planning Support Systems"; McCluskey and Franzsen, "Land Value Taxation."

30. See, for instance, Goldstein, "Reproduction of Race."

31. Tomba, "Differentials of Surplus-Value," 33.

32. Acuto, "Global Science for City Policy"; Geho, "Evaluation," 235–40.

33. Nunlist, "Virtual Valuation," 10.

34. Gottinger, "Computational Model."

35. TEC, "Transact Energy Introduces Z.E.W.O.P."

36. Chang and Pires, "Systems Analysis for the Future."

37. Elsaid and Aghezzaf, "Framework for Sustainable Waste Management."

38. Petts, "Municipal Waste Management."

39. Morrissey and Browne, "Waste Management Models."

40. To be sure, many waste-management designers began going beyond the matter of landfilling and exploring alternative practices toward the turn of the century. Some models were developed to consider a wider variety of options, including waste reduction, when calculating economic and environmental impact. But the administrative scale needed to implement these models has stymied their integration into government agencies. See Davy, "Fairness as Compassion"; and Tralhão, Coutinho-Rodrigues, and Alçada-Almeida, "Multiobjective Modeling Approach."

41. Su et al., "Inexact Multi-objective Dynamic Model."

42. Sumathi, "GIS-Based Approach."

43. Anwar et al., "Optimization of Solid Waste Management."

44. Siddiqui, Everett, and Vieux, "Landfill Siting."

45. Dillon, "Race, Waste, and Space."

46. Bullard, "Race and Environmental Justice"; "Toxic Wastes and Race"; "Rio Declaration."

47. Pulido, "Geographies of Race and Ethnicity II."

48. Petts, "Municipal Waste Managment"; Zurbrügg, "Assessment Methods for Waste Management."

49. Heiman, "Waste Management and Risk Assessment."

50. Chavis, "Foreword," 3–6.

51. Jung et al., "Landfill Site Selection."

52. For instance, the US Environmental Protection Agency removed such reports from its website during the administration of President Donald Trump.

53. Chavis, "Foreword," 3.

54. Sasao, "Estimation of the Social Costs."

55. Singh, *Black Is a Country*, 223.

56. See Martuzzi, Mitis, and Forastire, "Inequalities, Inequities, Environmental Justice."

57. Harper, Steger, and Filčák, "Environmental Justice and Roma Communities."

58. Hiramatsu et al., "Municipal Solid Waste Flow."

59. Petts, "Municipal Waste Management," 826–27.

60. Ferreira da Silva, "1 (Life) ÷ 0 (Blackness) = $\infty - \infty$ or ∞ / ∞."

61. Hiramatsu et al., "Municipal Solid Waste Flow," 951.

62. Datta, "New Urban Utopias of Postcolonial India"; Datta and Odendaal, "Smart Cities."

63. Hiramatsu et al., "Municipal Solid Waste Flow."

64. Cointreau-Levine, "Private Sector Participation."

65. Contrary to the proclamations of many Indian officials who promote algorithmic waste management, Vinay Gidwani and Rajyashree Reddy, in "The Afterlives of 'Waste,'" demonstrate that the informal sector has in some circumstances been more efficient in waste disposal than have municipal and private services.

66. Ngwane, "Xenophobia and Capitalist Urbanisation Processes."

67. Figueroa, "GIS Technology Improves Delineation"; Laberis, "Property Appraisal System."

68. Gilmore, Golden Gulag, 28.

69. Bledsoe and Wright, "Anti-Blackness of Global Capital," 12.

70. Brenner, "Debating Planetary Urbanization," 1–5.

71. Vanolo, "Is There Anybody Out There?"

72. Zuboff, Age of Surveillance Capitalism.

BIBLIOGRAPHY

Acuto, Michele. "Global Science for City Policy." Science 359, no. 6372 (2018): 165–66.
Amin, Ash, and Nigel Thrift. Cities: Reimagining the Urban. London: Polity, 2002.
Anwar, S., S. Elagroudy, M. Abdel Razik, A. Gaber, C. P. C. Bong, and W. S. Ho. "Optimization of Solid Waste Management in Rural Villages of Developing Countries." Clean Technologies and Environmental Policy (2018) 20: 1–14.
Bahl, Roy, and Johannes F. Linn. Urban Public Finance in Developing Countries. New York: Oxford University Press, 1992.
Bledsoe, Adam, and Willie Jamaal Wright. "The Anti-blackness of Global Capital." Environment and Planning D: Society and Space 37, no. 1 (2019): 8–26.
Bonds, Anne. "Race and Ethnicity I: Property, Race, and the Carceral State." Progress in Human Geography 43, no. 3 (2018): 1–10.
Brenner, Neil. "Debating Planetary Urbanization: For an Engaged Pluralism." Environment and Planning D: Society and Space 36, no. 3 (2018): 1–21.
Brenner, Neil, and Christian Schmid. "Towards a New Epistemology of the Urban?" City 19, no. 2/3 (2015): 151–82.
Bullard, Robert. "Race and Environmental Justice in the United States." Yale Journal of International Law 18, no. 12 (1993): 319–35.
Cardullo, Paolo, and Rob Kitchin. "Being a 'Citizen' in the Smart City: Up and down the Scaffold of Smart Citizen Participation in Dublin, Ireland." GeoJournal 84 (2019): 1–13.

Chang, Ni-Bin, and Ana Pires. "Systems Analysis for the Future of Solid Waste Management: Challenges and Perspectives." In *Sustainable Solid Waste Management: A Systems Engineering Approach*, 849–94. New York: Wiley, 2015.

Chavis, Benjamin. "Foreword." In *Confronting Environmental Racism: Voices from the Grassroots*, edited by Robert Bullard and Benjamin Chavis, 3–7. Cambridge, MA: South End.

Cointreau-Levine, Sandra. "Private Sector Participation in Municipal Solid Waste Services in Developing Countries." In *Urban Management Programme*, 47–52. Washington, DC: International Bank for Reconstruction and Development, 1994.

Datta, Ayona. "New Urban Utopias of Postcolonial India: 'Entrepreneurial Urbanization' in Dholera Smart City, Gujarat." *Dialogues in Human Geography* 5, no. 1 (2015): 3–22.

Datta, Ayona, and Nancy Odendaal. "Smart Cities and the Banality of Power." *Environment and Planning D: Society and Space* 37, no. 3 (2019): 387–92.

Davy, Benjamin. "Fairness as Compassion: Towards a Less Unfair Facility Siting Policy." *Risk* 7, no. 99 (1996): 99–108.

DePalma, Anthony. "Reassessments Hit Homeowners Hard." *New York Times*, May 15, 1988. https://www.nytimes.com/1988/05/15/realestate/reassessments-hit-homeowners-hard.html.

Dillon, Lindsey. "Race, Waste, and Space: Brownfield Redevelopment and Environmental Justice at the Hunters Point Shipyard." *Antipode* 46, no. 5 (2014): 1205–21.

Elsaid, Sarah, and El-Houssaine Aghezzaf. "A Framework for Sustainable Waste Management: Challenges and Opportunities." *Management Research Review* 38, no. 10 (2015): 1086–97.

Erbam, Diego Alfonso, and Mario Andrés Piumetto. *Making Land Legible: Cadastres for Urban Planning and Development in Latin America*. Cambridge, MA: Lincoln Institute of Land Policy, 2016.

Ferreira da Silva, Denise. "1 (Life) ÷ 0 (Blackness) = ∞ − ∞ or ∞ / ∞: On Matter beyond the Equation of Value." *E-Flux* 79 (2017): 1–18.

Figueroa, Roberto A. "GIS Technology Improves Delineation of Valuation Neighbourhoods in Regina." Paper presented at the Fourth Annual Integrating GIS and CAMA Conference, 1–8. Miami Beach, FL, 2000.

"First Nations Agriculture Needs Assessment." British Columbia Ministry of Agriculture, 2012. www2.gov.bc.ca/assets/gov/farming-natural-resources-and-industry/agriculture-and-seafood/farm-management/farm-business-management/first-nations-agriculture/first_nations_agriculture_needs_assessment.pdf.

Geho, Medard Lucas. "An Evaluation of the Application of Computer Assisted Mass Appraisal in Tanzania." *Journal of the Language Association of Eastern Africa*, 2, no. 2 (2014): 235–51.

Gidwani, Vinay, and Rajyashree N. Reddy. "The Afterlives of 'Waste': Notes from India for a Minor History of Capitalist Surplus." *Antipode* 43, no. 5 (2011): 1625–58.

Gilmore, Ruth Wilson. *Golden Gulag: Prisons, Surplus, Crisis, and Opposition in Globalizing California*. Berkeley: University of California Press, 2007.

Goldstein, Alyosha. "On the Reproduction of Race, Colonialism, and Settler Colonialism." In *Race and Capitalism: Global Territories, Transnational Histories*, 42–51. Los Angeles: Institute on Inequality and Democracy, 2017.

Gottinger, H. W. "A Computational Model for Solid Waste Management with Applications." *Applied Mathematical Modelling* 10 (1986): 330–38.

Graham, Steve, and Simon Marvin. *Telecommunications and the City: Electronic Spaces, Urban Places*. London: Routledge, 1996.

Graham, Stephen. "Software-Sorted Geographies." *Progress in Human Geography* 29, no. 5 (2005): 562–80.

"Guidance on International Mass Appraisal and Related Tax Policy." International Association of Assessing Officers, 2013. www.iaao.org/media/Standards/International_Guidance.pdf.

Harper, Krista, Tamara Steger, and Richard Filčák. "Environmental Justice and Roma Communities in Central and Eastern Europe." *Environmental Policy and Governance* 19, no. 4 (July–August 2009): 251–68.

Harris, Lee. "'Assessing' Discrimination: The Influence of Race in Residential Property Tax Assessment." *Journal of Land Use and Environmental Law* 20, no. 1 (2004): 1–60.

Heiman, Michael K. "Waste Management and Risk Assessment: Environmental Discrimination through Regulation." *Urban Geography* 17, no. 5 (1996): 400–418.

Hiramatsu, Ai, Yuji Hara, Makiko Sekiyama, Ryo Honda, and Chart Chiemchaisri. "Municipal Solid Waste Flow and Waste Generation Characteristics in an Urban-Rural Fringe Area in Thailand." *Waste Management and Research* 27 (2009): 951–60.

Jung, Sukwan, Tomoaki Miura, Michael Robotham, and Gregory L. Bruland. "Landfill Site Selection by Integrating a GIS Analysis with an Economic Analysis: A Case Study of Oahu, Hawaii." *Journal of Solid Waste Technology and Management* 39, no. 2 (2013): 114–32.

Kamarudin, Norhaya, and Dzurllkanian Daud. "Computer-Assisted Mass Appraisal (CAMA) Application for Property Tax Administration Improvement in Malaysia." Presented at International Federation of Surveyors XXV International Congress: Engaging the Challenges—Enhancing the Relevance, Kuala Lumpur, June 16–21, 2014.

Kitchin, Rob. "Continuous Geosurveillance in the 'Smart City.'" Dystopia, DIS Magazine, 2015. Accessed January 8, 2022. http://dismagazine.com/dystopia/73066/rob-kitchin-spatial-big-data-and-geosurveillance/.

Laberis, Bill. "Property Appraisal System to Ease Inequities." *Computerworld*, March 30, 1981, 45.

Leng, L. S. "Mass Appraisal for Property Tax Purposes in Singapore." In *Computer Assisted Mass Appraisal: An International Review*, edited by William J. McCluskey and Alastair S. Adair, 339–55. Burlington, VT: Ashgate, 1997.

Liu, Sing-cheong, Mark Wang, Bo-Sin Tang, and Siu-wai Wong. "What We Do and Can Do for a Living: Expanding the Role of the Real Estate Profession." *Journal of Property Investment and Finance* 25, no. 5 (2007): 468–81.

Luque-Ayala, Andrés, and Simon Marvin. "The Maintenance of Urban Circulation: An Operational Logic of Infrastructural Control." *Environment and Planning D: Society and Space* 34, no. 2 (2015): 191–208.

Martuzzi, Marco, Francesco Mitis, and Francesco Forastire. "Inequalities, Inequities, Environmental Justice in Waste Management and Health." *European Journal of Public Health* 20, no. 1 (2010): 21–26.

McCluskey, William J. "A Critical Review of Computer Assisted Mass Appraisal Techniques." In *Computer Assisted Mass Appraisal: An International Review*, edited by William J. McCluskey and Alastair S. Adair, 1–26. Burlington, VT: Ashgate, 1997.

McCluskey, William J., and Riel C. D. Franzsen. "Land Value Taxation: A Case Study Approach." Cambridge, MA: Lincoln Institute of Land Policy, 2001.

McElroy, Erin. "Property as Technology: Temporal Entanglements of Race, Space, and Displacement." *City* 24, no. 3 (April 2020): 1–18.

Melamed, Jodi. "Racial Capitalism." *Critical Ethnic Studies* 1, no. 1 (2015): 76–86.

Melamed, Jodi. *Represent and Destroy: Rationalizing Violence in the New Racial Capitalism*. Minneapolis: University of Minnesota Press, 2011.

Morrissey, Anne J., and Jim Browne. "Waste Management Models and Their Application to Sustainable Waste Management." *Waste Management* 24 (2004): 297–308.

Ngwane, Trevor. "Xenophobia and Capitalist Urbanisation Processes in Johannesburg's 'African' Townships." Spotlight On. *International Journal of Urban and Regional Research*, 2017. IJURR.org. Accessed December 20, 2021. https:// www.ijurr.org/spotlight-on/race-justice-and-the-city/xenophobia-and -capitalist-urbanisation-processes-in-johannesburgs-african-townships/.

Nunlist, Tom. "Virtual Valuation: GIS-Assisted Mass Appraisal in Shenzen." *Land Lines*, October 2017, 8–13. https://www.lincolninst.edu/sites/default/files /pubfiles/virtual-valuation-lla171003.pdf.

Ong, Aihwa. *Neoliberalism as Exception: Mutations in Citizenship and Sovereignty*. Durham, NC: Duke University Press, 2006.

Peña, Sergio, César M. Fuentes, Luis E. Cervera, and Vladimir Hernandez. "Planning Support Systems: A Computer-Assisted Mass Appraisal (CAMA) System for Ciudad Juarez, Mexico." *Journal of Property Tax Assessment and Administration* 9, no. 4 (2012): 25–40.

Petts, Judith. "Municipal Waste Management: Inequities and the Role of Deliberation." *Risk Analysis* 20, no. 6 (2000): 821–32.

Pulido, Laura. "Geographies of Race and Ethnicity II: Environmental Racism, Racial Capitalism and State-Sanctioned Violence." *Progress in Human Geography* 41, no. 4 (2017): 524–33.

Ranganathan, Malini. "Thinking with Flint: Racial Liberalism and the Roots of an American Water Tragedy." *Capitalism Nature Socialism* (2015): 17–33.

"Rio Declaration on Environment and Development." United Nations General Assembly, August 12, 1992. www.un.org/en/development/desa/population /migration/generalassembly/docs/globalcompact/A_CONF.151_26_Vol.I _Declaration.pdf.

Robinson, Cedric. *Black Marxism: The Making of the Black Radical Tradition.* Chapel Hill: University of North Carolina Press, 2000.

"Rural Property Tax Systems in Central and Eastern Europe." Food and Agriculture Organization of the United Nations, 2002. www.fao.org/3/y4313e /y4313e00.htm#Contents.

Safransky, Sara. "Geographies of Algorithmic Violence: Redlining the Smart City." *International Journal of Urban and Regional Research* 44, no. 2 (2019): 200–218.

Sasao, Toshiaki. "An Estimation of the Social Costs of Landfill Siting Using a Choice Experiment." *Waste Management* 24, no. 8 (2004): 753–62.

Sepulveda, Cristian, and Jorge Martinez-Vazquez. "Explaining Property Tax Collections in Developing Countries: The Case of Latin America." In *Decentralization and Reform in Latin America*, edited by Giorgio Brosio and Juan Pablo Jiménez, 223–59. Northampton, MA: Edward Elgar, 2012.

Siddiqui, Muhammad Z., Jess W. Everett, and Baxter E. Vieux. "Landfill Siting Using Geographic Information Systems: A Demonstration." *Journal of Environmental Engineering* 122 (1996): 515–23.

Singh, Nikhil Pal. *Black Is a Country: Race and the Unfinished Struggle for Democracy.* Cambridge, MA: Harvard University Press, 2005.

Smith, Neil. *The New Urban Frontier: Gentrification and the Revanchist City.* London: Routledge, 1996.

Su, J., B. D. Xi, H. L. Liu, Y. H. Jiang, and M. A. Warith. "An Inexact Multiobjective Dynamic Model and Its Application in China for the Management of Municipal Solid Waste." *Waste Management* 28 (2008): 2532–41.

Sumathi, V. R., Usha Natesan, and Chinmoy Sarkar. "GIS-Based Approach for Optimized Siting of Municipal Solid Waste Landfill." *Waste Management* 28 (2008): 2146–60.

TEC. "Transact Energy Introduces Z.E.W.O.P. to International Waste Optimization Conference in Brazil." TransAct Energy Corporation, November 9, 2017. http://transactenergycorp.com/zewop2016/author/actiondvzewop.

Tomba, Massimiliano. "Differentials of Surplus-Value in the Contemporary Forms of Exploitation." *Commoner* 12 (2007): 23–37.

Townsend, Anthony. *Smart Cities: Big Data, Civic Hackers, and the Quest for a New Utopia.* New York: W. W. Norton, 2014.

"Toxic Wastes and Race in the United States." United Church of Christ Commission for Racial Justice, 1987. uccfiles.com/pdf/ToxicWastes&Race.pdf.

Tralhão, Lino, João Coutinho-Rodrigues, and Luís Alçada-Almeida. "A Multi-objective Modeling Approach to Locate Multi-Compartment Containers for Urban-Sorted Waste." *Waste Management* 30 (2010): 2418–29.

Vanolo, Alberto. "Is There Anybody Out There? The Place and Role of Citizens in Tomorrow's Smart Cities." *Futures* 82 (2016): 26–36.

Zuboff, Shoshana. *The Age of Surveillance Capitalism: The Fight for a Human Future at the New Frontier of Power*. New York: PublicAffairs, 2019.

Zurbrügg, Christian. "Assessment Methods for Waste Management Decision-Support in Developing Countries." PhD diss., Università degli Studi di Brescia, Facoltà di Ingegneria, 2013.

III Aesthetics

REIMAGINING THE SITES OF CULTURAL MEMORY

Nuclear Antipolitics and the Queer Art of Logistical Failure

We broke the earth and now we fall through time.
because marching on a line we thought was forward
only called up the urgency of the abyss.
ALEXIS PAULINE GUMBS, *M ARCHIVE*, 2018

Several days after the August 6, 1945, atomic bombing of Hiroshima, my grandmother Hideko Kono entered the city to search for her husband and twelve-year-old son. She had evacuated months earlier to another town with her three younger children and received news of the bombing from her eldest son, Shigemi, who was fourteen years old and had survived the blast. By the time she reached Hiroshima, her husband, Michitoshi, had already died in the hospital, and she was unable to recover the body of her twelve-year-old son, Hiromi. In the collection of Tanka poetry recounting her experience of the devastation, my grandmother wrote with finality, "In Hiroshima / All living things have ended."[1] Seventy-one years later, during President Obama's 2016 visit to Hiroshima—the first such visit by a sitting US president—his speech made no apologies for ending all living things in Hiroshima. Instead, the meaning of Hiroshima was safely delimited to the moral quandaries of technological modernity. "In the image of a mushroom cloud," he asserted, "we are most starkly reminded of humanity's core contradiction . . . [that] our ability to set ourselves apart from nature . . . also give[s] us the capacity for unmatched destruction." Hiroshima's lesson, he summarized, was that "technological progress without an equivalent progress in human institutions can doom us."[2]

This essay sets out to challenge the technological universalisms invoked by Obama that fold Hiroshima into a morality tale of scientific progress, one that resonates contemporary narratives of the Anthropocene, an epoch in which humankind has achieved a disastrous level of geologic agency through its pursuit of technological modernity. The atomic bombing of Hiroshima is often periodized as the onset of the Anthropocene, initiating an irreversible surge in global human activity often characterized as the Great Acceleration.[3] I question the normativity of this periodization as well as what I view as the scalar politics embedded in the symbolism of the atomic bomb. In challenging nuclear universalisms, I pursue alternative forms of representation that do not rely on visual transparency to contest the ahistorical nature of global memory culture, which Katherine Lawless describes as the tendency to "translate historical forms of exploitation into universal narratives of suffering." In the case of Hiroshima, this means concealing the "slow violence of nuclear energy regimes by reducing nuclearity to the moment of explosion."[4] Shifting attention away from the spectacularity and radical uniqueness of nuclearism, I probe the largely unseen, banal violence of uranium mining undertaken on Indigenous lands. From the vantage point of the extracted and irradiated wastelands of nuclear modernity, I argue that technopolitics structure a postwar transformation of global power relations. In this case the antipolitical frame of technopolitics reveals the coordinated expansion and technological intensification of imperial state power that is secured through its simultaneous *depoliticization*. Hence, relations previously constructed around the colonizer and the colonized have since been reconstituted as depoliticized, technopolitical relations shaped by nuclear modernity. These technopolitical arrangements maintain imperial power structures in the aftermath of global decolonization movements insofar as power relations between the colonizer and colonized have been transformed and reproduced as relations between the nuclear and non-nuclear.

Transparent visibility structures what Lisa Yoneyama refers to as a "nuclear order of knowledge," one that limits the meaning of the atomic bomb to periodization: ending World War II and beginning the Cold War.[5] The visuality of nuclearism enables what Manu Vimalassery [Karuka], Juliana Hu Pegues, and Alyosha Goldstein describe as "colonial unknowing," whereby the slow violence of uranium mining is otherwise effaced by the spectacular violence of Hiroshima.[6] A large part of this unknowing occurs through the largely invisible, colonial sites of uranium mining. What is obscured from this order of knowledge is how the Belgian Congo and the Canadian Northwest Territories supplied the majority of the uranium for the atomic bomb that was detonated over Hiroshima, as well as the plutonium that was used in the bomb that exploded over Nagasaki. High-grade uranium from the Belgian Congo's Shinkolobwe mine was shipped to New Jersey and enriched in Canada, along with uranium from the Great Bear Lake region of the Northwest Territories. Thus, in playing with the homonyms *nonsite/nonsight*, I explore the ways in which colonial capitalism designates Indigenous lands as *nonsites* of nuclear modernity, making them available for what Traci Brynne Voyles calls "wastelanding." As she elaborates in her important work on uranium mines on Navajo lands, "the 'wasteland' is a racial and spatial signifier that renders an environment and the bodies that inhabit it pollutable."[7] These are sites that are deemed unproductive, backward, and peripheral to the technological superiority of the global North but are nevertheless mined for resources while toxic waste is dumped or left abandoned.

Another difficulty in reordering our knowledge of Hiroshima is rooted in postwar geopolitics and the Cold War. Shaped by the US occupation of Japan and in the shadow of the Cold War, public commemoration of Hiroshima in Japan and the US has largely served to obscure or evacuate its historical context and political significance. Japan's postwar economic ascendancy has largely deflected US responsibility for the human cost of the atomic bombs. As Yoneyama has shown, what is obscured by the Hiroshima museum's universalizing message of peace are the atrocities Japan committed in its quest for imperial power in Asia, Japan's postwar Cold War alliance with the United States, and a larger context of global warfare.[8] As Benedict Giamo summarizes, "Hiroshima has become a facile trope for atomic victimization and pacifism."[9] Moreover, global pleas for nuclear disarmament and "No More Hiroshimas" altogether elide the existence of Japan's many nuclear reactors while overlooking the sixty-seven nuclear tests conducted on the Marshall Islands over a twelve-year period, the largest of which was equivalent to a thousand Hiroshima-sized bombs.[10]

Although the Hiroshima Peace Memorial Museum and Park assails visitors with messages of peace and appeals to a world free of nuclear arms, these messages are undermined by Japan's embrace of nuclear power technology. Under the guise of Dwight D. Eisenhower's "Atoms for Peace" campaign in 1953, Japan's early adoption of nuclear power was compelled through secret collaborations between US foreign intelligence and conservative Japanese politicians and the business elite. Before the Fukushima Daiichi nuclear power plant meltdown in 2011, Japan had sixty nuclear reactors, the largest number in Asia, and had plans to generate 50 percent of all power from nuclear energy by 2030.[11] Although Japan has since been forced to scale back, shutting down twenty-seven reactors and limiting nuclear power to 20–25 percent of total energy by 2030, the truth is that a nuclear-free future is nowhere to be found on Japan's time horizon. The contradictory morality that surrounds nuclear energy and nuclear weapons is a refraction of a deeply embedded imperial regime of energy extraction. The antipolitical character of energy technopolitics similarly animates Japan's continual refusal to be accountable to the victims of its fascist imperial regime in Asia, as much as the United States continues to justify the atomic bombing by claiming it saved lives and ended the war.

In the United States the visual spectacle of a ballooning mushroom cloud remains the primary symbol of nuclear destruction that both aestheticizes and anesthetizes many Americans' engagement with the event, whereas the larger plutonium bomb that exploded over Nagasaki three days later has largely been relegated to an afterthought. Correspondingly, much of the historiography of the atomic bomb has focused on the technological and political ingenuity of the scientists involved in the Manhattan Project. Gabrielle Hecht refers to this bias as a form of *nuclear exceptionalism* that remains focused on First World electricity and military production, geographically delimited to the Cold War superpowers and Europe. She calls us to "witness the obsession with the historical minutiae of 'the decision to drop the bomb,' the endless stream of biographies of Manhattan Project scientists, and the insistence on the uniqueness of moral dilemmas posed by atomic activities." Following Hecht's reflection that "standing in an African uranium mine makes the contingent character of nuclearity much more visible," I attempt to disrupt the self-evident character of nuclearism by situating Hiroshima in a history of colonial capitalism rooted in energy extraction, from coal and oil to uranium.[12] Finally, by exploring these questions through an analysis of visual art by the Hiroshima-based artist Takahiro Iwasaki, I explore the racial and colonial dimensions of the atomic unconscious that probe the structural rather than the spectacular, and the violent social relations embedded in and required by energy infrastructures. Without such a materialist perspective, as Lawless notes, "we are left with the false radiance of a moral revolution whose advocates sit on the winning side of nuclear history and whose discourses serve the interests of postcolonial capital."[13] Iwasaki's sculptures refract the haunting "urgency of the abyss" that condition the extractivism required for war and energy.[14]

Fueling Primitive Accumulation

In a 2019 interview with Rachel Ablow, Elaine Scarry attempts to account for the pervasive misconceptions about nuclear weapons and to grapple with the question "Why is it so hard to think about nuclear war?"[15] Most people are unaware that 93 percent of nuclear weapons are owned by the United States (6,500) and Russia (6,850), whereas the remaining are owned by seven other nuclear states: France (300), China (280), UK (215), Pakistan (140–150), India (130–140), Israel (80), and North Korea (10–20). None are owned by Iran or Iraq.[16] Scarry responds to Ablow's question with Mohandas K. Gandhi's aphorism "You can wake a man who's asleep, but you can't wake a man who's pretending to be asleep." The implication here is that if the population is pretending to be asleep, "we are morally culpable . . . complicit with the genocide that's standing in the wings waiting to happen."[17] Although it may be true that most people are unconscious of the scale and distribution of nuclear weapons, the inability to be awakened to these facts is shaped by the way neoliberal technopolitics intersect with global energy-extraction regimes.

In order to explore the conditions that shape a nuclear unconscious, this section delves into the "hidden abode" of uranium production as it exists in relation to coal and oil energy extraction. By tracking the continuities and discontinuities between these energy regimes, I propose that we can begin to answer the question posed to Scarry. What becomes clear in the evolution of these unrenewable energy sources is the parallel evolution of increasingly undemocratic and authoritarian modes of political organization. The shift from coal to oil eroded the power of organized labor, whereas uranium extraction encouraged the creation of extremely exploitative labor regimes in a variety of settler colonial, postcolonial, and neocolonial settings. Much of this antidemocratic shift was attributable to the materiality of coal and oil and their unique systems of extraction and distribution. The Janus-faced nature of uranium, branded as either exceptional (as a source of apocalyptic destruction or energy salvation) or banal (as an unremarkable source of radiation that is found everywhere, more common than tin and five hundred times more bountiful than gold), has made possible the most-authoritarian technics that sustain a nuclear unconscious.[18] Unlike coal, which requires minimal if any processing after it has been mined, uranium ore must enter a complex system of processing and refining in order for it to be usable as reactor fuel or as a weapon. Given the properties of uranium, nuclear energy and weapons production are most amenable to highly centralized, authoritarian systems of control. Nuclear power is incongruous with any notion of an energy commons, and its technopolitical operations involve the suppression of democratic and egalitarian forms of political organization.

If we shift our focus away from the spectacle of nuclear destruction, our understanding of the colonial and imperial significance of uranium is best understood through the historical evolution of coal and oil extraction. To make this clear, I apply Karl Marx's theorization of primitive accumulation to demonstrate how shifts in energy regimes provide an important window on the racial politics of extractivism, dispossession, and labor exploitation that animates the colonial entanglements of nuclear modernity. Marx's conceptualization is particularly useful for approaching historical transition as a contingent and often unfinished and indeterminate process. In his original formulation, Marx presented "so-called primitive accumulation" as a challenge to nineteenth-century bourgeois economists who saw the European transition from feudalism to capitalism as the historical *emancipation* of serfs from feudal domination—liberated as "free laborers." What Marx elaborates is the incredible violence of this transition, which entailed the mass expulsion of the peasantry from communal lands and the wholesale destruction of villages. Far from an emancipation, Marx explains, this "history of expropriation is written in the annals of mankind in letters of blood and fire." In other words, direct extra-economic force is a requirement of capital, from the commercial transformation of land into agriculture to the genesis of industrial capitalism. These movements depended on brute force and "bloody legislation." Outside of Europe, in Africa, the Americas, and Asia, colonial dispossession and enslavement were the primary operations of primitive accumulation: "The discovery of gold and silver in America, the extirpation, enslavement and entombment in mines of indigenous populations of that continent, the beginnings of the conquest and plunder of India, and the conversion of Africa into a preserve for the commercial hunting of blackskins, are all things which characterize the dawn of the era of capitalist production. These idyllic proceedings were the chief moments of primitive accumulation."[19] Violent racial and gendered conquest, not emancipation, thus characterized the historical transition from feudalism to capitalism.

Rather than tying the violence of primitive accumulation to historical moments of transition, I incorporate both Rosa Luxemburg's and Cedric Robinson's important reformulations of Marx's framework in order to establish how imperialist racial violence is endemic to capitalism. What Luxemburg demonstrates is that capitalism's ongoing survival depends on the ongoing, violent primitive accumulation of noncapitalist spheres—regions "outside" the capitalist relation. She explains that "capital cannot accumulate without the aid of non-capitalist organizations. Only the continuous and progressive disintegration of non-capitalist organizations make the accumulation of capitalism possible."[20] For Robinson, who challenges the linear developmentalism of Marx's account of transition, European feudalism never vanished but rather continues to haunt capitalism. He writes that "capitalism was less a catastrophic revolution (negation) of feudalist social orders than *the extension* of these social relations into the larger tapestry of the modern world's political and economic relations."[21] Whereas Luxemburg clarifies the structural violence required by capital accumulation, Robinson discusses how feudalism continues to shape capitalism. In other words, conquest in the Americas was less a "prehistory" of capitalist modernity than its fundamental expression, a world order that requires the continual conversion of noncapitalist social relations into market ones through the violence of slavery, imperial expansion, and genocidal dispossession.

Although Marx's rendition of primitive accumulation suggests that land expropriation transformed the peasantry into wage laborers, the story is different outside Europe. As Dene political theorist Glen Coulthard clarifies, "The history and experience of *dispossession*, not proletarianization, has been the dominant background structure shaping the historical relation between Indigenous peoples and the Canadian [and US] state."[22] Importantly, it is the colonial capitalist state—not capitalists per se—that executes the violence of primitive accumulation that "hasten[s], as in a hothouse, the process of transformation."[23] As William Clare Roberts explains, because the state is a parasite of capital, it is "the state [that] executes and enforces expropriations that capital needs but cannot itself carry out."[24] From this view, the extra-economic violence of primitive accumulation is simultaneously structure and stage, both a structural requirement and a temporal precondition for capital to accumulate. These reconstructions of Marx's framework clarify how the state exercises extra-economic violence, defined as an amalgamation of military, administrative, legal, and debt-trapping tactics that form the preconditions of spatial accumulation through land expropriation, extraction, and abandonment. Thus, extra-economic predation, fraud, and violence form the fundamental economic irrationality of capitalism that takes the state form.

In the most violent apartheid states, such as Israeli Occupied Palestine, the transparency and normativity of settler colonial state violence recall

Marx's characterization of colonial capital accumulation as "dripping from head to toe, from every pore, in blood and dirt." Outside of these horrific sites of state terror, however, primitive accumulation occurs against the backdrop of liberal democratic governance without the repressive force of militarized state violence. State violence may not function as a regulative norm that oversees the process of colonial dispossession, but these operations have not simply withered away, autopiloted by the "silent compulsion of economic relations."[25] We are left, then, with a *gap* that mediates colonial structures of domination that Coulthard describes as "neither 'blood and fire' nor the 'silent compulsion' of capitalist economies [that] can adequately account for the reproduction of colonial hierarchies."[26] As a partial response, I propose that this gap is enabled by colonial technopolitics, an antipolitical mode of governmentality that, as James Ferguson puts it, "expand[s] the exercise of a particular sort of state power while simultaneously exerting a powerful depoliticizing effect." The nuclear industry is perhaps an exemplary form of the "antipolitics machine": "depoliticizing everything it touches, everywhere whisking political realities out of sight, all the while performing almost unnoticed its own preeminently political operation of expanding state power."[27]

The Colonial Power of Logistics

By placing uranium extraction on a continuum that includes coal and oil extraction—rather than the Manhattan Project—we open a view of how technopolitics functions as a form of colonial power originally embedded in logistical supply chains in the twentieth century. This section builds on the work of Timothy Mitchell, who tracks the way shifting labor relations in the coal and oil industries affected broader movements toward and away from democratic politics.

Until the 1800s, the energy required to sustain human life came almost entirely from renewable resources: solar power was converted into grain for food, into grasslands to raise animals, into forests to provide firewood, and into wind and water power for transportation and machinery. Because these renewable energy sources are widely distributed, human settlement tended to be dispersed along rivers, near pastures and woods. The emergence of coal energy in the early 1800s shifted these social relations dramatically, initiating a brutal stage of primitive accumulation. The switch to coal enabled the concentration of population in cities because people no longer needed to live in proximity to pastures and woods for energy. The growth of cities and the need for mass production created a demand for raw materials and new markets that were sustained through the brutality of colonialism and slavery. As Mitchell explains, "In acquiring lands for sugar and cotton production in the New World, Europeans had relied on the total dispossession of the local population and the importing of slave or indentured workforces."[28] In other words, the energy that powered industrial modernity and progress went hand in hand with the primitive accumulation of Indigenous land and African bodies.

By the nineteenth century, coal extraction also enabled forms of labor mobilization and social empowerment. Because of the "dendritic networks" of coal production, branches of production and distribution were interconnected with railways, dockworkers, and ships.[29] Because coal miners were literally beyond the view of any above-ground company overseer, which also gave miners increased autonomy and authority in their subterranean work, the general strike became a powerful weapon for organized labor, which could assert leverage over distribution choke points. Seizing the political power of the strike that could paralyze critical energy nodes of the nation, coal miners led the demand for higher wages, better living conditions, safety, and expanded democracy. Between 1881 and 1905, coal miners struck three times more than workers in other industries. This period also saw an unprecedented level of interracial labor-union mobilization and communist organizing in the US South. In Robin D. G. Kelley's study of the remarkable record of labor activity in Alabama, where 55 percent of the coal miners were Black, the period between 1881 and 1936 saw 603 strikes, more than half of them taking place between 1881 and 1905. Despite employers' racist tactics, violence, and exploitation of convict labor, Kelley notes that "during both the 1904 and 1908 coal miners' strikes, black workers were in the majority."[30] The concessions of large industrial firms and oligarchs to allow expanded forms of white welfare democracy and universal suffrage ultimately weakened interracial working-class mobilization. And despite the advances made by interracial coalitions in coal mining, it also remains true that labor mobilization, in and of itself, could never dignify the sheer misery, danger, and environmental costs of extractive labor. As Jasper Bernes aptly puts it, "The infrastructure of the modern world is cast from molten grief."[31]

The postwar shift from coal to oil presented a countervailing force to the democratic gains won by organized labor. Although Marx does not explicitly delineate the forms of abandonment that are tied to primitive accumulation, the expansion of US imperial power in the shift to oil initiated the long and steady decline of coal—and the abandonment of communities tied to coal mining and coal-fired power plants. Coal-generated power currently constitutes less than a quarter of US electricity and continues to fall precipitously. The shift to oil represented a massive geopolitical reorientation in energy extraction and distribution.

The shift to oil is rooted in postwar labor suppression. In war-devastated Europe, US planners found a way to defeat the power of coal miners by converting Europe's energy system from coal to oil. Europe's lack of oil fields necessitated shifting energy production out of Europe entirely to the Middle East. The United States sent materials to the Persian Gulf to construct a pipeline from eastern Saudi Arabia to the Mediterranean, which delivered large quantities of oil into Europe. Despite labor strikes in different oil-producing regions around the world, the material properties of oil and physical location of its extraction diminished the power of organized labor. At the point of extraction, oil extraction prompted a different organization of labor. In contrast to coal, oil was extracted through pressure, which required a smaller workforce that worked above ground, under the constant supervision of managers. The distribution of oil diverged from coal as well. Because coal is heavy, requiring labor-intensive underground mining, it remained primarily a localized source of energy, with very little of it crossing oceans. The relative lightness of oil, on the other hand, enabled its distribution by sea, reducing labor needs and eliminating the power of organized labor to strike to create choke points in the energy-distribution system. The movement of oil across oceans also meant that labor regulations could be circumvented. As Mitchell explains, shipping companies could escape labor laws because "transoceanic shipping operated beyond the territorial spaces governed by the labor regulations and democratic rights won in the widespread coal and railway strikes."[32] Unlike the dendritic branches of the coal supply chain, oil flowed unpredetermined in a grid-like pattern in which multiple pathways were available to avoid choke points. Unlike coal transported by rail, oil tankers could quickly be rerouted toward alternative sites, away from sites overtaken by striking laborers or industry nationalization movements. Of course, the cost of this increased flexibility was environmental devastation caused by oil spills.

If capitalism constructs social relations defined by scarcity, the birth of the transnational oil corporation functioned as a quintessential long-distance mechanism for limiting the supply of oil, "transforming post-war carbon energy abundance into a system of limited supplies." Beginning in

1943, the United States began issuing payments to Saudi Arabia to restrict the production of oil, which the US presented as vital to its national security interests during World War II. Scarcity was also manufactured by expanding US demand for massive amounts of energy. This was achieved by replacing six-cylinder engines with v8s in US automobiles, whereas white urban flight was enabled by commuter freeways and the construction of suburbs. As Mitchell recounts of the significance of postwar automobility, cars "helped engineer something larger—carbon-heavy forms of middle-class life that, combined with new political arrangements in the Middle East, would help the oil companies keep oil scarce enough to allow their profits to thrive."[33]

To summarize, the militancy of coal miners was partially based on the autonomy and expertise that miners were able to exercise underground prior to mechanization and on their ability to exploit the vulnerability of coal's dendritical supply-chain network. In contrast, because workers in oil extraction remain above ground, power was distributed upward to managers, engineers, and marketers. The expansion of technical "expertise" through research and development energy sectors and marketing divisions further diminished any expertise or autonomy associated with the oil-extraction worker. Transoceanic shipping dramatically expanded the networks of distribution and enabled the evasion of national labor and tax regulations. The ability of oil tankers to make last-minute route changes also made it possible to avoid regions of labor militancy.

In order to secure these arrangements in the unequal distribution of power—in terms of both energy and labor—an entire imperial infrastructure of extra-economic violence was built into this structure. The sale of enormous quantities of arms from the United States to suppress labor dissent and populist uprisings was put in place by Washington to secure the flow of dollars and Arabian oil. Looking back, as Mitchell observes, "if the emergence of the mass politics in the early twentieth century, out of which certain sites and episodes of welfare democracy were achieved, should be understood in relation to coal, the limits of contemporary democratic politics can be traced in relation to oil."[34] The physical properties and geopolitics of coal and oil had a major impact on the power of labor and its democratizing potential. As we see in the shift from coal to oil, the production of technological expertise generally diminished the power of workers involved in extractive labor. The control of oil by fewer and fewer "experts," the deployment of military violence to secure arrangements for the production of oil, and the imperial ruse of "national security" coalesced into a denialist US imperial ideology that consigned the label of "undemocratic" and backward to non-Western oil-producing nations.

It is on this terrain of accumulative violence and the increasing disempowerment of labor that we can approach uranium as source of both military and electrical power. Unlike coal, which requires minimal if any processing once it is extracted, oil and uranium require significant processing, again distributing labor power upward into the hands of technical experts: managers, engineers, and scientists. In order for uranium to be used as a weapon or for fuel, its extracted form must undergo multiple stages of processing. Uranium is first mined as ore, processed into yellowcake, and then converted into uranium hexafluoride. From this point, if you need to construct a bomb, uranium hexafluoride is enriched to 90 percent; alternatively, if you need to produce fuel, uranium hexafluoride is enriched to 3.5 percent. Prior to enrichment, each stage of preparation produces tailings, the low-grade uranium waste that is cast off.

If the social relations of oil extraction and distribution disempowered labor and manufactured scarcity to empower and enrich the transnational corporate class, the social relations of uranium extraction distribute power upward in even more unscrupulous ways. Although fuel and energy supply chains have long been central to military campaigns and national security, the dual purpose of uranium heightened the level of authoritarian, technocratic control over its extraction and distribution. Whereas state-supported oil corporations negotiated scarcity through monopolistic and cartel arrangements such as the Organization of the Petroleum Exporting Countries (OPEC), uranium was placed under US *monopsony* power. In the immediate aftermath of World War II, US efforts to preserve its status as the only nuclear superpower that could subdue the spread of communism involved monopolizing the supply of uranium through the formation of a uranium monopsony. In 1946 Congress passed the Atomic Energy Act, which gave the Atomic Energy Commission (AEC) the power to act as the sole buyer and regulator of uranium ore, which effectively controlled the production and pricing of uranium. As Stephanie Malin explains, "Monopsonies create power dynamics that mirror those of monopolies . . . [whereby] the single purchaser of a commodity controls the terms of trade and largely shapes markets for the commodity, dictating prices for goods and often determining how they will be used or redistributed."[35] Such were the autocratic conditions for the postwar roller coaster of accumulation and abandonment that has ravaged uranium-extraction sites and poisoned mining communities in Colorado, Utah, and New Mexico, sacrifice zones exploited to benefit the development of military and energy technology.

Uranium is the ideal motif for Western imperial power because of its interweaving of economic and military domains of power. As part of the production of Cold War technocratic expertise, the race for uranium was veiled in secrecy and highly classified state operations. Secrecy and monopolistic and monopsonistic logistical controls over the supply chain are at the root of technopolitical authoritarianism, particularly in shaping and shifting the ideology of nuclearity. As a renewed mode of primitive accumulation after Hiroshima, Western states exploited their "highly classified" technopolitical authority to quell socialism and movements for decolonization, such that "the Atom bomb [could act] as a substitute for colonial power."[36] In the United States the AEC's monopsonistic control over the industry predictably led to the overproduction of uranium, which resulted in ruinous devaluation. Millworkers, prospectors, and independent miners described the commission as a "dictatorship in a democracy." As communities dependent on the uranium boom were completely abandoned, left to contend with the industry's long-term effects of toxic contamination and illness, the United States shifted to making large purchases of uranium from Canada and overseas.[37]

Nuclear Neoliberation

Beyond the corruption of uranium's commodification within the United States' imperial war-finance nexus discussed above, the nuclearity of uranium was also subject to highly ideological technopolitical manipulation. The United States could not monopolize the supply of uranium given that lower grades of uranium were widely available, so uranium's secret power diminished—along with its nuclearity. Beginning in the 1960s, by shifting emphasis toward the financial axis of the war-finance nexus, uranium was born again as an ordinary commodity that wasn't "nuclear" until it had undergone substantial processing. No longer subject to monopsonistic control, uranium was neoliberated, subject to the invisible hand of the market. The "Atoms for Peace" campaign rebranded uranium as a source of peaceful energy that would spur economic development in Third World nations. In 1968 the Treaty on the Non-Proliferation of Nuclear Weapons invoked human-rights language to declare that the peaceful use of nuclear power was a fundamental right that was essential to developing areas of the world. Yet the "free market" was an imperial ruse for the politics that governed uranium's market. As Hecht outlines, "Invoking the 'free market' validated a political geography in which imperial powers could continue to dominate former colonies after independence."[38] Here monopsony-driven pollution and the free-market protection emerge as two sides of the same imperial coin for maintaining power over natural resources. In this light, the depoliticization of uranium through so-called market liberalization was chiefly an antipolitical operation: depoliticizing uranium in order to maintain and expand Western imperial control over it.

Despite centuries of documented hazards associated with uranium extraction, part of the antipolitical technical authority of the International Atomic Energy Agency (IAEA) was to completely extricate uranium ore as a nuclear source, *exempting* extraction zones from any regulatory protections, inspections, or safeguards. Uranium was not deemed "nuclear" unless it had already undergone significant conversion and processing. Excluding uranium mines and the workers, the IAEA classified a "principal nuclear facility" as a "reactor, a plant for processing nuclear material irradiated in a reactor, a plant for processing nuclear material irradiated in a reactor, a plant for separating the isotopes of a nuclear material, a plant for processing or fabricating nuclear material." As a result, as Hecht explains, "By the 1970s . . . the nuclearity of uranium ore and yellowcake had plummeted."[39] What this classificatory operation accomplishes is to racially and colonially segregate the technologically modern nuclear industry on one hand and a primitive mining industry on the other. Thus, the harm of uranium mining was diminished to the harms of mining in general, not the radioactive harms associated with the nuclear industry. Buttressed by the postwar ideology of peaceful economic development and human rights, Western imperial authorities expanded their command of uranium-extraction sites while rendering workers disposable, beyond the scope of "nuclear protection." The coloniality of nuclear discourse comes clear, as Hecht discusses, in the fact that the invasion of Iraq in 2003 was premised on the discovery that Iraq had obtained "yellowcake from Niger" and was therefore "nuclear." Yet neither Niger nor Gabon nor Namibia was ever reported as "being nuclear," even though these nations accounted for more than one-fifth of the uranium that fueled power plants in Europe, the United States, and Japan that year.[40] Nevertheless, "yellowcake from Niger" was automatically linked to weapons of mass destruction, as was the central justification for the war.

The technopolitical production of "nuclear" modernity effectively erased racialized, Indigenous labor through the legitimation of an imperial scale. Here scale emerges not as an objective or neutral orientation but as a deeply politicized mode of analysis and praxis. Connecting uranium production to the previous discussion of coal and oil extraction, then, we observed how the latter industries saw a progressive disempowerment of labor. In the case of uranium mining, however, extractive labor not only is disempowered but *disappears altogether* from the technopolitical scale of nuclear modernity—even as that labor is subject to the exploitative forces of imperial governance from which it is erased and obscured. This means, for instance, in the former French colony of Gabon, the mines from which uranium is extracted to fuel France are not subject to European regulatory or safety standards. Yet, in a neocolonial sleight of hand, when Gabon's uranium crosses borders to French processing plants, that uranium becomes ultramodern and thus "nuclear," and only then subject to international regulation. As Hecht observes, "When Gabon's uranium became nuclear fuel, it switched nationalities, enabling France to assert national energy independence through nuclear power."[41] Here France's continued "postcolonial" control over Gabon's resources reproduces the colonial relation that both exploits and erases the Indigenous African labor that motors the metropole.

Disappearing Scales

The practice of scalar segregation, what Johannes Fabian would refer to as the spatial "denial of coevalness,"[42] is an imperial operation that maintains the continued wastelanding of racialized and Indigenous lands— lands that are taken off the map of nuclear modernity and its regulatory protections yet are subject to market laws. As a testament to the erasure of one of the world's richest sources of uranium, the Shinkolobwe mine in the Democratic Republic of the Congo, Tom Zoellner notes that "Shinkolobwe is now considered an official nonplace."[43] Shinkolobwe's disappearance is a legacy of Western imperial control over the region, one that began under the brutal regime of King Leopold II of Belgium, who expropriated the Congo as his own private estate from 1885 to 1908. Leopold acquired the "Congo Free State," a nation seventy-five times larger than Belgium itself, during the European scramble for Africa under a humanitarian ruse of ending the Arab-controlled slave trade. Once in power, Leopold turned the country into a massive forced-labor camp occupied by his security corps, the ruthless Force Publique, which severed hands, kidnapped, murdered, and raped the Congolese to coerce high yields of rubber extraction. Historian Adam Hochschild estimates that ten million Congolese were killed under Leopold's "humanitarian" regime.[44] Never once setting foot in the Congo, Leopold amassed a billion-dollar personal fortune from the thousands of tons of rubber sap tapped by forced Indigenous labor, which was then exported to feed the many industries requiring rubber, including cars, bicycles, and telephone wires. Upon his death in 1909, the government of Belgium took over, leaving mostly intact the king's regime of forced labor administered by the Force Publique, which now operated on behalf of monopoly companies, the largest of which was the Union Minière de Haut Katanga. In the region of Katanga, large quantities of bismuth, cobalt, tin, zinc, and eventually uranium were extracted by local Congolese workers under a system of debt slavery. When sought-after radium was discovered in a uranium-rich hill in Katanga in 1915, the mining company forced "more than a thousand African laborers to dig into what would turn out to be the purest bubble of uranium ore ever found on earth."[45] With the discovery of nuclear fission in 1938, uranium was transformed from a worthless waste product to a prized commodity. When the Nazis invaded Belgium, the Union Minière moved its headquarters to New York and transferred 1,250 tons of uranium to Staten Island, where it would sit in obscurity for more than two years before being sold to the Manhattan Project. During the war, under a shroud of secrecy to evade Axis powers, Congolese workers labored around the clock to send hundreds of tons of uranium to the US every month. In many ways, it was the exploited Congolese workers who were directly if inadvertently responsible for installing the United States as the new global hegemon. Isaiah Mobilo, chair of the Congolese Civil Society of South Africa, aptly observes that in assisting the United States in the race to build an atomic bomb, "Shinkolobwe decided who would be the next leader of the world."[46]

The colonial counterpart to Shinkolobwe was the Eldorado mine in Canada's Northwest Territories, on the shores of the Great Bear Lake in the appropriately named Port Radium. Between Shinkolobwe's and Eldorado's 2,500 and 1,000 tons of excavated uranium, respectively, these mines produced the majority of uranium used in the burgeoning nuclear industrial complex of the United States. In Port Radium, Sahtu Dene "coolies" transported sacks of radium and ore from the mine onto barges that would eventually be refined in Ontario for use in the Manhattan Project. Despite government knowledge of the harmful effects of radiation exposure, workers labored unprotected while radioactive waste contaminated their lake, and the mine was left unremediated for decades. They worked without knowledge of their participation in the Manhattan Project. In the midst of the Canadian government's continual denial of responsibility for the postwar cancer epidemic, the Sahtu Dene sent a delegation to Hiroshima to apologize to ethnic Korean survivors of the atomic bombing. As Indigenous peoples who were also devastated by their exposure to nuclear radiation and environmental contamination, their trip to Hiroshima exposed the corresponding racist logic of imperial violence that undergirded the lethal exploitation of Sahtu Dene laborers and the annihilation of nonwhite peoples in Japan. Their presence in Japan violated the impersonal political abstraction intended by what filmmaker Raoul Peck describes as "killing at a distance."[47] President Harry S. Truman's comment two days after the bombing of Nagasaki diverted responsibility on the grounds of the inhumanity of the racial enemy: "When dealing with a beast, treat it like a beast. It's totally unfortunate, but it's still the truth. Indeed, there is no more to say."[48] In stark contrast to the apology offered by the Sahtu Dene to victims of the atomic bombing, the long-standing imperial logic of the United States justified accumulation by nuclear atrocity.

After the war, pollutable Indigenous land in the Congo and the Northwest Territories became "protectable" and thus subject to new rounds of imperial governance, from the CIA-backed assassination of Patrice Lumumba, the first democratically elected leader of the newly independent Democratic Republic of the Congo, to the massive expansion of state control over the Northwest Territories in Canada to pave the way for nonrenewable resource development.[49] The cancers that devastated communities in the Northwest Territories and in Katanga were actively disconnected from radiation exposure from mining and transport labor. Cancer, after all, is part of the epidemiological infrastructure of modernity: it is a "First World" disease. Of cancer-ridden African mining communities, Hecht observes that "many researchers have assumed that Africans simply don't live long enough to contract most types of cancer."[50] In 2005 the Canadian Deline Uranium Table's report—which contracted parts of its study to nuclear industry scientists—refuted any connection between spikes in cancer rates and heightened exposure to radiation when the Port Radium mine was open from 1942 to 1960. Instead, the report blamed the victims by attributing elevated cancer rates to the racially pathologized behaviors of smoking and drinking. The memory of past tragedy was sanitized and replaced with a future of economic prosperity through uranium mining. Then, after having opposed all future uranium mining until past issues related to the Port Radium mine were resolved, in 2008 the Dene-controlled Deline Land Corporation signed an amended agreement with the mining corporation Alberta Star granting it full authorization to permit the company's iron, oxide, copper, gold, and uranium exploration and drilling activities. Port Radium's rhetorical rebirth out of the wasteland of tragedy into a site of resource development demonstrates, as Yoneyama observes, the "uneven burden that the nuclear complex has placed on racialized and indigenous communities."[51] These technopolitical modes of social coercion serve to further dispossess Indigenous communities under the colonial subterfuge of modernization. This adds meaning to the way that colonial dispossession is interlinked with the erasure and disposability of exploited Indigenous labor, amplifying the significance of Kelley's point that "they wanted the land *and* the labor, just not the *people*."[52]

The Queer Art of Logistical Failure

The question posed to Elaine Scarry about why it is so hard to think about nuclear war raises issues of perception and representation. One of the ideas I've attempted to present in this chapter is that the very question of the "nuclear" is always/already bound up in the imperial production of energy infrastructures, technologies, and geographies that rely on the disposal and disavowal of exploited Indigenous labor in the nonsites of energy extraction. The ongoing primitive accumulation of Indigenous lands in the Northwest Territories and the Democratic Republic of the Congo is placed beyond "nuclear" representation. Insofar as nuclear power secures modern imperial power, it bears some resemblance to capital itself, as that which "organizes history but is unrepresentable within it."[53] When uranium is situated alongside the extraction of coal and oil, we see the progressive disempowerment and disappearance of labor and the rise of authoritarian social relations to manage the supply and distribution of energy resources. These operations require the coordinated imperial maintenance of resource-rich former colonies, settler colonies, and neo-colonies. What we see is that the energy supply chain itself has become so deeply entangled in Western imperial militarism that uranium is far from exceptional—it is merely the most recent source of energy to shape contemporary geopolitics and the global supply chain. As Deborah Cowen explains, supply-chain management in the post–World War II era is the direct legacy of military logistics and strategy. In other words, corporate and military logistics became increasingly enmeshed in the transition to oil and the rise of petroleum warfare. Cowen underscores that "logistics is no simple story of securitization and distribution, it is an industry and assemblage that is at once bio-, necro-, and antipolitical. . . . The banal and technocratic management of the movement of stuff through space has become a driving force of war and trade."[54] In many ways, *circulation*, as distinct from production and consumption, has taken on particular importance in the totality of capital, even as it remains a sphere whose representation is as banal as a shipping container—a far cry from the mysteries of the hidden abode of production or the fetishism of commodities. In this light the shifting nuclear status of uranium emerges as an appropriate symbol for the seemingly commonplace but in fact highly politicized circulatory operations of the global energy supply chain.

Returning again to the question of why it is so hard to think of nuclear war, this concluding section delves into a consideration of the scalar representation of energy infrastructures, particularly the role that the concept of the Anthropocene has played in visualizing global energy infrastructures at grand, panoramic scales: massive landfills, marble quarries, tailings ponds, and coal mines. A visual archive that exemplifies this scale is renowned Canadian photographer Edward Burtynsky's *Anthropocene* project, which includes a series of photographs and film collaboration with Jennifer Baichwal and Nicholas De Pencier. However, rather than providing a cognitive mapping of society's relation to capitalist totality, his large-scale topographic photography may instead reflect what Cowen describes as the "bio-, necro-, and antipolitical" operations of logistics itself. Alberto Toscano and Jeff Kinkle connect these scalar aesthetic features to the "art of logistics," clearing a path to trace capitalist linkages between photographs of military and environmental ruin. Drawing on the military-inspired framework for the optimal circulation of goods, the visual culture of logistics similarly emphasizes symmetry, minimalism, smoothness, and flow. These are ultimately aesthetic modes of obfuscation and disarticulation, which Toscano and Kinkle describe as "chains of dissociation."[55] Drawing on Allan Sekula's critique of the sale of military aerial photography on the art market as the "unqualified beautification of warfare" in postwar cultures,[56] logistical aesthetics enables a depoliticized, detached gaze that "appears symptomatic of a certain affinity between 'cold' modernism and military antihumanism."[57] Specifically, what aerial images of war landscapes

and energy wastelands have in common is that their "paradoxically pho-
togenic character stems in many ways from its inadvertent mimesis of a
modernist, minimalist geometry whose rules of representation are already
deeply incorporated into the grammar of artistic form."[58] The aesthetic effect of collapsing documentary impact into modernist visual modalities is
that, as Sekula observes, "a landscape possessed of humanly made features
can be translated into the realm of a nonreferential abstract geometry."[59] Hence,
expansive panoramic views of ecological ruin, often without people, convey an aesthetic grandeur that effectively dehumanizes the human-altered
landscape. This is the effect of what Toscano and Kinkle refer to as a "bad
abstraction" that ensues from the "depersonalizing symmetry and scale
over exploitation, friction, or indeed waste and consumption of energy,
human and machinic."[60] Thus, the human-altered logistical landscape is
curiously absent of any human trace, which corresponds to the way the
anthropogenic discourse relies on an abstract, racially unmarked "humanity" as the primary driver of ecological disaster. In this sense, visions of the
Anthropocene universalize humanity through its visual absence.

Large-scale topographic photography of ecological ruin may then reinforce the idea that geological rather than historical time is what really
matters, because it envisions capital as a spatialized form devoid of human
labor. Toscano observes that in human-absented depictions of capitalist
environmental ruin, there is a haunting sense that dead or past labor—not
living labor—is the central subject of contemporary capitalism: "The quantitative past represents past labor precisely by erasing its very traces. And
yet this drive to extinction is also behind the overpowering of our praxis
and our imaginations by dead labor—or capital spatialized and experienced
as the absence of labor, the absence of 'us.'" The marginalization and forgetting of living labor resonate strongly with the disempowerment, disposability, and erasure of Indigenous extractive labor, giving new significance to
the omnipresence of "dead labor" in the visual culture of human-absented,
human-altered landscapes. Here Toscano emphasizes the immense quan-
tity of past labor that "dominates the present" and how the invisible circuits
of capital are "spatialized as the absence of labor."[61] However, such scalar
representations of space make visible the quantities of past dead labor *but
not as past, not as history.* In other words, we see quantities of the past congealed in fixed capital but in a manner that "forgets the qualitative past, the
existential nature of the work, its origins and contexts, 'the traces of labour
on the product,' in favor of the quantitative present."[62] Toscano notes that
"the disappearance of the past is also the form of its massive unconscious

presence."[63] Like the aestheticization of war photography, our abiding attraction to human-altered, human-absented, logistical landscapes reflects a "closure of the space of politics and experience by capital, nation, and the state"[64] and a forgetting of history and of the qualitative past. A world in which the ratio of dead labor dramatically overwhelms living labor is expressed as the absence of humanity in the wastelands of capitalist circulation. Contrary to an aesthetics of cognitive mapping, logistical landscapes perform an unmapping of our relation to social totality.

By highlighting the radioactive nonsites of nuclear modernity, my objective has been to suggest that nuclear war and environmental devastation are entangled in the evolution of energy extraction, shaped by the technopolitical operations of primitive accumulation. In addition, the practice of imperial scale enables the material disarticulation and erasure of human labor that mirrors the "chains of dissociation" embedded in the military art of logistics. As a counterpoint to the "ruin porn" offered by cultural practitioners of the Anthropocene, the miniature sculptures and dioramas by Hiroshima-based artist Takahiro Iwasaki present alternative insights on energy infrastructures in the shadow of nuclear modernity. In his 2011 *Out of Disorder (Cosmo World)* series, in the collection of the Yokohama Museum of Art, miniature landscapes are constructed entirely out of detritus: hair, towels, toothbrushes, fibers and threads from old clothing. The miniature rendering of transmission towers, power plants, and industrial cranes in fiber and hair speaks to the heightened instability and fragility of Japan's energy infrastructure in the aftermath of Fukushima, presented as dioramas that serve as contact zones of nuclear past and present. Through his reuse of refuse that draws in themes of intimate, gendered histories and what Jack Halberstam refers to as the "queer art of failure,"[65] Iwasaki's artwork recasts sites of ecological abandonment as rich sites of accumulated bodily forgetting. His artwork implies that the recognition of the phantomlike objectivity of capital begins with the memory of a qualitative past. This offers an aesthetic that is distinct from the visual culture of the Anthropocene, where representations of ecological disaster are oriented toward an absent future rather than a human past.

The small scale of Iwasaki's sculptures requires that the viewer engage with multiple views, enabling what he calls a bird's-eye and a frog's-eye view of each landscape. As such, the effect is not a distanced panorama but rather a close encounter with the lightness and intricacy of the sculptures themselves, once again reinforcing the qualitative past of artistic craft involved in making the sculptures. The melancholic tone evoked by the

FIGURE 8.1. Takahiro Iwasaki. *Out of Disorder (Cosmo World)*. 2011. Hair, dust. Collection of Yokohama Museum of Art. ©Takahiro Iwasaki. Courtesy of ANOMALY.

sculptures is related to the reuse of materials, such as remnants of kimono, that have been cast off—a subtle reminder of their failure to function as the use values for which they were originally intended. However, the failure highlighted in their reuse is also what illuminates what is otherwise imperceptible in the commodity form. In a passage from *Capital*, Marx elaborates on how the only way we can perceive the past labor congealed in our products is when they fail or alert us to their imperfections: "It is by their imperfections that the means of production in any process brings to our attention their character of being the products of past labour. A knife which fails to cut, a piece of thread that keeps snapping, *forcibly remind us of Mr. A, the cutter, or Mr. B, the spinner*."[66] Failure therefore counteracts the chains of logistical dissociation, here highlighting the material connections that constitute the qualitative human past embedded in our products and environment. This resurrection of the qualitative past overrides the spatial forms that emphasize the quantitative present. Moreover, in the use of discarded materials, the sculptures' emphasis on the failure to be useful (as originally intended) represents a queer human temporality that resists absorption into the abstract temporality of the commodity form. Thus,

Iwasaki's sculptures offer a representation of social totality that harnesses the discarded past to imagine a repurposed future. Found materials are intricately and meticulously reanimated as energy landscapes and open up a view of dead labor's social past.

Iwasaki's investigations into energy and waste are linked to Hiroshima's atomic past. In particular, his incorporation of dust and hair references his hometown of Hiroshima, a city reborn "out of the ashes" of the atomic bomb. Hair also takes on deathly symbolism because hair loss was one of the effects of exposure to nuclear radiation. One of the repeated motifs that occupy Iwasaki's small-scale landscapes is the Ferris wheel (see figure 8.1), which is constructed out of black hair. Iwasaki was first inspired to build a miniature Ferris wheel in the aftermath of the Fukushima nuclear power plant disaster. When the tsunami landed, Iwasaki was in Yokohama as the electrical outage turned everything dark. He was walking past an amusement park and was stirred by the immobilized Ferris wheel. A symbol of postwar determination of industrial development, the amusement park and its sudden de-animation in this moment became an index of decadent ruin. The Ferris wheel's construction out of hair reconceptualized the nuclear meltdown as the second coming of Hiroshima, its spiderweb features evoking tensile infrastructures of death. In Iwasaki's sculpture, its microscopic scale holds within it a larger universe of disordered social relations. Yet in the resurrection and reanimation of bodily detritus, his sculpture also initiates a reappropriation of forgotten time against the technopolitics of imperial accumulation.

NOTES

1. Kono, "Genbaku no Uta."

2. Obama, "Text of President Obama's Speech."

3. DeLoughrey, *Allegories of the Anthropocene.*

4. Lawless, "Mapping the Atomic Unconscious," 41.

5. Yoneyama, "Hiroshima Re/Traces."

6. Vimalassery, Pegues, and Goldstein, "On Colonial Unknowing."

7. Voyles, *Wastelanding.*

8. Yoneyama, *Hiroshima Traces.*

9. Giamo, "Myth of the Vanquished."

10. Nixon, *Slow Violence*.

11. World Nuclear Association, "Nuclear Power in Japan."

12. Hecht, *Being Nuclear*, 13.

13. Lawless, "Mapping the Atomic Unconscious," 49.

14. Gumbs, M *Archive*, 140.

15. Ablow, "Interview with Elaine Scarry," 112.

16. Stockholm International Peace Research Institute, SIPRI *Yearbook 2021*.

17. Ablow, "Interview with Elaine Scarry," 113.

18. Zoellner, *Uranium*, 49.

19. Marx, *Capital*, 875, 896, 915.

20. Luxemburg, *Accumulation of Capital*, 416.

21. Robinson, *Black Marxism*, 10 (emphasis added).

22. Coulthard, *Red Skins, White Masks*, 13.

23. Marx, *Capital*, 916.

24. Roberts, "What Was Primitive Accumulation?," 544.

25. Marx, *Capital*, 926, 899.

26. Coulthard, *Red Skins, White Masks*, 15.

27. Ferguson, *Anti-politics Machine*, 21, xv.

28. Mitchell, *Carbon Democracy*, 17.

29. Mitchell, *Carbon Democracy*, 38.

30. Kelley, *Hammer and Hoe*, 5.

31. Bernes, "Between the Devil and the Green."

32. Mitchell, *Carbon Democracy*, 38.

33. Mitchell, *Carbon Democracy*, 38.

34. Mitchell, *Carbon Democracy*, 254.

35. Malin, *Price of Nuclear Power*, 35.

36. Hecht, *Being Nuclear*, 23.

37. Malin, *Price of Nuclear Power*, 40, 41.

38. Hecht, *Being Nuclear*, 33, 34.

39. Hecht, *Being Nuclear*, 33.

40. Hecht, *Being Nuclear*, 13.

41. Hecht, "Interscalar," 131.

42. Fabian, *Time and the Other*.

43. Zoellner, *Uranium*, 2.

44. Hochschild, *King Leopold's Ghost*.

45. Zoellner, *Uranium*, 5.

46. Quoted in Swain, "Forgotten Mine."

47. Peck, *Exterminate All the Brutes*.

48. Truman, "Harry S. Truman's Decision."

49. Coulthard, "From Wards of the State?," 65–66.

50. Hecht, *Being Nuclear*, 42.

51. Yoneyama, "Hiroshima Re/Traces."

52. Kelley, "Rest of Us," 269.

53. Toscano and Kinkle, *Cartographies of the Absolute*, 3.

54. Cowen, *Deadly Life of Logistics*, 4.

55. Toscano and Kinkle, *Cartographies of the Absolute*, 190.

56. Quoted in Toscano and Kinkle, *Cartographies of the Absolute*, 205.

57. Toscano and Kinkle, *Cartographies of the Absolute*, 209.

58. Toscano and Kinkle, *Cartographies of the Absolute*, 204.

59. Quoted in Toscano and Kinkle, *Cartographies of the Absolute*, 205 (emphasis mine).

60. Toscano and Kinkle, *Cartographies of the Absolute*, 127.

61. Toscano, "World," 114, 116, 113.

62. Jameson, quoted in Toscano, "World," 113.

63. Toscano, "World," 116.

64. Toscano and Kinkle, *Cartographies of the Absolute*, 232.

65. Halberstam, *Queer Art of Failure*.

66. Marx, *Capital*, 289.

BIBLIOGRAPHY

Ablow, Rachel. "An Interview with Elaine Scarry." *Representations* 146 (2019): 112–34.

Bernes, Jasper. "Between the Devil and the Green New Deal." *Commune*, April 25, 2019. https://communemag.com/between-the-devil-and-the-green-new-deal.

Coulthard, Glen. "From Wards of the State to Subjects of Recognition? Marx, Indigenous Peoples, and the Politics of Dispossession in Denedeh." In *Theorizing*

Native Studies, edited by Audra Simpson and Andrea Smith, 56–98. Durham, NC: Duke University Press, 2014.

Coulthard, Glen. *Red Skin, White Masks: Rejecting the Colonial Politics of Recognition*. Minneapolis: University of Minnesota Press, 2014.

Cowen, Deborah. *The Deadly Life of Logistics: Mapping Violence in Global Trade*. Minneapolis: University of Minnesota Press, 2014.

DeLoughrey, Elizabeth. *Allegories of the Anthropocene*. Durham, NC: Duke University Press, 2019.

Fabian, Johannes. *Time and the Other: How Anthropology Makes Its Object*. New York: Columbia University Press, 2002.

Ferguson, James. *The Anti-politics Machine: Development, Depoliticization, and Bureaucratic Power in Lesotho*. Minneapolis: University of Minnesota Press, 1994.

Giamo, Benedict. "The Myth of the Vanquished: The Hiroshima Peace Memorial Museum." *American Quarterly* 55, no. 4 (2003): 703–28.

Gumbs, Alexis Pauline. M *Archive*. Durham, NC: Duke University Press, 2018.

Halberstam, Jack. *Queer Art of Failure*. Durham, NC: Duke University Press, 2011.

Hecht, Gabrielle. *Being Nuclear: Africans and the Global Uranium Trade*. Cambridge: MIT Press, 2012.

Hecht, Gabrielle. "Interscalar Vehicles for an African Anthropocene: On Waste, Temporality, and Violence." *Cultural Anthropology* 33, no. 1 (2017): 109–41.

Hochschild, Adam. *King's Leopold's Ghost: A Story of Greed, Terror, and Heroism in Colonial Africa*. Boston: Mariner, 1999.

Kelley, Robin D. G. *Hammer and Hoe: Alabama Communists during the Great Depression*. Chapel Hill: University of North Carolina Press, 1990.

Kelley, Robin D. G. "The Rest of Us: Rethinking Settler and Native." *American Quarterly* 69, no. 2 (2017): 267–76.

Kono, Hideko. "Genbaku no Uta: Tanka of the Atomic Bomb." Translated by Yumie Kono and Ariel Sulllivan. Nagano, Japan: Mokuseisha, forthcoming.

Lawless, Katherine. "Mapping the Atomic Unconscious: Postcolonial Capital in Nuclear Glow." *Mediations* 31, no. 2 (2018): 41–54.

Luxemburg, Rosa. *The Accumulation of Capital*. Mansfield Centre, CT: Martino Publishing, 2015.

Malin, Stephanie. *The Price of Nuclear Power: Uranium Communities and Environmental Justice*. New Brunswick, NJ: Rutgers University Press, 2015.

Marx, Karl. *Capital*, vol. 1. New York: Penguin, 1976.

Mitchell, Timothy. *Carbon Democracy: Political Power in the Age of Oil*. New York: Verso, 2011.

Nixon, Rob. *Slow Violence and the Environmentalism of the Poor*. Cambridge: Harvard University Press, 2013.

Obama, Barack. "Text of President Obama's Speech in Hiroshima, Japan." *New York Times*, May 27, 2016. www.nytimes.com/2016/05/28/world/asia/text-of-president-obamas-speech-in-hiroshima-japan.html.

Peck, Raoul, dir. *Exterminate All the Brutes*, part 3. HBO, 2021.

Roberts, William Clare. "What Was Primitive Accumulation? Reconstructing the Origin of a Critical Concept." *European Journal of Political Theory* 19, no. 4 (2020): 532–52.

Robinson, Cedric J. *Black Marxism: The Making of the Black Radical Tradition.* Chapel Hill: University of North Carolina Press, 1983.

Stockholm International Peace Research Institute. *SIPRI Yearbook 2021: Armaments, Disarmaments and International Security.* "World Nuclear Forces." https://sipri .org/yearbook/2021/10.

Swain, Frank. "The Forgotten Mine That Built the Atomic Bomb." *BBC.* August 3, 2020. https://www.bbc.com/future/article/20200803-the-forgotten-mine -that-built-the-atomic-bomb.

Toscano, Alberto. "The World Is Already without Us." *Social Text* 34, no. 2 (127) (2016): 109–24.

Toscano, Alberto, and Jeff Kinkle. *Cartographies of the Absolute.* Alresford, UK: Zero, 2015.

Truman, Harry. "Harry S. Truman's Decision to Use the Atomic Bomb." Accessed June 15, 2021. www.nps.gov/articles/trumanatomicbomb.htm.

Vimalassery [Karuka], Manu, Juliana Hu Pegues, and Alyosha Goldstein. "Introduction: On Colonial Unknowing." *Theory and Event* 19, no. 4 (2016). muse.jhu .edu/article/633283.

Voyles, Traci Brynne. *Wastelanding: Legacies of Uranium Mining in Navajo Country.* Minneapolis: University of Minnesota Press, 2015.

World Nuclear Association. "Nuclear Power in Japan." Accessed February 17, 2022. https://world-nuclear.org/information-library/country-profiles/countries-g -n/japan-nuclear-power.aspx.

Yoneyama, Lisa. "Hiroshima Re/Traces: Radiontology and the Strategies of Coconjuring." Paper presented at Revisiting the Nuclear Order: Technopolitical Landscapes and Timescapes Conference, Paris, June 11–12, 2018.

Yoneyama, Lisa. *Hiroshima Traces: Time, Space, and the Dialectics of Memory.* Berkeley: University of California Press, 1999.

Zoellner, Tom. *Uranium: War, Energy, and the Rock That Shaped the World.* New York: Viking, 2009.

Erasing Empire: Remembering the Mexican-American War in Los Angeles

To the brave men and women [who] with trust in God faced privation and death in extending the frontiers of our country to include this land of promise.

INSCRIPTION, FORT MOORE PIONEER MEMORIAL, 1957

The title of a recent book, *How to Hide an Empire,* invites us to explore the historical geography of the United States, its national identity, and how we map the past.[1] Besides framing the United States as an empire, the title implies ongoing attempts to obscure such processes. Scholarly efforts to rethink the past and present were energized in 2020 when activists began removing statues honoring colonizers and white supremacists en masse.[2] The topplings sparked a vibrant public discussion: How do we understand the United States as a country that began as a business venture and replaced Indigenous peoples by any means necessary? What does it mean that the United States conquered hundreds of nations but disavows an imperialist identity? What is the significance of centuries of racial slavery and our refusal to grapple with its ballast? In this moment, cultural memory and the history of racial capitalism merged.

This essay explores the cultural memory associated with the Mexican-American War as one chapter in the history of racial capitalism. Imperialism is fundamental to US capitalism and history but is rarely acknowledged. The United States has largely eschewed an imperialist identity in order to distinguish itself from European modes of empire. Instead, it has crafted an identity as a nation of immigrants in order to avoid having to contend with a past steeped in slavery, conquest, and racial violence. When imperialism is acknowledged, it is limited to late nineteenth-century conquests "abroad" and framed as benevolent and anomalous. This strategy overlooks US imperialism toward Native nations and Mexico while sanitizing the past.[3]

Imperialism and settler colonization were the means by which the United States acquired its territory and were crucial to the development of capitalism.[4] These were racialized processes that were enabled and justified by white supremacy. I define white supremacy as a set of attitudes, values, and practices emanating from the belief that white people and Europe are superior to people of color and non-European places.[5] Although white supremacy includes violence and hatred, far more pervasive is the insistence that whites are of greater value than nonwhites. Lisa Marie Cacho reminds us that value is a relational category: value is produced only in relation to something else.[6] Thus, the devaluation of one group is predicated on the overvaluation of another. Regardless of words and sentiments, the actions of Europeans, including Spanish, French, and English colonizers, have consistently reflected the belief that white lives are of greater value than those deemed nonwhite (itself a shifting category). Because they are considered to be of greater value, whites' needs and desires have consistently taken priority over those deemed "nonwhite."

Imperialism has been overlooked in analyses of contemporary capitalism, as the editors explain in this book's introduction. Aside from such traditions as world systems theory, histories of capitalism tend to privilege countries, metropoles, and free labor while processes in the periphery receive less attention. Nonetheless, imperialism enabled the development of capitalism by providing critical elements, including semi-proletarianized labor, crops, resources, and land.[7] Although earlier scholars, such as Frantz Fanon, understood imperialism as racialized, the racial capitalism framing allows more robust analyses. Central to this is Brenna Bhandar's work on racial property regimes. Bhandar argues that colonialism and modernity were predicated on twin processes: the production of racial subjects and private property ownership. Key to this development was the "ideology of improvement," which legitimated particular forms of property and ownership—those stemming from English common law—while delegitimating others. In short, racial ideology justified the taking of land that did not adhere to sanctioned forms and giving it to settlers who would "improve" it. The ideology of improvement embodies one of the driving logics of settler colonization and imperialism: "It is the systematic devaluation or pathologization of non-Anglo-European land and property relations that form the driving rationale for territorial aggression and cycles of accumulation fueled by expansive and ongoing forms of dispossession."[8]

Given its history as a settler empire, the United States, like all nations, forged a national identity and narrative that justify its actions. Thus, we celebrate pioneers, pilgrims, and plantations while "forgetting" the social relations that initially produced them. Forgetting, of course, is a form of remembering, one that is central to hiding an empire.[9] In this essay I examine how historical sites commemorating the Mexican-American War (1846–1848) in Los Angeles County erase empire while affirming US innocence and benevolence.

The Mexican-American War and Imperialism

In the United States, outside of Chicana/o/x studies, the Mexican-American War is a "forgotten war."[10] Propelled by manifest destiny in the 1840s, the United States offered to purchase land from Mexico. Mexico refused. Unable to accept "no," President Polk sent troops into disputed territory, knowing it would provoke a response from Mexico. The United States subsequently invaded Mexico, won every major battle, and acquired over half a million square miles. The Treaty of Guadalupe Hidalgo was signed in 1848, and the United States paid Mexico $15 million to compensate it for the loss of half its territory.

The war was divisive in the United States precisely because it was imperialist and racist.[11] More than fifty thousand men volunteered, greatly outnumbering regular militia. Support in the South was strong because the planter class hoped to expand slavery, but there was opposition in the Northeast. Many public intellectuals considered it a racist, imperialist land-grab and believed that its justification was manufactured. Indeed, Henry David Thoreau wrote *Civil Disobedience* in response to the war. Even some proponents of manifest destiny opposed it because of the "undesirable" character of Mexicans: "Annexation of the country to the United States would be a calamity. Five million ignorant and indolent half-civilized Indians, with 1,500,000 free negroes and mulattoes . . ."[12] Despite such sentiments, presidents Polk and Tyler understood that the majority of the United States supported western expansion, so they pursued the war.

As an imperialist act, the war contributed to capitalist development in several ways, including Pacific access, territorial expansion, and solidifying the white nation. A major US goal was continental reach, specifically coastal access, which figured prominently in the nation's imagined racial geography. In 1862 Wisconsin senator James Rood Doolittle described one vision: "Emancipation with colonization [back to Africa], homesteads for white men in the territories of the temperate zone, homesteads for colored men in the tropics, with a railroad to the Pacific to bind together our eastern and western empire."[13]

Coastal control allowed the United States to ward off encroaching European powers and enabled trade by eliminating the need to sail around las Américas. Control of the Pacific was essential to the development of California (at this writing, the fifth-largest economy in the world), global trade, and military operations. Currently, almost 60 percent of US global trade flows through the twin ports of Los Angeles.[14] Indeed, it is difficult to imagine the contemporary United States without the Pacific Coast.

A second and closely related goal was the land itself, specifically 525,000 square miles of Mexican territory. Prior to the war, Mexico's border reached as far north as Oregon and as far west as Colorado. The land offered mineral wealth, the possibility of a transcontinental railroad, and homes for settlers. It is difficult to overstate the significance of the railroad to capitalist development: Not only did it transport goods across the country, but it facilitated global trade.

More pressing than the railroad, however, was land for white settlers. The push for westward expansion came from both Washington, DC, and white settlers themselves, though not always in unison. White settlers not only wanted land but, as they pushed the boundaries of the frontier, also sought to be reincorporated into the white US nation. This dynamic created an oscillation between settlers acting autonomously and state-sanctioned expansion.[15] Texas epitomizes this dynamic.

Although settler colonization is a demographic project, the process of western settlement intersects with racial capitalism in various ways. For example, offering millions of acres to settlers precluded the United States from having to address mounting class and regional tensions.[16] Or consider slavery: geographic expansion was vital to the slave economy, and many southerners considered western expansion essential. Indeed, a major impetus for the Texas Revolution (1836) was Texans' desire for slavery, which Mexico had outlawed (1829).[17]

A third contribution of the war to racial capitalism was the consolidation of the Anglo-Saxon race.[18] Reginald Horsman argues that prior to the war, whites were more fragmented in the racial hierarchy. The war was pivotal in uniting whites as Anglo-Saxons in opposition to Mexicans, Indigenous peoples, and African Americans. Because the United States was a consciously white nation until World War II,[19] conquering nonwhite peoples posed a problem: how do such peoples fit into a white nation?

Although the United States wanted Mexican territory, it did not want its people. Indeed, the war racialized Mexicans and, by extension, other Latina/o/x peoples. The popular press supported the war, and magazines and newspapers portrayed Mexicans as racial mongrels, greasers, dirty, and morally unfit for independence.[20] Such attitudes helped justify conquest under the guise of "uplifting" Mexico. Consequently, the United States debated what portion(s) of Mexico to take based on its population. One option was a complete takeover, but this was rejected because of Mexicans' "undesirability." In the end, the United States took half of Mexico's territory but only 1 percent of its population.

The treaty and annexation altered the racial formation of the United States in profound ways.[21] Concerned for its people in the newly conquered territory, Mexico negotiated various protections, including land, religious, and citizenship rights, as well as legal whiteness. Knowing the United States was a white supremacist country, Mexico sought to safeguard ethnic Mexicans by having them declared legally white. Although it is understandable why Mexico would insist on whiteness, it's important to realize that Mexico, as a former Spanish colony, was itself a white supremacist country with a long history of anti-Blackness and anti-Indigeneity.[22] The treaty actually marked the intersection of two distinct but overlapping white supremacist racial formations. Consequently, declaring Mexicans to be white did offer some protections, but it also reproduced white supremacy. Laura Gómez has argued that conferring whiteness on Mexicans created a potential "wedge" population, with deep implications for Indigenous nations and African Americans.[23] Nevertheless, the veneer of whiteness afforded only limited rights, including partial citizenship in Arizona and New Mexico. Indeed, both states were denied statehood for years because of their large Indigenous and Mexican populations.

In short, white supremacy was integral to the Mexican-American War, including its formulation, execution, justification, and treaty negotiations. Likewise, the war played a profound role in the development of US and global capitalism.

Arguably, current struggles over how the United States remembers white supremacy began in 2015, when Bree Newsome climbed a South Carolina flagpole and dismantled the Confederate flag.[24] Thus began a public struggle around "memory work," the deliberate process of engaging with the past by considering its ethical and normative dimensions.[25] Cultural memory denotes how we choose to represent the past, including who, what, and where is commemorated, the nature of such representations, and what is silenced. Hegemonic forms of cultural memory, such as celebrating Confederate soldiers and pioneers, not only build the white nation but also act as barriers to transformative memory work.

Historical places are sites of cultural memory and potential memory work. Experiencing the connection between *where* something occurred and *what* happened there can produce a potentially transformative experience. Places can produce visceral experiences leading to a reframing of historical events, as seen in Holocaust memorials and the Whitney Plantation Museum.[26] Both are designed to foreground what was previously erased.

Given its history of settler colonization, genocide, slavery, and empire, the United States has crafted a cultural memory that denies its true origins. Denial is central to settler empires because the truth would require the nation to fundamentally rethink its origin story and identity, a prospect that is deeply threatening to many. Instead, US cultural memory is characterized by "forgetting": "American culture is not amnesiac but rather replete with memory, [and] cultural memory is a central aspect of how American culture functions and how the nation is defined. The 'culture of amnesia' actually involves the generation of memory in new forms, a process often interpreted as forgetting. Indeed, memory and forgetting are co-constitutive processes; each is essential to the other's existence."[27] Thus, forgetting is never innocent but always performs important work. If the Mexican-American War is "forgotten," we must ask why. Michael Van Wagenen contends that forgetting eases the US conscience of having to remember an unfair and racist war. I argue that "forgetting" erases empire, white supremacy, and racial violence writ large. The Mexican-American War is but one instance of forgetting. Conversely, when it is remembered, it is characterized by white innocence and benevolence. Walter Hixson calls such virtues "good works" and argues they are part of settler fantasies and necessary to create a serviceable past.[28]

Transition narratives are key to the US cultural memory of the Mexican-American War. These are discourses that explain shifts in racial property regimes. As Laura Barraclough writes, "Transition narratives reframe the experience of conquest in a way that recuperates the legitimacy of the colonizing force and its social and cultural precepts, thus securing hegemonic rule in conquered territories through appeals to a shared heritage."[29] The effectiveness of transition narratives is evident in their hegemonic nature: we are largely oblivious to them. Taken as a whole, historical markers overwhelmingly reflect hegemonic narratives that affirm white innocence.

Narrating the Mexican-American War in Five Scenes

Although the Mexican-American War covered a vast area, the fighting was concentrated in several places, including Matamoras, Mexico City, Veracruz, and what is now Arizona, Texas, and California. Los Angeles played a crucial role. Not only was the last battle fought there, but Mexico surrendered and the terms of the Treaty of Guadalupe Hidalgo were negotiated there. Consequently, one might expect to see numerous monuments and markers commemorating the war. There is a total of five.[30] However, more important than the number is how the war is represented.

The sites employ three strategies to erase empire. First, sites focused on the military dimensions of the war are devoid of any social context. Second, the violence of the war is largely evacuated, including widespread violence against Mexican civilians. Third, the ethical dimensions of the war, including its fabricated rationale, the attack on Mexican sovereignty, and its imperialist nature, are never mentioned. Rather, the ethical superiority of the United States is highlighted because it compensated Mexico $15 million for the loss of land (i.e., good works). The US desire for continental dominance is portrayed as inevitable and unproblematic, whereas the racialized nature of the war is unspoken. Instead, the cumulative narrative is one of manifest destiny, in which expansion, US military prowess, and Anglo-American culture are valorized and conquest is inevitable and beneficial to all.

BATTLEFIELDS

I begin with two battlefields. However, I first wish to reflect momentarily on the memorialization of battlefields themselves. Although such places are obviously fundamental to any war, the Mexican-American War included pervasive and extreme violence against civilians.[31] Because such warfare is illegal and morally difficult, it undercuts tropes of uplift and benevolence and is never mentioned. Hence, memorializing battlefields is an act of erasure because it implies that the violence was limited to formal military engagements. It was not.

The first site is the Battle of the Rio San Gabriel, located in Montebello, about ten miles southeast of downtown Los Angeles. It exemplifies both a military focus and the significance of landscape. This site sits on a bluff on the western side of the San Gabriel River that affords an excellent view of the eastern San Gabriel Valley. On the bluff is a cannon covered by a shelter overlooking the river (see figure 9.1). At the site the strategic nature of the river becomes readily apparent. This is significant in a place such as Los Angeles, where the terrain has been bulldozed and paved, making it difficult to discern the pre-urban geography of the region. This particular portion of the San Gabriel River has not been concretized (although there are spillways on both sides), and one can clearly see the landforms and appreciate why a battle was fought here.

The photo suggests a pastoral view of Los Angeles, but the area is, in fact, surrounded by industrial parks, multi-unit housing, and major roadways.

FIGURE 9.1. Battle of the Rio San Gabriel (California Historical Landmark 385). Author photograph.

It is only because the riverbed is part of the region's flood-control system that it still exists intact.

Both the narration and design of the site foreground military dimensions of the war. The plaque reads: "Near this site on January 8, 1847 was fought the Battle of the Rio San Gabriel. Between American forces commanded by Capt. Robert Stockton, US Navy Commander-in-chief, Brig. Gen. Stephen W. Kearny, US Army, and Californians commanded by General Jose Maria Flores." There is no context for the war, why the two countries were fighting, or even the outcome of the battle. For those not familiar with California history, there are no clues as to what happened and why. Given the careful curation of the site and its durable features, we must assume that the erasure of empire was also deliberate.

The next site is La Mesa Battlefield. Located in an old industrial section of Vernon, several miles south of downtown, it sits on a north/south railroad easement, enabling one to glimpse the vastness of the Los Angeles plain (see figure 9.2). In 1847 Mexico mounted its last battle of the war, the Battle of Los Angeles, from here. Mexican soldiers marched into Los Angeles proper and were outgunned by US forces. This defeat was the basis for their eventual surrender. The marker consists of a tall pole, which likely once flew a flag, and a plaque at its base, which has been vandalized. In addition to the abandoned condition of the site, its location is problematic: there is no precise address. I had to park at the closest intersection and search for it on foot. It is impossible to know what transpired at the site without previous knowledge.

Because of the marker's location and defacement, Vernon built a new marker at its city hall in 2018. The plaque reads: "During the United States Occupation of California in the Mexican-American War, La Mesa served as a campsite for the Californio forces under General Castro in the summer of 1846. The last military encounter of the California front was fought here on January 9, 1847. Also known as the battle of Los Angeles." Once again, the text addresses only the military dimensions of the battle. Despite Vernon's replacement marker, the abandonment of the original marker suggests a general disregard for the memory of the war.

FORT MOORE PIONEER MEMORIAL

Fort Moore is not an officially recognized site but a public art installation. The memorial is a bas-relief honoring the raising of the US flag and is dedicated to the US soldiers who fought in the war (see figure 9.3).

FIGURE 9.2. La Mesa Battle-
field (California Historical
Marker 167). Photograph by
Audrey Mandelbaum.

Besides the raising of the flag, the sculpture depicts scenes of US settlement. Fort Moore is located on the northern edge of downtown Los
Angeles. Although thousands of cars pass it daily, few likely know what
it is, given the relatively unknown history of the war, the site's disrepair,
and its location near a freeway and away from foot traffic. Fort Moore
refers to the hill on which the memorial is built. The fort was built in
the aftermath of the war, and one of Los Angeles's first lynchings occurred there. Today the hill is a parking lot, with the sculpture serving
as its front.[32] The memorial itself has several components, including
the bas-relief, a dedication pillar, and a pool. When I first visited the
site in 2016, the pool was rusty and abandoned, but by 2020, it had been
refurbished.

Fort Moore is distinctive because unlike the previous sites, it provides
some context for the war. The monument has limited text and images of
soldiers, pioneers, and Anglo-American settlers. The scenes represent the
evolution of the region from US conquest to the 1950s, when the sculpture
was completed.

FIGURE 9.3. Fort Moore Pioneer Memorial, Los Angeles. Photograph by Audrey Mandelbaum.

The monument valorizes US conquest, culture, and history. Underneath the primary image, of soldiers raising the flag, is text that reads, "On this site stood Fort Moore built by the Mormon Battalion during the War with Mexico. This Memorial honors the troops who helped to win the Southwest. The flag of the United States was raised here on July 4, 1847 by United States Troops at the first Independence Day celebration in Los Angeles." Flag raising, of course, is one of the most iconographic symbols of conquest.

Adjacent to the flag-raising scene are three smaller images. First is a quasi-bucolic scene of a pioneer with a cow, covered wagon, house, and trees. The caption states: "On ranchos where herds of cattle ranged pioneers built homes and planted vineyards and orange groves." Because cattle are associated with the Mexican era and oranges are distinctly American, the sequencing illustrates Bhandar's ideology of improvement.[33] Anglo settlers believed that Mexicans were lazy, cattle ranching was unproductive, and irrigated agriculture was an improvement.

The next two images highlight technology and overcoming nature. The transportation scene features a white settler, a stagecoach, and a railroad. As the text notes, "The Prairie Schooner stage and iron horse brought many settlers who made Los Angeles a city." Because settler colonization is about replacing Native population(s), how they arrived is deemed important.

Anglo settlers believed that Mexicans, like Indigenous peoples, would simply disappear: "That the Indian race of Mexico must recede before us, is quite as certain as . . . the destiny of our own Indians."[34]

The final image features the power grid and one of the water-transfer projects that allow Los Angeles to support millions beyond its natural carrying capacity. The scene includes a nuclear, heteropatriarchal family, underscoring the extent to which Anglo settlement is dependent on the mass manipulation of nature: "Water and power have made our arid land flourish[;] may we keep faith with the Pioneers who brought us these gifts." Technological innovation, a form of goodness associated with manifest destiny, was especially valued in the 1950s during the Cold War.

Despite their limited role in the war, the Mormon Battalion looms large. Van Wagenen has suggested that Mormons lobbied for inclusion, including raising funds for the memorial.[35] Given their history of facing persecution, Mormons are dedicated to historical preservation and use cultural memory to ensure that their contributions to the nation, especially settlement, are recognized.[36] Although Mormon participation in the war was minimal, it illuminates the scope and complexity of US expansionism. In 1839 Mormons were forced to flee Illinois and elsewhere because of religious persecution. Upon crossing the Rockies, Mormon leader Brigham Young declared Salt Lake Valley as their new home. However, given the difficulties of moving a population more than two thousand miles, various groups became stranded. Needing assistance, they asked the US Army for help. The army responded by requesting five hundred volunteers to form a battalion for the war. In exchange, the soldiers' wages would be diverted to support the larger Mormon exodus. Young agreed to such terms, hoping that the arrangement would offer positive public relations, help shield the Mormons from further persecution, and provide needed resources. Here we can see how the US military leveraged religious discrimination to extend its empire, actively displacing Native persons and Mexicans in the process. Consequently, the Mormons were involved in at least two dispossessions: the Native peoples of what is now Utah, including the Ute, Shoshone, and Paiute, and both Native peoples and Mexicans in southern California.

Mormon contributions to building a wagon trail in the Southwest are celebrated as part of manifest destiny in the inscription on the sculpture: "The march to Santa Fe and the opening of the first wagon road to the Pacific helped end the isolation of the west and inspired the Gadsden Purchase of 1888." Roads, as a form of transportation, are essential to conquest, settlement, and expansion. Despite the fact that many wagon roads were built on Native trails, only the Mormons are mentioned. This is yet another way of "forgetting" the fact that other peoples had lived in the region for centuries. Also significant is the West's depiction as isolated, which reflects an imperialist perspective. Presumably, isolation was not a problem for Native peoples. Indeed, they probably longed for the "isolation" of the pre-Hispanic era.

Fort Moore performs significant ideological work. First, it uncritically celebrates territorial conquest. The true motives for the war are never mentioned but are implicitly referenced, as "extending the frontiers of this country." This indicates a powerful sense of entitlement and righteousness. Not only did the United States feel entitled to this land, but its expansion is seen as an unquestioned good. Neither Native peoples nor Mexicans are mentioned, so presumably the memorial is speaking to white settlers—the central subjects of the US nation. Once again, "the performance of good works" is essential to the transition narrative and settler fantasies.[37] Second, the memorial ignores previous peoples, both Indigenous and Mexican, and posits US actors as the only ones with agency. Anglo-Americans supposedly built Los Angeles, despite the fact that the Spanish conquered the area in 1771 and the Tongva had lived in the region for at least five thousand years prior to that. This is especially egregious when one considers the importance of water to the region and the profound knowledge and labor invested by Spanish, Mexican, and Indigenous peoples in harnessing water. Dismissing previous water infrastructure and technology not only erases previous civilizations but also reinscribes Anglo-Americans as the sole bearers of technological progress.

NEGOTIATING PEACE

The final two sites represent the conclusion of the war: the Catalina Verdugo Adobe and Campo de Cahuenga. They center negotiations, the treaty, and troop withdrawal, all of which are equated with peace. Mexican and US representatives negotiated elements of the Treaty of Guadalupe Hidalgo at the Catalina Adobe in Glendale. Supposedly, the representatives sat underneath a massive oak tree (roble de paz, or peace tree) and conducted their work. The site has been converted into a bucolic, lush 1.3-acre park that offers picnic spaces and an inviting place to visit. The site's buildings and landscaping are carefully tended and evoke the "Spanish fantasy" myth.

Coined by Carey McWilliams, the myth refers to Anglo-Americans' efforts, beginning in the late nineteenth century, to portray the Mexican and

Spanish eras as idyllic in order to promote the region and fashion a usable past. The Spanish fantasy myth can be seen in plays, festivals, architecture, and historical preservation.[38] There are at least two crucial power dynamics at work in the myth. First, it overlooks the devastation that the mission system brought to the Native peoples of the region. Consider that more than six thousand Indians are buried at the San Gabriel Mission, just east of Los Angeles. The fact that many died from disease does not make their deaths any less connected to colonization—Europeans brought displacement, disease, and death.[39] The second power dynamic associated with the myth is the act of curation itself: Anglo-Americans appropriating and reconfiguring Native, Mexican, and Spanish history. Historically, they have done so to articulate a distinct regional identity and to sell the region, a form of boosterism. For example, an old carreta (cart) has been repurposed as a planter (see figure 9.4). Likewise, ollas and metates (water jugs and grinding pads) are strategically placed around the garden as decorative items. Such placements underscore the faux nature of the site: ollas and metates were/are everyday tools that Mexican and Indigenous peoples have used for centuries. Here, they are severed from their normal context and have become part of the Spanish fantasy myth, echoing earlier examples, including Charro Days, Ramona, and the Mission Play.[40] Although the site does acknowledge Mexico in a sanitized and romantic way, there is almost no information on the substance of the treaty and why there was a war.

The final site is Campo de Cahuenga. This is the largest, most elaborate, and most developed site devoted to the war, and it is the only one that offers a counternarrative (albeit off-site). Campo de Cahuenga is California Historical Marker 151 and Los Angeles Cultural Historic Marker 29. Because it is situated across from Universal Studios (Los Angeles's top tourist destination), it is the only historic site which regularly attracts significant numbers of visitors. The site consists of a carefully tended adobe, an archaeological dig, picnic tables, and a small museum dedicated to telling the Anglo-American version of the war, especially its conclusion. A handout titled "Meet me at the Campo!" lists the many historical events associated with the site:

The Campo de Cahuenga is the birthplace of California and the place where the dream for a continental United States (Manifest Destiny) was realized. It is also a monument to peace, where the agreement leading to the end of the Mexican-American war was signed. It is a monument to the unification with the United States, as one of the first Overland

FIGURE 9.4. Catalina Verdugo Adobe. Photograph by Audrey Mandelbaum.

Stagecoach Stations in California. Finally, it has played an important role in American history, having served as a Union fortress and garrison during the American Civil War, giving it a significant place in the history of the great American struggle to become a United States of America. Indeed, the Campo is one of the most historic sites in America.

Such an uncritical celebration of manifest destiny signals an earlier era of historical preservation and the work of amateur docents. Certainly, a professional contemporary team would offer a more balanced view. But it is precisely the site's community-based nature that reveals its hegemonic nature. In fact, the majority of historical sites are developed and managed by amateurs. It is only the largest and most significant sites, such as Monticello, or those managed by the National Park Service, that employ professional staff and are more inclusive.

Campo de Cahuenga is known as the site of Mexico's "capitulation," which is an ambiguous word meaning "surrender" and ostensibly used in order to avoid having to reference an actual war. The site features a series of large panels that explain why the United States entered the war and explaining the outcome. Hence, it is the only historical site that narrates in detail why the war occurred. It is steeped in manifest destiny. For instance, the panels state that the United States entered the war because other colonial powers, namely England and France, desired California, and the United States could not let anyone else own it. Accordingly, it asked Mexico to sell it, but Mexico declined. At that point, "hostilities" ensued. Here, the United States is framed as vulnerable and acting reasonably, rather than as an empire committed to economic and territorial expansion. Indeed, such actions were considered entirely reasonable under the Monroe Doctrine.

Another panel, focused on the war itself, stated that at one point "Californios were resisting the US's forces." This struck me as odd: if the US and Mexico were at war, how could the Californios be seen as "resisting" US forces? Resisting implies that control and domination have been asserted—to resist is to challenge acknowledged authority. In reality, Mexicans were *defending* their land and people. I asked a docent about this interpretation, and a discussion ensued. One docent suggested that there was tremendous chaos at the time and that "resistance" really meant "chaos." Another explained that the Californios were resisting Mexico because Los Angeles was a forgotten outpost and harmed by Mexican policies. Still, she acknowledged that there was some "rebellion" against the Americans. In a rather stunning moment, another docent said, "It's not like they were at war." Realizing the implausibility of such a statement, someone from the San Fernando Historical Society suggested that perhaps the docent didn't think there was a war because a battle was not actually fought at Campo de Cahuenga. This conversation shows some of the mental gymnastics that are required to reconcile hegemonic narratives with facts and rational analysis.

An even deeper form of denial and disconnect occurred when a woman with a group of teens asked if any of them knew what *capitulation* means. No one volunteered an answer, but one girl responded that "I am only interested in US history." This is yet another remarkable assertion: Is Campo de Cahuenga outside of US history because it is also Mexican history, and therefore "foreign"? If it is not US history, how did Los Angeles become part of the United States? Does she believe that only Anglo-Americans are the bearers of US history? Regardless of the logic undergirding her statement, the idea that Los Angeles is outside of US history effectively erases empire by simply eliminating transition narratives. The absence of such narratives leads to the conclusion that it was always so.

Campo de Cahuenga is the only historical site in Los Angeles where the conquered "talk back." Almost everything was in English, but there was at least one bilingual brochure. However, it was not commensurate with the English one. The English version referenced the "American Acquisition Period," while the Spanish version called it "el pería/oodo de la Conquista Norteamericana" (the period of North American conquest). The Spanish version foregrounds power and domination, through *conquista*, whereas the English version employs the neutral *acquisition*.

But the real place where Mexican/Chicana/o/x and Indigenous voices can be seen is at the Metropolitan Transit Authority train stop. Universal Studios is on the Red Line, a rail line running from downtown Los Angeles to North Hollywood. The train station is below ground and, like most stops, features public art. The installation is called *Tree of Califas*, by artist Margaret García and architect Kate Diamond (see figure 9.5).[41] The project features four massive pillars telling the history of the region and specifically the war. The story is told chronologically through brightly painted ceramic tiles on each pillar from Indigenous and Mexican viewpoints. The first pillar is devoted to Spanish conquest, Indigenous people, the mission system, and Mexico. There are some rustic scenes, but García shows the enslavement of Indigenous peoples, indicating their coercion and oppres-

FIGURE 9.5. *Tree of Califas*. The legend reads: "Robert F. Stockton. Stockton threatened the citizens with dire punishment should they fail to cooperate with the new government." Source: Author photograph.

sion by the Catholic Church, and explains that Mexico promoted secularization in order to acquire mission lands. The second pillar explores the initial battles of the war, and the third depicts key figures in the war, including women. The tiles underscore the violence and force associated with the war, reminding us that this was, in fact, an actual war. Numerous tiles feature guns, swords, bloody bodies, and severed limbs. The final pillar focuses on Mexico's surrender.

Tree of Califas marks the Chicana/o/x/Mexican presence in two ways: first by offering a counternarrative of the war and second in the art itself. The aesthetic is deeply Chicana/o/x, as seen in its palette, materials, bilingual text, and Mexican iconography, such as calaveras, cactus, and religious symbolism. Although the mosaic is not on the grounds of Campo de Cahuenga, it is a genuine effort to complicate the story.

On the Significance of Cultural Memory

I wrote this chapter amid fierce national debate regarding cultural memory and the racial past. While this engagement is an essential first step, I worry it is only scratching the surface, as much of the activism seems to center on individuals. Activists advocating for the removal of monuments commemorating colonizers and enslavers routinely state that they are offensive, painful, and unwelcoming. Many argue that such figures should not be honored, while others insist that the values such men embody no longer represent the US, or at least what we should aspire to. Building on such concerns, scholars have documented the degree to which white property-owning men are commemorated and argue for more equitable representation.[42]

Perhaps this focus on individuals—both whom we honor and how we respond to their being honored—should not be surprising, given the individualistic nature of US culture. Nonetheless, such a focus eclipses the opportunity to fully grasp the processes, including racial capitalism, colonization, and imperialism, that created this territory and country. Rather than focusing on individuals, we would do well to interrogate the actual landscapes within which these processes were produced and embedded. Studying the commemorative landscape of events like the Mexican-American War offers a window into a much larger set of power relations. As the geographer Pierce Lewis wrote, "The landscape is our unwitting autobiography."[43]

Research for this essay was made possible by a Guggenheim Memorial Fellowship.

1. Immerwahr, *How to Hide an Empire*.

2. "Monuments and Memorials Removed."

3. On denying empire, see Jacobson, "Where We Stand"; Kaplan and Pease, *Cultures of United States Imperialism*; Immerwahr, *How to Hide an Empire*; Williams, *Tragedy of American Diplomacy*; and Karuka, *Empire's Tracks*.

4. Recent analyses of US empire include Frymer, *Building an American Empire*; Ran, *Two Faces of American Freedom*; Saler, *Settlers' Empire*; Patnaik and Patnaik, *Capital and Imperialism*; and Hixson, *American Settler Colonialism*.

5. Against equating white supremacy and colonization, see Byrd, *Transit of Empire*.

6. Cacho, "Racialized Hauntings."

7. Wallerstein, *Historical Capitalism*; Patnaik and Patnaik, *Capitalism and Imperialism*.

8. Bhandar, *Colonial Lives of Property*, 7; Fanon, *Wretched of the Earth*; see also Launius and Boyce, "More Than Metaphor," 168. On contracted conceptions of capitalism, see Singh, "Race, Violence"; and Glassman, "Primitive Accumulation." Regarding slavery, see Baptist, *Half Has Never Been Told*.

9. Sturken, *Tangled Memories*.

10. Van Wagenen, *Remembering the Forgotten War*. The war and its aftermath were central to early Chicanx studies: Acuña, *Occupied America*; Griswold del Castillo, *Treaty of Guadalupe Hidalgo*; Barrera, *Race and Class in the Southwest*; Montejano, *Anglos and Mexicans*; De Leon, *They Called Them Greasers*; Pitt, *Decline of the Californios*; Ramos, *Beyond the Alamo*; Gómez, *Manifest Destinies*; Monroy, *Thrown among Strangers*. Subsequent work highlighted gender and interracial formations: Almaguer, *Racial Faultlines*; Chávez-Garcia, *Negotiating Conquest*; Castañeda, "Sexual Violence in the Politics"; Benavides, "Californios! Whom Do You Support?"; González, *Refusing the Favor*.

11. On regional and class tensions, see Streeby, "American Sensations."

12. Streeby, "American Sensations," 4.

13. Quoted in Frymer, *Building an American Empire*, 149.

14. Port of Los Angeles. "By the Numbers."

15. Dunbar-Ortiz, *Indigenous Peoples' History*; Wilm, *Settlers as Conquerors*.

16. Streeby, "American Sensations"; Grandin, *End of the Myth*; Ostler, *Surviving Genocide*.

17. Burrough, Tomlinson, and Stanford, *Forget the Alamo*. Mexico also invited US settlers to move to Tejas in 1821 to help dispossess Native peoples.

18. Horsman, *Race and Manifest Destiny*.

19. Melamed, *Represent and Destroy*; Winant, *World Is a Ghetto*.

20. Rivera, *Emergence of Mexican America*, chapter 2.

21. Gómez, *Manifest Destinies*.

22. On Mexican white supremacy, see Martínez, *Genealogical Fictions*. On Mexican anti-Indigeneity, see González, *This Small City*; and Guidotti-Hernandez, *Unspeakable Violence*. On overlapping racial formations, see Saldaña-Portillo, *Indian Given*.

23. Gómez, *Manifest Destinies*.

24. Holly and Brown, "Woman Takes Down Confederate Flag."

25. Hirsch, *Generation of Postmemory*; Sturken, *Tangled Memories*; Gómez-Barris, *Where Memory Dwells*.

26. Modlin et al., "Can Plantation Museums?"; de la Loza, *Pocho Research Society Field Guide*. On place and cultural memory more generally, see Till, *New Berlin*; Foote, *Shadowed Ground*; DeLyser, *Ramona Memories*; and Dwyer and Alderman, *Civil Rights Memorials*. Of particular note is Project Reset, a major initiative to rethink southern tourism based on antiracism. See www.tourismreset.com.

27. Sturken, *Tangled Memories*, 2.

28. Van Wagenen, *Regarding the Forgotten War*. On goodness and white innocence, respectively, see Hixson, *American Settler Colonialism*; and Inwood, "'It Is the Innocence.'"

29. Barraclough, *Making the San Fernando Valley*, 11.

30. The war is ancillary to a few other sites in Los Angeles.

31. Hixson, *American Settler Colonialism*, chapter 5.

32. On Fort Moore, see Brown, "Fortifications and Catacombs."

33. Bhandar, *Colonial Lives of Property*.

34. Quoted in Dunbar-Ortiz, *Indigenous Peoples' History*, 118. See also Pitt, *Decline of the Californios*.

35. Van Wagenen, *Remembering the Forgotten War*, 169.

36. For example, see Ensign Peak Foundation.

37. Hixson, *American Settler Colonialism*, 20–22.

38. McWilliams, *North from Mexico*, chapter 2. Studies of the Spanish fantasy myth include Deverell, *Whitewashed Adobe*; Kropp, *California Vieja*; Carpio, *Collisions at the Crossroads*, chapter 1; and DeLyser, *Ramona Memories*.

39. For detailed discussion on disease and Native peoples, see Edwards and Kelton, "Germs, Genocides."

40. Deverell, *Whitewashed Adobe*; Kropp, *California Vieja*; DeLyser, *Ramona Memories*.

41. Metropolitan Transit Authority, "Tree of Califas."

42. Monument Lab, National Monument Audit.

43. Lewis, "Axioms for Reading."

BIBLIOGRAPHY

Acuña, Rodolfo. *Occupied America*. New York: Harper Collins, 1972.

Almaguer, Tomás. *Racial Faultlines*. Berkeley: University of California Press, 1994.

Baptist, Edward. *The Half Has Never Been Told: Slavery and the Making of American Capitalism*. New York: Basic Books, 2014.

Barraclough, Laura. *Making the San Fernando Valley: Rural Landscapes, Urban Development, and White Privilege*. Athens: University of Georgia Press, 2011.

Barrera, Mario. *Race and Class in the Southwest*. Notre Dame, IN: University of Notre Dame Press, 1979.

Benavides, José Luis. "'Californios! Whom Do You Support?' *El Clamor Publico's* Contradictory Role in the Racial Formation Process in Early California." *California History* 84 no. 2 (2006): 54–73.

Bhandar, Brenna. *Colonial Lives of Property*. Durham, NC: Duke University Press, 2018.

Brown, Jason. "The Fortifications and Catacombs of the Conquests of Los Angeles." In *Latitudes: An Angelenos' Atlas*, edited by Patricia Wakida, 73–84. Berkeley, CA: Heyday.

Burrough, Bryan, Chris Tomlinson, and Jason Stanford. *Forget the Alamo: The Rise and Fall of an American Myth*. New York: Penguin, 2021.

Byrd, Jodi. *The Transit of Empire*. Minneapolis: University of Minnesota Press, 2011.

Cacho, Lisa. "Racialized Hauntings of the Devalued Dead." In *Strange Affinities: The Sexual and Gender Politics of Comparative Racialization*, edited by Grace Hong and Rod Ferguson, 25–52. Durham, NC: Duke University Press, 2011.

Carpio, Genevieve. *Collisions at the Crossroads: How Place and Mobility Make Race*. Berkeley: University of California Press, 2019.

Castañeda, Antonia. "Sexual Violence in the Politics and Policies of Conquest." In *Building with Our Hands*, edited by Adela de la Torre and Beatriz Pesquera, 15–33. Berkeley: University of California Press, 1993.

Chávez-Garcia, Miroslava. *Negotiating Conquest: Gender and Power in California, 1770s–1880s*. Tucson: University of Arizona Press, 2004.

de la Loza, Sandra. *The Pocho Research Society Field Guide to L.A.: Monuments and Murals of Erased and Invisible Histories*. Seattle: University of Washington Press, 2011.

De Leon, Arnoldo. *They Called Them Greasers: Anglo Attitudes toward Mexicans in Texas, 1821–1900*. Austin: University of Texas Press, 1983.

DeLyser, Dydia. *Ramona Memories: Tourism and the Shaping of Southern California*. Minneapolis: University of Minnesota Press, 2005.

Deverell, William. *Whitewashed Adobe: The Rise of Los Angeles and the Remaking of Its Past*. Berkeley: University of California Press, 2004.

Dunbar-Ortiz, Roxanne. *An Indigenous Peoples' History of the United States*. New York: Basic Books, 2014.

Dwyer, Owen, and Derek Alderman. *Civil Rights Memorials and the Geography of Memory*. Chicago: Center for American Places, 2008.

Edwards, Tai, and Paul Kelton. "Germs, Genocides, and America's Indigenous Peoples." *Journal of American History* 107 (1): 52–76.

Ensign Peak Foundation. Accessed May 1, 2021. https://ensignpeakfoundation.org.

Fanon, Frantz. *Wretched of the Earth*. New York: Penguin, 2001 (1961).

Foote, Kenneth. *Shadowed Ground: America's Landscapes of Violence and Tragedy*. Austin: University of Texas Press, 1997.

Frymer, Paul. *Building an American Empire: The Era of Territorial and Political Expansion*. Princeton, NJ: Princeton University Press, 2017.

Glassman, Jim. "Primitive Accumulation, Accumulation by Dispossession, Accumulation by 'Extra-Economic' Means." *Progress in Human Geography* 30, no. 5 (2006): 608–25.

Gómez, Laura. *Manifest Destinies: The Making of the Mexican American Race*. New York: New York University Press, 2007.

Gómez-Barris, Macarena. *Where Memory Dwells: Culture and State Violence in Chile*. Berkeley: University of California Press, 2009.

González, Deena. *Refusing the Favor: The Spanish-Mexican Women of Santa Fe*. New York: Oxford University Press, 1999.

González, Michael. *This Small City Will Be a Mexican Paradise: Exploring the Origins of Mexican Culture in Los Angeles, 1821–1846*. Albuquerque: University of New Mexico Press, 2005.

Grandin, Greg. *The End of the Myth: From the Frontier to the Border Wall in the Mind of America*. New York: Metropolitan, 2019.

Griswold del Castillo, Richard. *The Treaty of Guadalupe Hidalgo*. Norman: University of Oklahoma Press, 1990.

Guidotti-Hernandez, Nicole. *Unspeakable Violence: Remapping US and Mexican National Imaginaries*. Durham, NC: Duke University Press, 2011.

Hirsch, Marianne. *The Generation of Postmemory: Writing and Visual Culture after the Holocaust*. New York: Columbia University Press, 2012.

Hixson, Walter. *American Settler Colonialism*. New York: Palgrave Macmillan, 2013.

Holly, Peter, and DeNeen Brown. "Woman Takes Down Confederate Flag in Front of South Carolina Statehouse." *Washington Post*, June 27, 2015. https://www.washingtonpost.com/news/post-nation/wp/2015/06/27/woman-takes-down-confederate-flag-in-front-of-south-carolina-statehouse/.

Horsman, Reginald. *Race and Manifest Destiny*. Cambridge, MA: Harvard University Press, 1981.

Immerwahr, Daniel. *How to Hide an Empire*. New York: Farrar, Straus and Giroux, 2018.

Inwood, Joshua F. J. "'It Is the Innocence Which Constitutes the Crime': Political Geographies of White Supremacy, the Construction of White Innocence, and the Flint Water Crisis." *Geography Compass* 12 no. 3 (2018): 1–11.

Jacobson, Matthew. "Where We Stand: US Empire at Street Level and in the Archive." *American Quarterly* 65 no. 2 (2013): 265–90.

Kaplan, Amy, and Donald Pease. *Cultures of United States Imperialism.* Durham, NC: Duke University Press, 1993.

Karuka, Manu. *Empire's Tracks.* Berkeley: University of California Press, 2019.

Kropp, Phoebe. *California Vieja: Culture and Memory in a Modern American Place.* Berkeley: University of California Press, 2006.

Launius, Sarah, and Geoffrey Boyce. "More Than Metaphor: Settler Colonialism, Frontier Logic, and the Continuities of Racialized Dispossession in a Southwest City." *Annals of the American Association of Geographers* 111 no. 1 (2021): 157–74.

Lewis, Pierce. "Axioms for Reading the American Landscape." In *The Interpretation of Ordinary Landscape: Geographical Essays,* edited by Donald Meinig, 11–32. New York: Oxford University Press, 1979.

Martínez, María Elena. *Genealogical Fictions: Limpieza de Sangre, Religion, and Gender in Colonial Mexico.* Palo Alto, CA: Stanford University Press, 2008.

McWilliams, Carey. *North from Mexico.* New York: Praeger, 1990 (1948).

Melamed, Jody. *Represent and Destroy: Rationalizing Violence in the New Racial Capitalism.* Minneapolis: University of Minnesota Press, 2011.

Metropolitan Transit Authority. "Tree of Califas." Accessed May 1, 2021. www.metro.net/about/art/artworks/untitled-garcia.

Modlin, Arnold, Stephen Hanna, Amy Potter, Bridget Forbes-Bright, and Derek Alderman. "Can Plantation Museums Do Full Justice to the Story of the Enslaved?" *GeoHumanities* 4, no. 2 (2018): 335–59.

Monroy, Douglas. *Thrown among Strangers: The Making of Mexican Culture in Frontier California.* Berkeley: University of California Press, 1990.

Montejano, David. *Anglos and Mexicans in the Making of Texas, 1836–1986.* Austin: University of Texas Press, 1987.

Monument Lab. National Monument Audit. Accessed January 7, 2022. https://monumentlab.com/audit.

"Monuments and Memorials Removed during the George Floyd Protests." Wikipedia. Accessed May 1, 2021. https://en.wikipedia.org/wiki/List_of_monuments _and_memorials_removed_during_the_George_Floyd_protests.

Ostler, Jeffrey. *Surviving Genocide: Native Nations and the United States from the American Revolution to Bleeding Kansas.* New Haven, CT: Yale University Press, 2019.

Patnaik, Utsa, and Prabhat Patnaik. *Capital and Imperialism.* New York: Monthly Review Press, 2021.

Pitt, Leonard. *Decline of the Californios.* Berkeley: University of California Press, 1966.

Port of Los Angeles. "By the Numbers." Accessed May 4, 2021. www
.portoflosangeles.org/tariffshurt.

Ramos, Raul. *Beyond the Alamo: Forging Mexican Ethnicity in San Antonio, 1821–1861*. Chapel Hill: University of North Carolina Press, 2008.

Ran, Aziz. *Two Faces of American Freedom*. Cambridge, MA: Harvard University Press, 2014.

Rivera, John Michael. *The Emergence of Mexican America*. New York: New York University Press, 2006.

Saldaña-Portillo, Josefina. *Indian Given: Racial Geographies across Mexico and the United States*. Durham, NC: Duke University Press, 2016.

Saler, Bethel. *The Settlers' Empire*. Philadelphia: University of Pennsylvania Press, 2014.

Singh, Nikhil. "On Race, Violence, and 'So-Called Primitive Accumulation.'" In *Futures of Black Radicalism*, edited by Gaye Johnson and Alyosha Lubin, 39–58. New York: Verso, 2017.

Streeby, Shelley. "American Sensations: Empire, Amnesia, and the US-Mexican War." *American Literary History* 13 no. 1 (2001): 1–40.

Sturken, Marita. *Tangled Memories: The Vietnam War, the AIDS Epidemic and the Politics of Remembering*. Berkeley: University of California Press, 1997.

Till, Karen. *The New Berlin: Memory, Politics, and Place*. Minneapolis: University of Minnesota Press, 2005.

Van Wagenen, Michael. *Remembering the Forgotten War: The Enduring Legacies of the US-Mexican War*. Amherst: University of Massachusetts Press, 2012.

Wallerstein, Immanuel. *Historical Capitalism*. London: Verso, 1983.

Williams, William Appleman. *The Tragedy of American Diplomacy*. Cleveland: World Publishing Company, 1959.

Wilm, Julius. *Settlers as Conquerors: Free Land Policy in Antebellum America*. Stuttgart: Franz Steiner Verlag, 2018.

Winant, Howard. *The World Is a Ghetto*. New York: Basic Books, 2001.

IV Rehearsing for the Future

Racial Capitalism Now: A Conversation with Michael Dawson and Ruth Wilson Gilmore

This conversation took place on March 30, 2019, at the end of the Racial Capitalism conference organized by the Unit for Criticism and Interpretive Theory at the University of Illinois, Urbana-Champaign. Most of the essays in this volume were presented at the conference, and this closing exchange between the two keynote speakers reflects on the conference presentations and their own role as scholars and activists in defining the field. The conversation concludes with their thoughts on the shifting ground of struggles against racial capitalism now. This discussion was facilitated by Brian Jordan Jefferson and Jodi Melamed.

BRIAN JORDAN JEFFERSON: Thank you, everyone, for coming out, and again I want to thank the Unit [for Criticism] and Susan Koshy for her stewardship and putting this together and of course the co-organizers, especially Lisa Cacho, for doing that presentation. And then a very big thank-you and round of applause for Sarah Richter and Alyssa Bralower, the graduate research assistants, for all their hard work. This is the last panel and will cover a lot of things I think a lot of us are looking forward to: "Racial Capitalism Now." We are delighted to have professors Michael Dawson and Ruth Wilson Gilmore here to talk about how we think about racial capitalism going forward and to put this into a contemporary context. I, and perhaps others in this room, might not have been in academia if it wasn't for their writings, so I'd like to thank them. Today we are going to see what happens when we put two great minds together. I'm excited myself, but before we start, Jodi would like to give a little anecdote to get the ball rolling.

JODI MELAMED: I want to say ditto to everything Brian just said in terms of their importance for bringing so many of us in the room here. And I did want to say that in addition to knowing both of them as legendary scholar-activists, I also know them both to be incredible conversationalists. I wanted to share one anecdote about each of them. The first is about Ruthie coming to Milwaukee in 2006 for a community conference at America's Black Holocaust Museum, which is coming back this year—the funding is there, which is amazing. I believe the talk itself was about two hours, and there were about four hundred to five hundred people there, mostly not students, mostly folks from around central Milwaukee. The official Q&A was about two and a half hours long, and then there was an unofficial three-hour Q&A. Ruthie did not leave until every person who wanted to talk to her had had their time. It was amazing. I was dead on my feet—I don't know how she did it. And then Michael convened an amazing racial capitalism workshop in Tuscany over the summer, and after a day of generously listening to and shaping, maybe, about six papers from morning until night, we were tired and I went to sleep, but Michael remained in deep conversation with the faculty and the graduate students there until three in the morning for three nights in a row. So we've got some great conversationalists here who are also very, very generous. Let's give them one round of applause to get started. Now our plan is to get them talking to each other, but we do also want, especially to the end, to open it up to questions from all of you. Brian and I have some questions to kind of keep prodding them to get things going, but maybe before and moving into the topic of "Racial Capitalism Now," I was thinking about how both of you share California. So maybe this is a New Yorker's question, but I was thinking about how both of you share California as a formative site of your thinking and activism, and I wonder how you would narrate your journey from those California times to your present thinking and concerns. I think that's a good place to start.

MICHAEL DAWSON: OK, I'll go first.

RUTH WILSON GILMORE: I'm older, but he was there first. [*Laughter.*]

MICHAEL DAWSON: If you're not going to play fair. I ended up in California as an undergraduate, and partly I also wound up in California because I started becoming interested in becoming an activist, in high school, particularly with the assassination of Dr. Martin Luther King. And fortunately I am now old enough to where being a Dawson doesn't mean anything, but being a Dawson in Chicago in the 1960s, 1970s—or for that matter the '40s or '50s—although I wasn't around then, meant that you were part of the ruling political machine in the city. And there is no way that a Dawson could be an antiwar activist, a Black Power Leninist. Nobody would trust me because everyone would think I was a police agent. So I had to go far enough away to school to where that name didn't ring too many bells, except maybe with the faculty.

I organized for about fifteen years and dropped out of school, worked in Silicon Valley, and started trying to understand why the Black Liberation movement was falling apart and, as Ruthie knows, it fell apart spectacularly and violently in the Bay Area. There was one summer where the Panther Party split—an organization that a lot of us at the time who were not members looked to. But it's also the same summer that an organization in Detroit, League of Revolutionary Black Workers, also split. So some of the major organizations that were trying to understand the intersection of white supremacy and capitalism in the United States were on the ropes in serious ways. Some of my work has thought about this. Some of the wounds were very much self-inflicted, but obviously the state was very much centered on trying to dismantle Black insurgency in the United States and globally. A lot of processes we saw were defensive actions in San Francisco in the 1970s. We saw Black neighborhoods disappear as gentrification began; at the same time that Black neighborhoods were disappearing, neighborhoods like Nihonmachi, the Japanese American neighborhood, were also gentrified, and those residents were also displaced. In the Bay Area there were active discussions and struggle between Indigenous, Black, Latinx, and Asian American activists trying to understand the different processes of—the word that Ruthie hates—racialization, but more precisely racial oppression, racial subordination.

I was trying to understand through the massive changes in the labor force at that time, massive changes in industry, technologies that had just begun to take off in Silicon Valley. And one thing that people forget about the Silicon Valley story is that it did not start with overprivileged teenagers hacking computers in their garages. It started with major corporations backing the Vietnam War, and Stanford was part of that. Stanford Engineering was part of that, and all the first wave of companies in Silicon Valley were also part of that. So we were trying to understand the relationship between imperialism, racial oppression at home, and capitalism, and the changes that were coming so rapidly we didn't have a handle on them. So how I got here today was very much as these movements and organizations started fracturing and coming apart, is when I finally did go back to school, it was to try to understand what had happened, what type of situation we were actually in. One of the tenets I have is that we did a lot of study of the Soviet Union, we studied China, we studied Guinea-Bissau, we studied a lot of different places, but we didn't study the United States very well. So trying to understand the political economy and the politics of the places we were trying to organize in was something I had been working on and something that, once again to throw it back to my roots, was thinking about political economy and race through this lens of what is now racial capitalism.

RUTH WILSON GILMORE: My trajectory is a bit different. I was born and grew up in New Haven, Connecticut, and I came to political consciousness as a kid because my parents were organizers and activists both in the traditional Race people way but my father was also quite a Left firebrand. He organized unions; he took over the New Haven chapter of the NAACP to use it as a respectable front to do all kinds of other things. They lost their charter but gained the things he was fighting for. So that was the context in which I came to consciousness, but then through all kinds of reasons that I won't share this evening, I wound up in California for the second time after bouncing through briefly in 1970—I was in the Bay the summer of 1970 during that long recession—bounced back to the East Coast, finished college, went to drama school and said, "The theater is not for me," and bounced back to the West Coast, where I met this guy [points to partner in the audience] and wound up spending a very, very long happy time there.

Like Michael, I was out of school for a long time—about seventeen years between when I finished my MFA and going back to school to do a PhD. In that time—we are talking about the late '70s until the early '90s—I watched with some amazement the entire landscape changing. So the things that Michael just spoke about were extremely evident, and anybody like Cheryl [Harris] who is from Los Angeles knows, that the contradictions in LA are right on the surface. You don't have to peel back one single layer to see them, even though because of the beguiling way that the mostly low-rise neighborhoods extend, it's hard sometimes to wrap our minds around the kinds of things that are abstractly represented, for example, in that last map that Cheryl showed us of the concentration of certain kinds of more recent predatory lending. So it was in the context of those changes, pretty much through then to the structural adjustments that kicked in in the late '70s and forward, that I started to do what led me to do what I talked to you about yesterday, that led me to do what I did, which is the reason you all know me.

I'll just say that this process of becoming involved in all different kinds of struggles for social justice, some of which involved students just getting access to higher education. And I will mention that two of the most famous Black Panther Party member assassinations were the assassinations of John Huggins and Bunchy Carter at UCLA, and what few people recognize is that the reason they were on campus that day, on a Saturday in January, was to argue about curriculum. They were students. They were arguing about curriculum and the direction Black studies ought to take. And Michael talked this morning about where Black studies went, which is not where it was intended to go at all. So, as you know, the FBI said the Black Panther Party is the most dangerous thing and it was dangerous not because they had guns, because everybody had guns. It wasn't the guns. It was the platform and the program and things like people arguing about curriculum, working with white people, etc., etc., etc. That's what made the party such a dangerous thing even though, as Michael said, it had internal contradictions that it also could not seem to resolve. The rest I think is kind of written up in my book, so I'm going to leave it there.

JODI MELAMED: Michael, do you want to respond to that?

MICHAEL DAWSON: One thing I would say: Black studies did in important ways have its start in California, and it came out of revolutionary movements in both northern and southern California, and there was a rich ideological debating ground—as we got into a little bit earlier today—mostly due to students. One of the most dangerous things, I think, about both the League of Revolutionary Black Workers and the Black Panther Party was their ability to make alliances across serious contradictions across racial and ethnic groups. If you ever get a chance to see the movie *Finally Got the News*, it's very much worth watching about the Detroit organizing. When I came back in December of 1969 for winter break, it was shortly after the assassination of Fred Hampton and Mark Clark in Chicago, and the city was on edge. The Panthers had organized across street youth organizations; they had organized hillbillies in one part of the city; they were working with Puerto Rican revolutionaries—Fred Hampton came out of the steel mills; that's where his family was from—and so people were trying to develop a type of analysis that could lay the basis for long-term alliances, solidarity, and organizing, and that's what was squashed pretty definitively.

But I think one of the things we shouldn't do, though, which is a danger probably more of my generation than of much younger people, is to romanticize that period. The level of homophobia and violence against women, for example, within the Panther Party was quite large. If you talk to a lot of the women cadre who survived that experience and who have written about it. So we have to learn from the mistakes of the past and realize that we are in new times, but history is still with us, as Cheryl [Harris] pointed out through Baldwin. So a lot of what happened during those times we are living with today.

BRIAN JORDAN JEFFERSON: One of the questions I wanted to ask given the type of work that you do and the disciplines that you are in and the times that you began your careers: what were some of the struggles or experiences that you had in doing work on what we now call racial capitalism? I have a political science degree, and I know [the discipline] is not the most hospitable place for racial theory. And I know my current discipline, geography, was not always as hospitable and may be not even now to this type of work. People of my generation might take it a little for granted that you can do this type of work, but how were your experiences?

RUTH WILSON GILMORE: Well, I'll be happy to start responding to that, and I think that you [points to Michael] were in a similar situation to me: we were not traditionally aged students. And I, for one, decided what I wanted to study, and I didn't decide that I wanted to study and write about prisons—that wasn't my goal. I wanted to learn very systematically how to think about things through political economy. I saw that as a huge gap in my knowledge. I could have done it in these reading groups that I talked about yesterday and as an autodidact or collecto-didact I was doing it, but also in my household we needed at least one pension to see us through our old age because we neglected having children to become a burden to.

MICHAEL DAWSON: That's what children are for?

RUTH WILSON GILMORE: Yeah!

MICHAEL DAWSON: Oh shoot! I got it wrong!

RUTH WILSON GILMORE: I can't believe that's news. So, having no children, I had to get a job. To get a job, I had to find something that I would enjoy doing as much as [my partner] Craig enjoyed what he did, which was, at the time, bookselling, and that didn't carry any type of pension other than Social Security. And as you all know, I'm a know-it-all, so know-it-alls are pretty well equipped to become teachers, and I love to teach.

So, I went back to school, and in looking around at different kinds of programs I announced to people whose advice I sought that I wanted to study political economy. I said it to Cedric Robinson, and I said it to different people. I said it to Clyde Woods, and Clyde said, "Political economy of what?" That is so typical Clyde, and I said, "That's a good question. Let me think." At the time I was an adjunct at UCLA teaching in African American Studies, and Clyde was doing an independent study with me; he was a PhD candidate at UCLA, talking through with me his ideas about the blues epistemology and planning in the Lower Mississippi Delta Development Commission. So I looked around, and I thought, Where can I do this? I looked at economics departments, and I realized I would die of old age before they would authorize me to do what I wanted to do, and I looked at some sociology programs, and there were a couple that looked somewhat likely. Somebody suggested planning, so I looked at a couple of planning departments, and in thinking about planning I rolled off to the Union of Radical Political Economists' summer camp, which is held in a camp. You know, you sleep in those bunks with the plastic mattress covers that squeak all night, and I met this really great regional economist called Ann Markusen, and I thought, I want to be able to do what she does! And I thought I would apply to Rutgers, where she taught at the time, and shortly after my summer camp experience, Craig and I made our way—every few years—to the Rethinking Marxism Conference at UMass Amherst, and we did what we do when we go to conferences: usually he goes one way, and I go another, and then we get back together later and share what we've learned. And we did that. We got back together, and he said, "You're going to Rutgers, but you're not going into planning, you're going into geography." And I was really taken aback because I hadn't taken a geography course since I was twelve years old, but I was also intrigued because in my geography textbook, figure this, during the Cold War in 1962, my geography textbook that was written by a Yale geographer and somebody else, had an entire section on socialist development and five-year plans. And I thought this makes perfect sense, I'm going to be a Communist. By the time I got to school, to answer the question, I knew that all I wanted people to do was to teach me really, really well how to do the things they knew how to do. I didn't come to just repeat what I already knew, as Marisol [LeBrón] said over dinner last night, but I also was not at all cowed or fearful of meeting their requirements, [or] of constricting the things that interested me and the methods that I wanted to use and the questions that I wanted to ask by fitting into a discipline. Perhaps, I might say, I chose a multidiscipline discipline to fulfill my ambitions.

MICHAEL DAWSON: I ended up in political science much more by default. I had been an African American studies undergraduate and an engineering major, and by the time I was thinking about graduate school, there were no African American studies graduate programs at the time, so I had to find a discipline. I wanted to study political economy—sound familiar [*looks toward Gilmore*]? And I looked at economics, and I had an econ teacher at Berkeley who said, "We'll kill you." He said, "You're really good, and I would love to have you as a student, but you will not survive our discipline." I thought this sounds like the type of advice that I should really listen to. So I did, and then I talked to another one of my teachers, Leon Litwack, in history, and he said, "History might be good. What do you want to work on?" and I said, "I want to work on the history of civil rights and the Black Power Movement." And he said, "That's not history. That's too recent."

RUTH WILSON GILMORE: Didn't pass the twenty-five-year rule?

MICHAEL DAWSON: Yes. So, I said, what else can I do? And then because I'm a partly lazy geek, I said OK, where can I study the type of Black movements I'm interested in and Black politics and play with numbers? Ah! Political science. And so that's where I ended up. Political science, I knew, was going to be hard because unlike sociology at the time, those who did [political science] often concentrated on institutions like the courts. I think we were the first generation of political scientists to study politics from below with a variety of methodologies. I mean it used to be called "Government," and they said we don't study politics, we study governance, and we were not interested in that. We were interested in subverting governance. We had to pretty much invent first the field of Black politics and then, with a lot of other people, the field of race and politics.

I did have the luxury in graduate school of studying political economy because I had a committee that was fairly high-powered, very high-powered actually: a Keynesian political economist, and a Marxist urban political economist, and a rational choice theorist all working with me. But then when I got to the University of Michigan, I was told by the graduate secretary, "Nobody does political economy here. Only Communists do." So I partly went down the public opinion route as a way to say, "Well, I'm going to get to political economy eventually, but I know we know very little about Black political movements and how Black people think about the world, so I'll start there." And that was legible to the people I was working with, and then we had to invent a new field.

RUTH WILSON GILMORE: And, actually, invention is one of the things that I take very seriously. And I won't say I have invented a field, but I have definitely trained now several generations of scholars who are doing things that scholars with geography degrees and American studies degrees were not doing before: asking questions differently and figuring out ways to combine methods to answer those questions and to manipulate the methods so that they could be expansive enough to answer the kinds of questions that we want answers for. And I'm very pleased by that, and sometimes I even feel proud about it, even though I also fear sometimes . . . [shakes head] . . . I just fear.

MICHAEL DAWSON: One thing I should make clear is that we didn't invent the field of Black politics. People had been studying that in HBCUs for a generation, going back to Ralph Bunche and people at Howard, Morehouse, and elsewhere. The race and politics field, though, had been defined as the racial attitudes of white citizens of the United States, and we said, "That's not race and politics. That's not how you study it." So we did change that to refocus it to the politics and movements of people of color, and one thing we started doing was bringing scholars from HBCUs into better-resourced universities.

RUTH WILSON GILMORE: Were you at Michigan with Cedric?

MICHAEL DAWSON: No.

RUTH WILSON GILMORE: No. You didn't overlap?

MICHAEL DAWSON: No.

RUTH WILSON GILMORE: This is the best story in the world. Cedric Robinson went from his first job, which was at SUNY Binghamton, to his second job—I think it was his second job—at the University of Michigan in political science. He arrived there, and there was maybe one Black student in the PhD program. He said, "Well!" and they said, "There aren't any. We looked." And he said, "Give me the admissions resources. We'll be right back." So, confident that Cedric Robinson couldn't find somebody who didn't exist, they let him and his little cadre of graduate students go out looking. They looked, and they looked, and they looked, and they got thirty Black students to apply to the PhD program at the University of Michigan. They were all admitted because the university was convinced they wouldn't come. And they all said yes. Turns out it was twenty-nine Black students and an Irish American kid who had gone to Howard, and the assumption was, on the part of Michigan, that if you go to Howard, you must be Black. It was twenty-nine plus one.

MICHAEL DAWSON: That was one of the reasons I took the job at Michigan, because there was a long tradition of Black graduate students studying race across the social sciences.

JODI MELAMED: You have both been amazing, insightful, decades-long critics of many different kinds of Lefts—reformist Lefts of all kinds. It strikes me that part of the utility of the racial capitalism concept rubric gathering us in hermeneutic, is that it lets us do those in a different way. I was wondering if you might say a few words—this could be in the vein of *What is the reformist Left we need to think about now?* It might be *What is the contradiction or negation of the negation that we need to produce?* And it might be in the vein of *what can we use racial capitalism—the kinds of skills, questions, and hermeneutics that we are developing under racial capitalism— to do what needs to be done?* So anywhere you want to run with those.

MICHAEL DAWSON: There are two parts to the question. I'll probably cheat and start with the slightly easier part of it, and that is the question of what should we be criticizing in various parts of the reformist and I think non-reformist Left today. I think the sad part is that a lot of what we are criticizing today is what we were criticizing fifty years ago. Well, I wasn't in the movement fifty years ago, but it's the same type of struggles that Harry Haywood, for example, talks about in the early Communist Party in the United States. The same type of struggles that in the middle 1960s that various Black revolutionaries had to think about or had to fight—well, by that time the Communist Party—the ideal that Black liberation and movements of people of color in the United States are revolutionary in their own right. They are not particularistic. They are not a distraction from the real revolutionary struggle. They are not dividing the working class—the working class has been divided since slavery. [Regarding the continuing struggle over that ideal,] for example, one of my colleagues in political science, who shall remain unnamed, has said that antiracist struggles, including struggles against the murder of Black people by the police, are by definition and in any form a neoliberal diversion from the true class struggle. It is insane.

The ideal that, in the other direction is that all we have to think about is race: everything is Black-centric—that we don't have to think about not just allies or but what are the other forms of oppression and domination both within and across Black communities. Those are still struggles that we have to carry out within the Left within various forms of political organizations. I'm relatively hopeful that the organizations that have been developing this decade are taking those struggles as central, those questions as central. They don't have answers yet, but they say they don't have answers, *and* they aren't quite as arrogant as some of my friends were when we were in our twenties. But I think they are asking some of the right questions.

RUTH WILSON GILMORE: What do I think? I think several things. One, that if we seriously want to enliven, and make useful, and keep useful the concept of racial capitalism, we have to get over thinking that what it's about is white-people capitalism. There *is* white-people capitalism, but that's not all of capitalism. And I think, as I started my talk with yesterday, that if we have learned anything from Robinson's book *Black Marxism*, it's that capitalism and racial practice codeveloped because the racial practice *was already there* and it had nothing to do with Black people. Do you understand? Nothing to do with Black people. Now, the fact that today we can detail in panel after panel and paper after paper how capitalism requiring inequality and racism enshrining inequality actually happen is important, but it isn't pushing the limit of how racial capitalism operates in general. And I think that if we wish to get out of any kind of particularistic trap, we must learn how to combine the specificity of the kinds of things we talked about here together for two days with the general trend of capitalism in the world today.

And it's all racial. Whether there are white people involved or not. Kimberly [Hoang,] correct me if I'm wrong, but I doubt C. K. Lee would say "racial capitalism" anywhere in her work—I know Cindy, and I think her work is fantastic. The work that is happening with the spread of the release, as it were, as Vijay Prashad puts it, of China, South Africa, Brazil, and India from the old Third World project, the release of those enormous political economies into the world has created new relations, as we know, of imperialism, of colonialism, and so forth. They have nothing to do with Europe and the United States. Although Europe and the United States are not off the hook. It's not like either/or. It's not like they are bad guys, and now we are not; that's not what I'm saying. What I'm saying is there is a world movement of racial capitalist relations. Those relations do not all emanate from the global North, from the Anglo-European, North American centers of power—economic and military power—and they matter, and they remain racial. If all the white people disappeared and capitalism stayed, it would remain racial. It remains racial.

So the problem is that we have to get rid of capitalism. And all of the "wait and wait and try every little thing" is that even though we know that if certain kinds of social and hierarchical relations and certain kinds of relations of practice can syncretize with capitalism, it means that capitalism can go away and what we are calling racism could remain. So getting rid of capitalism means transforming the world into a new series of economic, political, and cultural relations. Or as Stuart Hall puts it, "redressing," which is to say reorganizing the global maldistribution of symbolic and material resources. Bit by bit by bit by bit. So I worry that even when we are talking about capitalism, we get stuck in a specificity and imagine that it is the entire world of capitalism that we must fight against, and that then makes for a slippery slope into thinking that the only thing to be fixed is racism, as though racism can get fixed on its own.

MICHAEL DAWSON: One thing I would add, and I guess this is a type of specificity but a very general one right now. I've been fascinated by some of the talks and papers that were presented on this issue today, and I think we need a much better understanding of financial capitalism, which is the capitalism that governs the world today in all parts of the globe. Part of understanding financial capitalism with respect to racial capitalism in particular is understanding how racial subordination works. Just as Saidiya Hartman, who was invoked by several of us over the last few days, detail the shifts in various types of political economy between slavery and early Jim Crow, what's been the shift into financial capitalism and how does this change the way that racial subordination, as just one phenomenon, takes place? For example, I used to work for a guy named Larry Summers, some of you may have heard of him, and he wrote a paper that was very well regarded in economics, where he makes an argument that the global North, and maybe China and maybe Japan, should ship all their toxic waste to Africa because it's the comparative advantage between countries. He's still very much focused on the global North as a concept because he still thinks Europe rules. Africa should be happy to receive the toxic waste and a little bit of money, and "we"—being a very specific "we" in this case—can get rid of the stuff that is poisoning our land, air, water, and people. That's a small example to think about how financial capitalism works globally in this era, but it's a type of analysis we don't have enough of, and we don't have a basic understanding of financial capitalism in this era.

RUTH WILSON GILMORE: And, actually, picking up from that—and y'all can see that Summers memo online and I think he used the term "ineluctable logic"? To put toxicities that will shorten people's lives in the places where people's lives are already shorter. It is an actuarial imagination. You know the first actuarial tables in the United States were developed where? Does anybody know? What workers?

AUDIENCE MEMBER: Slavery?

RUTH WILSON GILMORE: No! Goodness no! The Irish digging the canals in upstate New York! And they actually had the shortest lives, those Irish workers, of anybody, because they weren't capital, which the slaves were. So the Irish were actually living shorter lives. Yep. That was the foundation for actuarial tables in the antebellum United States.

But in any event, considering then the vulnerabilities of the surface of the Earth and the people who inhabit the surface of the Earth, something that we have invoked in various ways, given our uninvited guestship here on this bit of the surface of the Earth, makes me think of two major issues that we haven't discussed deeply but have come up in various ways in our talks here. One has to do with climate change and the environment and the other has to do with landgrabs. Climate change and the environment are issues that many people in this room are concerned about, and we already know, as several people said in presentations, that climate change significantly affects people who are more vulnerable in the first place, whether because they live in coastal cities or for other reasons are vulnerable to drought and other kinds of disasters. And we all know, because we've been taught this over and over again, there is nothing natural about a natural disaster, they are all social and political as well.

As you might recall, for a while Ecuador had one of those benign autocrats, Carrera, at the head of the government, and Ecuador wrote a new constitution conferring absolute and inviolable rights to the land as well as to various Indigenous communities and so on and so forth. It was not in any way perfect, but it was a really surprising document to have been produced in the twenty-first century anywhere. One of the things that Carrera's government tried to do was to offer to the wealthy of the world an opportunity to pay Ecuador to leave the oil in the ground. They tried to actually financialize a moral gesture. This goes back to the moral and ethical things we've been trying to talk about. Nobody wrote a check. Nobody wrote a check, so the oil came out of the ground. These are things that are enormous and enormously important problems that people, who are not necessarily nice people like Carrera, have tried to figure out resolutions to that are not resolvable within the logic of capitalism as differentiated as that logic actually is across the surface of the Earth. That's something that is obviously essential because I think that it is clear that new regimes of articulation and new forms of—I'm going to use that word that I hate—racialization will emerge because of climate change and the ways that people will be pushed and pulled from where they are at to where they need to go, which is to say to high ground or to somewhere there is water. That's one whole series of issues that are also quite vibrant issues in the United States or here in North America.

And the second has to do with land grabbing, and land grabbing is a very constant growing problem on the Earth's surface. And places that have land scarcity but a lot of money like Saudi Arabia, and places that have a lot of land but also a whole lot of people like the People's Republic of China, are both involved in taking control. Effective ownership is effective control. So we will say taking ownership, without being able to define it specifically, of land in many places in order to produce food, or in central California, in order to grow hay for the show horses of Saudi elites or to grow certain kinds of crops for export from central California to China. Landgrabs are also a feature of the investment strategy of TIAA-CREF [Teachers

Insurance and Annuity Association of America–College Retirement Equities Fund], which many people here will be dependent on when they retire, and TIAA-CREF has been identified as participating in the dispossession of people, making peasants landless, dispossessing Indigenous people in many parts of the world. We had a small conference about this at my center at CUNY a few years ago, and there were reports and so on and so forth that have come out about that.

MICHAEL DAWSON: One of the topics that we touched on several times today but we didn't discuss as centrally is the question of democracy and how capitalism is allergic to democracy. One example that fits into those themes that we've been talking about during this conference is drawn from the work of Hannah Appel, who is an anthropologist at UCLA. She is studying, among other things, the type of contracts that American corporations and British corporations are writing in Africa that essentially indemnify them against democratic change or environmental protection in those countries. In other words, they are saying, "You have to guarantee us a certain output (whether it's extraction volumes of minerals or energy resources or what have you), and it doesn't matter if you have a change in government or if the people in your country decide that this is not a good policy for them. You have to indemnify us for twenty-five, thirty years." One of the strategies that American corporations are pursuing in other parts of the world is to make sure and guarantee that democracy will not matter when it comes to their ability to expropriate.

RUTH WILSON GILMORE: There's a guy who's got a relatively new institute or foundation or whatever it's called. I think his name is Nicolas Berggruen. Anybody here heard of him? His outfit is now behind a very high wall somewhere in the greater Bel Air area of Los Angeles. Berggruen is one of those people, like the people Kimberly Hoang was describing, who doesn't live anywhere. Meaning he can live wherever he wants to, in hotel room after hotel room, anywhere on the surface of the Earth. He makes tons of money doing something. He set up a research foundation that is extremely wealthy and funds pilot projects to change how governments work, and for a while Craig Calhoun ran this thing. I mean somebody you all know ran it, but Craig left and went to Irvine, I think. One of Berggruen's ideas has been that at the highest level, assuming that nation-states remain nation-states, the federal or national government should be one that reproduces itself the way that boards do in corporations. All right, so it should be self-reproducing; democracy has nothing to do with it, it's only a matter of technical expertise. But lower down, sort of to keep everybody feeling like they are participating, if you can touch somebody, then you have a democratic relationship, so that we can be democratic if I can touch Michael.

There are numerous, numerous white papers written and published on the Berggruen website[, and] all kinds of people have been consultants to this foundation, including [former US secretary of state] Condoleezza Rice and [former California governor] Jerry Brown. And some of the realignment of a variety of different governmental functions that have happened in California in recent years, although based in California on the realignment of mental health care during the [Ronald]Reagan governorship, but the more recent realignment that happened when Jerry Brown was in his second round of being the governor, were pilots that were rather seriously thought through and theorized within the context of that foundation. So everybody in the United States who worries about criminal justice stuff likes to point a finger shivering at ALEC [American Legislative Exchange Council] and what ALEC has done. ALEC has done some things, but there are a whole lot of other think tanks and political scientists, excuse me [points to Dawson], on all kinds of faculties around the country, who are having enormous influence on the official way that the official changes in governance and governmental structure are unfolding, and that is one of them.

BRIAN JORDAN JEFFERSON: We were going to open it for questions, but I have one quick question myself. I'll open it up to questions, but I'll ask the first one.

MICHAEL DAWSON: Is that a type of democracy? [Laughter.]

BRIAN JORDAN JEFFERSON: You've both talked a lot about teaching and students and your experience in sending people off into the world, and I was just wondering what trends you see with your students today and thinking back to when you were in school, and what excites you about what you see with graduate students and undergraduate students today—and if anything concerns you.

MICHAEL DAWSON: Well, one trend which is positive but one that is anxiety-producing, at least for my graduate students, is that when I was in graduate school you would go into the discipline you were trained in. The great majority of my students who take academic careers are not ending up in political science departments. They are ending up in gender studies departments, in Chicano studies, in Black studies, and I think American studies, in some cases. So, on the one hand, as someone who was trained as an undergraduate in a multidisciplinary environment of Black studies and noticing that multidisciplinary approaches give them more freedom to ask the types of questions that they want to, this is something I think is quite positive.

It does mean that, and this is the negative side, that political science and the social sciences, in general, are becoming less friendly to the type of work we are doing. So it is not just a matter of choice; it's a matter of trying to find some type of relatively reasonable space where people can do their work. One of the other really strong, really positive strengths, even [St. Clair] Drake said, "Dawson has to make a choice between being an activist and a student." And I said, "You didn't!" But both the undergraduates and graduate students I'm working with see that as a nonstarter, and, in general, that's what they want to do. We aren't going to tell them not to do their activism; now we can help them figure out how the two can complement each other and should complement each other. But once again I've found that student activism is very much tied to their intellectual and political projects. That is very positive.

RUTH WILSON GILMORE: I completely agree with you. My students have gone off into such a wide variety of departments. I still can't believe it. I have more students teaching in English departments than any other kinds—American studies, planning, geography, sociology, and so on. And as Michael said, not only do I not discourage people who come to study with me from doing their activism, my whole job, my whole mission, is to figure out how to put things together for them to pursue something so that they can produce some kind of knowledge that's useful for the struggles that they are involved in. And those struggles usually change because the temporality of doing a PhD—even though it might be five years, six years, seven years—and the temporality of certain kinds of struggles in social justice are not the same. One can set out to do a doctorate that's going to be useful for this struggle, but that struggle is going to be altogether different by the time that person's done, and yet there is going to be useful knowledge produced.

One of the things that I do with PhD students that I highly recommend to those of you who teach PhD students or those of you in the room who are doctoral students and still in coursework, is I teach studio courses and—this I learned from the great Ann Markusen—

I'll set out a problem, a general problem. A few years ago, it was policing. We used a database from the *Guardian* where they counted all the people killed by cops in the United States, and I highly recommend people look through it because things that people say about police killings and the raw, empirical facts of police killings are not identical in most cases. So we chose five places in the United States where people were more likely to be killed by cops than anywhere else, and Albuquerque was one of them. It's a really, really deadly place, and if you are a Native American person, it is a really, really, really deadly place. I think it's one in five homicides in Albuquerque is a cop killing an Indigenous person. One in five homicides. So students get together, they plan a research project, they do it in conjunction with people on the ground wherever this place is, who might be doing some work around this project. They go out and they do the research, and they use the skills they are developing as researchers to make the project come into being. So I have students who do GIS [geographic information systems]. I don't do it, so they do it. So they figure out how to use GIS. Other people do ethnographies, so they figure out how to use that and so on and so forth. Whatever their methods are, they can perfect them in the class. They work as a group, so they have to cooperate. Grades are not an issue for me—if you do your work, you'll do fine. Then we have "clients," which is to say the social justice movements of greater New York come at the end of the semester, and we present our work and get a critique. This is a really good thing to do. Among other things, it makes it very obvious that the classroom is not walled off from the street but rather is continuous with the street and with the community. It also means that we are held to some very high standards for the kind of work that we do because we don't just report it to each other, but we also report it to people we don't know, and it's also really exhilarating to do work that quickly and do it well.

BRIAN JORDAN JEFFERSON: We can open it up to Q&A.

AUDIENCE MEMBER: Thank you both for all your information and everything you've shared with us today and all the remarks over the past couple of days. I had a couple of questions, and they are both very different, so I guess you can choose. Talking about how we use our work and the things that we do in making the classroom a place that is not mysterious or opaque, what are some of the places outside of academia where we can take our skills and take our work and make it shareable and intelligible and useful? And my other question is, how do we expedite all that needs to happen to save people from the environmental degradation and threats that we are facing while also not de-emphasizing the humanity that is at stake and just make it about the environmental? Because I feel so many of the things we are facing are so imminent and they've been happening and they are going to keep happening, but we've also got these very real threats to lives that are not always directly alway relatable to the environment, but it all comes full circle. So whichever one of those you want to attend to.

JODI MELAMED: Because we only have ten minutes, if we could take about three more questions and let them respond in the group.

AUDIENCE MEMBER: I'd like to extend that first question that you had and the role of higher education institutions. I think Marisol LeBrón had talked about how racial capitalism works within the spaces that we are having these conversations in. What do we do now in these situations where a lot of labor is going to be required and not so much in the future? What are your thoughts on the role of racial capitalism within the university structure?

AUDIENCE MEMBER: First, thank you so much for your history of work, and thank you so much for being here. History certainly has told us that big transformations happen when people are coming together. I would like your advice, suggestions on communication within, between, together, and what strategies would you recommend? There are people in biology and people in communication who are talking about communication just being a driving force of change. And the other is what would you suggest for helping us together create visions, possibilities for the future, because I think that when we can do that together, we have the opportunity to work toward and, well, create shared goals if possible and work toward them?

MICHAEL DAWSON: I'm going to start in the middle, I guess. Well, one of the questions was how do we think about universities specifically, but also more generally in a changing economy where technology is taking jobs away, how do we think about work? How do we think about how we function? I think in part—this is also related to the last question as well, the visions for the future—what we have to do is to put everything on the table. You have to put family, you have to put work, and it's not necessarily about getting a better job or protecting the jobs we have, but you have to reimagine work itself and how that gets shared and how we get rewarded. Is it a bad thing that we have more leisure time? We've been trained to think—and I know I'm guilty of it—that if we aren't working every second of the day that we are messing up, but how do we think about how life itself should look? And that means we are reimagining basic institutions from work to family and, of course, to education as well. I think we were talking a little bit about this at lunch, about the need to, from the bottom up, have people imagine what type of world they want to live in, as opposed to the top-down models we had during a good part of the twentieth century. The one caveat we have to think through, and one of the areas that I think progressive movements have failed is the question of organization, is how we organize ourselves sufficiently to be able to take ideals from the bottom up and implement them as platforms for struggle without becoming autocratic, without becoming too bureaucratized, without becoming too centralized, without becoming antidemocratic. One of the other areas where I think there has to be an extraordinary amount of experimentation, in addition to the various types of economic forms we want to experiment with, is with organizational forms for struggle.

RUTH WILSON GILMORE: Definitely. Well, thank you all for your final questions. I think the best way to think about universities is as crossroads, and that is what they are. Universities exist to enable the reproduction of certain kinds of relations, but they are contradictory because they actually cannot guarantee that kind of reproduction, however much they are designed to do so. So what we know over history, for example, is that over the early part of the twentieth century, many of the most influential thinkers and organizers who were parts of cadres that brought about revolutions in their colonized places, met in universities—and I don't mean that the university therefore is some sort of necessary precondition to being a revolutionary—but they did. They met, they combined because of the segregated housing rules, and they all lived together, which was the case of all the colonized people who were being trained to be part of the professional-managerial class of the Portuguese empire. They all lived around the corner from my apartment in Lisbon because they weren't allowed to live with the other students. So [Amílcar] Cabral and [Agostinho] Neto and others they got together, they had underground study groups, and they planned their revolutions in school and with other people. So universities as crossroads is an important thing. Figure out who you can learn from, and if you read [Frantz] Fanon carefully, you can see that some of the formations that Fanon tells us to take seriously, we can understand universities through those other formations such as the military, which I don't recommend, but it is another place where people who otherwise wouldn't meet each other can meet. That's the first thing.

Second of all, obviously universities have resources, even modestly resourced universities, such as the University of Illinois, [and] where I teach—CUNY. Whereas Michael teaches in Chicago, which is fabulously wealthy, and you can fly 350,000 miles to do your research, which is great. But now we are going to be able to use that research for other things. It wasn't like Chicago planned to use that money against but rather for. The second thing is that education is crucial and there are all sorts of different ways that people become educated, and *Finally Got the News* is a great film that shows people who finally did some grassroots collective education. I participate with people who all over the world do things like pop-up universities, and they do charettes so people will get together and kind of design the world that they want to live in as part of the struggle against a particular thing. So we are trying to stop that toxic-waste incinerator, but part of that is to open consciousness by doing some work that gets beyond the idea that the only thing that we can do (maybe) is to stop that, but rather we can design a whole world. But to get to that world we are going to have to stop it. That's a completely different way of being in the world, which would also require different kinds of organization and organizational strategies.

The third thing I want to say is discourse is a real problem and, specifically, the ways that certain types of commonsense consciousness congeals around all different types of problems. When one says "prisons" in the USA, nine people out of ten hear "private prisons." They are not private, but that's what people hear. When one says "prisons" in the USA, nine people out of ten hear "labor." That's not what it's about. That's a little bit of what it's about, but it's mostly not what it's about. So discourse is a real problem—how to get people to think again what they thought they already knew are things that we have the time and relative luxury to try to figure out with different kinds of communication systems, and mobilization, and images and so forth. And I think that the artist [Cameron Rowland] that Cheryl [Harris] is working with is one of the people who can make us just stop and think again, which is important. And the final thing I want to say is that as I was listening to some of the more dire things that all of us were talking about these two days, my mind just kept wandering to the fact that in the mid-1930s—'35 or '36, I forget what year—there was this conference in Paris on fascism. So three years after Hitler was elected and Mussolini had long been in charge in Italy, and you know things were happening in Japan and so forth, there was a conference on fascism, and one of the people who participated in that conference was Walter Benjamin, who famously took his own life when he realized he couldn't get across the border and get away, get out of the snare of being sent back to the Third Reich. And sometimes I feel like these conferences that we are having are conferences like that one, where things are already terrible and they are about to get so much more terrible, and we do have to talk about it, but I wonder, and I fear—this is why I said I fear earlier—that somehow we might lose the urgency that we actually should all be incited into feeling completely by being together. One of the reasons I worry about us reciting the horror instead of rehearsing freedom is that we can recite the horror all the way into the camps, that reciting the horror doesn't keep us away from the camps. Whereas knowing we are rehearsing the freedom urgently because—I'm a Brechtian— there is this epic that's unrolling, and we don't know where it's going to end, but everything that we do—including holding this symposium—is happening in the context of everything we are talking about. We are here not in a university but here in society and in the social order. And I really thank everybody again for organizing this so that we can have these exchanges.

MICHAEL DAWSON: One thing I would add to that is, I think, that rehearsing the horrors is often what we are trained to do. But one of the things I was thinking and then I realized I was thinking incorrectly was that we need some victories, but the problem is we don't communicate our victories; we don't share the victories; we don't put them in the proper context, and that's one thing that the civil rights movement did very well. You have a little victory here, and other people across the state or in some place else would hear about it. That's how you build successful movements, and that's what we also need to do. We also need to start talking about what does work. Not just what's wrong, but what does work, and that way what does work make that as widely available as the horror stories that are justly capturing our attention as well.

JOANNE BARKER (LENAPE) is professor of American Indian studies at San Francisco. She is the author of *Native Acts: Law, Recognition, and Cultural Authenticity* (2011) and *Red Scare: The State's Indigenous Terrorist* (2021), and the editor of *Sovereignty Matters: Locations of Contestation and Possibility in Indigenous Struggles for Self-Determination* (2005).

JODI A. BYRD is a citizen of the Chickasaw Nation of Oklahoma and associate professor in the Department of Literatures in English at Cornell University. Byrd is the author of *The Transit of Empire: Indigenous Critiques of Colonialism* (2011), and their work has appeared most recently in *Social Text* and *South Atlantic Quarterly* and in Joanne Barker's *Critically Sovereign: Indigenous Gender, Sexuality, and Feminist Studies* (Duke University Press, 2017).

LISA MARIE CACHO is an associate professor of American studies at the University of Virginia. Cacho's scholarship interrogates the ways in which human value is both ascribed and denied relationally along racial, gendered, sexual, national, and spatial lines. Her book *Social Death: Racialized Rightlessness and the Criminalization of the Unprotected* (2012) won the John Hope Franklin award in 2013 for best book in American studies. Her most recent publications can be found in the *Boston Review, Social Text*, and *American Quarterly*. Currently, she is writing a book examining police killings in the United States.

MICHAEL DAWSON is John D. MacArthur Professor of Political Science at the University of Chicago, where he serves as the founding director of the Center for the Study of Race, Politics and Culture. His recent books, *Behind the Mule: Race and Class in African-American Politics* (1994) and *Black Visions: The Roots of Contemporary African-American Political Ideologies* (2001), won multiple awards, including the Ralph Bunche Award from the American Political Science Association for *Black Visions*. Dawson has published numerous journal articles, book chapters, and opinion pieces and is currently finishing an edited volume, "Fragmented Rainbow," on race and civil society in the United States, as well as a solo volume, "Black Politics in the Early 21st Century."

IYKO DAY is Elizabeth C. Small Associate Professor of English at Mount Holyoke College. She is currently chair of gender studies and critical social thought and a faculty member in the Five College Asian/Pacific/American Studies Program. Day is the author of *Alien Capital: Asian Racialization and the Logic of Settler Colonial Capitalism* (Duke University Press, 2016), and she coedits the book series Critical Race, Indigeneity, and Relationality for Temple University Press.

RUTH WILSON GILMORE is professor of earth and environmental sciences, and American studies, and the director of the Center for Place, Culture, and Politics at the Graduate Center, CUNY. She also serves on the executive committee of the Institute for Research on the African Diaspora in the Americas and the Caribbean. Cofounder of many grassroots organizations, including the California Prison Moratorium Project, Critical Resistance, and the Central California Environmental Justice Network, Gilmore is author of the prizewinning *Golden Gulag: Prisons, Surplus, Crisis, and Opposition in Globalizing California* (2007) as well as *Change Everything: Racial Capitalism and the Case for Abolition* (2022), *Abolition Geography* (2022), and a collection (coedited with Paul Gilroy) of Stuart Hall's writing on race and difference (Duke University Press, forthcoming).

ALYOSHA GOLDSTEIN is professor of American studies at the University of New Mexico. He is the author of *Poverty in Common: The Politics of Community Action during the American Century* (2012), the editor of *Formations of United States Colonialism* (2014), both published by Duke University Press, and the coeditor of *For Antifascist Futures: Against the Violence of Imperial Crisis* (2022). He has coedited special issues of *South Atlantic Quarterly, Theory and Event, Social Text,* and *Critical Ethnic Studies* and is completing a book on US colonialism, racial capitalism, genealogies of Black and Native dispossession, and the politics of law and redress in the colonial present.

CHERYL I. HARRIS is the Rosalinde and Arthur Gilbert Foundation Chair in Civil Rights and Civil Liberties at the UCLA School of Law. She is the author of groundbreaking scholarship in critical race theory, including "Whiteness as Property" (*Harvard Law Review*), and her work has also engaged issues of race and Indigeneity. She received UCLA Law School's Rutter Prize for excellence in teaching in 2018, and from 2019 to 2020 she was a Fellow in Law and Public Affairs at Princeton. Current projects include the revision of the late Derrick Bell's seminal text, *Race, Racism and American Law* (1970), as well as work on the relationships among race, debt, and property.

KIMBERLY KAY HOANG is an associate professor of sociology and the director of global studies at the University of Chicago. A central focus of her work is understanding the gendered dynamics of deal brokering in Southeast Asia's emerging markets. She is the author of *Dealing in Desire* (2015), which won several prestigious book awards, and *Spiderweb Capitalism* (forthcoming). Her prizewinning articles have appeared in a wide range of journals, including the *American Sociological Review, Social Problems, Gender and Society*, and the *Journal of Contemporary Ethnography*.

BRIAN JORDAN JEFFERSON is an associate professor of geography and geographic information science at the University of Illinois, Urbana-Champaign. His works explore computing technology, capitalism, and the state. He is author of *Digitize and Punish: Racial Criminalization in the Digital Age* (2020).

SUSAN KOSHY is an associate professor of English and Asian American studies and director of the Unit for Criticism and Interpretive Theory at the University of Illinois, Urbana-Champaign. She is the author of *Sexual Naturalization: Asian Americans and Miscegenation* (2004), which won the Choice Outstanding Academic Title Award. She is coeditor of *Transnational South Asians* (2008) and a special feature in *PMLA* on "Monolingualism and Its Discontents" (2022). Her articles have appeared in *PMLA, American Literary History*, the *Yale Journal of Criticism, Boundary 2, Differences, Diaspora, Social Text*, and several anthologies. She is completing work on a book manuscript titled "Manifest Diversity."

MARISOL LEBRÓN is an associate professor of feminist studies and critical race and ethnic studies at the University of California, Santa Cruz. She is the author of *Against Muerto Rico: Lessons from the Verano Boricua* (2021) and *Policing Life and Death: Race, Violence, and Resistance in Puerto Rico* (2019), as well as the coeditor of *Aftershocks of Disaster: Puerto Rico before and after the Storm* (2019). She is also one of the cocreators and project leaders for the Puerto Rico Syllabus, a digital resource for understanding the Puerto Rican debt crisis.

JODI MELAMED is an associate professor of English and Africana studies at Marquette University. She is the author of *Represent and Destroy: Rationalizing Violence in the New Racial Capitalism* (2011) and has published in a wide array of journals and editions. She is a coeditor (with Jodi Byrd, Alyosha Goldstein, and Chandan Reddy) of a special volume of *Social Text* on "Economies of Dispossession: Indigeneity, Race, Capitalism" (Spring 2018). Her articles have appeared in *American Quarterly, Boston Review,* and *Critical Ethnic Studies.* She is currently coauthoring a book with Chandan Reddy titled "Operationalizing Racial Capitalism: On Liberalism as Command Power."

LAURA PULIDO is the Collins Chair of Indigenous, Race, and Ethnic Studies and Geography at the University of Oregon, where she studies race, environmental justice, and cultural memory. She has written numerous books, including *Environmentalism and Economic Justice: Two Chicano Struggles in the Southwest* (1996); *Black, Brown, Yellow and Left: Radical Activism in Los Angeles* (2006); and *A People's Guide to Los Angeles* (with Laura Barraclough and Wendy Cheng) (2012). She has received numerous honors, including the Presidential Achievement Award from the Association of American Geographers and Ford and Guggenheim fellowships.

undermined by, 22, 37, 55, 162–63, 169, 178, 325–26; dispossession as core feature of, 8, 60; exchange, exploitation, and expropriation, interdependence of, 8, 10, 13; extra-economic force as central to, 8, 22, 262–63, 267; financialized, 7, 13, 18, 20–21, 170, 322–23; global, 3, 51–52, 131–33, 152, 288; imperialism as enabler of, 285; naturalization of racial tendencies, 2–3, 97; as racial capitalism, 1–2; real estate, 170, 175, 235; stages, theory of, 2, 5, 8, 25–26n14, 263; twin processes of, 285; violence, relation to, 7–9, 12, 20; white-people, 2, 321. *See also* capital; colonial racial capitalism; racial capitalism

capital-positing and capital-preserving violence, 8–9, 12, 20

Capitol Security (Puerto Rico), 213–20

care work, 64, 193

Caro, Xiomara (student activist), 216–17, 222, 224

Carrasquillo, José A. Rosa (police officer), 211

Carrera, Rafael, 324

Carter, Bunchy, 315

Carter, Jimmy, 135

Central Pacific Railroad Company, 50

Chakravartty, Paula, 96–97

Charron-Chenier, Raphael, 119n47

charters, 41–42, 44–45, 49

Chauvin, Derek, 160

checkerboarding, 48–49

Child Welfare League of America, 69

China, 133–35; property-assessment software, 234, 239; US rivalry with Vietnam, 138–39, 152

Chochenyo Ohlone, 34–35

Choudhury, Nusrat, 174

cities, 232; European Union, 242; growth of, 264–65; state-capital relations in context of, 234. *See also* property-assessment software; smart technology; waste management software

citizenship, 47–48, 50, 102–3, 288

Civil Disobedience (Thoreau), 286

Civil Obedience Act, 186

Civil Rights Act of 1866, 105

Claims Resolution Act (2010), 48

Clark, Mark, 316

climate change, 323–24. *See also* wastelands

coal extraction, 22, 260–62, 264–66, 268

coercion, 299–300; administrative, 162, 164; compulsion of economic relations, 8–9, 66–67, 264; and debt, 92–94; extra-economic force, 8, 14, 22, 262–63, 267; of labor, 17, 94,

97–104, 117n30, 120n61, 271–72, 274; race, relation to, 92–98. *See also* violence

COINTELPRO repression, 185

Cold War, 259, 269

collective life, 4, 11, 48–49, 98, 159–60

Collins, Booker, 181

colonialism: atom bomb as substitute for, 269; capitalism as a colonial relation, 4–5, 7; First World/Third World divide, 2, 131–32, 151; franchise, 6, 13; neocolonialism, resisting, 151–53; Vietnam and legacies of, 133–35, 147. *See also* colonial racial capitalism; settler colonialism

colonial racial capitalism, 6–7; administration as dominant form of, 15; and charters, 41–42, 44–45, 49; communities damaged by, 24; and emerging markets, 142, 153–54; framework of, 7–14; informal economies, 188–91; liberalism as central to, 163; logistics of, 18, 264–69; necropolitical logic of, 72, 112; policing as enforcement of, 167; and smart technologies, 232, 234; and social reproduction, 10, 13; and waste disposal, 239. *See also* administration/administrative power; capitalism; police violence; policing; racial capitalism

"colonial unknowing," 15, 22, 258–59

"colorblind" law, 70, 95

"Combating Public Disorder" law (Florida), 183–84

commemorations, 15, 21–23, 259; of battlefields, 290–92; and cultural memory, 284–85, 289–90, 295, 299, 301. *See also* Mexican-American War

commodities: debt as, 95, 97; racial subordination as, 17–18, 95

commodity form, 22, 278

Communist Party, USA, 320–21

Communist Party of Vietnam, 136, 139, 142

Community Collaborative Committee (Milwaukee), 174

computer-assisted mass-appraisal software (CAMA), 234–38, 244

Concepcion, William (police officer), 212

conceptual art, 88–89, 89, 112–13n1, 113n4, 113–14n6

Conquest by Law: How the Discovery of America Dispossessed Indigenous Peoples of Their Lands (Robertson), 41

"consent," 102, 163

Constitution, US, 36, 42; contract clause, 42–44; Fugitive Slave Clause, 98, 100; "Indian tribes" in, 37. *See also* Amendments to the US Constitution containment strategies, 208

contract clause, US Constitution, 42–44

contracts: and debt peonage, 102, 116–17n29, 117nn30–31; between Flint and Detroit Water Sewer District (DWSD), 107–9, 111–12; restrictions on states, 36, 42–44, 48, 50, 56n23

convict leasing and chain gangs, 17, 89, 89–91, 97–98, 102, 105, 115n15

corporations: as "artificial beings," 45; centralization and entitlement to access tribal lands, 41–45; corporate-federal collusion, 54, 57n32; Fourteenth Amendment rights, 36, 46, 49–53; global ownership structure, 148, 149; introduction to, 35–37; legal definitions of, 6, 16, 36. *See also* tribes

Coulthard, Glen, 4–5, 25n11,14, 60, 263–64

Cowen, Deborah, 274–75

credit, 93, 96–97

"creditworthiness," 96–97

criminalization: of BIPOC life, 11, 90, 114–15n13, 168–75; of community defenders and those they defend, 187–91; contemporary laws against protest, 182–84; of debt, 95, 97, 114–15n13, 116n25, 119n48; of "disposability," 166–68, 170–71, 176, 183, 185, 187, 191, 208; of Indigenous peoples, 166–67, 172; of peaceful assembly, 182–83; plea bargains, 177, 198n51; and police discretion, 169–76, 197n20; Public Law 280, 69, 172; regulation of pregnancy, 65; of resistance, 24; "resisting arrest," 177, 179–82, 183; role of in world system, 162; of self-defense and activism against police violence, 176–87; separation between criminal control and conquest, 166–67; and sexual exploitation of Black women and girls, 189; sorting people for capitalist care or destruction, 19, 162–63, 168. *See also* violence

criminal justice system, structure of, 176–77

cultural memory, 22, 284–85, 289–90, 295, 299, 301

curation, as appropriation, 297

Curtis Act (1898), 48

Datta, Ayona, 243

Dawson, Michael, 15, 23–24, 311–32

Day, Iyko, 21–22

death, premature, 19, 21, 77, 160–61, 167, 176; criminalization of defenders against, 187–91; as expectation, 166; and waste management software, 241–42, 244

debt, 14, 17–18, 88–128; abstraction of, 95, 97, 100; and accumulation, 95–98, 100, 102, 111–12; after abolition, 101–6, 116–17n29; as asset, 95–96; asset-stripping, 92, 94, 111; and Black geographies, 98, 106, 120n56; and bond issuance, 108–9, 111–12, 118n34; and collectivities, 98; as commodity, 95, 97; "creditworthiness," 96–97; criminal legal, 95, 97, 114–15n13, 116n25, 119n48; emancipation, compensated, 93, 100, 116–17n29, 117n30; and enslavement, 98–101; as essential structure and relation, 93–98; as extraction, 95, 106, 112; and Flint water crisis, 17, 98, 106–12, 122n84; foreclosure, 48, 120n59; fugitives as runaway capital, 100; incarceration through, 90–91; neoliberal reliance on, 95, 97, 106, 119n42; "new debtors' prisons," 95; "pay to stay" fees, 92, 94; predatory inclusion, 96, 119nn46–47; predatory lending, 103, 120n53, 315; racial subordination as commodity, 17–18, 95. *See also* dispossession; incarceration

debt peonage: Black, 17, 94; convict leasing and chain gangs as, 17, 89, 89–91, 97–98, 102, 105, 115n15; Indigenous, 14, 17, 97, 100–101; Mexican, 102–3; outlawed, 94–95, 118n39

decolonization, 4, 15, 25, 60, 151, 160, 178, 258, 269

Deer, Sarah, 68

dehumanization, 12, 216, 241, 276–77

Deline Land Corporation, 274

democracy, 193, 265; Atomic Energy Commission's undermining of, 269; bank and multinational corrosion of, 33, 35–37; capitalism and undermining of, 22, 37, 55, 162–63, 169, 178, 325–26; nation-state as self-reproducing, 325–26; as performance that conceals, 55; welfare, 265, 267

Democratic Republic of the Congo, 271

Deng Xiaoping, 136

Denning, Mark, 159–60, 195n2

De Pencier, Nicholas, 275

depoliticization, 22, 166, 184; of nuclear power, 258, 264, 270

Detroit, Michigan, 315–16; bankruptcy and water crisis, 110–11, 123n90; market-value assessment software used, 237–38

Detroit Water Sewer District (DWSD), 107–12

developmentalism: and Flint water crisis, 106, 111; and nuclear energy market, 269–70; reconfiguration of, 3, 131–33, 154n3; and smart technology, 238–39, 243; three racial truths of, 2–3

Diamond, Kate, 23, 300, 300–301

difference: management of, 15, 163–64, 223; programming racialized, 3, 243–45; regional,

Flynn, Edward, 173
Forbes, Jack D., 52
Force Publique (Belgium), 272
foreclosure, 48, 119n46, 120n59
foreclosure crisis (2008), 33–37, 54, 75
foreign direct investment (FDI), 18–19, 136–38, 137, 140
Foreign Investment and the Reproduction of Racial Capitalism in South Africa (Legassick and Hemson), 62
Fort Moore Pioneer Memorial, 23, 284, 292–96, 294
Fortuño, Luis, 208–12, 220
Foucault, Michel, 119n48
Fourteenth Amendment, 105; rights of corporations, 36, 46, 49–53
Fox6 Milwaukee, 188
fractionated inheritance laws, 16, 48–49, 61, 72–76
France, 133–34, 271, 299
franchise colonialism, 6, 13
fraud, US government, 33, 37, 41; democracy as cover for, 55; land speculation by wealthy officials, 43–44
Frazier, Darnella, 160
freedmen, and due process clause, 50
"freedom dreams," 193, 195
free markets, 126, 163, 237, 269–70
French Indochina, 134
Fugitive Slave Act of 1850, 99, 100, 104
Fugitive Slave Clause (US Constitution), 98, 100

Gabon, 270, 271
Gadsden Purchase (1888), 295
Gandhi, Mohandas K., 261
García, Margaret, 23, *300*, 300–301
General Allotment Act (1887), 16, 36, 45, 48, 61, 73
Genesee County, Michigan, 107–9
genocide and genocidal policies: adoption policies as eliminatory appropriation, 72; depopulation of Indigenous peoples, 101; against Indigenous peoples of California and Nevada, 52–53; police killings in Albuquerque, 328; sterilization campaigns against Indigenous women, 68
gentrification, 238, 244, 313
geographic information systems (GIS), 234, 328
geography of human settlement, 264–65
Georgia, 42–44, 46
Giamo, Benedict, 259
Giap, Vo Nguyen, 134

Gilmore, Ruth Wilson, 2, 13, 90, 91, 94, 115n11, 115n18, 115n20, 232; conversation with Dawson, 15, 23–24, 311–32; on criminalization, 11, 166, 168
global capitalism, 3, 51–52, 131, 152, 288
global financialization, 62; corporate ownership structure, 148, *149*; foreign direct investment, 18–19, 136–38, *137*, *138*, 140; offshore structures, 133, 136, 141, 148, 152–53; tax issues, 142, 145–47. *See also* emerging and frontier markets
Global South, 6–7; and property-assessment software, 236, 239; racial capitalism perpetuated in, 18–19; and waste management software, 240, 243
Golden Gulag (Gilmore), 91
Goldstein, Alyosha, 258
Goldtooth, Tom B. K., 33, 37
Goldwater Institute, 70, 71
Gómez, Laura, 121n71, 288
Gómez-Barris, Macarena, 10–11, 18, 153
Gonzales, Antonio, 179
"good works," narrative of, 286, 289, 290, 295–96
Gore, Ellie, 10
governmental structure, 326
Gramsci, Antonio, 64
Gray, Freddie, 168
Great Acceleration, 258
Great Lakes Water Authority (GLWA), 110–12
Griffin, Demetrius, 195
"grounded relationalities," 65
Guadalupe, Ana (UPR-RP chancellor), 229n40
Gumbs, Alexis Pauline, 257

Halberstam, Jack, 277
Hall, Stuart, 64, 322
Hamilton, Dontre, 179
Hammer, Peter, 107
Hampton, Fred, 316
Han Dynasty, 133
Harris, Cheryl I., 17, 314, 315, 316, 331
Hartman, Saidiya, 93, 114n12, 117n30, 322
Harvey, David, 66–67, 79n27
Hawaii, 51, 54
Haywood, Harry, 320
Heaggan-Brown, Dominique, 186
Hecht, Gabrielle, 260, 270, 271, 273
heir's property, 14, 16–17, 61, 73–77
Hemmens, Craig, 165
Hemson, David, 62, 78n6
Hiroshima, 22, 257–60, 273, 277–78
Hiroshima Peace Memorial Museum and Park, 259

Morgan, Jennifer, 64–65
Mormon Battalion, 295–96
mortgages, 120n59; backed by enslaved persons, 99–100; subprime loan crisis, 15, 17, 96–97; and tenancy-in-common property, 74–75
multiculturalism, neoliberal, 167, 170, 196n14, 237

NAACP, 314
Nagasaki, 259, 260, 273
Nagle, Rebecca, 72
Nast, Heidi, 4
National Association of Black Social Workers, 70
National Forum (South Africa), 61–62
national security rhetoric, 135, 245, 267–68
nation-state, 9, 19, 42, 169, 239, 325–26
Native Lands Act (South Africa, 1913), 62
naturalization: of inequalities, 1–2; of racial tendencies, 2–3, 97
nature, manipulation of, 294–95
Nazis, 272, 332
necrocomputation, 242
necropolitical logic, 72, 112, 275
neocolonialism, resisting, 151–53
neoliberalism, 4, 15, 18, 66, 152; carceral forms of, 92; debt as central to, 95, 97, 106, 119n42; multicultural, 167, 170, 196n14, 237; nuclear, 269–71; in Puerto Rico, 208, 210, 212, 227–28n9
neoslavery, 92
Netherlands, 42
neutrality, claims of, 15, 21, 164; and debt, 90, 95, 96
New England Mississippi Land Company, 43–44
New Orleans, *Slaughterhouse* lawsuits, 49–53
Newsome, Bree, 289
New York City, 237, 244, 247n22
New Zealand child removal policies, 68
Nguyen, Nhi Ba, 153
Nguyen, Tu, 139–40
Ngwane, Trevor, 244
Nhat, Nguyen Duc, 140
Nichols, Robert, 5, 166–67
91020000 (Rowland), 89, 89–92, 115n18
Nitty II, Frank (Frank Sensabaugh), 182, 192–95, 198n59
Nixon, Rob, 17
noncapitalist social forms, expropriation of, 9, 63, 66–67, 263
nonsite/nonsight, 22, 259, 271, 274, 277

Noonan, Jacqueline, 123n90
nuclear power, 257–83; as antipolitical/depoliticization of, 22, 258, 264, 270, 275; atomic bomb as substitute for colonial power, 269; and colonial power of logistics, 264–69; international regulation, 270–71; Manhattan Project, 260, 272–73; nuclear exceptionalism, 260, 261, 274; nuclear neoliberation, 269–71; nuclear unconscious, 261; periodization of, 257–58; and primitive accumulation, 261–64, 265, 269, 274, 277; scalar politics of atomic bomb, 258, 271–74, 276; slow violence of, 258; technopolitics, 22, 258, 260, 261, 264, 279; weapons, 260–62, 268–75, 277. *See also* uranium mining

Obama, Barack, 138, 257–58
Occupy Oakland, 33–35
"Occupy Talks: Indigenous Perspectives on the Occupy Movement, The" symposium, 37
Occupy Wall Street (OWS) movement, 15, 33, 54–55
O'Connor, Reed, 71
offshore capital structures, 133, 136, 141, 148, 152–53
oil extraction, 260–62, 264–68
Omnibus Act (1910), 48
1 percent, 33, 54–55
one-third world and two-thirds world, 131–33, 154n3
Ong, Aihwa, 234
Organización Socialista Internacional, 221
Organization of the Petroleum Exporting Countries (OPEC), 268
Out of Disorder (Cosmo World) (Iwasaki), 22, 277–79, *278*
ownership, 61, 285; aboriginal titles, 40; global structure of corporations, 148, *149*; partition of heirs' property, 14, 16–17, 61, 73–77; possession held in abeyance, 76; trust titles, 48. *See also* land; property

pacifist politics, 259
Pan Africanist Congress, 1
pandemic of 2020, 24
Paro Nacional del Pueblo (People's National Stoppage), 209, 210
"partition," 232
Patrick, Monica Lewis, 110
peaceful assembly, attempts to criminalize, 182–83
Peck, John, 44
Peck, Raoul, 273

queer art of failure, 277–79

race: accumulation and reproduction, pivot
   with, 61–66; coercion, relation to, 92–98;
   multiple views of, 152; not synonymous with
   skin color, 2
racial capitalism, 285, 314, 316; Black women,
   dependence on, 9–10; capitalism as, 1–2;
   colonial capitalism as, 7; and reformist Left,
   320–21; in relation to reproduction, 61; scholarship on, 320–22, 329; social reproduction
   of, 60–87; South African origin of term, 1, 5,
   25n1, 61–62. *See also* colonial racial capitalism
Racial Capitalism conference (University of
   Illinois, Urbana-Champaign, 2019), 311
"racialism," 62–63, 114n11
racialization, 4, 23, 162–64, 242, 313, 324
Racial Justice Program (ACLU), 174
racial property regimes, 285, 290
racism, 193; as core feature of capitalism, 1–2,
   61, 63, 76, 90, 93, 114n11; environmental, 241;
   institutionalized, 218; in Puerto Rico, 208,
   218–19; without capitalism, 322
Radio Huelga (Strike Radio), 210
railroads, 46, 50–53, 287
Ramírez, José Laguarta, 228n10
Ramírez, Roberto José Thomas, 214
real estate capitalism, 170, 175, 235
Reconstruction period, 14, 17, 45, 46–49
Reddy, Chandan, 6, 18, 196n17
Red Nation Rising (Bordertown Violence Working Group), 169
Regional Comprehensive Economic Partnership, 139
regional difference, 238, 239, 243, 244
regulatory opacity and transparency, 140–41,
   144
renewable energy sources, 264
reproduction: accumulation and race, pivot
   with, 61–66; adoption and removal of
   Indigenous children, 16–17, 68–72, 77, 79n29;
   always-contingent politics of, 65; "productive" work vs., 10; simple and expanded, 63.
   See also social reproduction
Republicans, and Yazoo Land Act of 1795, 43
Reséndez, Andrés, 100, 121nn64–65
resistance: algorithmic abolitionist thinking,
   21, 245–46; block-party protest, 191–95;
   decriminalization of self-defense, 162, 179–80;
   effectiveness of small acts, 192; by Indigenous
   communities and peoples, 5–6, 11, 159, 183;
   by the land, 12; living life as, 168; love as, 162;

177–78, 192–95; as loving action, 162, 177–78,
   192–95; Milwaukee uprisings, 20, 159–60, 179;
   to narratives of colonial racial capitalism,
   163–64, 191–92; to neocolonialism, 151–53;
   pintata ("paint-in"), 206–7, 224; possibilities for, 13–14; redressing capitalism, 322;
   revolutionary movements, 180–82; social
   justice movements, 24, 54–55, 328; victories,
   communicating, 332; to violence work, 19–20,
   176–87. *See also* University of Puerto Rico
   student strikes; uprisings
Rethinking Marxism Conference (UMass
   Amherst), 317
Reyes, Wayne, 160
Rhodes, Alexandre de, 133
Rice, Condoleeza, 326
"right of way" laws, 46, 50
rights: equal protection of corporations as
   "persons," 49–53; liberal rights regime, 18, 93;
   trade rights, 16, 36, 38, 41–42, 44–45, 49
Rio Declaration of Environment and Develop-
   ment (1992), 243
riots, redefinition of, 183
Ritchie, Andrea, 171
Rivera Clemente, Maricruz, 215
roads, 295–96
Roberto, Giovanni (student activist), 214,
   216–19, 225
Roberts, Dorothy, 65
Roberts, William Clare, 263
Robertson, Lindsay G., 41
Robinson, Cedric, 1, 23–24, 114n11, 243, 262–63,
   317, 319–20, 321; "racialism," 62–63
Rodríguez, Benjamin, 215–16
Rodríguez, Dylan, 196n14
Rosselló, Pedro (governor), 208
Rowland, Cameron, *89*, 89–93, 113n4, 113–14n6,
   115n18, 331
rubber, coerced production of, 272

Safransky, Sara, 237
Sahtu Dene laborers, 272–73
Sandefur, Timothy, 71
San Francisco, computer-driven dispossession,
   238
San Gabriel Mission, 297
San Gabriel River, 291
Saudi Arabia, US payments to, 267
savings, vs. profit, 92, 107–8, 116n22
Scalia, Antonin, 88, 90
scandal, 54–55
scarcity, manufactured, 266–68

Scarry, Elaine, 261, 274

Schermerhorn, Calvin, 99

scholarship: Black studies, 25–26n14, 315, 327; feminist social reproduction theory, 64–65; and graduate students, 326–28; Indigenous studies, North American, 4–5; political economy/science, 317–19, 326–27; racial capitalism, study of, 320–22, 329

Seamster, Louise, 119n47

Seigel, Micol, 195n7

Sekula, Allan, 275, 276

settler colonialism, 13, 15–17, 77, 120n59; apartheid states, 1, 61–62, 163–64; children, taking and trafficking of, 68; denial as central to, 289; dispossessive regimes of accumulation, 3–5, 7, 66–67; "good works," narrative of, 286, 289, 290, 295–96; improvement, ideology of, 285–86; initial conceptions of, 62; mission system, 297; reactionary backlash against reforms, 68, 70–72; replacement of Indigenous populations, 294–95; of South Africa, 1, 5, 61–62; transition, narratives of, 289–90, 296, 299; of United States, 7, 60–61, 285–87. See also colonialism; imperialism; Mexican-American War

sex-trade economies, 189–90

Shariff, Nayyirah, 109, 110

Shesky, Rusten, 186

Shinkolobwe (Democratic Republic of the Congo), 271

shipping, 266

Shoemaker, Jessica, 74

Silicon Valley, 313–14

Simulacra and Simulation (Baudrillard), 55

Singh, Nikhil, 65, 242

Sino-French War, 133

Sino-Vietnamese War (Third Indochina War), 135

Slaughterhouse cases, 49–51

slavery: afterlives of as ongoing in United States, 67, 92, 101–2, 114n12; in Belgian Congo, 272; children, market in, 68; and debt, 98–101; dispossession after, 14, 17, 98–101; financialization of enslaved Black body, 100; Indigenous peoples, enslavement of, 100–101, 120n61, 121nn64–65; Mexico outlaws (1829), 287; neoslavery, 92; surrogacy/slavery nexus, 65; Texans' desire for, 287

slow violence, 17, 22, 258

smart technology, 15, 232–54; accumulation through, 233–34, 239, 242–46; beyond algorithm, 245–46; market-value assessment

(MVA) software, 237–38; "platform urbanization" rhetoric, 237; programming racial difference, 3, 243–45; and racial inequality, 233–34; regional difference, 238, 239, 243, 244; self-monitoring and reporting technology (SMART), 233; and social differentiation, 21, 232–33, 236–39, 241–45; used to combat discrimination, 237; value determinants, 236–37. See also property-assessment software; technopolitics, colonial; waste management software

Smith, Neil, 234

Smith, Sylville, 179, 186

Snyder, Rick, 107, 122n84

social justice movements, 24, 54–55, 328

social media, 24, 212, 214, 220

social movements, 47, 210, 217, 330

social relations: and "forgetting," 286, 289, 290; inequalities as inputs into, 233; production and conservation of, 64; scarcity as defining feature of, 266–68; of uranium, 268. See also inequalities

social reproduction, 9–10, 60–87; and 1887 General Allotment Act, 16; as dialectical relation, 76–77; as embodied, 10; feminist theory of, 64–65; "productive" work vs, 10. See also reproduction

"society," Westernized, 6

solidarity, 206, 217, 246; building coalitions, 226–27; with community leaders, 220–21; of Puerto Ricans with students, 20, 223–24

South Africa, 1, 5, 25n1, 61–62, 78n6

sovereignty: and allotment policy, 73; denationalization of state, 151; Indigenous, 16, 39–40, 48, 71–72, 159; US, as counter-sovereignty, 169; Vietnam's reassertion of, 19

Soviet Union, 135, 136

Spain, 51–52, 101

Spanish-American War, 51–52

"Spanish fantasy" myth, 296–97, 298

spatial dynamics, 2; Black geographies as wasteland, 98, 106, 120n55; of capitalism, 63; denial of coevalness, 271; erasure of dead or past labor, 276–78; smart governance algorithms applied to, 21, 242, 244

speculative logic, 143, 151

Standing Rock uprisings, 183

Stanford University, 314

"state of nature," 39

statues of colonizers, removal of, 284, 289, 301

Stop and Frisk: Balancing Crime Control with Community Relations, 173

strikes, 265–67. *See also* University of Puerto
Rico student strikes

structural adjustments, 315

student movements. *See* University of Puerto
Rico student strikes

subprime loan crisis, 15, 17, 96–97

Summers, Larry, 323

supply-chain management, 274–75

Supreme Court decisions, 56n12, 56n23; *Adarand Constructors, Inc. v. Pena*, 88; *Adoptive Couple v. Baby Girl*, 70; *Brackeen v. Bernhardt*, 70–71; *Cobell v. Salazar*, 48; *Dred Scott v. Sandford*, 116n29; *Fletcher v. Peck*, 36, 42, 44; *Johnson's Lessee v. McIntosh*, 36, 39–42; *Santa Clara County v. Southern Pacific Railroad Company*, 36, 45–46, 50–51, 53; *Slaughterhouse cases*, 49–51; *Trustees of Dartmouth College v. Woodward*, 36, 44–45

surplus labor, and incarceration, 91, 94,
115–16n20

"surplus" lands, 48–49, 73, 91

"surplus" populations, 3, 8, 11, 94, 115n18

surplus value, 63

Taylor, Keeanga-Yamahtta, 96, 119n46, 120n56

Teachers Insurance and Annuity Association of
America-College Retirement Equities Fund
(TIAA-CREF), 324–25

technopolitics, colonial, 258, 261, 279; as antipolitical/depolitical, 22, 258, 260, 264, 270, 275;
"highly classified" authority, 269. *See also*
smart technology

terra nullius, 16, 67–68, 296

Theft Is Property! (Nichols), 5–6

Thirteenth Amendment, 46, 91, 101–2, 115n14

Thomas, Clarence, 70

Thoreau, Henry David, 286

Toscano, Albert, 275, 276–77

Trafficking Victims Protection Act (2000), 190

transitions: of African Americans from chattel
to constitutional citizens, 102–3; to carceral
neoliberal forms, 92; from coal to oil to uranium, 22, 261–68, 271, 274–75; from convict
leasing to chain gang, 89–90, 115n15; police
budgets rerouted, 183–84, 199n67; settler
narratives of, 289–90, 296, 299; shift to oil,
266–67; socialist, in Vietnam, 136. *See also*
Mexican-American War

Trans-Pacific Partnership (TPP), 19, 138–39

treaties with Indigenous peoples between 1778
and 1871, 36, 37–40; Cherokee removal treaty
of 1835, 43; and Indian Appropriations Bill

of 1871, 48; international law violated by US,
39–40; and land-development companies, 41,
42–43; suspension of, 39–41, 45; US violation
of, 39–40, 52

Treaty of Guadalupe Hidalgo (1848), 52, 103,
286, 288, 290, 296

Treaty of Paris (1783), 39

Treaty on the Non-Proliferation of Nuclear
Weapons (1968), 269

Tree of Califas (Garcia and Diamond), 23, 300,
300–301

tribes: considered irrelevant in constitutional
law, 47, 51; as corporations with limitations,
54; introduction to, 35–37; legal contortion of
Indigenous nations into, 41; legal definitions
of, 6, 16, 36; and persons, 45–53; rearticulated as legal and economic structure, 45; as
sovereign nations, 39. *See also* corporations;
Indigenous communities and peoples;
Indigenous nations

Trivedi, Somil, 177

Trudeau, Justin, 139

Truman, Harry, 273

Trump, Donald, 19, 138–39

Trump administration, 185

Trung sisters, 133

trust titles, 48

Turner, John Kenneth, 101

Tyler, John, 286

Uniform Arrest Act, 165–66, 185, 197n20

Uniform Partition of Heirs Property (2010),
75–76

Union Miniere de Haut Katanga, 272

Union of Radical Political Economists, 317

United Nations, 235

United States: afterlives of slavery as ongoing
in, 67, 92, 101–2, 114n12; Army's leveraging of
Mormons, 295–96; child removal policies, 68;
China, rivalry with, 138–39, 152; corporate-
federal collusion, 54, 57n32; denialist imperial
ideology of, 267–68, 284–85, 289; and forced
Congolese labor, 272; forgetting of social relations, 286, 289, 290; genocidal policy against
"Indians," 52–53, 68, 72, 101, 328; global
capitalism, plunge into, 51, 52; imperialism of,
33, 35–36, 53–54, 67, 267–69, 284–87, 289–92,
295, 299; Iraq, invasion of, 270; manifest destiny narrative, 103, 286, 290, 295–99; and oil
extraction, 266–67; Reconstruction period,
45, 46–49; sacrifice zones for uranium mining, 268–69; settler colonialism of, 7, 60–61,